Kenneth Clark

Kenneth Clark

A BIOGRAPHY

Meryle Secrest

Weidenfeld and Nicolson
London

Grateful acknowledgement is made to the following: to Michael Colefax, for permission to quote from letters of Lady Sibyl Colefax; to Catriona Williams, for permission to quote from letters of Sir Colin Anderson to the author and for family photographs; to Anne Graham Bell, for permission to quote from a letter of Frank Graham Bell; to Lady May, for permission to quote from the letters of Sir Owen Morshead; to Dr Russell Martin, for permission to quote from a letter of Robert Martin; to Sir Francis Watson, for permission to quote from a letter of C.F.Bell; to Judith Gairdner, for permission to quote from a letter of Dr William Tenant Gairdner to the author; to Sir William Keswick, for permission to quote from his letter to the author; to John Piper, for permission to quote from his letter to Lord Clark; to Christopher Smith, for permission to quote from a letter to the author; to John Sparrow, for permission to quote from a letter of Sir Maurice Bowra; to Henry Moore, for permission to quote from his letters to Lord Clark; to James Lees-Milne, for permission to quote from his published diaries and letters to the author; to Reg Snell, for permission to quote from his memories of Winchester and Kenneth Clark; to Brian Pye-Smith, for permission to quote from his letter to the author; to Michael Lubbock, for permission to quote from two letters; to Barbara Halpern, for permission to quote from published and unpublished letters of Mary Berenson and Alys Russell; to John Russell, for permission to quote from letters of Logan Pearsall Smith to Lord Clark; to Dr C.I.C.Bosanquet, for permission to quote from his Winchester memoirs; to Mrs Loftus-Potter, for permission to quote from a letter of the late Judge Douglas C.L.Potter to the author; to Collins, Publishers, for permission to quote from the unpublished diary of Harold Nicolson; to Sybil, Dowager Marchioness of Cholmondeley, for permission to quote from a letter of the late Sir Philip Sassoon; to the Earl of Crawford, for permission to quote from his father's letters to Lord Clark; to Peter Green, for permission to quote from his letter to the author; to G.R.Mitchell, for permission to quote from his letter to the author; and to Rev. Prof. N.W.Porteous, for permission to quote from two letters to the author. Photographs by courtesy of the Estate of Lord Clark.

First published in Great Britain in 1984 by
George Weidenfeld & Nicolson Ltd
91 Clapham High Street, London sw4 7TA

Copyright © Meryle Secrest Beveridge, 1984

All rights reserved. No part of this publication may be reproduced, stored in a retrieval system, or transmitted in any form or by any means, electronic, mechanical, photocopying, recording or otherwise, without the prior permission of the copyright owner.

ISBN 0 297 78398 X

Typeset and printed in Great Britain
at The Pitman Press, Bath

For my husband

Contents

Illustrations

For the outer sense alone perceives visible things
and the eye of the heart alone sees the invisible.
RICHARD OF SAINT-VICTOR (d. 1173)

Preface

Saltwood, the castle in Kent which Kenneth Clark bought in the 1950s, included a handsome building separate from the main house in which he housed his library. Once the Archbishop's audience hall, the room overlooked the inner bailey, the towers and grey stone battlements.

One entered a door in a wall and ascended a winding flight of stone steps to a vast and lofty hall, the vaulted and carved ceiling of which had been faultlessly restored by a previous owner. There was evidence everywhere of a discriminating taste: tapestries, sculpture, *objets d'art* and oriental carpets, but the thousands of beautiful books, row on row, around the walls, were the principal witnesses. Examining them at random one found part of the library willed to Kenneth Clark's son Colin by the American novelist Edith Wharton: the complete works of Balzac, for instance, along with the works of Diderot, *Vingt ans après* by A. Dumas, works of Flaubert and François Villon. There was every kind of art book imaginable: catalogues of Dutch painters, treatises on early German art, classical sculpture, Bernini, Fantin-Latour, Toulouse-Lautrec, Calder, Renoir and Corot.

There were slender books of poetry, books of reference, and novels by British authors of the 1920s and 1930s. One book in particular on the life and work of Honoré Fragonard, published in Paris in 1889, was inscribed 'For K – With Love for Xmas and a very special wish for 1946'. It was from Mary Kessell, a British artist of the 1940s and 1950s. Many of the books were obviously priceless and so it was sad to find them spotted with mould or literally wet, their leather bindings crumbling and infested with bookworm; the stone walls seeped with moisture and a particularly bitter, penetrating chill, despite the warmth outside. One's breath froze on the air. One forced open a window, kneeling on a seat of palest silk that was rotted into tatters.

Kenneth Clark had worked in a small study directly overhead, conveniently close to his magnificent source material. His spacious desk, its drawer stuffed with old love-letters and decomposing boxes of After Eight mints, showed other evidence of the master's presence. Among the objects on its broad surface were a collection of smooth stones, placed with great care, beside gilt and marble candelabra. Wherever one's eye rested there were visual delights: a carved fireplace, curtains of gilt brocade, a grandfather clock of inlaid wood, no longer running, and, on either side of the fireplace, matching female sculptures executed with a fastidiousness that would have pleased Botticelli. There were beautiful pieces of pottery, old vases and a glass-fronted bookcase full of art catalogues. The room, however, had the same air of dusty neglect as the one beneath, of thought left in suspension, an illusion that was heightened by the tendency of the grandfather clock to begin ticking whenever a footstep jolted it into action, then stop disjointedly.

Another room in the same wing, the card room, housed some of Kenneth Clark's archives. We had discussed the idea of a biography a decade before and, whenever we met, which was often, I filed away further notes dealing with his career, ideas and preoccupations. By the time he had definitely decided that I should write his biography we were on easy terms. So it seemed natural that I should be given access to the numerous files of essays, speeches, manuscripts, notebooks, family albums and letters in his cabinets at The Garden House, the bungalow he had built on the edge of the castle moat, and where he lived in later years. There was, however, a great deal of additional material in the castle itself, older files, more personal letters. One autumn afternoon in 1978 we went to unlock the sanctum sanctorum. Our guide was Margaret Slythe, Kenneth Clark's sometime librarian, a sharp-eyed, teasing and perceptive friend of many years' standing.

The room was filled with a jumble of family memorabilia: old appointment books belonging to his first wife Jane, picture postcards, children's diaries, more letters and a great many files dealing with Kenneth Clark's years at the National Gallery, the Arts Council and elsewhere. One small trunk was jammed with newspaper clippings, torn and yellowing. There was a larger trunk full of family photographs. The three of us wandered around, picking up old postcards of Wales, forcing open file drawers and pausing briefly to inspect an area of the room where it seemed evident that there had been a recent bonfire. What had been burned? His letters to Jane had been found, but where were her letters to him? He looked by turns vague, wise and preoccupied. 'Ah!' he said and changed the subject. There were, nevertheless, plenty of clues to be assembled from the scattered fragments thrust in drawers and I could not hide my excitement. What was truly entrancing was the trunk of photographs: Jane posing for Man Ray, Jane in court dress, Jane with the twins Colin and Colette, Jane laughing up at her son Alan, Jane with short bobbed hair, her eyes impudently amused . . . We were uncovering one buried and forgotten treasure after another when Mrs Slythe happened to look in Kenneth Clark's direction and was beside him instantly. 'Perhaps you'd like to go back to the house?' she said gently. I caught the merest glimpse of his overwhelmed look; then he was gone.

MERYLE SECREST
Walpole, New Hampshire

1 Young Man Running

'Happy and Glorious
Not too Uproarious
God save our K.' – SIR OWEN MORSHEAD

Late in the morning one New Year's Day a young and immaculately dressed man ran up the steps of the National Gallery in London and entered its doors for the first time as director. One can set the opening scene almost too well, thanks to Whistler or those Neo Realist film-makers who pursued the labyrinthine course of their heroes' lives past clangorous traffic, groping pedestrians, bedraggled pigeons and billowing fog, using a palette of infinite greys. A face would appear in a blur, then hover in disembodied outline before disappearing into the ocherous, choking fog as the doors flapped and swung. The principal actor in this particular drama, however, merely jotted a skeletal reference in his diary for 1 Jan. 1934 to that fog, the worst for several years. To his private feelings there was no clue.

At the age of thirty Kenneth Clark had been invited to leave his post as keeper of the Department of Fine Art at the Ashmolean Museum in Oxford, itself a position 'many middle-aged men would have been satisfied to achieve', wrote his contemporary, Peter Quennell, and had taken the giant step to directorship of the National Gallery. The telegram offering him a five-year term of office arrived in the summer of 1933, when he was still only twenty-nine years old. He was the youngest man ever to be appointed at that time. 'Everything in life for you has gone so smoothly & beautifully & happily,' his friend, the famous hostess Sibyl Colefax wrote on New Year's Day 1934. 'I want it to continue so for always.'

There was no doubt that, as he hurried up that flight of steps in that anonymous London fog, Kenneth Clark was one of the most discussed, praised and envied young men in the British art world. Looking at the past, one found a rich man's child, brought up in isolated splendour amidst philistine Victorian bad taste, with a precocious love of art. By the age of nine or ten he was rehanging all the

I

paintings on his father's walls and confidently pronouncing upon them. He had vowed to become an artist and clung to his declaration throughout some exceptionally unhappy years in public school. Then, as his ambitions turned to writing about art, he was discovered, encouraged, literally rescued by two men who were to have an incalculable influence upon him. In later years, he would become famous as an administrator, connoisseur, spokesman, television personality and, most of all, writer: a figure of major importance in the art world.

All this was in the future when, in January 1934, Kenneth Clark, 'sharp-beaked, dark, bird-eyed, alert', took his decisive steps into the limelight. He had not only 'arrived', at the age of thirty, but he had appeared on the scene without a single ruffled hair or misplaced phrase. He was full of energy, authority and a most intimidating confidence. 'People of my generation thought it was a marvellous appointment,' commented the art dealer Sir Geoffrey Agnew. As for Kenneth Clark, he had hardly dared to breathe the words that to become director of the National Gallery had been his dearest ambition.

London's National Gallery, which was one of the first public collections, now about 150 years old, was founded with great opposition, particularly from artists. Constable is said to have declared, 'Should there ever be a National Gallery which is talked of, it will be the end of art in England.' Sir Thomas Lawrence and others were equally antagonistic, perhaps because these painters were afraid that a taste for Old Masters would prejudice their sales. Their fears did not materialize. At the urging of George IV, the government bought about forty paintings from a famous collection belonging to a Russian émigré banker, and a building was designed with a commanding view of Trafalgar Square, Nelson's column and numberless generations of pigeons. 'Wilkins's Pepper-pot', it was called, a derisive reference to the neo-classic dome and heavily columned front its architect had favoured. The quips were forgotten in the years to follow, as Parliament consistently approved handsome funds for acquisitions. The nation, it was decided, must own a complete historical collection. It became an Englishman's duty to offer a family heirloom to the National Gallery first, and the collection of treasures grew handsomely. By the time Kenneth Clark arrived, it was magnificent.

What hung on the walls was one matter; in terms of administration the Gallery was a shambles. Kenneth Clark succeeded Sir Augustus Daniel who, it was said, was 'a pure scholar . . . a retired country gentleman'. Others were less polite. Lord Lee of Fareham, who had been responsible for Kenneth Clark's appointment, commented that Daniel was retiring 'after five years' tenure of the post which had been without parallel for sheer incapacity and a kind of malignant timidity'. It was no secret that affairs at the National Gallery had been bungled for years. What another director, Sir Charles Holmes, called the 'strangling' of the National Gallery could be traced to an infamous Minute of Lord Rosebery's, adopted in 1894, by which the powers of the director were effectively nullified. From that time onwards the pettiest of decisions had to be referred by the director to his Board of Trustees. Holmes's predecessor retired, a broken man. Holmes himself soon found that the director's opinion seemed 'neither to be asked nor expected'. Such cavalier lack of respect from the trustees was matched by the staff. The keeper, in particular, theoretically a subordinate, had broad powers and guarded them with enthusiasm.

By the late 1920s the staff at the National Gallery were in a state of permanent rebellion against the trustees in general and the director in particular. Lord Lee, who had retired as chairman of the Board of Trustees in 1933, felt himself to be a victim of an '. . . ineradicable spirit of faction which had always permeated the staff'. Lord Balniel, who was to become chairman, commented feelingly that 'the whole place seems to be haunted by jealousies and intrigues and incompetence', adding that 'when National Gallery troubles arise they are Hydra-headed, Medusa-haired, Gorgon-eyed and Harpy nasty'.

The idea that some free-floating spirit of psychic ill-will inhabited the corridors, was seriously entertained. The eminently sensible Holmes wrote that, although he did not believe in such things, 'there must be something queer about the place. Only a few months ago I learned the experience of a most distinguished Trustee . . . a leader in every grave political contest for twenty years or more. Not one of his major activities took so much out of him as a Board Meeting at Trafalgar Square.'

The rows continued even though a Royal Commission, called in 1928, concluded that the director ought to be made the Gallery's chief administrative officer. This rudimentary notion was not put into effect until Kenneth Clark had been in office for almost a year, in November 1934. He was therefore walking into a job which one man after another had confessed himself unable to endure, one in which all actual power belonged to his trustees, and in which his subordinates thought he should act as a figurehead and leave the real work to them. The painter Philip Wilson Steer wrote to congratulate his young friend, while commenting privately that he supposed a young man would not mind a hornet's nest so much at that age. He would never have taken the position had he known the truth, Kenneth Clark wrote later – much later.

Within four years Kenneth Clark had been knighted, was living in a grand house in Portland Place and had made a secure position for himself as spokesman for the arts. Despite the predictable battles and in the face of a staff mutiny, he had triumphed. He appeared to be a man in full possession of his world and himself; indomitable. 'Many people would envy such a "success story",' the *Manchester Daily Express* commented rapturously.

The triumphs had not cheered him. In the summer of 1938 he wrote to his mother-in-law gloomily about the fact that he was almost thirty-five years old and approaching the middle of his allotted span. This was presumably the age at which Dante Alighieri, the fourteenth-century Florentine poet, found himself in a dark wood in which the path was lost. Dante, as one of the chief magistrates of Florence, had attempted to rule justly in the midst of violent political struggles, but was convicted in absentia, dispossessed and banished; left to wander through the villages and woods of Italy and wrestle with fearsome divisions inside himself.

It is clear that Kenneth Clark was beginning to feel an acute conflict of interests. On the one hand, he longed to write something of real worth and thought it ought to be possible to write about art with perception and insight. It was obvious that the longer he continued as a public servant, the less chance he had of developing as a writer.

On the other hand, he enjoyed his work. There was something intoxicating, to his rapid and restless mind, about administration. Compared to writing it was ridiculously easy. Even though he did not think he had much to boast about, enough people had reassured him on this point to make him believe he ought to remain. Yet he also confided, this time to his mother, that apart from its paintings, he absolutely detested the National Gallery. While knowing what he really wanted, or thought he wanted, he had accepted an invitation to remain there for a further five years as if sabotaging his own deepest desires and setting himself on the one course he deeply doubted. However, the fact that Kenneth Clark chose to describe his dilemma in terms of the *Divine Comedy*'s dark metaphor would seem to show more than simple confusion over objectives.

If, as the psychoanalyst Erik H. Erikson writes, human nature can best be studied in a state of conflict, Kenneth Clark's sense of being lost in a dark wood is a pivotal moment. To judge from a fascinating study of the lives of 310 painters, composers, poets, writers and sculptors, it is not unique. The death rate among such men and women, according to Elliott Jaques, suddenly increases between the ages of thirty-five and thirty-nine. Some creative artists surmount this and go on to work with greater maturity and insight than before; others, like Rossini, stop altogether. That there is such a pivotal period in mid life seems well established, as is the fact that the crisis is experienced more intensely by people of pronounced, even if unrealized, creativity. Those who are faced with such a crisis, according to Jaques, are actually confronting their own death, which they experience unconsciously as a fantasy of immobilization and helplessness. At this moment of profound depression, unresolved problems of childhood and adolescence can return with renewed force. Like pale ghosts they menace the adult feast, unwelcome spectres from a troubled past. In the case of Kenneth Clark that past was more than usually strewn with obstacles and beset with phantoms, ones that he had been taught to fear. Such emotions, he had learned in childhood, were to be avoided and suppressed since, if one did not keep the most vigilant control, they would, as his mother believed, erupt with disastrous consequences. For an example of what might happen if one did not exercise such absolute control, he had only to look at his father.

2 The Clarks of Paisley

'Sweetly blew the breath from the roses
And the birds swung and sang in a tree
While I sewed, and my lover sat holding
My white spool of Clark's O.N.T.' –
American advertising jingle, 1880s

One crossed a faultless expanse of gravel and stopped beside an imposing façade, which faced avenues of trees radiating from the front door like the spokes of a wheel, as far as the eye could see. The house was known as Sudbourne Hall and was owned by that *bon vivant*, the man who broke the bank at Monte Carlo, Kenneth Mackenzie Clark, always called K.

One entered a massive, high-ceilinged hall, which, if not exactly ordered over the telephone, may have had its origins in an equivalent Edwardian fashion. Kenneth Mackenzie Clark bought the eighteenth-century house, then a plain rectangular brick structure with a neo-classical exterior, on eleven thousand acres of the best shooting land in Suffolk, and called in an architect to improve matters. He then went abroad. For such an architect there was only one safe passage through the shoals of choices and he took it: the wealthy style. That style was expressed in terms of dark shiny woods, sumptuous fabrics and colours, curves, gilding and other elaborate ornamentation, one which took its cue from the antique rather than the contemporary.

Wealth, birth and manners, one author has said succinctly, were the qualifications for entrée into society in that halcyon period before the Great War. Kenneth Mackenzie Clark did not have, and would have scorned, the qualifications of birth, but had nothing to apologize for in manners or money. Some concept of his fortune can be gained from the fact that, when he married, he owned a small London house in Grosvenor Square, where the American Embassy now stands, a mansion in Perthshire, two yachts, and was about to buy Sudbourne Hall.

Sudbourne Hall, which was torn down in 1951, had some fifty

rooms – thirty-six bedrooms (thirteen of them for servants), eight bathrooms and six reception rooms. Of the three Adam fireplaces, one was somewhat damaged, probably during the Second World War when the house was used as a battle school by the War Department. There was a fine wooden porch and the doorway had a curious, interesting leaded fanlight – all demolished. But the pride of the house was its hallway and staircase, said to have two hundred and fifty pillars on the balustrading, each with a different carving in the Italian-ate manner. Week-end guests who crossed that vast expanse of Oriental carpeting, whose eyes might have rested briefly on a flam-boyantly carved grandfather clock, a gateleg table filled with photo-graphs and flowers, and a Scottish landscape painting on the far wall, would have mounted that panelled staircase, with its vistas of ferns and Greek marble statues, and made their way to one of the bedrooms. On the very edge of the servants' wing, had they advanced that far, they would have found a green baize door, beyond which was a nursery. In it was a baby boy, Kenneth Mackenzie Clark, always called K.

Sudbourne Hall was bought in 1904, a year after the young K was born on 13 July 1903. In one of the leather-bound photograph albums there is a picture of his proud mother, holding up a tiny white bundle with a pug nose and querulous little face. She has the baby at arm's length and from her expression one sees it all: the sense of pride in ownership – the way one displays a pedigree puppy, taking care to maintain a distance in case it should disgrace itself in one's lap. The correct distance.

The night nursery had a brass bedstead and, on its walls, a pattern of Kensington Palace roses. Up to the age of five, that pattern of roses was the young K's single memory. No memory of mother or father; no memory of that all-important figure, his nanny, who would be in command when he, attired in a sailor hat, a cape-collared coat and white gloves, and tucked around with fur, was deemed ready for inspection in his perambulator. When there were so many faces to remember they went past in a blur, and so the two-year-old K stared out solemnly beneath his extravagant hat, as if momentarily puzzled into silence.

There are numerous photographs of Kenneth Clark at this stage of his life: K, scarcely out of the cradle, fitted into a wickerlike contraption on top of a horse; K in a large cap and knee-length trousers with a cricket bat at the ready; K, with bony knees and pathetically thin legs, on the deck of a ship beside a dog, and K, in long stockings and short trousers, seated far from his mother on a wall as if mutely resigned to the distance between them. Repeatedly one sees the same expressions, which vary from a kind of wordless indignation to baffled sadness – the look of the bewildered child.

Another photograph shows the young boy leaning against his father's legs. There is a paternal hand on his shoulder, the fingers delicately touching his neck, while the other arm cradles a pugnacious-looking dog. The boy brings one hand up to meet his father's and, with the other, he holds the dog's paw, to link the figures of animal, child and man in a circle of enclosed warmth.

He saw his parents at the traditional time, that is, for an hour between afternoon tea and dressing for dinner. His mother, Margaret Alice (known by her second name), was the youngest of the six children of James McArthur of Manchester, formerly of Paisley, and a cousin of her husband's on his mother's side. There was a great deal of intermarriage between the McArthurs, who were Quakers, and the Clarks, so it was natural that, when Kenneth Mackenzie Clark decided to marry, he should choose this girl who had, in the fashion of genteel daughters brought up to do nothing, lived a quiet life in Godalming, with her mother, two older unmarried sisters and an eccentric unmarried brother, Fowler, whom she detested. They cannot have met very often, according to their son, 'but my father always said that he took a fancy to her from the start and was determined to marry her'.

Little is known about the McArthurs except that they had no money and were supported by their son-in-law. Even so, Alice, though moving from relative obscurity to affluence, was said to have married beneath her. They were wed in London in October 1900 when Alice was thirty-three and her husband thirty-two. After a decent interval Alice gave birth to a boy. It was a Caesarean delivery. She never had another child.

Everything about her manner suggested decorum and reticence: the unassuming way she stood, almost shrinking back, on the deck of her husband's yacht, the *Katoomba*, in leg o'mutton sleeves and simple black skirt; or sat in a wicker chair, uneasily balancing a large and unbecoming hat over her untidy hair, her manner indicating unregenerate plainness and an impenetrable shyness. She had, her son recalls, a love of words. She once confessed that, while feverish, she had written a play imitating George Bernard Shaw. On rare occasions when she managed to overcome her reserve, she could talk animatedly and amusingly. Perhaps the most revealing aspect of her nature is illustrated by an incident which took place during the Second World War, when she sat knitting in the library of her son's house in Hampstead. Thinking that she smelled smoke, Alice Clark calmly rose and retired to another room. In a matter of moments the library floor collapsed. Someone eventually summoned the fire brigade. One pictures a retreating back, the impassive face, and a myopic refusal to see the obvious.

Alice had a real horror of emotion. She would not listen to music and feared going to church in case she might be so affected as to feel something. Christmas was anathema for the same reason. She came, it would seem, from a family that had placed effective taboos on any demonstration of emotion and for whom correct behaviour, reticence and exquisite politeness were all. One presented an impregnable façade to the world and if unruly feelings escaped they were sternly suppressed or, if that were not possible, ignored.

What united his parents, their son said, was their lack of the least social pretension and their bright-mindedness. There is no question that Alice adored her husband. She lived only for him. As a result her son, who could not remember being touched by his mother, felt 'very much neglected' by her. The remark was made with a detachment uncoloured by resentment. Other feelings can be glimpsed in his manner of describing the objectionable way wealthy parents banished their children to boarding schools at the first available opportunity. It was not enough that he was being brought up by a succession of servants. He must be removed altogether.

There was, her son said, a fund of buried sensuality in his mother, which found an outlet in food. One must wonder how much of it was ever channelled into the act of sex. In that respect one knows as little about her husband. Kenneth Clark also said, 'My father once told me that he liked tarts, but I couldn't bring myself to ask which kind.' He also said that his father had been delighted to be much sought after before marriage and that he ceased to be a ladies' man only because his wife would not let him out of her sight. There is a photograph of Kenneth Mackenzie Clark in the south of France in later life walking jauntily along the street with a very pretty woman on his arm and Alice Clark at an equable distance. What is certain is that Kenneth Mackenzie Clark was his wife's temperamental opposite: a gregarious, emotionally mercurial and generous man, a Churchillian figure. Like that British statesman he had launched himself into life. At the age of fourteen he had left school to accompany one of his brothers to Australia, a country that so entranced him that he named a yacht *Katoomba* in remembrance. After a stay in New Zealand he returned to join senior members of the family business. His son thought that his father had held down a job for only two years but this seems inaccurate, since in 1890 he went to Russia on the firm's business and was still employed six or seven years later.

Kenneth Mackenzie Clark, with his large and beautifully shaped head, his eccentricities (he was inordinately proud of his legs and seized every sartorial excuse to display them), his mountebank hats and his swashbuckling cigars, is an ingratiating figure. While he, too, left his son in the care of servants, it is evident that he took his parental role much more seriously than did his wife. He was the one who took the young K to the water's edge to show him the fish flickering below, or dug into the business of making a sand castle while his son, arms akimbo, watched critically. He was the one who provided tireless demonstrations of his miraculous conjuring skills. Rabbits would appear and disappear out of hats and guests' watches would be eaten. He was the best fun in the world.

All the pastimes thought proper to a gentleman were taught to the young K. Kenneth Mackenzie Clark played billiards or snooker every night of his life and his son was entranced. Golf was another game the young K dutifully learned and enjoyed enough to pursue into adulthood. Sailing, the family passion, was exciting, but that other favourite water sport of his father's, angling, a dreadful bore (although one tried to like it). Then there was learning to shoot. K was also taught to ride, the one sport his father did not practise. A sequence of photographs, from babyhood, shows the squirming child perched on a horse, and the same look of outraged protest. One day an ancient pony, guaranteed incapable of acceleration, was found for the young K to ride. He mounted reluctantly. It walked a few steps and lay down. The Clarks, obviously, were not fated to be horsemen.

The company that had made Kenneth Mackenzie Clark so rich is one of the most distinguished in the British textile industry. Its origins go back to the mid eighteenth century, when a farmer from Renfrewshire named William Clark died at the age of forty-three, leaving a widow, Agnes, and six small children. His wife gave up the farm and moved to Paisley, centre of the Scottish weaving trade, apprenticing her eldest son Allan as a weaver. James, aged six, became a draw-boy, standing hour after hour at a loom, pulling warp threads through heddle loops. In due course James became a master weaver, married, and installed his family at the aptly named No. 10 Cotton Street.

Handloom weavers like James Clark needed a constant supply of smooth twine, always made of silk, for the loops through which the warp threads were passed. James Clark first made his own silk loops and then, in partnership with his brother Patrick, began to sell them from No. 10 Cotton Street. Just as his business as a weaver's furnisher was beginning to prosper, fate intervened. It was 1805, the year of Nelson's great victory against Napoleon, the Battle of Trafalgar. Its effects threatened to be catastrophic for the master weavers of Paisley since Napoleon, in retaliation, placed an embargo on European trade with Britain. This effectively cut off the supply of silk from Hamburg for the manufacture of the crucial heddle loops. The cotton industry had been growing rapidly in Britain, but no one had so far managed to invent a method of making cotton thread which could replace silk in the heddle loops. Patrick Clark, however, was determined. After hours of ingenious experimentation, he devised the first satisfactory cotton heddle loop. The weavers were saved.

The Clarks soon realized that their new cotton would make a sewing thread as well, one that had distinct advantages over the silk and linen thread then in use. Their inventiveness had a further sequel. At the time sewing thread was sold in hanks or skeins, which the sewer wound into little balls, as one winds a hank of wool. A thread as fine as cotton presented almost intractable handling problems, but another Clark had the notion of winding the thread onto a wooden spool. In 1813 the Clarks opened their first cotton thread factory in Paisley. It was to make that town the most important manufacturing centre for cotton thread in the world. The boast was, 'It's Paisley thread that holds the world together.'

Those Scottish upstarts, the Clarks, had to decide whether to join the ranks of the nineteenth-century industrialists scrambling for entry into the British upper classes, or maintain their status as 'being in trade'. They chose the latter course: better to be honest thread families respected by a town than social climbers whose base strivings cost them their self-respect. When Maundy Gregory, Lloyd George's chief agent in the sale of honours, suggested to Kenneth Mackenzie Clark that a title, that *sine qua non* of entry into the right ranks, was obtainable for a price, he was told to go to hell.

The Clarks therefore stayed in Paisley and sent branches of the
family to the New World to set up thread companies in Newark, New
Jersey. They were well liked. John Clark of Gateside (there are so
many Johns, Jameses, Williams and Roberts in each generation that it
is necessary to refer to a Clark by his place of origin), a great-uncle of
Kenneth Clark, was a lifelong bachelor who created a family of
friendships around him. He had an inscription carved in stone at the
entrance to his conservatory : THE ORNAMENTS OF MY HOUSE ARE MY
FRIENDS. (A wit amended that inscription to 'fiends'.) He was Uncle
John to countless children, went shooting and played whist and
billiards, and was a great yachtsman and angler. He was also known for
his generosity. He gave the town of Largs on the west coast of Scotland
a much-needed hospital, spent £30,000 to rebuild a church, repaired the Esplanade and maintained a soup kitchen. But then they
were all generous. The descendants of a Renfrewshire farmer had, by
the 1880s, given their birthplace a town hall, a free public library, an art
gallery, a museum, an observatory, public gardens and school recreation grounds. At least one Clark (George) had a statue erected in his
honour.

The Clark tradition of benevolent paternalism extended to the mills
they managed. They steadily improved working conditions, instituted
benefit and pension schemes and organized summer picnics and excur-
sions. William Clark in particular pioneered the practice of giving a
Saturday half-holiday for workers who, in the 1880s, regularly worked
a twelve-hour day, six days a week. He took such an indefatigable
interest in their well-being that he visited every employee on sick
leave, to satisfy himself that the invalid was receiving proper care. Such
largesse by the Clarks was invariably accompanied by a commendable
lack of self-promotion. It was philanthropy by stealth.

Paisley in the 1880s was a town in transition. On the one hand there
still existed descendants of the early weavers, small businessmen who
set up shop in their own thatched cottages, thrifty, abstemious and
law-abiding, proud of their town and their own skills. Their numbers
were steadily declining, however, as the hand-looming trade was
engulfed by mass manufacturing. As the mills expanded, so did the
hordes of men and women workers who jammed into the wretched
tenements, and whose one recreation was drinking.

By the nineteenth century, alcohol and its excesses had become a
serious social problem. Some Paisley citizens, bent on self-improve-
ment, spent their precious hours of free time in the library, while

others, down around Paisley Cross, reeled on the pavements on Sunday afternoons. One day in court Bailie (alderman) James Clark of Chapel fined a shopkeeper £3 after his wife was found to be hiding eight gills of whisky, forty-five bottles of ale and eight bottles of porter. Bailie Clark was, like Kenneth Clark's great-uncle John, a lifelong teetotaller. When not imposing sentence in court, he could be found on the temperance platform, describing alcohol as a serpent, adder, canker, plague, poison, roaring lion, fiery dart and rank weed.

Then Kenneth Mackenzie Clark (whose father, another Bailie named James, this time of Ralston, was one of the four major stockholders) joined the Clark Thread Company beside his uncles, Stewart Clark of Kilnside and John Clark of Gateside. This was in about 1890, when he was just twenty-two years old. He was soon sent, with a delegation of other thread manufacturers, to negotiate in St Petersburg for the sale of thread to Russia. The trip was a success and, on his return, he was put to work negotiating, with his uncles, the sale of the Clark mills to a larger rival, J. & P. Coats Ltd of Paisley – about which there had been rumours for decades. Negotiations dragged on through the early 1890s, culminating in 1896, when Kenneth and Stewart Clark (John Clark having died two years before) sold the family firm for the then magnificent sum of £2,585,913. Shortly thereafter Kenneth Mackenzie Clark lost interest. 'He thought to himself, if business interferes with your pleasure, give up business,' his son commented drily.

Kenneth Mackenzie Clark was, like his Uncle John before him, punctual to a quixotic degree. Uncle John had been known to make an appointment for 8 minutes to 9 a.m., and the visitor who did not keep Greenwich Mean Time was in for a shock. It was said that if Uncle John were on a yachting trip, and found himself arriving at port two hours before his announced appearance, he would anchor outside the breakwater for two hours and wait. As for Kenneth Mackenzie Clark, another great yachtsman who loved to read Conrad's yarns about the sea, a race against time was his idea of real sport. In 1901, he entered his yacht, the *Kariad*, in a race to prove he owned the fastest yacht in Scotland.

Yachting had been, for decades, the preferred amusement of rich industrial families in the west of Scotland. It was a tradition of the sea in that part of Scotland, where innumerable sea lochs are sliced by bleak headlands, that the Clyde estuary provided a paradise for the amateur sailor. Uncle John had several first-class yachts (one of

them, ninety-five feet long, took a crew of eighteen and had a saloon
of white and gold, with ebony and gold furnishings) while the leading
members of the Coats family built equally resplendent vessels which
were virtually floating houses. Kenneth Mackenzie Clark's *Kariad*, at
eighty feet, was racing against James Coats's *Sybarita*, which was
ninety feet on the waterline and was therefore given an eight-minute
handicap. The course was forty miles down the Clyde and back, the
purse £500.

When the morning came for the race, a heavy gale was blowing and
both yachts set out with topmasts housed and sails close-reefed, the
Kariad barely behind the *Sybarita*. The smaller yacht proved so difficult to shake off that the *Sybarita*, in defiance of the winds, let out an
extra reef and made it to the finish through a hailstorm, two minutes
and forty-three seconds ahead of her rival. The force of the storm
had, however, ripped twenty feet of copper sheathing from both sides
of the *Sybarita*'s bows. Workers in the Coats factory celebrated the
victory, while workers in the Clark factory pointed out that it had
been won at the cost of damaging the yacht. What Kenneth Mackenzie Clark thought is not recorded.

By the turn of the century, only Kenneth Mackenzie Clark and his
older brother, William Campbell, were left in what had been a family
of nine children. The whisky bottle, Kenneth Clark wrote, had
claimed everyone else. This seems a slight overstatement (it is known
that at least one of the brothers, James Alexander, died in Colorado
Springs after a collision overturned his carriage), but it is certainly
true that they died disastrously soon: Christina at the age of twenty-
two, Clara Clark Baxter at twenty-six, Norman at twenty-nine, John
George at thirty-eight ... The Paisley split between the upright and
comatose seemed uncannily mirrored, in the Clark family, between
those ruled by stern morality and those who were rebelling against its
dictates. 'Oh, Mr Clark, you'll have a wee whisky with me?' was the
accepted method of business negotiation in those days. By the time
his son was born, Kenneth Mackenzie Clark was a confirmed drinker.

3 Keeping Secrets

'Never imagine that children who don't say, or
ask, don't know. In their blank eyes and
heedless ears is hidden their attempt to make
away with what they cannot swallow. Unable
to become shock-proof except by cutting off
response, they must go deaf and blind.' –
ROSAMOND LEHMANN

The site once occupied by Sudbourne Hall is bare nowadays. Gone
are the flights of steps, the brick columns with their stone pilasters,
the cupid-ornamented fountain, the roses and the bay windows.
Grouped around a courtyard, only the stables remain, of unadorned
brick but with an occasional fanciful touch – a domed turret and a
beautifully proportioned archway – to tease the eye with the
unexpected.

Even in Kenneth Clark's childhood few horses were kept, but there
were several cars, including a Rolls-Royce, two Delaunay-Bellevilles
and a Panhard. He went to look at them every day and perhaps this is
why his first memory of childhood was of a motor race in the park,
staged in honour of his fifth birthday. The great disappointment of
the day was that the cars did not start at the same moment, tearing
across the gravel and racing hell-bent down those dwindling perspectives of chestnut, elm and beech, but sedately took turns. The
winning car was a neighbour's Mercedes.

He remembered how difficult it was to learn to read and, like
Charlemagne, thought he would never master the art, but the rewards were worth the effort. Chief among them were a series of books
written by Bertha Upton, a British woman living in the United States,
and illustrated by her daughter, Florence, which Kenneth Clark
believed had a profound influence on his character. The name 'Golliwog' (with its overtones of 'polliwog', an American word for tadpole)
was the perfect choice for the shaggy-haired black doll the Uptons
had invented. Golliwog became a transatlantic sensation after the
first book was published in 1895 and sequels followed until 1909.

He never forgot Golliwog, who lived on harmonious terms with five wooden dolls. Later he described Golliwog as an eternal optimist, forever setting out on some great adventure, only to be overcome by disasters. To be constantly chivalrous and gentlemanly, like Golliwog, even though forever floored by fate: the message made a deep impression upon the young K. The linoleum floor of the nursery was the ideal place to build elaborate architectural triumphs, using an array of pediments, arches, columns and bases. The resulting inventions were displayed to those visitors who could be cajoled into admiring them. Of guests there was a ready supply, since the main reason for the family's presence at Sudbourne was the shoot.

The sport of fox-hunting had always been the prerogative of aristocrats. Stalking the fields with a gun and a dog in search of rabbit, pheasant or partridge was considered the proper amusement of 'inferior persons' according to Bishop Latimer. However, by the turn of the century, advances in gun design, new railway lines which could take guests deep into the country and, most of all, the example of the Prince of Wales, who was an excellent shot, had radically changed the picture. It became the height of fashion to shoot whatever could be persuaded to run or fly in front of a gun. And, indeed, the manner of persuasion had radically changed.

In the old days gentlemen walked through the woods and shot the birds they disturbed. Now the gentlemen stayed put while small armies of 'beaters' manoeuvred the flocks in the right direction. To guard further against disappointment birds were expressly reared for the slaughter (some twelve thousand pheasants a year at Sandringham, the Prince of Wales's estate). They were destroyed in equally impressive numbers. The more one shot, the higher one's rank and the closer in fraternity to the Prince of Wales.

It was an expensive sport, but income tax at that time was about 5d. in the pound, and men like Kenneth Mackenzie Clark could afford to be lavish. Indeed, it was considered an advantage to be invited by the *nouveau riche* rather than the aristocracy, since the former would be more likely to have adequate plumbing (though Sudbourne Hall, with only eight bathrooms, was disappointingly lax in that regard). In this respect there is a story about one hostess who was entertaining King Edward VII for the first time and had spent a fortune on redecorating her house. She ventured to ask whether everything was to her monarch's liking. 'The King thought for a moment, and then said it might be an idea to put a hook in the bathroom door.'

Guests invited to Sudbourne would take the train from London to Wickham Market station on Monday or Tuesday evenings, where they would be picked up in the Delaunay-Bellevilles. The cars would scrunch up to the entrance and the young K would hang over the banisters, sniffing the deliciously unfamiliar aroma of petrol, assessing the furs and counting cigars, eager to see how many familiar faces he could find. Next morning, the guns and their ladies would appear for breakfast at 9. The men would be immaculately attired in Harris tweed shooting suits, usually jackets and waistcoats worn with knee breeches and long socks, made by the wearer's own tailor to his specification. The royal family, and particularly King George v, always wore shooting spats on the field, and these had been adopted by other crack shots. It was considered smart for the men to breakfast standing. The menu was likely to include boar's head and cold turkey as well as the usual scrambled eggs and bacon, kidneys, kippers, scones and marmalade.

Given the implicit assumptions of the shoot: its emphasis upon skill, its manly overtones, its exclusivity, even its social necessity (since no Englishman could protest that he did not shoot if he wished to be invited for the week-end), it was only a matter of time before a gun would be placed in the hands of the young K. At the age of ten he stood in line with his father, waiting for the moment when those feathered targets wheeled over their heads. Then he aimed and fired. To see dead and dying pheasants whacking down in their hundreds was bad enough. Then, however, his father took him hare shooting in the marshes near Sudbourne, and he was horrified to discover that the animals, when wounded, screamed in agony. That experience turned him into a confirmed opponent of blood sports.

Some of the most famous hosts in England, it was said, hardly troubled to serve their guests anything more for lunch than a squashed sandwich in a paper bag. However, at Sudbourne, as at Sandringham, it was customary to have a proper lunch out of doors, served with ceremonious disregard for wet turf and ants. The ladies would join the guns at one of the thatched pavilions in the woods, built expressly to hold a party of fourteen, and the feasting would begin: oysters and liver pâté, steak and kidney pudding, cold turkey, ham, treacle tart, double Cottenham cheese and then, in case there were any corners left to fill, a marvellously indigestible plum cake. The guns sometimes drank more than they should, and the afternoon's performance would not compare with that of the morning. Later, there would be moody silences at the billiard table, interrupted by the crash of soda syphons diluting gargantuan glasses of whisky, while the women drank tea. Every evening there was another stupefying meal after which the guests would grope their way to bed. Or rather, the male guests did so.

Ladies at these parties may have wilted, but hardly from fatigue, since they were barred from shooting. They therefore went for walks, wrote letters, took drives or, less often, and braving clouds of acrid smoke, went to watch the shoot. Their hostess, Alice Clark, could always be found seated near her husband. Or they changed clothes yet again, since a shooting party required an elegant breakfast outfit, usually of velvet or silk, then tweeds for lunch with the guns and two chilly afternoon drives. Drinking tea called for an extravagant gown, and dinner for an all-out affair in satin or brocade. Since it was considered bad form to be seen in the same clothes twice, and since most shooting-parties lasted for four days, this involved an outlay of sixteen outfits for a single house-party.

The continual parade of colours, textures, patterns and designs had an immediate lure for the young K. After tea he would be sent to bed with his usual prunes and junket, but not yet to sleep. After the ladies had changed for the last time that day they would present themselves and good-humouredly parade around while he decided who should win a prize. Watching others dressing up was all part of some elaborate game, linked in his mind with a host of delightful pastimes because, in those days, guests were expected to entertain as well as be entertained. The age of the parlour baritone was over, but magical tricks were considered high social accomplishments. Kenneth Clark dressed up himself when, each winter, his parents visited Cap Martin and he appeared at the annual Battle of Flowers, attired as a bird or perhaps an elegant huntsman. Among his other delights were visits to the Casino at Mentone where conjurors, jugglers, acrobats and stuntmen demonstrated their prowess for two hours. He liked the men who balanced chairs on their heads, and no one was more critical than he of the way rabbits were drawn out of hats. He would go home and write plays of his own, with his Golliwog and teddy bear as actors. Then his mother and guests would have to come and watch while he, loving acting and the attention, entertained them.

He had another favourite occupation. From the age of about seven onwards he kept himself amused by rehanging the paintings on the walls of Sudbourne Hall. No one seems to have thought it strange that a boy of his age should occupy himself in this way and no one tried to prevent him. The only problem appeared to be finding a servant willing to help. That usually meant Sam, whose only clear duty was to iron the newspapers – a relic of the early days of the nineteenth century when newsprint arrived wet. He and Sam did not try to rehang the larger items (*Murthley Moss* by Sir John Millais, or *Bathers* by Fred Walker), but the rest, and there must have been at least a hundred, were taken down and reshuffled every month; the instinct to organize and rearrange was already well developed.

Guests who had arrived early in the week had usually left by Saturday. That left Sunday, to be devoted to Kenneth Mackenzie Clark's other passion, his prize animals. These had their antecedents in 1898 when A.H.E.Wood bought the estate and founded the Sudbourne Stud Farm. Wood kept only pedigree stock and, after Kenneth Mackenzie Clark bought the estate in 1904, he concentrated on breeding work horses, called Suffolk Punches, which became world famous. The young K loved to go and inspect the handsome winners of so many silver cups on dark shining bases. Invariably, as he ran his hands over the heavy brown roundness of the horses' glistening bodies, he thought of conkers (horse-chestnuts) – forming yet another indelible visual impression.

He was always asking to be driven to Aldeburgh in the governess cart, although his parents did not understand why and neither did he. The fragile water-colour palette of the Suffolk coast, with its wandering woods giving way to sandy commons, its estuaries and marshes, its evanescent greens and pearled silvers, became the standards against which all other landscapes would be measured. Once there, he would roam around the beach looking for pieces of amber (he never found any) and picking up fistfuls of pebbles. He would end his fruitless search for amber by buying a piece in Mr Stephenson's shop, then return home in the company of an elderly and bewhiskered groom, his pockets full of the fast-fading pebbles.

Stays at Sudbourne lasted from the start of the pheasant-shooting season on 1 October until the end of January, when the Clarks moved to the French Riviera. There Kenneth Mackenzie Clark was, his son recalled, amazingly lucky at gambling. After a handsome win he would buy elaborately decorated hats for his lady friends, order quantities of linen from the Grande Maison du Blanc to appease Alice, and his son would find piles of gleaming gold coins in the dip of his father's bed in the mornings.

After 20 April it was considered social suicide to remain on the Riviera and Kenneth and Alice Clark would repair to Marienbad, or Carlsbad, for the ritual of a cure. There, their son remarked, they ate and drank only twice as much as people do nowadays. He would be sent back to the vast silence of Sudbourne Hall.

He denied that he ever felt lonely. His was the absorbed solitude of the only child, too engrossed to notice the vacant chairs, inventing games in which he was the actor, audience and stage. There was Golliwog. There were three or four teddy bears. There was a blue frog named Jacqueline and a live parrot, bought in Monte Carlo, that sat on his shoulder as he walked around the garden, and whom he dearly loved. In short, he amused himself and, when the silence became noticeable, filled it with the sound of his own voice. By early manhood he had formed the habit of talking to himself on long walks. That such apparent self-sufficiency might have concealed a need for human dialogue that had not been expressed is suggested by Kenneth Clark's recollection that, from an early age, he played on the floor with his parents' collection of porcelain. These became his toys and from then onwards he placed small *objets d'art* as if they were engaged in a conversation.

What Kenneth Clark feared far more than being left alone were the times when some well-meaning adult would arrange to have other children play with him. He did not know what to do with them. They made fun of his teddy bears, his bricks and toy soldiers. They teased and twisted his wrists. After several hours of this kind of jollity he could not wait to be alone.

Unprepared as he was to deal with childish hostility, the young K was even more at a loss when faced with that of the Sudbourne servants. Whatever resentment they felt for Kenneth and Alice Clark was concealed until it could be vented upon their hapless son. He claims that he was actually fed rotten food: worm-eaten cheese, curdled milk, rancid butter and bitter fruit. Meanwhile, in The Room in which the butler, cook and housekeeper ate in dignified separation from the Servants' Hall, he could not help knowing that they ate the best food his father's money could buy.

Even if one discounts such acts of petty meanness, the diet of an Edwardian child was likely to be dismal, according to Marghanita Laski, writing on domestic life in *Edwardian England, 1901–1914*. Ignorance virtually ensured that no child of whatever class would be properly fed. Rich children were filled with stodge, never saw fresh fruit, and a thin, nervous, easily nauseated child might be force fed on cream and thickly sliced bread and butter. All his life Kenneth Clark dreamed at least once a week about splendid meals: 'Wonderful meals: jugged hare, venison, figs with *prosciutto* . . .'

Early in June they would travel to London, where his parents had leased a flat at 25 Berkeley Square, and he would be taken to see Squire Bancroft, George Alexander and Gerald du Maurier in the plays of J.M.Barrie and Charles Hawtrey. There Kenneth Mackenzie Clark paused briefly, *en route* from the soberer pleasures: yachting at Cowes, fishing for salmon in Scotland and grouse shooting on the Scottish moors. It was an agreeable year, brought to its fitting conclusion on 1 October, with the start of a new pheasant-shooting season and the return to Sudbourne. Shaw would have called it a lifetime of happiness, adding, 'No man alive could bear it: it would be hell on earth.'

Kenneth Mackenzie Clark usually drank gin in the morning. In those days it was considered rakish to want Scotch so soon, but a gin and tonic was acceptable. Later in the day he would consume half a bottle of whisky in public and considerably more off-stage. He also drank a bottle of champagne a night as befitted a man who could have been mistaken for that great personality of the Edwardian music halls, Champagne Charlie. He drank every day but some days more than others. 'I have a great many memories of my father being in bed with a bad leg, as it was called,' Kenneth Clark recalled.

Those were the terrible times when, all the guests having left, Kenneth Mackenzie Clark would go to bed for three days or sit at dinner plunged into an intimidating gloom. At times like these one's normally ebullient and responsive father had turned into a rather 'alarming uncle'. Whenever the drunken binges were too frequent the young K and his mother would have to take his father to a London nursing-home at 9 Mandeville Place, run by a sinister lady named Miss Gordon. The 'drying out' process was never lengthy but there were many trips to Mandeville Place.

Kenneth Clark never ceased to find his father's behaviour puzzling, even baffling. He stoutly maintained, to the end of his life, that nothing was wrong. His parents were wonderfully happily married. The only problem, as he saw it, was that his mother tried to intervene. Her sole ambition in life became to stop her husband's drinking – an aim never to be fulfilled, since he died of cirrhosis of the liver. She would become aggrieved and resentful, pull a miserable face, beg and plead and burst into tears. Kenneth Clark could still see her pale, tear-swollen face and hear her agonizing reproaches. 'If she could once have had a drink with my father things might have gone better. But she never touched a drop.'

On the occasions when his father became unusually drunk his first thought would be to get a pony trap and go to the nearby village of Orford to call on his mother-in-law. 'I would have to get in with him and we'd be swaying all over the road and driving on the grass. Somehow we would arrive.' They would be met by his mother's two lady-like sisters and the well-born Mrs James McArthur, née Sarah Jane Flintoff, that lady of granite-like breeding and adamant good manners. None of them would see anything amiss. Perfect courtesy and perfect pretence.

Silence was the code followed by any Edwardian family with a position to maintain. Such matters were a family secret because to have revealed the truth would have been too humiliating. Kenneth Clark recalled other occasions when, for instance, *en route* to their house in Scotland, they would stop overnight in Edinburgh at the North British Hotel and his father would choose that moment to become particularly drunk. Rather than face Alice's martyred expression, his father would take over a sofa in the hotel drawing-room and make himself as conspicuous as possible. No doubt he called too loudly for the waiter or tipped over his glass. Perhaps he launched into his fertile repertory of music-hall songs, one of which began, 'Am I a man or am I a mouse?'

Guests would make their views known. The hotel staff would be summoned and the wife informed. She would not appear but, in the tradition of Victorian melodrama, of waifs sent to knock on doors of pubs, would despatch her son. He, a small figure, completely unable to dislodge his father, would have to brave the silent barrage of eyes and rouse him. Finally, with the help of a porter, Kenneth Mackenzie Clark might be persuaded to stagger into the hotel lift, mumbling 'An old dog for a hard road'.

There were similar occasions in London, whenever they visited the flat in Berkeley Square. Kenneth Mackenzie Clark would repair to his club after dinner and invariably get drunk. A messenger would be sent and young K, aged eleven or twelve, would have to go there, get his father into a taxi and somehow get him up to bed. He said, 'I couldn't explain to people what a dear old boy he really was, and I felt terribly embarrassed and never got used to it.' Perhaps the most

difficult thing of all was that he could not confide in anyone. 'That was
the trouble.'

When one's father has lost control and one's mother refuses to act,
the son must take charge. One must somehow stop him from driving
off the road and endangering both their lives. One must brave the
firing-line of hostile eyes and assume the burden. *Noblesse oblige*!
Didn't Golliwog, that intrepid hero of Florence and Bertha Upton,
present an example of chivalry more compelling than the Knights of
the Arthurian legend? Didn't grandmother pretend not to notice
when his father staggered in drunk? How infinitely grateful his father
was for her kindness and tact! He could and must take charge of the
father he loved, if only to spare him those incessant reproaches.

Was the child told not to tell, or was it merely assumed by those
around the young K that he would never ask questions and never
breathe a word? 'We must be clear on the issue that many vows of
silence are self-imposed,' writes Thomas J. Cottle in a study entitled
Children's Secrets. 'And if the phrase "vows of silence" rings with a
monastic sound, then it is an apt description. For many children,
themselves practically stricken by the mental illness of a parent, have
chosen to live an almost monastic existence . . . Children's loyalty to
parents, taking, as it does, many forms, often seems remarkable.'

Children who take on the burden of a family secret, such as alco-
holism, which family members somehow make the child believe will
bring about their humiliation, shame or personal ruin if the truth is
ever known, are marked and marred by the experience. The child
leads his life in a world of 'as if', that is to say, 'as if' the parent is
perfectly normal, 'as if' he does not drive recklessly, 'as if' he isn't
suffering from a hangover and 'as if' he isn't making a public spectacle
of himself in the rooms of a club. However, the act of assuming an
adult burden, in order to spare his mother and protect his father from
himself, 'often causes the secret-keeper to feel shame', Cottle writes.
'It seems ironic that the act of secret-keeping should represent a
process whereby people not only prevent shame from spreading . . .
but . . . take the shame into themselves.' It is as if the child himself
becomes an accomplice in the act, guilty by association.

Or, to turn the analogy around, it is as if the boy can see that the
adults are deluding themselves, yet, out of loyalty to the emperor,
insists that he can see clothes. Such a preserving of what he knows to
be false obliges a child to disown his true feelings and hypocritically
pretend to those he does not have. Whatever fear, grief or shame he

feels must be smothered, at least in public. He becomes the confused and helpless victim of a game he never asked to join.

Later, Kenneth Clark was to decide that those obligatory acts of rescue had made him precociously closed-off and on the defensive. He had sensed that such a child will become wary of any kind of intimate relationship, with its potential for so much pain. Holding on so tightly to a secret can put the child into a psychological isolation booth. 'One stands alone with one's secret; there is no one to hug . . . If no one touches me, I am not loved. If I cannot express my feelings, I am unlovable . . .'

He became afraid of the dark. His old nursery, with its brass bedstead and wallpaper of Kensington Palace roses, was familiar and comforting, but when he graduated to a more grown-up bedroom, he became convinced that it was haunted. Whenever he closed his eyes, sharp images of witches and goblins would rise up, those monsters from the scourge of the infant imagination, Arthur Rackham. The more tired he was, the more vivid and sharp were the long pointing nails, the accusing fingers. His eyes would fly open, seeking the comforting outlines of a headboard, a lamp, an end table. Such reassurance had been forbidden by the law of governesses, in this case Miss Frankish. There was to be no night light for Kenneth Mackenzie Clark, also called K. He was too old.

Children who are chronically under the pressure of fearful expectations often become more tense at night. Instead of protective figures and the reassurance of familiar outlines there is only an empty room and an impenetrable dark. Such children are, in short, left to the mercy of their own hostile impulses, which many a youngster can face only with the help of loving adults, who can make it clear to him that his angry feelings are not as overwhelming as he, in his panic, thinks they are.

K begged for a chink of light that would put those images of inner terror to rout, kill them off, but the adults were adamant. He was left to do battle with his demons alone.

4 Moments of Vision

'It is through ... Art and Art only that we can
shield ourselves from the sordid perils of actual
existence.' — OSCAR WILDE

In the nineteenth century Sudbourne Hall belonged to Sir Richard
Wallace, illegitimate son of the wealthy Marquess of Hertford, who
had inherited several handsome properties, including houses in
London and Paris. Since Wallace was an assiduous collector, one
assumes that a representative sampling of his paintings, armour,
furniture and *objets d'art* found their way into Sudbourne Hall.

Wallace was, as Kenneth Clark was to describe him, a *grand amateur*, one who was determined to surround himself with the most
sumptuous and costly of ambiences. It was not enough that a picture be
a genuine Rubens or Watteau; it must be the finest in the master's
œuvre. What Wallace tended to like was a polished and elaborate
surface, and this showed itself in his collection of Sèvres porcelain and
enamel snuff boxes. When faced with paintings that did not fall into the
category of safe masterpieces, Wallace was led astray by this penchant
for shiny surfaces, closely allied with his taste for agreeable subjects
and beautiful bosoms. The result was a disastrous accumulation of
works by Jean Baptiste Greuze, the eighteenth-century exponent of
light-hearted fluff, and not a single painting by Jean Baptiste Chardin.

No mementoes of the Wallace talent for enhancing life remained at
Sudbourne when it was acquired by the Clarks, save for some characteristically luxurious game books, of green morocco ornamented with
gold pheasants and partridges, which the host would present to his
shooting-party guests. There were, however, several books which had
belonged to Wood, the previous owner, on the library shelves and, in
fact, the library was the nicest room in the house. It had seven full-sized
sofas and four armchairs, or was it the other way around? A child
might be happy there for hours contemplating the pewter kettles in
back issues of the *Connoisseur* or looking at *Punch*.

The moment at which the young K decided to become an artist

cannot be known but it must have been during those hours in the library that he conceived his ambition: to have a drawing accepted by *Punch*. The priggish jibes of du Maurier merely bored him and the drawings of Leech left him cold. Charles Keene was another matter. This particular artist had qualities the young K was beginning to appreciate vividly: a love of all that was rarefied, subtle and understated in style, allied to a lively sense of humour. Keene was particularly good at 'sending up' drunks.

Perhaps the decision in favour of art was in the air, a legacy of Sudbourne and one of its distinguished owners. There is no doubt that its newest owner, for all his shortcomings, genuinely loved art. Kenneth Mackenzie Clark's eye was unschooled and he sometimes made some disastrous choices, or bought modest examples of an admired school, at that time the Barbizon. However, he had the good sense to admire works by Théodore Rousseau and J.F. Millet. He had personally known the Scottish painter Sir W.Q. Orchardson and, when he died, bequeathed to his son at least one painting that he loved ever after: *The Last Dance*. He also gave his son an important piece of advice. 'Don't spend your money in silly ways,' he said. 'Save up and buy a nice picture.'

On 25 December 1910, when K was seven years old, he received a present that was to become his favourite book. It was a large volume on the Louvre and contained fifty colour plates. The reproduction was poor but nevertheless gave him some idea of classical European painting. He admired one work so much that he tried to copy it: *Il Condottiere* by Antonello da Messina. This portrait of a man in three-quarter face, with wide cheekbones, a strong nose, stubborn mouth and lustrous eyes, was an arresting study with dramatic contrasts, but not what one would expect to fascinate a boy of his age.

He was not, however, the usual seven-year-old. He had a special gift, an unusual sensitivity towards works of art. The fact that, at the age of seventy, he could close his eyes and reel off the names of paintings he had first seen in his Louvre book some sixty-three years earlier, demonstrates the retentiveness of his visual memory. It also reveals a willingness to examine a work of art far more intently than most adults are prepared to do, let alone children. Years later, when faced with the problem of explaining the power of art to a more or less indifferent audience, he spelled out the process that evolved from those long hours of solitary study in the library of Sudbourne Hall.

First, he wrote, there was the immediate impact made by a

masterpiece, the kind of impression that would make itself known even if one were on a bus travelling at thirty miles an hour and had glimpsed the painting in a shop window. That first shock of awareness must be followed up by a close inspection of every inch of the canvas, appreciating the nuances: the harmonies of colour and passages of fine descriptive drawing. However, one could not sustain such concentration for much longer than one could enjoy the smell of an orange which, in his case, was a couple of minutes. The usefulness of historical knowledge was that it kept one's attention fixed on the work while one's senses had time to revive. This inevitably happened. At length his own eye would become so saturated that everything he saw was charged by the impression he had received. He would find himself looking at a room as if it were a Vermeer, at the milkman as if he were drawn by van der Weyden, and at the logs on the fire as if designed by Titian.

That innate responsiveness was to have unexpected rewards. Years later he described an astonishing experience. An object on which he was gazing seemed to detach itself from its background and take on an intense inner meaning. Such a revelatory, almost mystical experience might have been akin to that described by Thomas Traherne, the seventeenth-century English poet, when he wrote that 'Eternity was manifest in the light of the day and something infinite behind everything appeared.' However, there were some important differences. Kenneth Clark cited the example of John Henry Newman, on his last day at Oxford, seeing with a sense of vivid poignance the snapdragons growing on the walls near his rooms, flowers that had provided the symbolic reassurance that he would stay at Oxford for ever. Then he cited Coleridge, for whom a moon veiled in mist was a symbol of his own psyche. What, in other words, made the object so mysteriously symbolic was its ability to evoke what Walter Pater described as some 'forgotten or hidden truth of my inner nature'. To experience such a moment was as close as most people could come to knowing how it felt to create a work of art.

Kenneth Clark's emphasis on the importance of his aesthetic gift was his way of conceding that he had felt short-changed by life. Alone at Sudbourne he would pedal away at the pianola for hours in the grip of the illusion that he was actually performing masterpieces, while tears of joy blurred his eyes. This was the same person who later wrote that he enjoyed storms at sea because he was too unfeeling to find them terrifying. By then the family taboo had taken its inevitable toll. But it was permissible, even expected, to be moved – to tears – by art. Art was his sole remaining emotional outlet and one he desperately needed. Art would sustain him where life had let him down. The Clarks, those 'absolutely worthless, irresponsible people', had passed on something valuable after all.

One of the most astonishing things Alice Clark ever did, as far as her son was concerned, took place when he was about seven years old. One morning, visiting K in the nursery, Alice discovered him in tears. He was being roundly scolded by his horrid German governess, Miss Frankish. Unseen, Alice Clark silently withdrew, but for once reacted. Next day the tyrant was gone. In her place was 'my darling Lam', the first woman who was, for two years at least, wholeheartedly his. She was his natural protector, for whom a crack of light at night seemed a perfectly reasonable request. Here at last was a reassuring figure, and also a playmate, someone with whom he could share his love for conjuring tricks, animals, dressing up, paintings and *Punch*.

The young K's ambition to become an artist like Charles Keene filled his mother with misgivings but his father was delighted. Not that Kenneth Mackenzie Clark ever had such an ambition for himself. The very idea was comical, his son commented, but he did have an artist's hands, and he loved the company of artists. As a member of the Arts Club he went every year to the annual banquet of the Royal Academy and liked to invite artists to Sudbourne for the week-end. He also seems to have shown a nice appreciation of his son's developing interests. After learning that K had attended, and loved, the Japanese exhibition at Shepherd's Bush in 1909, he produced a really wonderful present. It was a large album of original Japanese drawings, a few of which were by Hokusai, the great eighteenth-century Japanese painter and creator of colour prints. K was entranced. He enthusiastically began to imitate the Japanese style and was still pleased with the results when he reviewed his work decades later.

Then Kenneth Mackenzie Clark commissioned Charles Sims to paint a portrait of the young K. It was the start of a friendship that was to end only with Sims's death. Sims decided to paint his subject paddling in a sandy cove, looking across the river Alde toward his favourite town, Aldeburgh. However, Sims's imagination failed him and he posed his subject, with a twisted torso and flailing arms, so ineptly that K looks as puzzled and uncomfortable as he did when, as a baby, he was perched on top of a horse. That the painting was a failure hardly mattered to the seven-year-old, who remembered glorious picnics in that sandy cove and the bliss of watching a fine artist at work.

Then K confided that his great ambition was to draw like Charles Keene. Sims thought that was all right, but Degas was a better model. Then Sims pronounced the unknown name of a French painter living in obscurity in Provence: Paul Cézanne. Imitate Cézanne, Sims advised; he was inexhaustible.

The method of learning to paint by imitating the masters has had a long history. Constable made pencil studies of the oil-painted land-scapes of Jakob van Ruisdael the better to appreciate the spatial divisions, weights and patterns employed by that Dutch artist. Dela-croix copied an etching by Goya, Jean Watteau a head by Rubens. Cézanne, Kenneth Clark's great love, taught himself to draw by copying the work of his predecessors and particularly that of Signorelli. But Signorelli's imagery (for instance, that of a man carry-ing another on his shoulder) was transformed by Cézanne, who used the motif in a totally new guise. Delacroix similarly transformed Goya, just as Watteau recreated Rubens in his own image. Men of genius can safely borrow from each other, but whether those of lesser talents have more to lose than to learn from the process is a moot point.

It is clear, however, that Kenneth Clark's instinctive desire to imitate the masters was ideally suited to develop his precocious ap-preciative powers. After Keene, his idol became Aubrey Beardsley and the way that artist achieved his effects completely absorbed him. By the age of nine or ten he was completely sure of himself. As confidently as he had taken down paintings from walls and put others in their places, he began to separate good pictures from bad ones. Grown-ups listened respectfully and nodded their heads.

Before being sent to boarding school, the young K could count on spending his summers in Scotland. Although he disclaimed having felt any great affection for his native land, it is evident that his father emphatically did, since every year he made the interminable trip back. After stopping at the rightly dreaded North British Hotel in Edin-burgh, Kenneth Mackenzie Clark and his wife would eventually arrive at Poolewe, where the river Ewe enters a tidal loch.

There the Clarks rented Pool House, stuffed with garishly slip-covered furniture and worn carpets, devoid of anything readable except Queen Victoria's *Leaves from Our Journal in the Highlands*. Their son found the house charmless, and so did his parents, because they soon abandoned it for their yacht, anchored half a mile out in Loch Ewe, leaving their son marooned in the house with Lam. That round of days spent fishing for non-existent salmon at Poolewe, surrounded by clouds of gnats, and lonely evenings at Pool House leafing through the reminiscences of Queen Victoria with Lam, reinforced Kenneth Clark's melancholic conviction that his parents did not want him with them. Morning after morning he would see them come chugging in on a launch – not to visit him but to fish. On the occasions when he was allowed on board his father's glorious yacht, the *Zoraide* (an old-fashioned steam vessel which was to become a patrol boat during the First World War and which miraculously survived), he would be rapturous. To be on board in the middle of a storm, when all the pots and pans in the galley went smashing to the floor, and waves thundered overhead, was the best fun in the world. At such moments of danger he was at his absolute best. An old public school friend, Sir William Keswick, remembered frequent trips of this kind, as well as one that almost ended in disaster.

On one of their days off, he said, he and K set out with another boy, called Grant, for Southampton, where they liked to charter small dinghies. This particular day they chose to sail for the Isle of Wight. They were in mid-passage when they were assailed by high winds and a stormy sea. 'Grant had the sense to be frightened, perhaps because he knew more. I wasn't frightened because I thought K knew how to sail. He kept telling us things like "Pull the sheets" and was completely calm. Somehow we arrived.'

Sending boys to school, Kenneth Clark implied, was a parental plot. Whatever the motive, it was an honourable English tradition, established in the days when the primary role of such schools was to provide recruits for the church. At one time these so-called public schools were divided into upper and lower divisions. Then in the latter half of the nineteenth century the idea took hold that it was best to educate the younger boys separately, out of the lustful reach of older boys, and the concept of the private preparatory school was born.

One of the most famous of the nineteenth-century headmasters, a man of towering personality and influence, was Thomas Arnold, headmaster of Rugby. His great-nephew, E.P. Arnold, was similarly famous and intimidating. At the end of the nineteenth century Arnold went into partnership with the Rev. Cowley Powles, a well-known schoolmaster and great friend of the rector and writer Charles

Kingsley, to run Powles's preparatory school for boys. Arnold moved to Wixenford, as the school at Wokingham in Berkshire was called, where he embarked on an ambitious building programme and continued, as his partner had done, to attract boys of notable, titled and wealthy parents. Some of them were Scots.

By the time the young K arrived at the school in which he was to spend the next five years of his life, E.P. Arnold had been replaced by a trio of headmasters, all partners in the enterprise: Philip Morton, Harold Wallace and Ernest Garnett. None of them had distinguished themselves as scholars, but this hardly mattered since they were so skilled in the art of appealing to wealthy status seekers. His parents were plied with drinks, taken on a tour of the school's manicured cricket pitches, its avenues of pleached limes and the arcadian spot in which, it was claimed, the boys ate *al fresco* in the summer. They were, predictably, impressed.

Morton, Wallace and Garnett would also contrive to name-drop. This was not difficult, since their pupils' parents were always wealthy and usually titled as well: a German princeling, briefly King of Albania, Field Marshal Sir Archibald Montgomery-Massingberd, Major-General Lord Sackville and General Sir Sidney Clive being among the former pupils. The Prince of the Belgians was there. The Clarks liked what they saw and K was enrolled.

No tears seem to have been shed as the eight-year-old K left Lam and Suffolk far behind to be deposited at Wixenford. He remembered no first-day-of-school misery, nor the trip on the train, nor the unfamiliar strangeness of new clothes, a trunk, pocket money, not even an agonized last look at his faithful and loving Lam. Nor did the sudden onslaught of boys (there were about seventy pupils enrolled in those days) fill him with the sick fear and distaste that had been his youthful reaction to strange children. He found them congenial and friendly. He never got into fights and seemed most offended that anyone should think he had. Far from being unhappy at home, he was suddenly happy again.

It was evident to him later that the standards of teaching at Wixenford were abysmally low. History was a blank – that teacher must have been unusually bad. Latin was not much better, English mediocre and, as a result, Kenneth Clark's spelling was always tentative. But then, Morton, Wallace and Garnett hardly expected their pupils to need good marks since it was assumed they would all go to Eton.

Geometry was a happy exception and so were the drawing lessons:

classes were held in a large half-panelled room filled with wooden chairs and desks, and with an old clock ticking on the wall. It looked like all the other classrooms except for its blackboard, where diagrams of *fleurs de lis* were more likely to be discovered than theorems. The art master, whom everyone called Tompy, was an amiable classicist who believed all problems of composition could be reduced to cubes, cylinders and cones. Such a spartan view of art seemed exactly right to K, who set to work enthusiastically building landscapes out of such materials. Tompy further endeared himself by encouraging K's imitative efforts and no doubt had some kind words to say to his parents. When the time came to say goodbye to Tompy, his pupil was distressed to discover how much it mattered.

Art was the main but not the only pleasure at Wixenford. There was the fun of editing the school newspaper and going to the weekly dancing classes considered indispensable for the future deportment of young gentlemen. There K also discovered musical theatre, writing the libretti, designing the scenery and casting the actors. There was the fun of the rackets court, planting his own garden and even cricket. Despite his conviction that he was a very bad slow bowler who never scored a run, his name survives on the cricket pavilion board as a member of the team of 1916. (The school is now called Ludgrove.) Even when his parents made it plain that he would not be going to Eton with all his friends, but to Winchester, he managed to remain in good spirits. The headmaster's report on the departing Kenneth Mackenzie Clark was most encouraging.

It was a free, happy life, clouded only by the times when he was sent to join his parents. Those dreaded holidays! How frightful for Edwardian parents to have a child in the house! It was more than they could bear. In his memory they were always in the South of France and he, lonely and shy, was travelling down on the *train bleu*, at the age of eleven or twelve, a mascot of the *wagons lits*, almost a joke figure, since he was always alone. This journey, he recalled, was made throughout the course of the First World War, even when the Germans were at the gates of Paris. He could not remember whether his parents actually met him at the station or whether, in a further gesture of indifference, they sent a trap to collect him. It never occurred to him to rebel, or think them extraordinary: 'I thought that was what people were like.' Thank heavens Lam was always waiting. 'She made my life.'

5 Winchester

'Doom! Shivering doom! Inexorable bells
To early school, to chapel, school again:
Compulsory constipation, hurried meals
Bulked out with Whipped Cream Walnuts
from the town.' – JOHN BETJEMAN

Kenneth Mackenzie Clark sent his son, Kenneth Mackenzie Clark, to Winchester for five years. Perhaps the moment has arrived to examine the fact that, even though the son bore his father's name and nickname, there seems to have been no attempt to differentiate between them. Only the obvious explanation that the blurring of outlines was intentional makes sense. There was to be a tradition established of hats, billiard games and guns, of men who gambled in Monte Carlo and came in from the sea with their moustaches coated with salt.

Unfortunately not a single letter from Kenneth Mackenzie Clark senior survives, and one can only venture that, having left school at fourteen, he was determined to give his son the educational advantages he himself lacked. Winchester, that great public school, was decided upon when the moment came to submit his son's name (when he was seven and a half). The decision was not altered when Kenneth Clark decided to become an artist, despite the unavoidable fact that English public schools do not encourage budding artists.

English public schools do, however, produce gentlemen. Again, too little is known about Kenneth Mackenzie Clark, except his scornful spurning of the purchase of instant status, his assertion that no man with a title ever wrote to him, except to ask for money, and his hatred of snobbery. As a member of the burgeoning middle class, he resented aristocratic exclusiveness and condemned the way the upper classes, in virtual control of the armed forces, the government and the church, bought and sold position with the arrogance of divine right.

However, he had already prepared his son for entry into a great public school by sending him to one of the most snobbish prep schools

33

in England. One has to take into account that contamination of aspiration which, Harold Nicolson declared in *Good Behaviour*, was the corollary of the Industrial Revolution and the moneyed rise of the middle class. As their numbers grew, the traditional divisions of upper, middle and lower class 'began to divide, and strange new fissures were observed. Instead of taking for granted the station into which they had been born, men and women began to be self-conscious about it and competitive.'

This would plausibly explain Kenneth Mackenzie Clark's country estate in Suffolk, another in Scotland, his villa on the Mediterranean, his yachts, his *pied-à-terre* in London and his correctly timed visits to each. These are not the actions of a Paisley Clark, a tradesman and proud of it, preferring to die an obscure death loved by his townsmen, but those of someone who is, however ambivalently, socially ambitious. And in fact the upper classes were adapting to some of the new realities. Mr Harrod (the department store owner) entertained academicians and parliamentarians at his shooting-box on Exmoor. The daughter of Sir Blundell Maple (governor of Maple & Co., upholsterers) had married a German baron and her father was seen in the best circles, while Sir Thomas Lipton (the grocer) had been a personal friend of King Edward VII. The privileged classes, it seemed, were quite prepared to accept the rising rich provided they were well-educated and amusing, and these graces could be obtained from the public schools. Since the school's revenues might depend upon it, headmasters were most agreeable.

Nevertheless, the late-eighteenth-century view lingered that no man could claim to be a gentleman if he worked, for as John Locke wrote, 'Trade is wholly inconsistent with a gentleman's calling.' That public schools intensified the manifestations of caste is undeniable. The teachers were chiefly responsible, since most were professionals of middle-class origins and social ambition. Whatever lessons in snobbery they omitted, the boys themselves, with their unconscious cruelty, supplied.

Kenneth Clark joined Winchester College for the second term ('Common Time') in the spring of 1917 at the age of thirteen and a half. He was slightly above average height and thin, with a crop of dark brown hair, a monumental forehead and close-set ears; saved from pronounced good looks by what one contemporary called his 'powerful, beaky nose'. He seems to have smiled little, perhaps because of teeth which remained irregular despite a corrective plate and painful tightenings. Photographs of the period show that the child's look of bewilderment, even indignation, has gone. Instead, the eyes are wary. Another contemporary referred to his disconcerting way of darting furtive, sideways looks. There is an oddly fixed set to the mouth and chin, that of someone accustomed to biting back a retort, and an air of watchful remoteness. Despite all of this he seems vulnerable. Perhaps it is his delicacy of feature, his slender frame, his hands stuffed dejectedly into pockets, a droop in his shoulder or the way he has turned his head to look at his photographer, as if hoping for nothing and expecting the worst.

In *The Old School Tie*, Jonathan Gathorne-Hardy observed that the practice of sending children away to school at a young age was apt to produce in them a vague sense of having done wrong: to a small child the only reason for this banishment was that he was not loved, and therefore not lovable. To a sense of isolation thus engendered must be added, in the case of Kenneth Clark, the experience of having had a mother who lived only for her husband, and a father who, however indulgent and warm, could be transformed at a moment's notice into a shameful spectacle. Lam's benign two-year reign has to be weighed against these powerful influences. There can be no doubt that he was constricted by his mother's coldness and afflicted by his father's illness. 'One stands alone with one's secret.'

To be tormented by unfulfilled emotional needs is intolerable unless one can somehow stop them by placing an emotional moat between oneself and others. This appears to have happened. By the time K arrived at Winchester he no longer looked for affection, nor was he in pain when his needs were not met. He had succeeded in keeping his emotions under control. Art was his single secret emotional outlet.

No fairy godmother with malign intent could have invented an atmosphere better designed to repress K's emotional life further than the school in which he found himself. The fact that such a school was several degrees less terrifying than it would have been a hundred years before was scant comfort to the boys who entered, endured stoically, left gratefully and, when memory was blunted and a nostalgic yearning for their adolescence had asserted itself, sent their sons to the same school. (Kenneth Clark never succumbed; his sons went to Eton.)

Eton, that most famous of all English public schools, might have its academic drawbacks; Winchester produced an intellectual élite. In

K's time the school was accustomed to gaining twenty to twenty-five scholarships to Oxford and Cambridge alone. (Scholarships to other universities were not thought worth recording.) The school was founded by William of Wykeham, Bishop of Winchester (the reason why former students are called Wykehamists) in 1382 as 'a perpetual college of poor scholars [sic] clerks,' and had, by the time Kenneth Clark arrived, an ancient tradition of politeness and learning. Its pupils were, it was said, trained in a single-minded passion for Greek, a rigid respect for tradition and a private language. There was the usual strong emphasis on sport. At Oxford and Cambridge, Wykehamists were known for being ambitious, single-minded and impenetrable. An Oxford don once said, 'You never know what a Wykehamist is thinking. In fact you never know if he's thinking at all.'

At Eton a boy was given a room, however small, of his own. At Winchester he was never alone. By day he studied with all the others in his House Room in a small cubicle, called a 'toys', derived from the French word *toise*, meaning fathom, or the amount of space allotted to each boy in College. In this cramped uncomfortable boxlike space the devoted scholar was expected to concentrate while life went on all around him: gramophone playing, ping-pong and raucous shouting. By night boys aged thirteen to eighteen shared the same freezing dormitories, called 'galleries', a wilderness of bare floors and staircases. They washed with the aid of basins and jugs of water and took cold baths in rows of metal tubs. These were kept 'topped up' by leaving the taps running, and emptied over the concrete floor when the next 'man' demanded his turn. Even the toilets were without doors.

Such total lack of privacy, it was thought, accounted for the Wykehamist's guarded manner in later life. The deliberate decision to leave no boy alone and unwatched was, however, designed to prevent older boys from seducing younger ones. For the same reason, younger boys were forbidden to talk to older ones, even to fraternize with anyone outside their own house. Reginald Snell, who was Kenneth Clark's junior by eighteen months and came to know him well, wrote that the school 'deprived us of our childhood: tenderness, and the desire to "play" which belongs to children, was abhorrent – we were neither called boys nor allowed to dress like boys.... Social deportment was controlled to the last detail: how you should speak (you weren't allowed to use the word "think" until you had been in the school for two years), what you should wear (including how many buttons of your waistcoat you might leave undone).' A boy might not refer to his father and mother in the ordinary human way but had to use the words 'pater' and 'mater' – just as one's sister and brother were 'frater' and 'soror' – at all times; a boy never dared let down his guard. 'To call another "man" by his Christian name was out of the question – it was a bit daring even to *know* it.'

Other dictates of conduct were implicit in the business of transforming young hooligans into gentlemen. Politeness must be beaten into them if necessary. Caning, at Winchester called 'tunding' (derived from the Latin *tundo*, to beat), was administered by the prefects, or older boys, frequently on the fags who served them. As a refinement the juniors were required to cut the ground ashes themselves, usually in 'Hell', a forbidding bank beside the river Itchen. Nominally the stick had to be thin enough to slip through the Headmaster's gold ring but such formalities were often dispensed with. Once the stick was ready the victim was told to 'stand round', i.e. bend double and touch his toes. He was then beaten on the bottom with the ground ash, 'six hard cutting strokes that I found very painful', wrote Reg Snell, who was beaten only once. (Snell's experiences at Winchester made him a lifelong critic. Three of his books on the failure of public schools and the need for reform were subsequently published at the Hogarth Press by Leonard and Virginia Woolf.)

Snell continued, 'A beating by the Headmaster (reserved for "grave offences", not necessarily sexual) was a much more serious affair; it was on the bare buttocks, and administered by a lash consisting of four sticks, and I can still recall with horror my first sight of the torn and bleeding skin when I met a senior in my House in the "tub room" the day after his punishment. I connect Sunday evenings, the favourite beating time, with the taste of the cocoa we had for Sunday supper . . . and the sound of thrashings that came through the closed door of the prefects' common-room.' Another contemporary, Graham Mitchell, later the Deputy Director General (1956–65) of the British Security Service (MI5), wrote: 'I can sum up in a word my memories of my first two years at Winchester: misery. They were without question the unhappiest years of what has been, on the whole, a very happy life. I contemplated . . . suicide.'

When he came to write his autobiography, *Another Part of the Wood*, Kenneth Clark minimized the experiences at Winchester. 'All intellectuals complain about their schooldays. This is ridiculous. The things that happen to them are nothing compared to the initiation rites of the Australian aboriginal and Indonesian people, nothing at all.' He denied that he was even particularly unhappy at Winchester. To appear self-pitying was against his inner code, but there was more to it than that. His reluctance to air his misery originated in his stance of detachment. Such things should not matter and he valiantly tried not to have them matter. It is evident, however, that Kenneth Clark never forgot the injustices at Winchester.

'I was never beaten before I went there. My darling Lam wouldn't have dreamed of it.' But, the moment he arrived, an older boy pounced on him for arrogantly speaking before he was spoken to, and lashed him with a ground ash cane. The night after his arrival another boy, himself an artist, took offence at the self-assured way in which this new man was discussing art and beat him again. He believed that they invented reasons. He was beaten at least twice a week, and this was bad because one needed several nights to recover. 'During the first year one was not allowed a cushion on the bench and one's bottom was awfully sore.' He remembers one prefect in particular, later a judge, whom he afterwards met in a club. 'He flinched a little bit I must say.' Etiquette appears to have dictated that neither man should ever refer to those incidents at Winchester. When contacted, the judge did not recall Kenneth Clark at first, but then remembered that the latter had struck him as somewhat arrogant.

Kenneth Clark reserved his greatest indignation, however, for another boy he met in later life – the father of one of his children's closest friends. This tormentor had actually dirtied the cups it was his duty to wash for the prefects, so as to be able to beat him for it. The injustice of that still rankled.

It was a miserable existence, even for someone as schooled in stoicism as himself, and he tried to become invisible. 'I lay low as much as I could. Never showed my face.' He was not successful. It was his misfortune to have Herbert Aris as housemaster, the man in charge of the Officers' Training Corps, which paraded and practised for war every week, and who was known, from his looks, as The Hake. He appeared to resent the fact that Kenneth Clark was not a gentleman. Sir William (Tony) Keswick, who was to become governor of the Hudson's Bay Company and a chairman of Matheson and Co., re-called that, 'Our horrid little housemaster used to come round in the evenings. K and I were doing preparation of a Latin translation for the next day. He would ask us if everything was all right. I can remember K saying, "Well sir, I should like to learn the piano," and the wretched little housemaster said, "I don't want boys here to learn the piano. We want boys to have a healthy life. You'll learn football." That was about the third day.'

From that moment on, it was obvious to Tony Keswick that here was another unhappy conscript. They met as soon as they arrived, in an enormous hall with a large table in the middle. Kenneth Clark was at one end and Tony Keswick at the other. Both were in tears. 'We looked at each other and began talking, and in a few minutes had forgotten our tears and were laughing. Then there was a roar like a tornado, like a train, and a horde of boys appeared. I can still remember K saying, "This is dreadful, isn't it?" and it was. It's the most vivid memory I have of him.'

They sat beside each other. Sir William Keswick remembers that every toys had a wooden partition, some 5 feet high, forming the back rest for the toys in front. On it, the new man was 'supposed to pin a photograph of your mum or your favourite footballer, or a bridge in your town. I had nothing and lived in fear that the head boy would notice and say, "Look here, Keswick, you won't conform."' A beating seemed certain. 'Then K said, "Don't worry. I have an envelope full of drawings." He reached into his pocket and pulled out drawings by Augustus John of Dorelia, and Sir William Orpen, that sort of thing. "Help yourself," said he, being the dear fellow he was. I had them for the rest of my career at Winchester, three charming Augustus John drawings, and they travelled with me for years.'

For Kenneth Clark, Winchester's saving grace was its eccentric and colourful headmaster, Montague ('Monty') Rendall. Like the Italian art historian Bernard Berenson, Rendall had visited Italy in early manhood and had fallen in love with Florence, including its art. Under Berenson's tutelage Rendall had spent two years assembling a collection of photographs for the school's new Museum of Natural History and Art, which opened in 1897. By the time Kenneth Clark arrived, Rendall had been giving a regular series of Sunday evening lectures on Italian art for a quarter of a century. Almost at once, Kenneth Clark began attending Rendall's lectures on Fra Angelico, Pisanello, Botticelli and Bellini, and was put to work studying the large wooden cases of photographs that Rendall had laboriously assembled. In an ocean of philistinism, here was a dolphin, an enchanted creature who dared to talk about beauty, who not only

tolerated eccentricity but encouraged it. Anyone who went to the
headmaster's lectures was immune from open derision and Kenneth
Clark never missed one. Years later he tried to express the debt of
gratitude he owed Rendall in a moving letter that was subsequently
published.

He already had the idea in the back of his mind that he wanted to
write about art, and was reading widely. His interest in aesthetics
naturally led him to Berenson's famous essays on the Florentine and
Central Italian painters of the Renaissance. Despite the author's
awkward style and the incomplete nature of his theories, Kenneth
Clark was so stimulated that he could not sleep for several nights. He
had realized that another book he had read, *The Drawings of the
Florentine Painters*, published in 1903, was in urgent need of
revision. He was the assistant Berenson needed, he decided, and
found himself saying so one day with more confidence than he felt.

Soon after he arrived Kenneth Clark went off eagerly to the home
of his new art master, Mr Macdonald. The master, who in his youth
had gone on sketching expeditions with Ruskin, was a well-meaning
but indolent aesthete whose pupils (art was an optional subject) had
dwindled to three. Here, however, was a new arrival, eagerness
itself. If Mr Macdonald was disconcerted at the news, he hid it well,
and particularly after the newcomer recognized two drawings on his
walls as being by the Japanese artist Utamaro. If the newcomer would
return in a week's time, Mr Macdonald said, indicating a Sheraton
bureau, there were lots of other Japanese drawings he could see.
Kenneth Clark accepted the invitation with enthusiasm. Those afternoons spent at what, for him, was the most wonderful of all pastimes,
went a long way to reconcile him to Winchester. It also reinforced
his secret inner conviction that, as long as he had such beauty in his
life, he would never succumb to despair.

Whenever Mr Macdonald deigned to take a class, the performance
was lacklustre. The drawing school was full of blatant nineteenth-
century imitations of Renaissance sculpture and the master set his
pupils to work drawing them – copies of copies. It was not exactly
inspiring, but it was art, so Kenneth Clark dutifully licked his pencil
and drew the fakes dozens of times from every angle. Whenever the
art master's absences were especially prolonged, Kenneth Clark took
over and 'ended up running the class'. Then he began to lecture on art
himself. One Sunday afternoon in the early summer of 1921, when he
was just eighteen, Kenneth Clark talked about pictures. He traced

the origins of frescos from the Byzantine period through the great flowering of art known as the Italian Renaissance and ending somewhat short of the Post-Impressionists. *The Wykehamist* noted that the paper was of great interest. The speaker's style was engaging, if somewhat marred by the frequency of his artistic and technical terms, too many of which were left unexplained.

For an adolescent of Kenneth Clark's acute sensibility, for whom visual sensation was almost a physical need, Winchester provided other avenues of escape. Thanks to Monty Rendall the school's interiors began to glow with bare shining floors, beautiful old pots and lamps, chests and masses of flowers. There was the Gothic chantry and its surrounding cloisters, where he could almost imagine himself visiting the backgrounds of the *Très Riches Heures*. This illusion was intensified in the Deanery, where he went to turn the pages of the Winchester Bible, the greatest English illuminated manuscript of the twelfth and thirteenth centuries, in a blissful dream. He immediately began to sketch the ruined Romanesque arches of the cathedral's south transept, and to draw Winchester's architecture became his new ambition. When the great master of architectural drawing, Muirhead Bone, came to the school, Kenneth Clark trailed behind him, and when Albert Goodwin, the water-colourist, also paid a visit, the young K was permitted to paint at his side. They sat in the Warden's Garden, recording the plane trees that arched over a brook and dangled their leaves in the water. At such a moment his chief desire might have echoed that of Ruskin, 'that the frost might not touch the almond blossom'.

Kenneth Clark was often ill during his first year at Winchester but, despite this, began to do well academically. He gained good marks during his first term and in the Common Time of 1918, a year later, took first place. By the time he arrived, compulsory Greek had been abolished, and he never studied it. Since, as Snell wrote, only the classicists, the real initiates, were considered truly 'of the family', Kenneth Clark was not considered a first-rate scholar. He did, however, take lessons in English literature as an alternative to Greek and studied Latin, for which he seems to have had a natural gift. His contemporary, Graham Mitchell, wrote, 'Some of us had to translate a late Latin poem into English verse. In it was the phrase "*potus cibique paucitas*". Clark's translation, "by limiting our daily fare", I still think to be felicitous.' There was a daily class of mathematics and

French and a smattering of science and German. He did not study history until his final year.

'History Bill', the Rev A.T.P. Williams, was, like 'Monty' Rendall, a teacher of genius with the gift of inspiring his pupils with his own passion for his subject. Kenneth Clark was soon in his Special History group and, along with Snell, listening raptly to History Bill's discourses on medieval history, monasticism, the feudal system, the crusades and trade, England under the Romans, the pre-Conquest years, the Norman Kings, British constitutional history since Anglo-Saxon times and British foreign policy. Perhaps these classes were gradually training a natural writer in the subtleties of the English language; in clarity of thought, forcefulness of expression and, above all, gracefulness of style. Whatever was happening came about unnoticed. One day Kenneth Clark, by now working towards a university scholarship, entered a history essay competition, the Vere Herbert Smith prize. He chose as subject the influence of the Puritans on England. He thought it a mediocre work; nevertheless, an un-suspected talent must have been evident, for he won the prize. He was 'absolutely amazed'. He added, 'For some mysterious reason it changed my life at age seventeen from being an artist to that of a writer.'

The decision may have been instinctive, but it was perfectly reasonable. If Kenneth Clark had any native artistic talent, it had been fairly well discouraged by the drudgery of reproducing all those cubes, blocks and pyramids at Wixenford, not to mention copying fake sculpture at Winchester. The harder he laboured the worse his work became, and he knew it. As an artist he faced a mediocre future, but as a writer, a connoisseur, an assistant to the world's leading art historian, the possibilities were enticing. He must have known, some-how, that he could improve on Berenson's writing style.

The hateful housemaster Aris had retired and his place was taken by H.A. Jackson, 'The Jacker', another eccentric who, for all his unpredictable opinions, took a somewhat more benign interest in his pupil's affairs. He suggested that K try for a scholarship to Oxford, not because he thought he would get one, but because he feared Kenneth Clark would not pass the entrance examination. Those who had tried for a scholarship were, he thought, treated more indulgently. Both of them were gloomily aware that, after an auspicious start, Kenneth Clark's academic prowess had been undistinguished. His place varied between fifth and seventeenth in a class of twenty-one pupils during the remainder of his time at Winchester.

'The Jacker's' notes on Kenneth Clark's progress during his last two years are enlightening. Common Time, 1921, was a fair report. Clark must not shirk the dull part of the work. In Cloister Time he was considered to be 'coming on' in character. 'The Jacker' suggested that his pupil try for Trinity College, Oxford, a name chosen at random because it sounded good – Jackson himself had been to Trinity College, Cambridge. Once again Kenneth Clark thought he had made a miserable showing and, again, the examiners thought otherwise. He won a scholarship. 'The Jacker' was most pleased. He did, however, feel it necessary to give his pupil some parting advice. Art was perfectly all right as a hobby but not as a career. He hoped his pupil would keep a sense of proportion.

Leonard Woolf observed in his autobiography, *Sowing: An Autobiography of the Years 1880–1904*, that he managed to be good enough at games to be left alone. Intelligence and hard work might therefore be judged an eccentricity, instead of being condemned as vice or personal nastiness. Something of the sort seems to have happened to Kenneth Clark. He was keenly interested in cricket and was a fast bowler for his House. In addition he was an excellent squash player and subsequently won a half blue in tennis at Oxford. Perhaps for these reasons, although he was not a favourite, he was not actually disliked, according to Tony Keswick.

However, he made his biggest mark as a runner. Winchester men were expected to make two long runs a week, one of them three and a half miles around St Catherine's Hill. Performances were monitored by the prefects and if the runner was too slow the ground-ash was liberally applied. Escaping from danger by a fast sprint was being forcefully inculcated and Kenneth Clark, abnormally thin for his age, and a natural runner, took off into the distance. Then one day, after this run, disaster struck: chest pains and collapse. He was admitted to the school hospital with pneumonia and sent home for a term.

He was dangerously undernourished but this was to be expected. C.I.C. Bosanquet, later Vice-Chancellor of the University of Newcastle-upon-Tyne, who met Kenneth Clark at Monty Rendall's art lectures, remembers that the students were always hungry. 'At that period it was still the practice of Housedons [Housemasters] not to provide any cooked food in the afternoon or evening. We were given a hot breakfast and lunch, but thereafter only tea or cocoa plus bread and butter (usually margarine).' Kenneth Clark recalled one midday meal consisting solely of the skins of boiled potatoes. 'We spent our whole time in search of food,' Sir William Keswick said.

> The only thing we could get was something in a tin like treacle, a kind of artificial milk. We used to make very nice bargains like, 'I will keep it in my larder if you will carry it in.' Our larders were a sort of burry with books on top and you slid things inside. The most horrible things would come out, dirty stockings stuck together with treacle. Dear K can't remember those sorts of things.
>
> I remember another occasion. As senior boys we were allowed to sit at the head of the table with 'The Jacker', our housemaster. One day we had a really terrible cabbage soup, more water than cabbage, and K said, 'Wake up, Keswick, and pass the Logie.' He was referring to a stream of the river Itchen closest to New Field, where we used to go and dig out the weeds. 'The Jacker' didn't think it was very funny and sent K out without his last course.

By the time Kenneth Clark became a prefect in 1922, his last year at school, the automatic assumption of command which was the aim of British public school training was ingrained. One more solitary, scared, inward-turning boy had metamorphosed into a member of the sceptical, analytical and demanding intelligentsia. There was no question about the formidable powers of his mind, no question either that he struck most people as forbidding. Graham Mitchell, a junior by two years, wrote, 'My attitude towards him is, I think, best expressed in the simple word "fear". He was impatient of stupidity, humbug and conceit.... [H]is general demeanour, if this is not a contradiction in terms, was one of urbane ferocity.' Those not intimidated, while respecting his intellectual superiority, considered him a loner. The immediate impression he gave, especially to men, became lifelong, and was contradicted only by close friends. These, like Reg Snell, while agreeing that Clark looked arrogant and fierce, 'the kind of boy the nasty sort of schoolmaster loves to humiliate', would insist that he was actually quite different: 'a considerate and wryly humorous companion'.

Whenever he felt himself to be in a hostile social situation Kenneth Clark's *hauteur* would become especially pronounced. And, at Winchester, even as privileged and pampered seniors, the way was still full of traps for those who had not been born gentlemen. Snell recalled hearing Kenneth Clark dismissed by schoolfellows as '"not really our sort", the word "trade" being dropped, almost in an under-tone, as if the person under discussion had an unmentionable disease'. The fact of an ignominious birth was shameful, and there was the further problem of taking friends home, knowing how dreadfully embarrassing his father could be when drunk. The late Sir Colin Anderson, who met Kenneth Clark at Oxford and became his lifelong friend, remembered Kenneth Mackenzie Clark as a 'jolly, friendly man, if somewhat tipsy'. Sir William Keswick's impression was that he could be charming or irrationally angry and that, at such moments, his son was afraid of him. 'He was a very cross old man once drunk.'

Some time in 1919, and for his last three years at school, Kenneth Clark became convinced that he was dying of paralysis. 'I never thought I would live to the age of thirty. I remember, when I proposed to Jane, saying, "I am afraid I may be dying of paralysis." It seemed to me absolutely natural and inevitable and during my last year at school it caused me a great deal of grief. It was pure neurasthenia, of course.' Life at Winchester, having compounded the problems posed by the atmosphere at home, had resulted in the fear that his emotions were becoming frozen. To remove oneself from one's feelings, to observe events, surroundings and others as if one were sitting in front row centre at the drama of one's own life is, in a way, the most radical of all attempts at inner equilibrium, and bound to produce the conviction that one's inner self is turning to stone.

In common with another fellow sufferer, Dr Johnson, Kenneth Clark launched on a course of immensely long walks in the hope that the fatigue would reassure him. His games of squash and tennis were similarly motivated, but the conviction of paralysis and death was unshakeable. In the case of Dr Johnson there was no doubt, Boswell wrote, that he felt himself 'overwhelmed with an horrible melancholia, with perpetual irritation, fretfulness and impatience; and with a dejec-tion, gloom and despair, which made existence misery'. In a pathetic attempt at self-control Johnson would force himself to walk to Birm-ingham and back, a distance of thirty-two miles, 'in the hope that it could shake him into exertions that would pull his mind away from itself into some kind of unified activity'. Johnson also became obsessed with the passage of time. 'Oh Lord,' he wrote in one of his journals, 'enable me ... in redeeming the time which *I have spent in Sloth* ...'

There is no question that the lives of public schoolboys were ruled by the clock. 'Chivvied and harried from dawn to dusk, continually kept at work they were bored by, yet rewarded for doing it, punished for not doing it – the compulsive doing of tasks became ingrained. The result is so obvious that scarcely a single social study mentions it – the English upper classes were absurdly over-conscientious.' As far as Kenneth Clark was concerned, a lifelong passion for punctuality was one of those strange quirks of character for which there seemed no explanation, although his father's punctual ways, the continual hounding at Winchester and, finally, the feeling of being pursued by an irrational yet terrifying fear, makes the trait fully understandable, even inevitable. Furthermore, if one suggests that a life of misery is bound to instil in the sufferer one overriding thought, that what he most wants to do is run away, then the origins of the two obsessions seem evident. Here was someone torn, on the one hand, by the conviction that he ought to run for dear life – believing that, if he did not stop moving, he would die – and the equal belief that he was doomed to die at the age of thirty no matter how far he fled. A malevolent fate had decreed illness and death as the only resolution of his impasse.

No wonder then that, while at Winchester, Kenneth Clark fainted while watching a performance of Ibsen's *Ghosts*.

6 Ghosts

'then I realized that my salvation lay in her, for
I saw the joy of life in her'. – IBSEN

Kenneth Clark fainted again, years later, watching another performance of *Ghosts* at the National Theatre. Flesh and blood had
remembered what the boy at Winchester, cold, hungry and horrified
at human behaviour, had forgotten.

Ibsen's play tells the story of Oswald, a young artist who returns
from Paris to spend the winter with his widowed mother and slowly
realizes that the father he has been taught to respect and admire is a
scoundrel. Only cowardice, his mother confesses, and fear of social
disapproval, have prevented her from allowing the truth to be
known. Now, however, she regrets it. 'It is not only what we have
inherited from our fathers and mothers that exists again in us, but all
sorts of old dead ideas and all kinds of old dead beliefs . . . They
[ghosts] must be as countless as the grains of the sands . . . And we
are so miserably afraid of the light, all of us.'

Then his mother learns that Oswald has inherited syphilis from his
father, the ghastly legacy of a wasted life. The innocent son is to be
sacrificed for the sins of the father. Oswald is, however, prepared
for the final onset of madness. When it comes, the son insists, his
mother must administer a lethal dose of morphia because, 'I never
asked you for life. And what kind of a life was it that you gave me? I
don't want it! You shall take it back!'

When Kenneth Clark first saw the play he could not remember
the exact moment that caused such a dramatic reaction but only that
he was deeply affected and disturbed by it. The second time he
fainted, at the National Theatre with his wife, it was the terrible end
to the play which 'knocked him flat', literally. He found himself
suddenly overwhelmed by memories of his family life: his dissolute
father, his mother who tried too hard, and he himself, innocent and
guiltless but feeling neither. The weight of his inheritance and the

menace of mental collapse and impotence were suddenly unbearably vivid. He fainted with horror.

In his book *Children's Secrets*, Thomas J. Cottle wrote that adolescents had many moments in which they wondered about their relative normality or abnormality. The concept of and concern with madness were no strangers to the adolescent imagination. What reassured an adolescent was the visible normality of his parents. The child's unspoken reassurance to himself was that if his parents were normal, then he would also be normal.

That Kenneth Clark should attempt to identify with his father was, then, a normal stage of development. From early childhood he shared his father's love of art. He tried valiantly to adopt his father's tastes, played billiards from childhood, admired his father's stables with their Suffolk Punches, and the Delaunay-Bellevilles, took up golf and sailing. He tried to fish, shoot and ride. He showed, from an early age, the same love of the music hall and the theatre and the same love of dressing up. An undated photograph, undoubtedly taken when Kenneth Clark was in his late teens, shows Kenneth Mackenzie Clark, the old dandy, standing with a cigar between his fingers and a large-brimmed hat planted at a defiant angle. His slim, elegant son poses beside him with an insouciant twist to his body, one hand on hip, a cane in the other, sporting a similarly rakish hat and a brim turned up at the identical angle.

The child looked to the parent for reassurance yet, as Kenneth Clark's reaction to *Ghosts* made clear, his fears about his father and hence about himself were catastrophic. Children commonly keep conflicting emotions at bay by separating their image of the loved and feared parent into airtight compartments. There is an exalted and admired father, who can be loved and adored safely, and there is a feared and hated father, who is someone else, and never the twain shall meet. However, in adolescence the uneasy compromise is liable to be disturbed and a boy likely to discover in himself violent feelings of hatred. Living, as Kenneth Clark did, with a stern and unbending mother in an atmosphere of claustrophobic moral rectitude, even to have entertained feelings of anger towards his father would have been inadmissible. The very idea would have 'floored' him.

As he got older, the fact that Kenneth Clark never lost his temper became a point of pride. Similarly, he would go to heroic lengths to resist being reminded of his father's less lovable qualities, although, as the following makes clear, he took them for granted in his twenties.

After he finally met Berenson in 1926, he earnestly assured B.B.'s wife that her husband's rages did not upset him in the slightest because they were far less intimidating than similar traits in his own father. He would also dismiss his adolescent fears of paralysis as 'pure neurasthenia', as if that explained everything. Yet his conviction that, like his father's brothers and sisters, he was doomed to an early death, did not lead to the outcome he feared. To have overcome it alone is a remarkable achievement; to have gone forward as steadfastly and brilliantly as he was to do is astounding. The outlet that art afforded for his feelings must have played a major role. A contributing factor was his stance of detachment that, despite its defects as a solution, had an important goal: to preserve his freedom. Somewhere, in the inmost recesses of his soul, he had to stay intact, even if the preservation of his integrity were a struggle to the death. If the price to be paid were a deadening of his real feelings, at least he was still alive.

Sudbourne had gone. The estate of eleven thousand acres, which required a staff of seventy in its heyday, had been sold. His father's income had declined; furthermore, shooting was out and fishing had come in. Sudbourne was bought in 1916 by a speculator whose only interest appeared to be one of the contents of the house, an enormous musical box that played drums. The Clarks lived on there until 1918. When they left, Kenneth Clark prudently took the best of Wood's books from the library.

Visiting the estate, now a farm, some sixty years later, Kenneth Clark walked towards the middle of an immaculately vast and empty lawn and said with a wave of his hand, 'That is the view you saw from the front door.' There again were the four avenues lined with chestnuts, elms and beeches, symmetrical symbols of expansion and attainment. Perhaps the central avenue, the obvious path, had been closed off and made useless, but the others were still there, those dreamlike metaphors of freedom and the mind's wide-ranging powers, leading one outward and away, toward infinite possibilities.

He walked back along a path to the stables and pointed out the game larder in which the day's bag was hung. He penetrated still further, toward a tangle of woods, once another sweep of immaculately kept grass. 'It is extraordinary to see how nature takes over; absolutely lost.' He found greenhouses, their glass long shattered, and once-cultivated rose bushes spreading like brambles among the undergrowth. He went down a ragged path threading towards a lake and a derelict bridge.

'I used to have canoe races with my friends down there. That', he said, indicating a heap of broken logs, 'was the boat house and here is the bridge. It's not in very good repair I must say.' Then he paused, caught up by the realization that Sudbourne was 'far and away' the most delightful house he had ever lived in. 'When I dream about Sudbourne, it is always the way it was.'

They moved to a large and unremarkable house in Bournemouth called The Toft and there Kenneth Clark uncomplainingly joined them, although he disliked the town. Then his father bought a vast Scottish estate, Shielbridge, consisting of the whole peninsula of Ardnamurchan from Loch Shiel to the point, some 75,000 acres. There the father fished while the son repaired to the miles of bog and his customary soliloquizing walks. Because he had won a history prize at Winchester and a scholarship to Oxford, he became momentarily convinced that he should become a historian. He plunged enthusiastically into Tacitus, Michelet's history of France and Carlyle's *Past and Present*, while making neat notes of all the books he planned to write. To become an art historian would, in any event, have seemed a hopelessly impractical goal. Even thirty years later, in 1950, when Kenneth Clark was describing himself as an art historian, the profession was non-existent in Britain. He could have studied in Germany, where *Kunstgeschichte* was an established profession, but his mind would have recoiled from the German fondness for an accumulation of factual detail at the expense of critical values. There was, in addition, his desire to do something worth while. He was enthusiastically ready to 'adore studying history'.

He was disappointed. Part of his frustration may have had to do with the tutorial system at Oxford in the 1920s. Undergraduates were under no compulsion to attend lectures. They studied a subject with the advice of a tutor who directed the course of study, prescribed essays and recommended books. Whether a young man did well or ill in any particular subject therefore depended, in great measure, upon his relationship with one man. Kenneth Clark's particular mentor was an amiable loafer with a livid complexion who was invariably ill according to a notice tacked up on his door whenever an undergraduate was due to appear. Kenneth Clark managed to get transferred to the care of another historian, G.N. Clark, later Sir George Clark, editor of the *English Historical Review*, but could not sustain his early enthusiasm. Perhaps it was because his tutor, although brilliant, was austere. Kenneth Clark was also lonely.

He had been unwilling to make his own choice of college and paid the price. Oxford's colleges had divided traditionally between those priding themselves on scholarly achievement and those which, like Christ Church, were dominated by hearties, sports-car drivers and champagne-party-givers. Trinity, almost the smallest of the colleges, where everyone knew everyone else, surrounded by acres of green quadrangles and gardens, and incorporating a beautiful Wren chapel, was exquisite enough for any aesthete, but less hospitable in its tastes. Peter Green, a contemporary, the son of a doctor in the Indian Medical Service, who also went up to Trinity in September 1922, recalled: 'We, as a college, were very interested in games and despite our small number, went head of the river, won the Rugby Football Cup, etc., and most members even if not good at games would come down and cheer us on, but Kenneth remained outside that part of college life.' Another contemporary, Douglas C.L. Potter, wrote: 'Most of us were paid for by our parents ... did not have to work unless we felt like it, were out to enjoy life, and neither knew nor cared how the university was run ...' Like others of his generation, he dismissed himself modestly as a 'Philistine', spending his time in 'rowing, running and jazz', and seldom even saw Kenneth Clark.

As at Winchester, his contemporaries disliked the air of 'Curzonian superiority', as another friend, Peter Quennell, described it. One remarked: 'To me, much younger, a musician rather than a painter, and not his intellectual equal, he was very formidable and somewhat cold.' Meeting him at about the same time, David Knowles, who became a Benedictine monk, taught mediaeval history, and was later a close friend, noted in his diary that the young man was certainly learned and fastidious, but almost chilly. Peter Green thought he must be much older, as did Christopher Eastwood, later an Assistant Under-Secretary of State at the Colonial Office. Eastwood, who was also a scholar and therefore took his meals with Clark at the scholars' table, remarked on his precocious learning and maturity of manner, which seemed more like that of a don of thirty-five or forty than an undergraduate.

Dr N.W. Porteous, another contemporary, wrote that they gradually became friendly 'and, although I suppose I must have seemed a

bit of a "Philistine" in my ignorance of music and art he never treated
me as such and, by being just what he was, he helped me to realize
that there was a magical world of artistic beauty which he instinctively
inhabited . . ..' Christopher Smith, another contemporary, also had
'from a certain distance, an immense admiration and . . . respect . . .
As an undergraduate he was extraordinarily mature and sophisticated in the best sense . . . and although I was one year senior to
him, I . . . felt like an overgrown schoolboy in his company. It was
not that he was the least condescending [but rather that] his tastes
were . . . so much more cultured than my rather commonplace and
philistine interests. His manner and his dress were impeccable.'

Someone had to break the ice. Among the first was a tall, amiable
young man who happened to be staying, along with Clark, in the New
Buildings at the Broad Street end in the front quadrangle just above
the Dean. Sir Colin Anderson recalled in a privately printed memoir,
Three Score Years and Ten, that, 'if our rooms hadn't been marooned
next to one another up a particularly cool, stone stair we would never
have met. He wasn't exactly in the centre of the Junior Common
Room set, while I was outwardly as muddy as any other oaf. I kept my
aesthetic core carefully hidden, just as I do today; but I suppose a
chink must have shown.'

In those Trinity College rooms of Kenneth Clark's one felt
immediately apart. The college provided standard chairs and curtains. These had been removed or transformed. 'The rest of us had
hunting or coaching prints or that Vermeer girl wearing pearls.
His were real paintings and objects.' Reg Snell remembers seeing
a print of Vermeer's *Girl in a Yellow Turban* over the mantelpiece
and, rather tucked away, a glorious Corot, bought at the Leicester
Galleries. Kenneth Clark had been buying art, most of it from the
Leicester Galleries, throughout his teenage years and had already
assembled an enviable collection. In those early years, when Post-
Impressionists were scarcely appreciated in England, the Leicester
Galleries held pioneering exhibitions of the work of Picasso,
Cézanne, Van Gogh, Gauguin and Matisse. Many bargains could
be found and Kenneth Clark usually spent less than £5.

There were, in that room of Kenneth Clark's off Broad Street, a
great many large and expensive books on art strewn about, and there
was the latest model gramophone. Sir Colin recalled, 'While we
played "Kitten on the Keys", he had Bartok. Even the drink was
different and more sophisticated. It wasn't the sort of room you could

have a blind [get drunk] in. He was cocooned in a civilization of his own up there.'

Kenneth Clark made a few cautious forays out of his cocoon. He joined the illustrious Oxford Union Dramatic Society, although he did not dare to strike up a conversation or actually act, and gave papers to a highbrow literary group, the Gryphon Society. Several men who heard him recall with some awe that his first paper was entitled, *A Not Too Improbable Aesthetic*. But then, those who did not think Kenneth Clark very rum for preferring Renoir to rowing, tended to be awestruck even when, they hastened to add, they learned from the exchange.

When Christopher Eastwood was preparing his own paper for the Gryphon Society on Jane Austen, Kenneth Clark offered to hear him read it. A discussion followed, during which the latter dropped the remark 'ordinary rather negative good taste', with a jaundiced look at the modest prints on Eastwood's walls. Eastwood was naturally hurt, but had the grace to see that the rebuke had merit and began to look at art with new eyes. Kenneth Clark began to give successful lunch parties in his rooms, dispensing the normal amounts of sherry and rather more than the usual number of records. 'I recall one incident which made a lasting impression on me,' another Trinity College graduate wrote. 'We had been listening to one of his gramophone records and I had made some derogatory remark about the music, when Kenneth suddenly burst out: "You're hopeless! Don't you like anything?" ... The effect of his outburst ... was to increase my admiration for him. I had discovered that the essence of the spirit of this man, with his superb intelligence, his exquisite refinement and discrimination, was *enthusiasm*.' Brian Pye-Smith had a similar memory: 'There was one occasion in my first term when he invited me to have coffee in his room after dinner and listen to his Mozart gramophone records and at the end of the first one [I remember] K saying, "Isn't that delicious?" I have the feeling that he thought I was not appreciative of the privilege for he never invited me again – but of course I was!'

The writer Cyril Connolly, who was a contemporary of Kenneth Clark's, eased his way into Oxford social life by alternating between humility and genial superiority. Kenneth Clark, seemingly intimidated, tongue-tied and perfecting his armour, to judge from *Another Part of the Wood*, was actually making his way with remarkable skill. The Dean of Balliol at that time was Francis Fortescue

Urquhart, a remarkable character universally known as 'Sligger' who, Connolly wrote, was the kind of man one could pinch, put one's arm around and call by his nickname. He held open house every night and had an inner circle of everyone who counted. Before long, Kenneth Clark was a member of that select group.

In the circles Kenneth Clark frequented, to find life a huge joke was almost as socially *de rigueur* as being skilled with a gun had been in his father's set. Another of his friends, Maurice Bowra, then in his twenties and already a don and scholar of repute, was an even more outrageous wit and somewhat more dangerous since, it was said, 'If disobliging jokes could not be made to someone's face, then behind his back would have to do.' Since Bowra slandered everyone almost as a matter of course, it was not long before he had prised some of his father's shameful antics out of Kenneth Clark and laughed them to scorn. This novel approach – no one had ever poked fun at his father before – brought such enormous relief that Kenneth Clark, who was no mean wit himself, held Bowra in special regard for the rest of his life. He was released at last – or thought he was.

In those years at Trinity College, from 1922 to 1926, Kenneth Clark seldom bothered to go to lectures and was left on his own apart from the weekly chore of writing an essay and reading it to a tutor. It was self-evident to him that one went to Oxford to educate oneself by conversation with one's intellectual superiors and pursue one's interests unhampered by such formalities as a weekly timetable. As he had done at Winchester, he set about making shrewd use of Oxford's advantages and minimizing, or ignoring, its shortcomings.

Sir Trenchard Cox, later director of the Victoria and Albert Museum, recalled that, when he was at Cambridge, he went to have tea with a great authority on glass, a Mr Quarrell, at the Burlington Fine Arts Club in Savile Row. He and his host were sitting in front of a fire when a young man entered and took a book off the shelf. Quarrell remarked, 'Did you see him? He's a most brilliant young scholar. You haven't heard of him but one day you will. His name is Clark.' Everyone seemed to be noticing this precocious young man and C.F. ('Charlie') Bell, Keeper of the Department of Fine Art in the Ashmolean Museum, was no exception. It was a great stroke of good luck.

Charlie Bell seemed to be an old man when Kenneth Clark met him in 1922. He was an intimidating figure, an acknowledged expert on Old Master drawings, who disliked visitors and ran his museum department as if it were his exclusive preserve. Edward Croft-Murray, retired Keeper of Prints and Drawings at the British Museum, who was another protégé of Bell's, recalled that Bell had a knack for spotting young talent and nurturing latent gifts. He was 'wonderfully generous', Croft-Murray said, but could be jealously 'exclusivist' in his affections and had a fiendish temper. Bell put the newcomer to work in a small room containing a large safe, inside which was a fabulous collection of drawings. Exquisite works by Michelangelo, Leonardo da Vinci, Correggio, Dürer, Rembrandt, Botticelli, Filippo Lippi, Pisanello, Holbein the Younger, Watteau, Van Dyck and so on, were crowned by a group of drawings by Raphael which is among the two or three richest collections of that artist's graphic work in the world.

The Ashmolean's collection of drawings – it owns an equally rare and valuable collection of prints – is remarkable enough to earn it an important place in the ranks of the world's great museums. That, however, is only a fraction of the holdings that have been acquired since the museum was established by Elias Ashmole, antiquary, virtuoso, collector and diarist, in 1677, to house his collection of curiosities. Paintings by such artists as Van Dyck, Sir Peter Paul Rubens, Sir Joshua Reynolds, John Constable, Vincent Van Gogh and Giovanni Battista Tiepolo, among others, are housed in a harmonious Greek Revival building of white and honey-coloured stone. Any budding art historian would consider himself blessed to be able to study there.

As has been noted, Alice McArthur Clark had never wanted her son to become a painter. She spoke darkly of the primrose path artists were fated to tread, dwelling at length upon the example of a friend's son who, having gone to live *la vie Bohème* in Paris, was constantly cutting loose in some shocking new way. If Kenneth Clark's father was very unhappy when his son abandoned his hopes, Alice Clark must have been visibly relieved. The clear evidence is that she hoped for great things. Gabriel White, who became a painter and was a director of the Arts Council, met Kenneth Clark at Trinity and, since his parents were living in Bournemouth at the same time as the Clarks, came to know him better than most people. He recalled that Mrs Clark was 'desperately ambitious for her son. She wanted him to go into politics. She wanted him to become Prime Minister. Art wasn't on the cards.'

Dr N.W. Porteous recalled going on a walk with Kenneth Clark while they were both still at Oxford, 'along Addison's Walk in the extensive grounds of Magdalen College. We must have talked about our respective future plans, because I distinctively [sic] remember that he told me he hoped to enter politics, perhaps by becoming secretary to a Minister.' If not politics, it was to be the family business. Writing in commiseration of Kenneth Clark's disappointing final examination results, Maurice Bowra commented, 'I am afraid it will mean your family driving you into the business and that would be terrible.' A few years later, after Kenneth Clark had graduated from Oxford and made his first visit to Bernard and Mary Berenson in Florence, that ambition had shifted. His parents were set upon his becoming a diplomat, Mrs Berenson told her sister Alys, the divorced wife of Bertrand Russell, and were opposed to a career in art as it 'has no prestige whatsoever for them and they would feel he was throwing himself away'.

Having ignored her boy as a child, Alice Clark was belatedly discovering that she had an exceptional son. That she wanted a great career for him is clear evidence that she had radically revised her estimate and was pinning on him what may have been hopes long frustrated and denied – for her husband, or herself. Kenneth Clark, typically, was avoiding a confrontation. After a lifetime of feeling ignored it is a heady experience to become a figure of almost magical potential in the eyes of a mother. He was understandably reluctant to disenchant her. To do something prestigious seemed to matter to her immensely and the one career he wanted was the one on which she placed no value. So why not please his parents, since nothing really mattered to him one way or another, or ought *not* to matter? Yet he was determined to write about the history and criticism of art, however deeply hidden that ambition might be. So, when he should have been concentrating on modern history, he was actually pursuing a contradictory path with tenacious single-mindedness. He might not openly rebel, but he would not be deflected.

One imagines him in a cramped back room, perhaps overcast with that delicate, greyish light that seeps through the autumn mists in England, oblivious of the cold, fingering pieces of paper once held by Raphael and Michelangelo, and thinking himself the luckiest man in the world. He was given a large paper edition of an old catalogue by J.C. Robinson, *Drawings by Michael Angelo and Raffaelle in the University Galleries*, and told to decide which were genuine and which fake. Bell encouraged him to make acid comments in the margins.

He later called it the best possible education in learning how to look, an apparently ironic comment in view of the distinct lack of direction he received. Bell's gift to Clark was, however, to realize intuitively how little help was necessary, seeing that here was someone who would instinctively reach towards the influences he needed. These innate gifts, though apparently those of a connoisseur, were far removed from the usual considerations, even those of the standard art historian. For Kenneth Clark, facts were interesting only for the conclusion that could be wrung out of them, and the question at issue for him was how to reconstruct the imaginative processes of a genius. So he stared at Raphael's drawing of a kneeling saint, made when the artist was in his late teens, until he could see how this artist had refined his visual sensations, so that the resulting work somehow corresponded with an inner vision. He looked at Michelangelo's drawings of muscular shoulders from the same perspective and, when he came to Rembrandt, felt he was seeing anew etchings that he had copied since he was fourteen.

It is impossible to know how much this self-taught aesthete was influenced by the example of other men, impossible not to suspect that one in particular had a great deal to do with the path he was forging for himself. Artist, writer, lecturer, broadcaster, theoretician and organizer, visionary and champion of artists – Roger Fry was the *beau idéal* of all that an energetic and enlightened person can do in the cause of art. The son of distinguished Quakers, Fry was a gifted art historian as well as dedicated artist and prominent member of the Bloomsbury set. He became the lover of Vanessa Bell whose sister, Virginia Woolf, was to write his biography. Fry achieved international importance in 1906 by becoming curator of paintings at the Metropolitan Museum of Art in New York. When he returned to England some years later, it was as critic, adviser to wealthy collectors, and organizer of the first Post-Impressionist exhibitions (1911 and 1913), introducing the British to the great French painters of the nineteenth century and that unknown genius, Cézanne.

While searching vainly through the library at Winchester for something readable, Kenneth Clark had come upon Roger Fry's books. After Ruskin's ornamented and labyrinthine style, it was a relief to turn to the beautifully simple language of Fry, with his consummate gifts of clarity and persuasive argument, whether he were dissecting a drawing by Daumier, a painting by Poussin or a Ch'ang bronze. Then, at Oxford, Kenneth Clark saw Fry in action, lecturing to a full house on Poussin and Cézanne, and was transported. Fry's persuasive voice and eloquent arguments were matched, it seemed, with an ability to see to the heart of things.

In reaction to Ruskin's emphasis upon moral values and subject-matter, Fry held that art's effect must depend solely upon the balance of forms with colours. All that mattered were the absolute integrity of the artist's intent and the purity of the aesthetic sensation. All other considerations: pictorial content, iconography, social and historical context, were meaningless, as far as Fry was concerned. By the time Kenneth Clark came to write an introduction to Fry's *Last Lectures*, in 1939, he believed that Fry's theories about pure form were the hardest to defend, and had long since lost interest in them himself. He had realized that Fry's aesthetic theories did not really represent his own experience; whereas he himself loved to linger over a particularly fine piece of drawing, an enchanting subject or a graceful composition, for Fry such factors were much less important than a kind of arid perfectionism.

Fry, Kenneth Clark also decided, was no painter. Even though he worked at it for forty years and cared much more deeply about his laboured, paint-encrusted canvases than the articles he dashed off, Fry's work refused to make an impression. However, he felt that he must be mistaken somehow, so he bought two drawings and a painting. This naturally endeared him to the artist, and an invitation to Fry's London house at 7 Dalmeny Avenue, Holloway, followed. They were fast friends until Fry's death in 1934. In their long conversations Kenneth Clark would have felt in sympathy with Fry's Quaker dislike of pretence and ostentation. He would have admired Fry's eagerness to defend young, misunderstood and neglected artists, and would have explored the inexhaustible subject of their joint love, Cézanne. He would have agreed about the catastrophic indifference of the British towards art and been convinced by Fry's passionate argument that art ought not to be the exclusive province of a wealthy few. Everyone, Fry said, was potentially capable of appreciating art.

Whenever Kenneth Clark was bored it showed, if not in his manner, then in his work. He received a second-class honours degree in history, a deflating experience that he dismissed with his customary self-deprecation. The trouble was, he wrote, that he was not clever enough, his way of disguising the fact that his commitment lay elsewhere. Completing his three-year course in modern history did, however, mean that he would now have to begin a career. At this critical juncture, Charlie Bell again came to the rescue with an extremely generous offer. The week before Kenneth Clark sat for his final examinations, he asked Bell what he should do when they were over, and was told that he should write a book on the Gothic revival. Bell, it appears, had made a great many notes on the subject which he would never use. Like many who are intensely self-critical, he applied his rigorous standards to others and was famous for the malicious annotations he made in the margins of others' books in an extremely tidy hand. He much preferred others to publish his knowledge, according to another protégé, because if the results were attacked, they would get the blame.

Kenneth Clark was taken aback, partly because he did not know what the Gothic revival was, and partly because he had half decided to concentrate on one of the great Italians. He found it an inspired suggestion just the same, so he rented rooms at 21 Beaumont Street near the Ashmolean, and set to work.

After desperately trying to come to terms with all the contradictory demands placed upon him by his public school, Cyril Connolly formulated what he called a Theory of Permanent Adolescence. In his view, those so educated remained in an emotional time-warp, 'adolescent, school-minded, self-conscious, cowardly, sentimental, and in the last analysis homosexual'. Kenneth Clark would have been likely to agree with every assessment except the last. From his earliest years at Wixenford when bold, jolly older girls took care of him at school dances, he had liked girls. He was then eleven years old and very susceptible, not so much to a particular girl, as to what she represented: that delicious and indescribable difference in which sexual attraction was mingled with the half-sensed charms of womanliness. He was, however, in love with fantasy since there was hardly any chance of meeting a real girl. The only one he could remember was Sybil, the daughter of the family doctor, later Lord Dawson of Penn, who came to Sudbourne with her father. She also visited Shielbridge a few times and both sets of parents seemed to think a match had been arranged. Perhaps Kenneth Clark did himself, although he was never particularly enthusiastic about it and never made the slightest move to approach a girl he suspected of fortune-hunting. Then one day Sybil made her feelings about his father's behaviour unmistakably clear, giving Kenneth Clark an excuse to end whatever understanding they might have had. After that there was no one else in his life. He kept his predilections so well hidden that, even in 1926, when he was deeply in love, no one at I Tatti, Berenson's villa, could decide which sex he preferred.

At Winchester boyish crushes were taken as a matter of course, but no good Wykehamist would admit to liking a girl. At Oxford women were segregated in colleges of their own. 'Undergraduettes lived in purdah,' Evelyn Waugh wrote in *A Little Learning*. 'Except during Eights Week girls were very rarely to be seen in men's colleges. The proctors retained, and in my day on one occasion at least asserted, their right to expel beyond the university limits, independent women who were thought to be a temptation.'

Enterprising Oxford men of that post-First-World-War generation contrived to meet women despite such obstacles. Women were allowed to entertain young men in the drawing-rooms of their colleges for bananas, cream and tea, if properly chaperoned, and a couple might be seen walking alone together if it were clear, from the golf clubs they carried, that they had a serious purpose in mind. Those less determined or more inhibited kept their feelings hidden. Kenneth Clark frequently glimpsed girls he liked at lectures (one of the few activities open to both sexes), but would never have summoned up the courage to approach any of them. One of the girls who, he thought, had a particularly sweet expression was named Jane Martin. He was bowled over. Then, in the summer of 1925, one of his friends, Gordon Waterfield, invited him to dinner at the Moorish Tea Room to meet his fiancée. She was Jane Martin.

Jane Martin was born Elizabeth Winifred Martin on 6 October 1902, a year before her future husband, in Dublin. 'Betty', as she was always called by her family (she renamed herself Jane at Oxford), was the daughter of a businessman, Robert MacGregor Martin, and a doctor, Emily Winifred Dickson. Dr Dickson, who was born on 13 July 1866 in Dungannon, County Tyrone, was descended from a long line of linen weavers and farmers who had emigrated from Scotland at the time of James I. Her father, Thomas Dickson, started a linen mill in Dungannon and was a Liberal Member of Parliament for almost seventeen years. Later he was a Privy Councillor. E. Winifred Dickson was the second youngest of six children and one of three girls. She was educated privately and showed, from adolescence, unusual poise and maturity. She nursed her mother through a year-long illness and, once her mother had to some extent recovered, decided to study medicine, with her father's active support.

The School of the College of Surgeons in Dublin had just been opened to women and she enrolled there in 1887, at the age of twenty-one. Examinations were easy, she decided. She matriculated in the old Royal University of Ireland, took her licentiateship in 1891 and an MB two years later, the latter with first-class honours. In the same year she was elected first woman Fellow of the Royal College of Surgeons in Ireland. Dr Dickson put up her brass plate in Dublin and went on to win further degrees, a mastership in obstetrics, and was appointed examiner in midwifery to the Royal College.

From the beginning Dr Dickson, one of the first two women doctors in Ireland, knew she had to be better than a man. Her standards of perfectionism may be glimpsed from her reproof to the Medical Women's Federation, decades later, about a minor error, that she had expected better from a *women's* organization. The Federation's secretary, Miss Mabel Rew, recalled that Dr Dickson would 'always stick up firmly for women doctors' rights', yet she could be 'aggravatingly self-effacing'.

Then, in December 1899, at the age of thirty-three, Dr Dickson became plain Mrs Martin and abandoned her practice. Her friend, Dr Mary Griscom, thought that she had married because she had just been appointed to the gynaecological staffs of two hospitals. 'It was a terrific responsibility, for her to start doing abdominal surgery, when she had never even assisted at such, and all her brilliant brain work and seeing good men doing them did not really help much, when one started in alone, taking human life in one's hands.' She suggested as much to Dr Dickson who replied, 'Maybe.'

Robert MacGregor Martin was ten years younger than his wife. Like her family, his was also in the linen business and came from Fife in Scotland. Both sets of grandparents knew each other and so it was natural that Robert Martin, on a trip to northern Ireland, should visit the Dicksons. Winifred was intellectual, introverted and single-mindedly set on a goal. Robert Martin, with his sleek, smooth head and even features, was a charming, talkative extrovert who loved golfing and winter sports. When he married, he was acting as secretary for the Irish Lace Depot, a centre for hand-made lace. Later he became managing director of a hand-made carpet factory in County Kildare and, during that relatively affluent period, owned the first car in the area, a 1908 De Dion Bouton. Two years after their marriage, in 1901, their first child, Russell, was born. Betty arrived a year later and then three boys: Kenneth, Alan and Colin, the last-named born when Mrs Martin was forty-four.

The Martins lived in different parts of Dublin until Betty was ten.
Dr Russell Martin remembers at least four houses. Later, there was a
large country house with a long avenue, 'Castle Warden', where they
played tennis, rode a donkey cart, kept cows, hens and a dog. Betty
was, her brother recalled, rather tomboyish as a girl and big for her
age; larger than any of her brothers. Their father was often away on
business trips. Then, at the outbreak of the First World War, he
enlisted and was sent out with a garrison battalion to India and Burma
for the duration.

Money was short. To pay for the children's educations, plain Mrs
Martin went back to being a doctor. She joined the staff of the County
Mental Hospital at Rainhill near Liverpool and then, when she was
denied married quarters (because she was a woman), put her children
into boarding schools. By then Betty was attending Malvern College
for Ladies. She never again lived in Ireland.

Jane, her future husband said, 'was fond of her father and indulged
him'. She also took his advice. Robert Martin was absolutely clear on
the principle that it was a wife's duty to subordinate herself to her
husband. Writing to his daughter from South Africa in the 1930s he
said: 'Once more I must repeat ... how deeply I admire you for
having taken the one correct line for a young wife, namely to act as a
help and companion to your Husband; to work through him and to
rejoice in his success. That is the only way. In Rhodesia and here I
have seen many evidences of wrecks caused by a reversal of this
policy; and *all* find this out when it is too late.' Whether Robert
Martin were making an oblique reference to his own marriage is not
known. In any case, Jane took the moral to heart.

There were those who saw Jane's mother as a woman of dauntless
courage and strength. 'How hard she worked!' her future son-in-law
commented. 'I hardly ever saw her smile.' If she was admirable, her
husband was a disappointment. Dame Alix Kilroy, later Lady
Meynell, described him as 'feckless and boastful, a show-off. He took
us both to Bond Street while we were at Oxford to buy Jane some
shoes at Pinet's. They cost four guineas, which was a frightful price in
those days. I had the distinct impression that Jane's mother was
expected to foot the bill.' Kenneth Clark called him 'an incredible old
fake. He was completely idle and penniless – he lived on his wife, who
was a very poor doctor, and latterly on me. To the great relief of the
whole family he was shipped off to Durban, South Africa, where he
lived for another thirty years or so.'

Alix Kilroy met Jane at Malvern. By the age of fifteen or sixteen Jane was, her friend recalled, rather short (she was 5′ 4″), with her mother's wide, flat face, gently pouting mouth and enormous eyes – what Diana Menuhin was to call 'Dog-in-the-Tinderbox' eyes, after the fairy tale by Hans Andersen. Her brown hair was pulled back into a single plait. Jane's face was too flat and her features too pronounced for prettiness, but this was more than compensated for by her expression of alert amusement and self-possession, almost impudence. She was charming and outgoing, generously nice to everyone.

Malvern College was, Alix Kilroy said, 'a horrible school with too many unreasoning rules'. For Jane, the game was to see how much one could get away with. Girls wore gym tunics and it was decreed that, when they knelt down, the tunic must touch the floor all the way around. Somehow Jane's tunic was always shorter than anyone else's. She was not deliberately defiant so much as high-spirited, impish, unconventional. If her friend Phyllis, 'the most wicked girl in the school', went to the races, then Jane would go with her, as much to champion her as join in her wickedness. Once she had arrived at Somerville College, Oxford, Jane's gaiety and warmth made her social success immediate. 'She was much more a natural Bohemian than a member of the smart set of aesthetes.'

Janet Adam-Smith, who became an author and literary editor of the *New Statesman*, met Jane at Somerville, when the latter was in her third year.

So here I was, and here was this extremely glamorous senior, charming in her looks and manner, who took me under her wing. Jane didn't have any money and used to appear at college dances looking splendid, having bought curtain material which she then draped around her in some highly original way. The legend was that it was held together with safety pins. Back in the 1920s the feeling was that if you were a serious girl at Oxford, you had to look serious, high-thinking and plain living. Jane, however, always looked feminine and delightful. Young men flocked around her. In those days, of course, there were strict rules and one was that in no circumstance could one have a man in one's rooms. Jane had a room on the ground floor, giving onto the garden, and a quite familiar sight would be a pair of trousers, the top half of which would be in Jane's room, so that she could always say he wasn't there!

Then there was the time when some Don came upon her walking on the towpath with a young man and Jane was reported to the woman principal. Jane said, 'But I was walking alone and he attached himself to me. What could I have done?' and the principal replied, 'You should pass it off with a laugh, Miss Martin, pass it off with a laugh.'

Many were the times when Jane stayed in London overnight for a dance and Dame Evelyn (later Baroness) Sharp would rumple her bed to make it look as if it had been slept in. In sexual matters Jane was strait-laced, almost prudish, according to Alix Kilroy. In those days girls did not have boy friends as such, but 'there were young men after us both. Once an aristocrat made advances to Jane and then transferred his attentions to me. Jane thought that extremely wrong and said, "You must cut him," so I did. Jane felt half-jilted by him and so I did it out of loyalty to Jane.'

From the start, Jane was very adaptable where men were concerned. 'I remember at Oxford she fell in with a tennis player, so she decided she'd be a tennis player too. When she married K she determined to become a connoisseur. I have no recollection of her having any interest in cultural matters before she met K.'

The most attentive of Jane's young men was Gordon Waterfield, the son of Aubrey Waterfield, a painter, and Lina Duff Gordon. At the turn of the century Lina, then living with her wealthy and over-bearing aunt, Janet Ross, near I Tatti, had married despite the latter's vehement objections. Lina was a good friend of Mary Berenson's and Aunt Janet had enlisted Berensonian support in her battle with her niece. (Lina Waterfield later told the story in her book, *A Castle in Italy*.) All that, however, was long ago. Gordon, an undergraduate at Oxford, found Jane 'amusing and fun and something of a Bohemian, prepared to take risks'. They would go boating in his canoe even though it was not allowed. 'Once I upset us both in a little river beside Magdalen College. We had to plough through the mud to get back but she was terribly good about it and never blamed me.'

At the same time Gordon Waterfield was seeing Kenneth Clark often. 'My uncle was paying to put me through Oxford and I was going into the cotton business as he had. My uncle was very excited to learn that I had met a Clark. But K was not very interested in the family firm, although he was interested in almost everything else. For instance, he knew about motor bicycles and what kind to buy.' They met at the Oxford University Dramatic Society, where both were members, and at the same parties. When Gordon Waterfield fell in love with Jane Martin, and then left to take a newspaper job in Cairo and learn the cotton business, it seemed natural that he should ask his friend to look after her.

By then Jane Martin had graduated from Somerville. She had failed her finals the first year and stayed an extra year. She gained a third-class Honours degree in history – 'I was no ornament to Somerville', she used to say – and took a teaching job at a private girls' school called Downe House near Newbury. Kenneth Clark wrote on notepaper embossed with the crossed flags of the yacht *Adventuress*, from 'The Clyde', to observe that Newbury was not far from Oxford and he would be delighted to drive down and take her on outings. He also sent her some tweed patterns she had asked him to get in London. He ventured to think that the checked pattern in two shades of purple would be the best choice. Then he invited her to come sailing. His father, he said, was planning to build an extremely large new motorboat, so there would be plenty of room for her. All the proprieties could be observed, he added, almost as an afterthought. Not too long after that he invited her to visit his rooms. He was in evident terror that his daring act would be discovered and, as luck would have it, 'Sligger' made an unexpected appearance. Kenneth Clark, in the best tradition of farce, shoved Jane into a cupboard, where she was obliged to remain for some time. Not surprisingly, she never quite forgave him for the importance he placed on appearances.

He found her enchanting. She might not know much about art, or revivals of the Gothic, but that was part of her charm. There was her self-assured way of encountering strangers, her warmth, kindness, generosity, sense of fun and the way she launched herself into life, just as his father had. Where he was shy, she was buoyant; where he was emotionally inhibited, she was spontaneity itself. He had long since foregone his exhibitionistic impulses; Jane, with wonderful panache, paraded hers. Where he felt himself to be diffident and secretive, she was stout-hearted and truthful. In battles, she expressed the anger he felt bound to conceal and disclaim. She adored him, defended him and protected him, just as Lam had done. He saw his salvation in her.

There was, however, the problem of Gordon, soldiering away on the *Egyptian Gazette*. How should he be told? Jane wrote offering to meet him in southern Italy to discuss their future. Gordon, however, could not get away from his newspaper and did not feel financially able to support a wife at that time. She behaved, he wrote later, 'very

straightforwardly and properly'. He thought he felt nothing but
relief. Far beneath the surface, Gordon was hurt that Jane should
prefer his friend. He said, 'I remember one terrible occasion when I
went to have dinner with them in London shortly after their marriage
and broke down. It was much too close quarters, so I left in a hurry. I
think now I was expecting too much of myself.'

On that fateful afternoon when Kenneth Clark went to ask Jane
Martin to marry him there had been some confusion about exactly
when he would arrive from Oxford and he was late. 'I remember
going down the hill towards her and catching a glimpse of her coming
up the hill through the trees. There was an expression on her face that
I had never seen before. She looked so terrible that I very nearly
turned around and left.'

He did not turn around. When they met, 'she was very sweet and
everything was all right. But I never forgot that look.'

7 I Tatti

'It is quite moving to see how Kenneth admires
B.B. Nothing is lost on that boy, he is so
marvellously cultivated that he can follow
intelligently almost every intellectual path that
B.B. opens. He says he has never before
been ... with any older man whose mind did
not seem poured into moulds.' –
MARY BERENSON

In September 1925 Bernard Berenson was at the pinnacle of his fame
as an expert on Italian Renaissance art. Although Kenneth Clark did
not know it then, 'B.B.' had been chief adviser to that famous and
controversial dealer Sir Joseph (later Lord) Duveen, for decades. He
received 25 per cent of the profits from a sale and his celebrated
initials, affixed to certificates, were eagerly sought by the American
millionaires willing to pay Sir Joseph's outrageous prices. As a result,
by the time Kenneth Clark met him, Berenson was ensconced in
ducal splendour in a villa outside Florence, I Tatti, the centre of a
worldly and ambitious milieu. To have dined with B.B. was worth
boasting about, if you were a young scholar. To receive the mark of
his favour was to have gained everything the art world had to bestow.

Berenson's famous writings on the Italian Renaissance had all been
published decades before. He knew that *Drawings of the Florentine
Painters*, while an admired work of scholarship, was particularly out
of date. Early in 1925 he thought he had found the assistant he needed
to prepare a new edition, Yukio Yashiro, a young Japanese scholar.
He complained that it was too bad his assistant would have to be a
'Jap' and not even a European, let alone an American. Fate, in the
form of an unlikely *deus ex machina*, was conspiring to have the ideal
candidate appear, prepared to do exactly what Berenson wanted.
That autumn of 1925 Charlie Bell invited Kenneth Clark to stay
with him outside Florence at the home of Gordon Waterfield's
intimidating Aunt Janet. Kenneth Clark said he would be charmed.

By the time the two men arrived at Aunt Janet's menacing villa,
Poggio Gherardo, not far from I Tatti on the hills above Settignano,

Kenneth Clark was as intoxicated by Italy as Monty Rendall and
B.B. had been before him. Bell, however, was suddenly taken ill.
The reverence in which Berenson was held in most circles of the art
world was not shared by him; to Bell the idea that one could be
dogmatic in such matters as connoisseurship amounted to a confidence trick. Left to himself, he would have stayed in bed. As it was, a
luncheon was planned for the next day and so he staggered out. He
already knew how much it meant to his protégé.

The villa of I Tatti had been reclaimed by the Berensons from
semi-dereliction at the turn of the century. A rectangular and
classically simple sixteenth-century house, it stood at an angle from
the road, almost completely hidden by *allées* of cypresses and ilex.
Long corridors and ample wall space presented ideal opportunities
for displaying the collection of Siamese, Egyptian, Chinese and Persian sculptures, *objets d'art* and quattrocento paintings that the
Berensons had collected over the years. The *pièce de résistance*,
however, was the library, crammed with books (B.B. liked to describe his villa as a library with rooms attached) and if the resulting
impression was somewhat intimidating, Berenson did not mind. He
liked the villa's bookish decor, giving the right ambience for a life of
leisurely study, one interrupted only by visitors. These came in
droves to lunch, tea, dinner and for the week-end as well.

At lunch, most people were talking in Italian which, at the time,
Kenneth Clark did not speak. Afterwards the party repaired to a
limonaia overlooking the formal garden and B.B. directed the newcomer to join him for a chat. By then the would-be disciple was
privately agreeing with Bell. Kenneth Clark liked his friends to be
warm and unpretentious, and above all, not to boast or put on airs.
Berenson seemed as vainglorious and boastful as it was possible to
be. His host, unaware of the negative reaction, was almost at the
door, bound for Vienna, when he paused and placed a hand on
Clark's arm. Then he invited him to become his assistant and help
prepare a new edition of the *Florentine Drawings*.

How could he turn down such a spectacular opportunity to fulfil the
dream of his adolescence? How could he possibly stomach Mr Berenson? How could he make his parents like it? How could he explain
himself to Bell? He was in such a state of turmoil that he became
literally ill. As he expected, the reaction at home was negative. By the
time he came to write his autobiography, he put it in the mildest
possible terms, but the reality was otherwise, to judge from the letter

he wrote to Mary Berenson a month later. The idea that he should propose giving up his shining prospects of a business or political career for the paltry world of art struck them with horror, he wrote. He absolutely must stay at Oxford for the rest of the year, but after talking himself hoarse he had finally won their agreement to let him spend his winter holidays at I Tatti.

The attempt seemed doomed to fail. Berenson surely needed someone who could begin immediately. But even if he did accept these conditions, would Kenneth Clark live to regret it? As for his parents, he was duty bound to please them. He was also discovering in himself a clear sense of direction and knew the consequences, if one allowed others to make decisions that one could only make one-self. He must have felt that without art, which alone could shield him from the 'sordid perils of actual existence', as Oscar Wilde wrote, he would go under. In his turmoil, almost paralysed by frustration, panic and anger that he dared not express, he had another crisis. He called it hypochondria. It culminated in an attack of jaundice. He went home to Bournemouth, stared at the yellow curtains in his parents' living-room, and felt more ill than ever.

The good news arrived that the Berenson offer would stay open indefinitely. Early in January 1926 he spent three weeks thinking about art, poking about in Berenson's library and talking of nothing else but art. To be in the company of people who looked benevolently upon his eccentricities instead of having to conceal them, as if they were a secret vice, was worth all the swallowing of dislike that it might cost him. But the enthusiasm was unfeigned, on both sides. 'Kenneth Clark is a very remarkable youth, so learned and with such good taste,' Mary Berenson wrote to her sister Alys. He had announced his intention of settling in Florence and devoting his life to working with B.B., 'but of course when a young man speaks about "devoting his life", it means, "two years and then see",' she wrote with prescience. They had advised him not to disillusion his parents but reassure them that he was learning languages so that, when he became a diplomat – their plan for him – he would be at an advantage. Mary Berenson added, 'He objects, "but it is a lie, I don't mean to take up a diplomatic career", but it will be wiser to tell them that two years hence.'

Kenneth Clark had also charmed Mary's brother, Logan Pearsall Smith, a literary stylist of some note and author of a few fastidious volumes: *Unforgotten Years, Trivia, More Trivia* and *All Trivia*. Smith reported to Alys Russell that the Englishman was the newest

favourite in court and that he had just come upon Clark 'sitting with
the B.B.s over a portfolio of photographs, emitting opinions about
them which they seemed to listen to with respect'.

Kenneth Clark did not realize, Logan wrote from I Tatti late in
January 1926, how greatly he was missed. 'I often wish you were here
to laugh with me over some of the more amazing incidents. I am
sometimes in that uncomfortable predicament suggested by Fon-
tenelle, when he said, "*la chose est risible, mais il nous manque des
rieurs*".' Subsequently, Logan thanked 'my dear Kenneth' for his
response and thought he did himself an injustice to apologize for it.
He had, Logan said,

> a very pretty epistolary gift. You should exercise it, as the habit of pouring
> out one's mind on paper is an excellent preparation for writing other
> things. This advice is good advice, though hardly disinterested, since,
> should the rage of writing seize you, I might hope perhaps to be among
> their recipients. I have only one criticism – or shall I say query ? – to make
> in this connection. The proposition which is inscribed in large letters on
> your envelopes, and forms as it were a sort of preface or portico to your
> communications – the statement that BRITISH GOODS ARE BEST – seems,
> when addressed to this Cosmopolitan villa, a little baldly put.

Returning to Oxford early in 1926, Kenneth Clark was again in
despair; he even contemplated running away. He was restrained by
the knowledge that he could not work on his Gothic Revival book
anywhere else and was reasonably sure he would be allowed to return
to Italy that summer. His dislike of Berenson's prima donna ways was
being tempered by the discovery that, in the right circumstances, no
one could be a more stimulating mentor. Just to talk with him was
exhilarating. Berenson really seemed to want him, and him alone.
The knowledge gave him the confidence he needed, for if the elder
Clarks were blind to the opportunity being offered, Kenneth Clark
certainly was not. For a tactician, he was turning to Mary Berenson,
who reiterated her conviction that, if necessary, parents must be
deliberately misled. She did not say so in as many words but her
intention was clear. Children, she wrote, must have no pangs of
conscience on this score since they plainly knew best. It was a doc-
trine which would have sounded daringly attractive to Kenneth
Clark.

Kenneth Clark's letters to the Berensons have a quaintly formal,
almost stilted quality, lit only occasionally with the irreverence and
bite that came to characterize his later writings. They artlessly

describe the rarefied world of a wealthy young aesthete as he stared out of his Oxford window onto the rain and fog while writing a discourse on Ruskin for the Gryphon Society, all the while dreaming of Italy and thinking up new ways to wriggle out of his parents' clutches. He was to spend the early summer in Dresden perfecting his German – at least that was the ostensible reason – then take up several months' residence with the Berensons and travel with them. They, completely nonplussed by his private life, and concluding that he was not a ladies' man, had arranged to have him share a flat with their English friend Cecil Pinsent, whose tastes were known to be pronounced, and Kenneth Clark politely agreed. He also asked Mary Berenson anxiously whether he ought to bring his chauffeur. It was absurd, of course, to have a chauffeur at his age. However, the man made a useful valet and was a marvellous mechanic in time of need, whereas his employer was a dud.

Arriving in Dresden, Kenneth Clark predictably rushed to the museum and worked there every day for three weeks. The Italian attributions were hopelessly out of date, he wrote. He had discovered a Rembrandt and been immodest enough to boast about it. Now he had five days left to gloat over some incomparable Dürers, Cranachs and Grünewalds. Fortunately he was not missing much in London; the only news was that the Piero *St Michael* had been cleaned.

During that erratic year K and Jane met during his stays at Oxford. The arrangement with Gordon was definitely off, marriage was definitely on, and Jane was composing hesitant letters in which she expressed her dutiful readiness to join her husband 'under the Settignano tree', as Mary Berenson put it. There was, however, the matter of Gordon's parents. The Waterfields had never quite thought Jane Martin good enough for their son, and that Jane should have attracted such a well-heeled suitor was a twist of the knife, as their eventual daughter-in-law, Kitty Waterfield, expressed it. For her part Mary Berenson could recall the days when Janet Ross ('Aunt Janet') had been enraged that Lina was marrying Aubrey Waterfield. Now here was Lina, behaving with Gordon's fiancée as Janet had with her. When he arrived in Munich, K found a letter from Jane with news of the latest Waterfield reactions. The Berensons had joined their camp, she wrote. K replied that he would take care of them, but Aunt Janet's nefarious ways were another matter. To think that someone as upright and straightforward as Jane was being labelled an unscrupulous fortune hunter – it was past belief.

In October he joined the Berensons in Milan where they visited the chief galleries before driving around northern Italy, hunting for art. Whatever they might think about Kenneth Clark's private life, the Berensons could not fault him as a travelling companion. 'He is the keenest sightseer I ever knew and extraordinarily intelligent. He never says a stupid thing,' Mary gushed to Alys from Vicenza and then, from Verona, 'I love to see Kenneth appreciate B.B.'s attitude to art and learning. We get on very well with Kenneth and hope he will be as great a success as Nicky [Mariano] . . .' Then K wired Jane, setting the wedding date for 10 January 1927.

He had not seen his fiancée for three months, yet he went to Rome for the Christmas holidays and did not return to London until the day before his wedding. Either the groom had definitely cooled on the idea or was avoiding something. The latter turned out to be the case. Sensing that there might be a head-on collision between his bride's innocent love of ceremony and extravagant display and his mother's horror of ostentation, not to mention emotion, a church . . . He must have quailed at the prospect. The only solution was to lie low.

The wedding turned out to be satisfactory, from his point of view: no wedding dress, no bridesmaids, no champagne, no organ, no reception and hardly any guests. Not surprisingly, his bride's spirits were cast down. She must have seriously doubted whether he really wanted to marry her. She had hardly seen him for months, and felt awkward and estranged. 'I remember them sitting on the sofa at St Ermin's Mansions on their honeymoon,' Alix Kilroy said, 'and Jane saying, "I still feel very polite".' Mary Berenson's concerns for Jane were 'on the money question, as he is really stingy', she told Alys. However, Jane had managed to get him into a church, St Peter's in Eaton Square, even though he asked for a registry office wedding. 'This begins well,' Mary commented with satisfaction. 'It won't do any harm for her to have the Upper Hand.'

Kenneth Clark was planning to take his bride to Sospel in the south of France, where his father had made him a present of a large hotel, and then they were to go on to Florence. Parental permission to study at I Tatti had been granted at last. Victory was sweet and, on his marriage certificate, the husband described his occupation as Art Critic.

Mary Berenson had arranged for the rental of a house near I Tatti, the Chiostro di San Martino. It adjoined a glorious Brunelleschian church, mercifully preserved, and dated from the quattrocento although a plaque on their bedroom wall went back to the year 682 when, supposedly, the blessed Andrew the Scot had died there. They arrived in February and found the house dreadfully cold and the drains stubbornly temperamental. However, it was wonderfully picturesque, the servants were a treasure and the cook sublime; the meals matched anything that the new tenant had ever been served in London.

Dealing with the Berenson and Waterfield affair was obviously the first order of business. Aunt Janet had been so amazingly rude to Jane that it was almost a joke. Berenson was another matter. The prospect of confronting him so terrified K that, on the verge of a visit, his knees literally gave way and he collapsed into a reclining chair. When they finally arrived, his fears were confirmed. Berenson placed Jane beside him and then, knowing that she spoke no German or Italian, talked across her in those languages at every meal. Just as things seemed hopeless, Berenson learned of Aunt Janet's behaviour and changed sides. Such outright rudeness was not to be tolerated. He dressed up in his best clothes and called upon Mrs Ross to deliver a formal protest.

Every morning, K took the tram to Florence, arriving at the door of the Gabinetto del Disegni as it opened, to work on the laborious revisions required for the new edition of the *Drawings of the Florentine Painters*. It was perhaps the most tedious work he was ever to undertake – a matter of checking sizes of drawings and catalogue descriptions – and went against his temperament, since minor details bored him. However, he was allowed to query the drawings' attributions occasionally. That was the whole point, since to become a connoisseur seemed the great goal of a lifetime.

Meanwhile Jane, who knew nothing about art, threw herself wholeheartedly into studying it. To teach someone as bright-minded as Jane was K's idea of relaxation. He was enjoying himself hugely and she was learning fast; before long, they would go into a gallery and she would suggest the name of an obscure artist to the director and be right. They travelled all over Italy, in love with its churches, museums and landscape, in love with their charming house, united in their enthusiasms. It was the best possible beginning for a marriage. It was to be their happiest time together.

K's future direction seemed so well established that he decided to give up his book on the Gothic Revival. He told Jane of his decision one day as they were walking in the grounds of I Tatti and she came to

a dead halt. The fact that she only vaguely understood the importance
of the book did not stop her from a sizzling defence of it. He had, she
pointed out, already written more than a third of the manuscript. He
owed it to Charlie Bell to finish what he had started. K contritely
agreed and abandoned work in Florence so as to spend an uncomfortable few months back in Oxford, where he needed to do further
research. They fled to Italy at the first opportunity and K went on
writing in the Chiostro di San Martino. Jane read every chapter and
then typed it on the I Tatti typewriter. She was reading Gibbon's
Decline and Fall in a sunny bedroom and resting a great deal; she had
just discovered she was pregnant.

While Jane stayed on in the Chiostro di San Martino, K, in the
early autumn of 1927, followed Berenson to Paris. Berenson's
periodic journeys to the great European capitals were taking on,
more and more, the aura of a Great Appearance. On this particular
occasion his visit was grander than usual since officials of the Louvre
had decided to pay him the ultimate compliment of taking down some
of the masterpieces from the walls and removing their protective
glass, the better to be inspected by B.B. With Kenneth Clark at his
side, the great man sat at a table beside a sunny window while one
masterpiece after another was laid before them. As a kind of *hors
d'œuvre*, they were first presented with the little *Annunciation* of
Leonardo da Vinci. Berenson had prepared an article claiming that it
was by Lorenzo di Credi, but the moment he saw it he changed his
mind. It could only be a Leonardo, he said.

That was enough of a treat as far as Kenneth Clark was concerned.
But then the officials entered bearing the famous *Fête Champêtre* by
Giorgione, its glass removed and the sunlight slanting across its exquisite surface. Kenneth Clark stared at the painting that he had
loved in reproductions since he was seven years old and thought he
had never seen anything so beautiful in his life. After such an experience, to look at contemporary art in the rue la Boétie was a dreary jolt
back to earth. The shops were full of dreadful works he would pay not
to own. Modern art, he realized, after a discussion with a group of
artists in a café, had reached an impasse because artists were in the
grip of unscrupulous dealers. Everyone knew that Vollard had
bought several hundred Cézannes for a total of £200 and was now
asking £10,000 each – such a huge profit seemed inconceivable. Now
of course every businessman in Paris was clamouring to own a
Cézanne. Similarly, there were some commendable Picassos for sale

at Rosenberg's for £10,000 each – large abstract designs. However, Rosenberg was saying that he would not sell his twenty-five best Picassos for any price since he stood to make a fortune from them eventually. Kenneth Clark, who at that time shared his mentor's low opinion of Picasso, hoped he would live to see the day when that bubble burst. People were going to look like idiots.

Most evenings he returned to his room in the courtyard of a *pension* at 5 rue des Pyramides for a solitary meal. The days dragged by. Fortunately Nicky Mariano came to the rescue with an evening on the town. First they had dinner in Berenson's private suite, exactly like Adolphe Menjou in *A Woman of Paris*, and then went to see a comedy, *Léopold le Bien-Aimé*. Going to see a play in a foreign language had the advantage that one was prepared to enjoy any joke that one could follow; since his grasp of French was improving, he was in stitches most of the time. If only Jane were there. If only she could have been with him at the Louvre at the magical moment when the *Fête Champêtre* stood with the light falling across it, revealing a whole range of unsuspected subtleties and delicate hues. How could he possibly enjoy something like that, he wrote, without his other half?

In November 1927 his bank balance was handsome. Altogether there was £600 on deposit for the spring, which would pay for the car and the baby, due in April. It must be born in England, they decided, but they left the Chiostro di San Martino sadly, almost in tears. While looking for a house they stayed temporarily in St Ermin's Mansions, Westminster. K was at work until lunch and from tea to dinner on his book, leaving barely two free hours a day in which to see things and people. His mother, who had recently had an operation (unspecified), looked very frail. She seemed edgy and prepared to dislike anything he suggested.

Then, on 13 April 1928, Alan Kenneth Mackenzie Clark was born. Kenneth Clark had taken Jane to the nursing home the night before. She was in excellent spirits and no pain. All that changed during the night and, due to the size of the baby's head, labour was prolonged and painful. Her husband, plainly out of his depth, tried to dismiss it as a normal delivery while commiserating with Jane. He made a passing reference to the baby in his report to Mary Berenson. No one paid it much attention, he said, so he assumed it was healthy. He found it an uncommonly homely child, although others who had seen

more newborns considered it handsome. He would place it as School
of Baldovinetti, and resembling the infant in the André painting.

His book, *The Gothic Revival*, was finished at last. Thanks to
Logan Pearsall Smith, who had gallantly offered to show the manuscript to Michael Sadleir of Constable's, publication was assured.
Fifteen minutes after Jane's baby arrived he delivered his manuscript
to the publisher's. They were exceedingly kind about it, he wrote.

By the 1920s everyone agreed that the Gothic Revival architectural
style, as common to the British landscape as trees and haystacks, was
abominable. While concurring, Charlie Bell thought the time had
come to relate such monstrosities to the literary and religious
movements of the time. So Kenneth Clark, taking the historical view,
set out to describe the evolution of the Gothic Revival through the
poetry, novels, comment and personalities of the eighteenth and
nineteenth centuries. The early chapters had been written too soon
after taking his final examinations to give him much pleasure in retrospect. However, after Jane had rekindled his determination, he
realized that he had left the book at its most interesting point, and
plunged into an examination of the Gothic Revival's most brilliant
exponents.

Although showing nominal deference to Roger Fry's theories of
pure form, and the theories of pure architectural values espoused by
Geoffrey Scott in his book, *The Architecture of Humanism* (1914),
Kenneth Clark avoided lengthy analyses because, he said, he had the
sense to see that this was not his forte. Rather he hoped to demon-
strate, by means of concrete examples, that form was a language and
that shapes could somehow be translated into words; even that
design could be interpreted as a state of mind. He wanted to see art as
a whole and, by drawing from a wide range of sources, to extract fresh
insights from unfamiliar juxtapositions.

In *The Gothic Revival*, published when Kenneth Clark was
twenty-five years old, one finds a writer whose style has remarkable
polish and self-assurance. Here was an independent, alert and penetrating mind, reassessing a forgotten architectural period with vigour
and originality. Like the Gothic novelists he described, he was in
revolt against stuffy and conventional opinion or, like Ruskin,
launching an attack on shams. With his first book he was demolishing
the commonplace and simultaneously breaking free from the mould
his parents' stifling beliefs and barren expectations might have forced
him into. The irony was that he set out to attack one view and ended

up with an implicit rebuttal of another. Originally, he wrote, he saw his book as a way of exposing what Geoffrey Scott called 'the ethical fallacy', and read the apologists of the period, Pugin, Ruskin and Gilbert Scott, to find evidence of such a fallacy in their work. But the more he studied the period, the more convinced he became that the conclusions he was looking for were false. In fact, soon after he began work on the subject, he came to see that the Gothic Revival had produced works of genius; the false Gothic of Fonthill, the Houses of Parliament, the tasteful Gothic of Temple Moore and Bentley. The greatest architects of the movement, he felt, were those his contemporaries thought the worst: Street and Butterfield. However, if he flew in the face of established opinion, would he be ridiculed? He solved the dilemma by equivocating, and settled on a tone that left him feeling ashamed of his cowardice while failing to satisfy his potential critics. These, he later wrote, attacked him anyway for making his digs far too half-hearted.

If he felt ambivalent about the book, many reviewers did not. They called it a brilliant, lively and informative account of one of the most absurd chapters in the history of English taste, and hailed the arrival of an important new writer. After the first reviews appeared, Alys Russell reported that the young couple were happily exploring and conquering London. Discerning people, she wrote, all liked his book and were anxious to meet this impudently intelligent young man.

They had settled on a house, 65 Tufton Street in Westminster, and moved there in the early summer of 1928. Since Kenneth Clark's father paid the bill, the house was chosen reluctantly after the idea that K and Jane should move to the countryside near Sudbourne was vetoed. Not surprisingly, K always disliked the house and, perhaps for that reason, made no attempt to reshape it to his developing tastes. He even declared that he was quite content with heavy mahogany furniture and large gilt frames, that these reminded him of his childhood, and that he would not feel at home in the stripped-down and polished rooms coming into vogue. Just the same he and Jane did redecorate their bedroom with a background more to their taste, a William Morris print – he found Morris's elegant arabesques so harmonious and restful that he was to use his designs ever afterwards – and furnished his study with some choice drawings from his growing collection, including ones by Correggio and Beccafumi.

Jane had looked very ill after Alan was born but, a month later, seemed much better, Alys Russell thought. However, 'nursing little

Alan is still very painful. He was soon brought in crying lustily for his
food, so I came away.' The baby had been christened, Kenneth Clark
told Mary Berenson. Just as his parents were giving their dutiful word
that he would renounce the sinful desires of the flesh, Alan produced
a quiet hiccough. He was healthy and thriving, and was already
waving his arms about and burbling at them in the most charming
way. He began life as 'Jane's baby', but quickly became 'our son'.

In pursuit of his future career as a connoisseur Kenneth Clark was
haunting the Bond Street auction houses and looking at everything
up for sale. He had battled his way into one of them recently and
found astonishing prices being paid for inferior Dutch paintings;
Italian works were a bargain by comparison. The dealer, Max Roths-
child, had a very interesting tempera head, part of a large picture
once owned by Charles I, that no one could positively identify.
Kenneth Clark was sending a photograph of it to Berenson without
the dealer's knowledge. His comment, that he never revealed his
association with Berenson to dealers, shows that, at some point
during his stay at I Tatti, he realized that Berenson was dealing in art.
That he had become one of Berenson's scouts is also clear from
another remark, made in connection with a Savile Gallery catalogue
that he mailed to I Tatti in the spring of 1929. He was sending it
although, he wrote, the names of Ghirlandaio and Verrocchio
notwithstanding, there was nothing for 'us'.

He kept telling Berenson that he was just about to return to work
on the *Florentine Drawings*. Since that project would not absorb all
his energies he was casting around for other ideas. He had sketched
out some thoughts about a book dealing with that conflict between
classicism and the baroque that had absorbed the Italian spirit during
the late sixteenth and early seventeenth centuries. Since this subject
arose from ideas which Berenson himself had suggested, the Great
Man naturally approved. His disciple set to work and, a few months
later, was refusing to be deflected by offers to publish his articles and
was collecting material for his study of classicism.

Despite his reassurances, Kenneth Clark had completely lost
interest in the *Florentine Drawings*. The fact was that he 'loathed the
pettifogging business of correcting notes and numbers and there will
be a lot of that to do if he means to help B.B.', Mary Berenson
complained to Alys Russell. For his part, Berenson was convinced
that he had made a poor choice. What he needed was careful
scholarship, not fancy writing. Both men kept postponing the matter.

Mary Berenson was convinced that it would all end in a deplorable quarrel. Then Kenneth Clark, in a conversation with W.G. Constable, happened to drop the word 'collaboration'.

The word somehow got back to I Tatti. It prompted a long letter from Berenson to say that a collaborator was not what he had in mind. Berenson was eager to know what progress Kenneth Clark was making on his new book. He hoped nothing would lure his pupil away from that. Kenneth Clark must devote his gift for scholarship and his literary talents to writing a 'milestone contribution' to the history of ideas. Berenson was confident that he was capable of it. Mary Berenson was less gracious. All that Kenneth Clark had wanted from his friendship with a great man was whatever glory he could get out of it. She told Alys Russell, 'He has an ungenerous, self-centred nature.' Her 'two years and then see' had been almost literally correct.

Kenneth Clark's interest in classicism, the baroque or anything else was supplanted by a new enthusiasm: Leonardo da Vinci. While studying at the Ashmolean, he had been intrigued by a small group of Leonardo's drawings he had found there, one a preparatory study for that artist's great painting, *The Virgin of the Rocks*. Then, during that first year of work for Berenson, he had looked at the six hundred folios (or sheets) by Leonardo in the royal collection at Windsor Castle. These drawings, whose subjects ranged from navigation, cities, botany and the human figure to natural disasters – earthquakes, deluges and explosions – were rendered with phenomenal clarity. All thoughts of what B.B. might have termed petty antiquarianism vanished. There was only one subject worth studying and that was Leonardo.

While at Windsor Kenneth Clark struck up a warm friendship with the librarian, Owen (later Sir Owen) Morshead. Morshead was just ten years his senior, had been a hero of the First World War (he won the MC and DSO), was married with three young children and, in 1926, had just taken up his post as librarian. The idea of preparing the first catalogue ever made of the King's great collection of Leonardo drawings was in the air and Kenneth Clark soon seemed the logical choice. The appointment came in 1929 when Kenneth Clark was twenty-six years old.

It might seem prosaic to begin with Leonardo today, Kenneth Clark wrote, as well as pretentious. However, at that time worthwhile books on Leonardo were few and far between. There were some serious problems of attribution and, astonishingly, the relationship between Leonardo's art and his writings had never been explored. The best work on the subject was *The Literary Works of Leonardo da Vinci* by J.P. Richter, but that had been published years before, in 1883, and made no reference to Leonardo's debts to his contemporaries, to the mass of books he read and, above all, his close connection with the Middle Ages. Leonardo seemed an isolated, superhuman figure. As he had with *The Gothic Revival*, Kenneth Clark saw an opportunity to do something innovative and seized it. However, the study of Leonardo involved more than simply giving up his work on the *Florentine Drawings* project. In effect, he had abandoned connoisseurship.

On a visit to Rome early in 1929, Kenneth Clark went to hear a lecture by an important new theoretician, Felix ('Aby') Warburg. If Berenson had reacted against nineteenth-century Academism by placing his emphasis upon aestheticism and 'tactile values', Warburg could be said to be in opposition to the doctrines of B.B. and his predecessor, Giovanni Morelli. For Warburg, paintings spoke in symbols, and the purpose of art historical research should be to unravel the riddles and put them in their historical perspective. Warburg's theories were to have a major influence on many people, including Kenneth Clark, since he would, in years to come, be obsessed by a painter's motifs, or recurring images. That lecture opened up new vistas for his listener, and acted as a necessary corrective to Berenson's 'life-enhancing' theories. If there had ever been a close link between the two men, it was loosening. Shortly after that, Kenneth Clark wrote to decline B.B.'s suggestion that he publish his attributions because, he said, he did not feel confident enough.

The moment had come, Kenneth Clark decided, to move closer to his work in the library of Windsor Castle. He and Jane had taken a great fancy to a charming house owned by friends of theirs beside the river Thames at Twickenham and found their own home in Westminster dingier than ever by comparison. Now that their son had an important new status as cataloguer of the King's drawings, the elder Clarks withdrew their objections to having him live in the country. He and Jane searched in Richmond, which was on the way to Windsor, and soon found the house of their dreams.

It was an early eighteenth-century house of red brick on Richmond Green which, since it stood on the site of the Tudor palace of Sheen, was named Old Palace Place. The Clarks prepared to move in the early autumn of 1930 and, for the first time, drew up plans to decorate

Alice Clark.

Kenneth Mackenzie Clark, the man who broke
the bank at Monte Carlo.

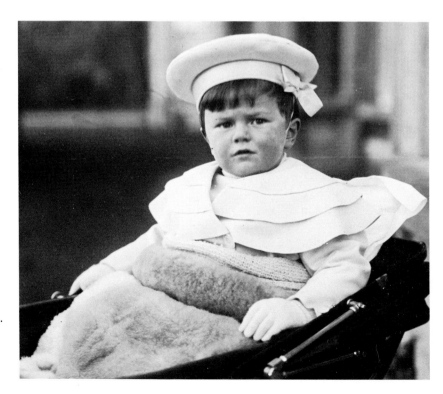

The young K.

Alice Clark and her son.

The elder K with his namesake.

The young K at the bat.

K as a boy.

K in adolescence.

Father and son, with an unidentified American relative.

Sudbourne Hall.

The main hall at Sudbourne,
transformed.

The library at Sudbourne.

Kenneth and Alice Clark out for a walk; their friends at right are not identified.

Jane Clark.

Kenneth Clark's drawing of Jane.

Jane Clark's sense of style in the late 1920s.

Alan Clark with the twins, Colette and Colin.

Queen Elizabeth attends a Myra Hess concert at the National Gallery with the director.

a house to their own tastes with the aid of John Hill, a young decorator from the London firm of Green and Abbott. The house's most beautiful room, a drawing-room 36' × 15' on the first floor, containing seven tall windows overlooking the Green, was hung with red silk. Its woodwork was painted green and gold. At one end was hung a large, pretentious Tintoretto, a portrait of a member of the Gonzaga family. There was a square, panelled entrance hall, three smaller reception rooms and, on the ground floor, opening onto the garden, a panelled sitting-room which they painted white. All-white curtains were designed by Green and Abbot with a motif of stencilled feathers and ribbons, and a carpet to match. The sofa and chairs were gold and the walls hung with the Clarks' growing collection of drawings.

In the course of their redecoration they found a complete Gothic mantelpiece dated 1655 in the dining-room, which had been part of the old palace. It had curled spandrels and, what was most rare, the original colouring and gilding. Two Florentine quattrocento bas-reliefs of angels were installed on either side of the chimneypiece. Many of the other rooms – there were ten bed- and dressing-rooms, for instance – had original cornices and fireplaces. Curtains were designed in off-white linen, with leaves superimposed in delicate greys – others were of deep blue satin with gold stars. Queen Mary was to admire these so warmly when she came to visit that they were called Queen Mary's curtains ever afterwards. As for the solid Edwardian mahogany, that was being replaced by the more elegant and graceful lines of Regency. From now on Kenneth Clark's houses would reflect his taste rather than his inheritance.

Old Palace Place, with its overtones of regal visitations, its carefully wrought interiors and its ambience of discrimination and luxury, was an idyllic setting. He took calmly the fact that he would be sought after, consulted and invited to some of the most exclusive parties in London. He travelled in his own chauffeur-driven limousine. He owned his own hotel in the south of France. He had already published a book and, at the age of twenty-seven, was at work on a study art historians twice his age would have drawn blood for. He was, in fact, off and running.

When, at Oxford, Jane had been imitated, admired and envied, her Bohemian friends had not minded that she was not 'grand'. Her marriage to Kenneth Clark had, however, catapulted her into a world where women dressed for dinner, exchanged gossip about couturiers, complained about their butlers and assessed pedigrees. Was she awestruck, as others were, or fiercely resolved to present the right façade in loyalty to this brilliantly clever man, this exquisite arbiter of taste whom she had married? Such speculations would be idle were it not for the fact that, after three years of marriage Jane, as Janet Flanner was to remark of Queen Mary in *London was Yesterday*, seemed to be devoting her energies to not being herself. Shortly after the Clarks moved to Richmond, Jane's old friend Alix Kilroy came for a visit: 'I shall never forget that weekend,' she said. 'They were extremely uncomfortable company, because they were putting on such a pose of being enormously knowledgeable. They'd throw out the name of Giorgione as if everyone should know it. The whole house was kept very cold for the sake of the pictures and one felt that these were more important than the people.' Their guest was thoroughly miserable and cut short her stay. It was not simply the atmosphere of frigid formality, but the change that had taken place in Jane. Then she wrote Jane an indignant letter. 'I saw her suddenly as rich, arrogant, a poseur. I was very young and still thinking that relationships ought to be honest, and started with poor Jane. I don't know how much she minded. I don't think she ever answered.'

Gordon Waterfield and his new wife Kitty, who met Jane in 1929, had a similar impression. Kitty Waterfield said, 'It seemed to me everything was going swimmingly, but Jane was uncomfortable.' Jane was 'putting on an act of what K wanted her to be, someone more original than anyone else by virtue of her looks and dress, who said all the right amusing, clever things, and who entertained impeccably. A paragon. She could never relax and be herself. Never. Any more.'

They were always together. Jane travelled with him to visit museums and picture collections in Paris, Edinburgh, Vienna, Munich, or Milan; to the hotel at Sospel, for a holiday, or to Shiel-bridge, to endure yachting trips with a tense face, since she hated being on the water. When Kenneth Clark was asked to give two lectures on the study of art history at London University, Jane scoured the city for an audience. Despite all her efforts, hardly anyone came.

'We' went to Paris to see the Byzantine exhibition and, although only there for three days, they worked so hard that they were exhausted. 'We' met, and disapproved of, a young man who was to review a Byzantine exhibition for the *Burlington* magazine while knowing nothing about it. Then 'we' were just off to Cambridge for a series of festivities organized by Sir Sydney Cockerell to celebrate the opening of his new wing at the Fitzwilliam. One could hardly fail to notice such a couple. And, in fact, Kenneth Clark's name was being raised again, this time in connection with a major exhibition of Italian art in London in January 1930. The idea had developed as the result of a friendship between Lady Chamberlain, wife of the former British Foreign Secretary, and the Italian Duce, Benito Mussolini, and was therefore, Kenneth Clark concluded, a calculated piece of Fascist propaganda. Nevertheless he was not as strongly opposed as Berenson was – some of the Great Man's reservations having to do with the wisdom of transporting so many masterpieces out of Italy – and accepted with alacrity when he was invited to assist W.G. Constable, who had just been appointed Assistant Director of the National Gallery, in organizing the exhibition.

Kenneth Clark thought it might arouse mild interest and was unprepared for the hordes of people who jammed the galleries and besieged him for tickets. They came to see, among other things, Botticelli's famous *Birth of Venus* along with eleven other Botticellis, a Neroccio from Yale, eight Piero di Cosimos including *A Forest Fire*, lent by Prince Paul of Yugoslavia, six Giorgiones, including his famous *The Tempest* lent by Prince Giovanelli of Venice, sixteen Titians, eleven Raphaels, ten Tintorettos (though not Kenneth Clark's), Fra Angelicos, Fra Filippo Lippis, Bellinis, Mantegnas, Signorellis, Piero della Francesca's famous portraits of the Duke and Duchess of Urbino, lent by the Uffizi in Florence, and thirty-six drawings by Leonardo.

Once the exhibition ended he edited the large, heavy, expensive two-volume catalogue. His collaborator on the project was Lord Balniel (later Earl of Crawford and Balcarres). The book took so long to appear and cost so much (six guineas) that its oblivion was practically guaranteed; Kenneth Clark called it a complete disaster. As usual, things were never as bad as he thought they were. The reviewer for the *Times Literary Supplement* gave the editors considerable credit for having unearthed much new material. Kenneth Clark received special mention for having deduced that a group of drawings traditionally attributed to Bellini could be shown, when compared with engravings, to be by Mantegna. There was the further bonus of a new friendship: with David Balniel, Member of Parliament, heir to an ancient and honourable Scottish title, owner of an art collection and a fine scholar. It was one that was to be crucially important to him. He had also entered the London art world.

As Charlie Bell had warned him when he first proposed to throw in his lot with Berenson, art historians were formidable enemies. From the very start of his career Berenson, immersed in the fiercely competitive game of saying who painted what, had managed to antagonize as many colleagues as he had made friends among the socially prominent and influential. He and Roger Fry had not spoken to each other for two decades and neither liked Charles Ricketts, the painter, sculptor, book illustrator and stage designer. Ricketts, in common with Fry and Berenson, had nothing good to say about Sir Robert Witt. Kenneth Clark ought to have been in trouble by the very fact of his having appeared on the scene so soon and with such spectacular ease. He was probably right in concluding that these fearsome adversaries did not see him as a threat to their livelihoods and therefore were prepared to treat him indulgently. He seemed to have hit upon just the right manner, friendly, amenable and detached. As he did while staying at I Tatti, he refilled the teacups, passed round the sandwiches and stayed out of trouble. And yet opportunities to enter the fray kept presenting themselves in a tantalizing way.

Two years before, in the autumn of 1928, Owen Morshead had tried to interest him in the post of assistant librarian at the House of Lords. There was a modest salary attached but unfortunately no likelihood of succeeding the librarian, a nice man in his mid forties. This seemed easier to resist than an offer, two years later, to join the faculty of Edinburgh University. Kenneth Clark was momentarily irresolute but turned it down. The indefatigable Morshead, determined to see his friend suitably employed, hoped aloud that Kenneth Clark would be appointed as first head of the Courtauld Institute of Art, then in its planning stages. Again nothing happened, but in the spring of 1931 came the best offer yet.

Charlie Bell was stepping down as keeper of the Department of Fine Art at the Ashmolean. Kenneth Clark had known for some time that Bell, who had been in fragile health for years, was thinking of retiring. He did not know that he was being forced out and, although he had been generously treated by Bell, could not help seeing that the cantankerous little man, who ran his department as if its holdings were his own private preserve, had serious drawbacks. He also knew that the search was on for a replacement but had not applied because his friend,

Leigh Ashton, had. He was therefore astonished to be offered the job. It was tempting, flattering, delightful even, and yet ... He wrote asking Berenson for advice.

Accepting the appointment certainly had its advantages, Berenson replied. None of them were worth it. He begged Kenneth Clark not to choose the path of one who curated, catalogued, made discoveries and haunted exhibitions. Kenneth Clark was destined for far greater things than that. He had a mission: to civilize mankind. It was a melodramatic appeal, but it reached that part of Kenneth Clark's nature that distrusted what he saw of the art world. After all, he too thought of himself as destined to become an interpreter and communicator. Becoming an administrator was not part of the plan and would only hamper him as a writer. Yet he accepted.

It was a wrong turning, he decided in retrospect. He had looked for a job simply because he did not want to disappoint his mother. Not a rising politician, not a brilliant diplomat – how lame it seemed simply to call oneself a writer! Having a title would justify his choice, as well as put paid to the parental conviction that he had thrown away a brilliant future. Perhaps it was then that he began to form the ambition, as he later wrote, to become director of the National Gallery – an idea so preposterous that he would only confide it to a few close friends.

He berated himself for being overly dutiful and conceited, but in any case he was a man divided. The role of administrator, with its ceaseless demands for action, had an irresistible lure for that side of him that sought compulsive activity. The irrational fear that he would die of paralysis at the age of thirty had to be allayed: 'In the middle of the journey of our life, I came to myself within a dark wood where the straight way was lost ...'

How nice it was to receive the museum guide, Alice Clark wrote from Shielbridge. They had been reading everything there was to learn about the Ashmolean in the *Encyclopaedia Britannica*, and that was not much. He certainly was not wasting any time. It had been a jolt to see the Saturday advertisement of Old Palace Place in *The Times*. She quite saw, however, that it must be sold as soon as possible. She also wrote about plans to have Alan and his nanny come and stay, while apologizing for bringing the subject up. It was wrong of her to be worrying him with such trivia when he had so much else on his mind. She just wanted him to know, she said, that his name was constantly on their lips. They were so impressed with him.

K and Jane bought another house (the Clarks were to own what Sir Colin Anderson termed a 'fidgety' number) called Shotover Cleve at Headington. Although Kenneth Clark called it ordinary and said its only virtue was rooms with uniformly good views overlooking the Thames valley, Alys Russell described it as 'a delightful white Italian villa with a lovely tame and wild garden', and covered with roses. Mrs Russell added that the Clarks owned two cars and had ten servants – with no one to clean the knives! Kenneth Clark told Berenson that they were rather glad to have left Richmond where even they had become tired of singing its praises. One could hardly do likewise for Shotover Cleve.

Jane, who had been mutinous about leaving Old Palace Place after having lived there for barely a year, nevertheless rose to the challenge of Oxford. To think that she would be able to shock the frumpish female intelligentsia with her expensive and daring wardrobe was a distinct consolation. She appeared periodically at the main entrance of the Ashmolean driving a small car, wearing a round white hat and riding breeches and 'looking frightfully smart', Edward Croft-Murray said. She was an 'angelic' hostess to her husband's friends: Leigh Ashton, John Sparrow, Cyril Connolly, Maurice Bowra and Bobbie Longden, knowing exactly how to make them feel welcome. She was equally gracious with his older, distinguished friends, such as the art critic, author, painter and sometime poet D.S. MacColl, and wrote letters praising his verses with just the right touch of awe.

The Clarks' Oxford dinners were formidable. 'K I disliked very much', Kitty Waterfield said of that period, 'because he'd try to be awfully nice to me and say, "You know the third picture on the right as you go into the National Gallery ...?" To someone who had no pretensions...' He seemed to have a way of offending people from the best of motives. Another friend recalls hearing that the wife of a peer who went to an early Oxford party and was seated on her host's right finally ventured a comment. He silenced her with a polite, 'Excuse me, but we want to hear what Clive Bell is saying.' She did not say much after that. Sir Isaiah Berlin recalled that, shortly after his arrival from Riga, when he met Kenneth Clark, he pronounced a French word and Kenneth Clark said innocently, 'Yes, foreigners do pronounce it that way.' Berlin added, 'I was very hurt.'

That Jane in particular had to present a flawless surface was apparent. A guest remembered hearing her at dinner make little forays into the subject of art, and then looking across at her husband 'and he'd make a sign to her and she would continue or sheer off the subject'. There is a story, no doubt apocryphal, that Kenneth Clark interrupted a conversation with John Betjeman about architecture to say, 'Don't talk about Norman Shaw to Jane, if you don't mind. She hasn't got to him yet.' From the exacting standards being set, they might all have been characters in a novel by Ivy Compton-Burnett; their acute and dazzling talk 'was a manual of evasive upper-class British conversation', as Janet Flanner wrote. Or perhaps the atmosphere at those conversational contests had most in common with the description Alan Pryce-Jones has drawn of the 1920s. That was a time, he wrote, when the creative spirit was on its mettle and addressing itself to people who kept on theirs, so that 'a cosy sensation of radiant intelligence' became the norm among clever young things. Being able to discuss Stravinsky's double fugues, or the origins of the Byzantine dome, or even the Gothic revival, made for a society that was brilliant and stimulating, but also competitive and more than a little ruthless.

Kenneth Clark plunged into life in what Berenson called his 'new toy shop'. He began, as he was to begin everywhere he went, by rehanging his collection. Even so he had a great deal of time left, he told B.B., as if to prove to his mentor as well as himself that he could go on being a writer. He had hired a clever young assistant who knew nothing about art but was adept at steering the local *bon ton* away from the keeper's office. And, when he was not working on his Leonardo catalogue, he was scheming to add to the holdings of the Department of Fine Art. One of his best purchases was the Piero di Cosimo *A Forest Fire*, for which he had helped provide the entry to the catalogue of the 1930 Italian exhibition. The owner, Prince Paul of Yugoslavia, was selling at a bargain figure and although Kenneth Clark would have loved to own it himself, he persuaded the National Art Collections Fund to buy it for the museum instead. He would also have loved to own an alluring ivory statue of Venus and Cupid by Peytel, which he acquired for the museum for an equally nominal sum. A further achievement was to persuade the University that the museum needed a gallery for seventeenth- and eighteenth-century paintings. To make sure the plans were carried out he advanced the money interest free.

There was only one discordant note: the end of his friendship with Charlie Bell. Bell had taken his forced resignation in favour of Clark with great generosity. He wrote that it was far better than being followed by a son of his own, 'for even in moments of the most soaring fantasy I never could imagine myself producing a son with your

intellect or sympathetic temperament'. He covered pages of notepaper with precise and voluminous instructions about the care and
handling of the department. He had not even minded that Kenneth
Clark would want to dismiss his assistant and appoint his own.
However, according to Sir Francis Watson, who perhaps knew Bell
better than anyone, the trouble began when Berenson made his siren-
song offer to Kenneth Clark and was accepted. Bell had strong pro-
prietary feelings and, Sir Francis believed, felt that Berenson had
snaffled his favourite. Added to this was the arrival of Jane and Bell's
loud assertion that he could identify the point in *The Gothic Revival* at
which his pupil's interests were deflected. It would not be difficult for
Kenneth Clark, now in charge of what had always been a closely
guarded domain, with his energetic interest in rehanging paintings and
letting in the outside world, to have made another false step in Bell's
eyes. He himself never knew what happened. The letters stopped and
it was rumoured that the man who delighted in the stiletto virtuosity of
his pen had annotated a copy of *The Gothic Revival* which ripped it to
shreds.

Early in 1932, despite bitter opposition, Kenneth Clark arranged to
have Roger Fry lecture on Cézanne at Oxford. While he was staying
with them Fry developed influenza and could not be moved. The
doctors feared it would become pneumonia. No sooner had Fry recovered than Jane, never a reliable driver, had a car accident. She hit a
lamp-post with such force that she knocked it over and overturned her
small car, a Wolseley Hornet. She ruined the car but crawled out with
nothing more serious than some ugly bruises. She might just have
known, at that date, that she was pregnant again.

Jane's father had been a twin and she correctly predicted them in her
own case. A boy, Colin, and a girl, Colette, were born on 9 October
1932. Maurice Bowra subsequently referred to them as Cols -ette and
-in. Alan and Colin were Clark family names and, by a fortunate
chance, also the names of Jane's brothers. It was another difficult and
protracted delivery. Following it, Jane contracted jaundice and her
recovery was slow.

That summer of Kenneth Clark's life passed in a blur. His father was
ill with cirrhosis of the liver and he was making periodic visits to Shielbridge. When he arrived in August he found that his father had eaten
his first food for weeks and even felt well enough to play a listless hand
of bridge. His mother insisted that Kenneth Mackenzie Clark was
going to recover; her son was under no illusions. Whenever his father

seemed well enough to be left, K went fishing for trout or took long walks over the hills. He was still trying to decide whether he had made a mistake in abandoning art. It might be worth taking it up again once he left the Ashmolean, if only to increase his appreciation for great works. The trouble about writing was that everyone else was so abysmally bad that it was easy to become conceited.

He returned to Shielbridge a few days after the twins' birth and found that his father, although looking better, had gone further downhill. His mind was so fuzzy that he seemed to think that his son was, instead, his brother Norman, who had died three decades before. Alice was the soul of patience. She somehow made sense of his father's obscure and muddled references to events that had happened long ago. K felt helpless. Then, when his father's mind cleared, he had a new cause for concern because his father talked about dying and upset his mother a great deal. When Kenneth Mackenzie Clark finally died, ten days after the twins' birth, Alice was desperate. She felt that her life was finished. She had bottled her feelings up for so long, she told her son, that they seemed atrophied, like an unused limb. Ten days after her husband's death she, too, became ill and was operated on for an unspecified ailment.

His father's death presented him with a flock of decisions. His mother was in a state of hysteria, refusing to discuss problems or let anyone else decide, but someone had to make plans for the Ardnamurchan estate. One soul had to be buried just as two new ones were entering the world. He spent the afternoon of his father's death in the billiard room, soothed and absorbed by the delicate calculations required and the satisfying click of the ivory balls.

What were his feelings as he stood there calculating his next moves? Anguish, at the loss of his loving, generous, erratic and self-destructive parent? Relief, that decades of pain and embarrassment had ended at last? Emotions too private to be revealed, secreted from view, just like a cache of the very best Havana cigars that his father had hidden away. Going through his father's effects he found them by chance and examined them reflectively. Although he had never smoked them, the penetrating and persisting aroma of a fine cigar was one of the memories he had associated with his father since childhood.

One can see him carefully rolling the leaf cap off the end with his fingers and placing a choice specimen ruminatively in his mouth. He was about to be thirty and still alive.

8 Getting Things Done

Ruhm streut ihm Rosen
Schnell in die Bahn
Lieben und Kosen
Lorbeer und Rosen
Führen ihn höher und höher hinan.* –
LUDWIG TIECK, *Die schöne Magelone*

On New Year's Day 1934 the new director of the National Gallery made his way through the doors to his office. He would have assessed it instantly with that rapid, flickering look which seemed to find nothing of particular interest and which scrutinized everything. One of his predecessors, C.J. Holmes, arriving eighteen years earlier, had found it full of broken and battered furniture and actually filthy. Kenneth Clark noted that it seemed large and light and the mouldings put into place since by the Ministry of Works quite horrid, but fortunately obscured, for the most part, by several large bookcases. Photographers and reporters found him bent intently over the papers on his desk, his hair impeccably groomed, wearing a faultless pin-stripe suit with a dotted tie. He had already toured the Gallery and greeted such dignitaries as Sir Robert Witt, a former chairman of the Board of Trustees, and a very friendly Lord Lee. The day was off to an excellent start.

On that singular occasion the Viscount Lee of Fareham would naturally have been among the first to appear. Lee, a short, hook-nosed man with a pince-nez and extremely formidable manner, had turned to the arts after failing to carve out a successful career in politics. And, soon after Kenneth Clark swam into his orbit (the two men had worked together on the Italian exhibition), Lee learned that he was about to lose his influence in the art world as well. He was being ousted from the National Gallery Board of Trustees, where he had served as chairman, in part because of his fondness for such

* Fame strews roses/Swiftly in his path./Love and caresses,/Laurel and roses/Lead him on higher and higher.

tactics as lying on the floor in a kind of fit when he did not get his own way. He was universally detested but, nothing daunted, Lee was angling to get back in, and had engineered Kenneth Clark's appointment for this express purpose. It was another of those bargains in which the protégé was uncomfortably aware of the pound of flesh to be exacted. In fairness to Kenneth Clark, when Lee did eventually return as a trustee it was through no fault of the director's. In any case, he had his own way of dealing with Lee. During one of the latter's temper tantrums, Kenneth Clark stood up and leaned across the table underneath which Lee was lying, to make a point to David Balniel. The latter objected, to which Kenneth Clark replied, 'That's all right; there's nothing like hitting a man when he's down.'

Journalists who interviewed Kenneth Clark that morning found him reluctant to discuss his ideas at such an early stage. He believed that the collection was so immensely rich (he later estimated its worth at £12 million) that it would be difficult to add many more works of a comparable value. He also thought the pictures might be better arranged. He had a few ideas. Almost his first act was to remove the massive portrait of Charles I on horseback by Van Dyck from its place of honour in the English room, where it dwarfed everything else, and place it at the head of the main staircase, commanding the entrance, 'as befits the first great English collector', the magazine *Country Life* noted.

The National Gallery was not permitted to exhibit works by living artists but Kenneth Clark hoped to show those of artists recently dead and, in particular, the French Impressionists. The Tate Gallery on Millbank was the logical place but, in the twenties and early thirties, two successive directors had done their best to prevent such paintings from entering that gallery, even as gifts. Kenneth Clark intended to make amends. Soon after his arrival, he hung a new gift in Room XXI, Manet's famous *Bar des Folies Bergères*, and placed Cézanne's *La Montagne Sainte Victoire* beside it. It was the first time a work by Cézanne had ever been seen in the National Gallery. There were several august comments in the papers on the fact that Cézanne had been considered practically an outlaw barely two decades before, and noting that the National Gallery was the most exclusive institution in the world. If it was a snub, the director ignored it. He was determined that the public should stop thinking of a gallery as a mausoleum for masterpieces but as a place where one might be accosted by new ideas, however curious.

Opening hours were an immediate concern. Attendance at the National Gallery had dwindled from some 670,000 a year in 1928 to 531,000 by 1934. Part of the reason was the introduction, early in the 1920s, of four days of paid admission. These were actually instituted to keep people out, in order that copyists might work without interruptions from the common herd.

There was another practical problem. Like most of the great European galleries at the time, the National Gallery had no artificial lighting and, in winter, the penumbral London light frequently made its contents indiscernible. At such moments guards were sent around to expel the viewers. Furthermore, the gallery's doors were closed at 4.30 p.m. daily, so that working people could only visit on week-ends. As soon as he took office Kenneth Clark vowed to improve matters. When vast crowds descended on London to attend two major football matches, the director decided to open the Gallery at 8 a.m., in case the football crowds could be tempted inside to reflect on the meaning of art before the kick-off.

His next venture was to promote the idea of artificial lighting. The possibility had been discussed for several years but always abandoned on the basis of cost. This time, Kenneth Clark managed to persuade the British Treasury to open its coffers, not just for lights but for the extra staff that would be required if the Gallery were to stay open three evenings a week. Then, at the grand opening, the Prime Minister, members of the Royal Family and other assorted dignitaries were invited to see the improvement for themselves, and compliments were rapturous. The lights had been so installed as to eliminate shadows and even colour balance had been taken into account. As a grand additional gesture, the Gallery's handsome portico was lit up for the first time to create a new focus of interest on Trafalgar Square. The symbolism was not lost on the press.

If, as Berenson predicted, there were to be spikes encountered in the job, these were hardly perceptible. Kenneth Clark had made it an immediate priority to woo the Board of Trustees. In addition to Lee's backing, he was to have the enthusiastic support of Sir Philip Sassoon, then chairman of the board, a wealthy, art-loving and socially prominent bachelor. By great good fortune David Balniel became a trustee a year later and was another solid Clark supporter. Kenneth Clark could not help remarking to B.B. that things were going very much more smoothly.

Early in his tenure he adopted a certain level tone towards the trustees in which he dispassionately weighed an issue's pros and cons. Speaking of a Foreign Office request to borrow paintings for a state dinner and take off the protective glass, he remarked that he personally was not opposed but felt bound to point out that the Gallery's regulations for loans specifically prohibited this. Or he might write that he had received a kind letter from the owner of a handsome Velazquez Virgin to say that she would never be able to give it up. This took a great load off his mind as the Gallery could not afford to buy it. It was just the right, laconic touch. At the end of his first year, Sir Philip Sassoon wrote to thank him for everything he had done. A new atmosphere had been created, one of exhilaration and excitement, thanks to the tact and skill of the director. As far as he could tell, Kenneth Clark told B.B., he was extremely fortunate in his staff, who had not resented his appointment and approved of his new ideas. He thought of himself as the manager of a large department store or a professional entertainer.

He was also receiving favourable notices from the press. The *Sphere* noted that a new broom was sweeping out the dusty corridors of the National Gallery, held by the capable hands of its young director who had, some months before, 'breezed' into that sombre fortress on Trafalgar Square. The *Manchester Evening News* declared that a revolution was taking place, led by a man who was Getting Things Done. The newspaper commented, 'Never, in any country, has so young a man filled such a great position. And justification ... is already provided by the reforms which Mr Clark has introduced and the new interest in the Gallery which he has aroused.'

Kenneth Mackenzie Clark had been buried in the Acharacle church graveyard near the house, Shielbridge, in which he died. Alice Clark had been persuaded to sell the estate and lived with her son and daughter-in-law at Oxford for a time, seeming a good deal stronger and more cheerful. However, his mother had no idea that anyone needed to work and had an almost Russian gift for spending his and Jane's time in aimless conversation. Despite his impatience, Kenneth Clark was discovering that his father's death had brought them closer. Having lost her reason for living, Alice Clark was, by degrees, resurrecting and transferring it to the son who had so spectacularly fulfilled all her hopes.

It was clear that he revelled in his new position. He told B.B. that the activity had gone to his head. He was so busy that his work took every atom of energy. He stayed at the Burlington Hotel in Cork Street during the week, while Jane looked for a house in London. There he entertained friends for dinner, such as Clive Bell, to whom he offered to show his paintings: Renoirs and some 'scraps' by Cézanne. Full days at the Gallery would be followed by lengthy dinners washed down with generous glasses of wine. One evening he and his friend Owen Morshead went to a banquet where they ate and drank far too much. They finally staggered home making the deserted streets echo with their shouts of laughter, he wrote in his diary. About a week later he dined with an acquaintance and sampled far too much of a delicious claret, vintage 1900. On the inevitable morning after everything went wrong and the problems of reorganizing Room XXIII were so intractable that he almost passed out. On another such day he went through the motions of working, writing a lecture and attending a reception at Burlington House while feeling like a walking corpse.

Then, a few months after his appointment, there came another demand on his energies: appointment to the post of Surveyor of the King's Pictures. Over the centuries the British crown had acquired some five thousand paintings of incomparable quality – forty-five paintings, fifty drawings and ten etchings by Canaletto alone, a collection of Old Master drawings at Windsor Castle that included famous Leonardos, prints, sculpture, porcelain, jewels, silver, furniture: the list was endless. Since the collection belonged to the Crown the taxpayer saw these treasures on rare occasions only. The finest works were divided between Buckingham Palace (closed to the public), Windsor Castle (partly closed and completely closed whenever the King was in residence), and Hampton Court, where the Royal Family no longer lived (always open). Hampton Court had the finest Italian and Renaissance works. The Holbeins, Van Dycks and Canalettos were at Windsor. Everything else was at Buckingham Palace.

It was an extraordinary opportunity and one that, before his appointment to the National Gallery, Kenneth Clark had been angling to get from the moment he heard that Collins Baker, then Surveyor, was planning to leave. Then he learned that King George v did not want anyone to rehang his collection: what he wanted was an expert who would tell him which paintings needed repair. Kenneth Clark formally withdrew.

There were other possible contenders, but the most eligible was

Tancred Borenius, a Finnish art historian who was a fine scholar and would have made an excellent courtier, Kenneth Clark thought. He also knew that, as long as Lord Lee bought Italian primitives with Borenius's advice, he did not acquire the best examples. The most serious charge against Borenius was that, in common with many other experts advising on sales, he was known to charge a fee for his certifications. The Lord Chamberlain was scandalized and Borenius's name was dropped.

Their Majesties returned to the idea of appointing Kenneth Clark, who continued to decline the honour. Then, some months after he had become director, King George v and Queen Mary made a personal visit to the National Gallery. No reigning monarch had ever been there before. There were boisterous crowds lining Trafalgar Square to cheer as the King, in a black top hat, and the Queen, in a dark coat liberally trimmed with fur, both using canes, mounted the steps. At the top the director, in a morning coat, hands gravely folded, awaited their arrival. It was Palm Sunday 1934.

George v got things off to a flying start by dismissing Turner as a madman. As for Cézanne's paintings, he wanted to attack them with his cane. He cheered up notably, however, before *Derby Day*, by William Powell Frith, the famous Victorian painting of the races which attracted such crowds, when it first went on view at the Royal Academy, that barriers had to be erected. The King remarked appreciatively on the numerous incidents depicted and regretted only that there had been no room to show the race itself. Queen Mary seemed to disapprove of these irreverent remarks, but unbent slightly. After pausing at the steps to enjoy the view of so many loyal subjects, the King and Queen made their departure. Shortly after that, the post of Surveyor was pressed upon the director who, having achieved his dearest ambition, saw no necessity for further honours. However, one could hardly resist a royal command. Kenneth Clark gave in.

One imagines Kenneth Clark on his daily tour of the Gallery, observing its activities with half-closed eyes and the peculiarly guarded, alert expression that was characteristic. He was making it his business to know everything that was happening. For instance, the two paintings visitors liked best were *The Nativity* by Piero della Francesca and *The Marriage of Giovanni Arnolfini and Giovanna Cenami* by Van Eyck. He made daily checks with the sales desk and took time to chat with the Gallery's attendants. Because of this he felt that nothing escaped him and that he knew every word a visitor let fall – or thought he did.

Every day was filled with appointments with people who had old masters to sell, they claimed. Although such offers were usually worthless, Kenneth Clark felt bound to see everyone, just in case. He was visiting dealers on the Continent, opening exhibitions, giving lectures and travelling all over Britain as he frantically tried to give equal attention to two jobs. Just after Christmas 1934 he collapsed. It was, his doctor said, 'a strained heart', and he ordered him to bed. His dear friend, the American novelist Edith Wharton, wrote that it was no wonder, after his heroic attempt to keep two lives going at once. She urged him to come to the south of France to convalesce. Instead he went to Brighton and had an agreeable time looking for antiques with Jane.

The Gallery was acquiring new works despite the director's original reservations. The purchase of one painting, *Crowning with Thorns*, by Hieronymus Bosch, had been opposed by almost everyone until the cleaning, when the transformation caused a general change of heart. In an interview the director learnedly discussed certain parallels between the fifteenth-century Flemish painting, with its allusive overtones, such as a spiked dog-collar around the neck of one persecutor of Jesus, and the modern vogue for Surrealism. So far so good, but then, some months after he took office, Kenneth Clark made his first mistake.

There was, he told Berenson, one purchase he longed to make since the school was unrepresented in the Gallery. This was a group of seven small paintings of scenes from the life of St Francis by Sassetta, the fifteenth-century Italian master, part of a large composition painted for the high altarpiece of the Church of San Francesco in San Sepolcro. Since the central panel, St Francis himself, was Berenson's prize possession, Kenneth Clark needed no persuading of the composition's worth. After reaching Duveen's hands, the little paintings were duly certified by B.B. as authentic and sold to Clarence Mackay of Long Island. Kenneth Clark knew that Duveen had probably bought the paintings for next to nothing – about £30,000. After investing a further £4,270 on restoration Duveen reportedly sold the paintings to Mackay for £100,000 – his profit on paper being £75,000. Berenson stood to receive his usual 25% of the net amount. In 1934 the gallery was told that Mackay was willing to sell at a loss and

Kenneth Clark somehow decided to offer £35,000. He knew that the paintings had been cleaned by Duveen but did not realize how extensively they had been reworked and repainted.

In *Another Part of the Wood* Kenneth Clark describes the meeting of the Board of Trustees at which Duveen blandly admitted the truth – that Mackay had never paid for the paintings. This should not have surprised the director. He knew what Duveen's sales tactics were like, and that certain prominent collectors had been allowed to decorate their walls with his wares, provided that they entertained often enough. However, the gallery was now in the highly embarrassing position of bargaining with its own trustee. This raised again the question of why an art dealer should have been appointed. Even Sir Philip Sassoon, Duveen's staunchest ally, was enraged. He did not dare let his mind dwell on the truth, he told his director, or they would have to carry him out feet first.

Had Sir Philip known exactly what the Board of Trustees was buying, he would have been apopleptic. Years after the purchase it was discovered that the little Sassettas had been retouched on a breathtaking scale. The panels had been sawn out of their frames, reduced in thickness to almost 0.5 cm from their original 4 cm, and heavy cradles fixed to the backs. Then they were reinserted in a different, and wrong, order, but not before they had been generously repainted. In one instance, a cloak was added to the arm of St Francis's father. Original paint in good condition was painted over and a soft resin varnish laid on – the Duveen gloss. It was, perhaps, no more than might be expected from Duveen, who was notorious for ruthlessly repainting his works to suit the tastes of his clients, but it had bothered even B.B., who privately complained about the crassness of the restoration. However, once Kenneth Clark expressed an interest Berenson kept his reservations to himself. Far from warning his former protégé, he told him that nothing would give him more pleasure than to see the paintings at the National Gallery.

In the autumn of 1934, Kenneth Clark asked Berenson whether he would be willing to write an article about the Mackay Sassettas for the *Burlington* magazine. He was referring to the practice, common in those days, for a connoisseur who had advised on the sale to confirm his opinion in an article. Although such a man might be judged leniently for the optimistic sales certificates he wrote – since everybody did it – the public act of a signed review was another matter. Kenneth Clark was therefore asking B.B. to make a real declaration of approval, and one that would support his own position. He thought, innocently enough, that writing about one of his particular interests for the National Gallery would strike his mentor as a highly desirable *coup de théâtre*. Besides, he was almost certain that the paintings had not been reproduced since they had been cleaned.

Berenson's reply was brief. His wife was so ill and his mind so taken up with other things that he feared it would be impossible for him to publish an article on the Sassettas. From then on there is no record that Kenneth Clark ever consulted the connoisseur about paintings he was buying for the National Gallery, through Duveen or anyone else.

Paintings that were bought for the collection were routinely cleaned before being exhibited. Thanks to Kenneth Clark's decision to establish a modern laboratory with the latest equipment, great strides were being made. Besides the new X-ray, ultra-violet and infra-red rays, all of which provided important clues, colour values could now be measured and the relative ages of mediums and varnishes tested by means of a polariscope and spectroscope. Microscopes, photo-microscopes and chemical analyses were being used to detect the slightest presence of paint in any material that might be removed.

Such new techniques had taken the restorer's art far from the days when pictures in big country houses were periodically handed over for the house carpenter to brighten up. He usually gave them an extra coat of varnish or oiled them to make them shine for a season, although they later turned black. Early restorers were, Kenneth Clark said in a speech on the aesthetics of restoration, helped by the fashion for discoloured varnish. By the eighteenth century, admired works by Titian, Van Dyck or Antonio Carracci, for instance, had been repainted for over a century. So many coats had been applied and had discoloured that, it was argued, because Titian's masterpieces were dark brown, a picture must be dark brown to be a masterpiece. One wit is supposed to have said, 'A good picture, like a good fiddle, must be brown.' After a cleaning of three paintings in the National Gallery in 1852 revealed other colours, there was a special government enquiry.

Kenneth Clark knew he would have to move with caution. Early in his tenure the rumour was published that he planned to clean Titian's famous *Bacchus and Ariadne*. He knew, however, that this was a much-damaged work and that the gravy brown of the old restorers at least provided a unity that allowed the design to retain some of its original effect. Nothing useful could come from its removal and he decided against it. However, the new expertise seemed to offer the promise that better-preserved works might be seen in all their original splendour for the first time in living memory and with almost no danger of damage. It was too good to resist.

He experimented with a few works, including El Greco's *The Agony in the Garden of Gethsemane* and Vincenzo Foppa's *The Adoration of the Kings*. Both came back from the laboratory looking unfamiliarly bright (he knew from experience that newly cleaned canvases always looked this way), but immeasurably improved. So he decided to tackle a more famous work, a portrait of Philip IV of Spain by Diego Velazquez. Velazquez painted several portraits of the king and since this full-length study was signed (as only a few of the painter's works were), it was assumed that Velazquez attached particular importance to it.

Kenneth Clark personally oversaw the removal of the painting's nineteenth-century varnish. He had been afraid to allow work on the head because it looked so flat, but this was found to be the fault of the discoloured varnish, which had also obscured much of the delicate brushwork. The removal of the brown mud had, for the first time, allowed one to see why the painting was known as 'The Silver Philip'. The director was enchanted by the transformation but not for long. The art critic of the *Daily Telegraph* went to see the painting and almost wept. The work had been carried out so drastically that its beauty had been seriously affected. The patina of age had gone and with it the master's touch.

The cleaning had its defenders. The painter Augustus John expressed his approval and a former professor of chemistry at the Royal Academy, after examining the painting with a magnifying glass, was satisfied that nothing had been damaged. There was no reason, a reader argued, why dirty and discoloured varnish should be allowed to obscure the beauty and technique of a wonderful painting. From the press reports, another reader had expected to find a choice example of the modern practice of 'flaying' pictures and found that a rather dull, if distinguished, work had been transformed into a masterpiece.

Kenneth Clark had won that round but it left him nettled and on the defensive. The main question, he concluded, in his speech about the aesthetics of restoration, was aesthetic: would the picture look more beautiful restored or unrestored? The answer, however, often depended upon the scientists. Since the National Gallery had

excellent professional advice, he hoped that time would put paid to
the notion that paintings were being tampered with just to see what
would happen. From then on he evaded the subject as much as he
could. A decade later, after he had left the Gallery and was asked to
intervene in a similar case, he declined. He was a bad ally, he wrote,
because some of the pictures cleaned during his régime were open to
criticism. He begged his friend to leave him out of it and not even tell
anyone that they had discussed the subject because no good could
come of it.

9 Fearfully Bolshie

'The vast majority of mankind is aesthetically
damned, and damned not for want of
opportunity or good-will, but by
predestination'. – ROGER FRY

When the artist and writer William Rothenstein first saw the work of
Jacob Epstein, a young sculptor, in London in 1907, he immediately
advised him to move to Paris. Everyone knew that, in terms of
acceptance, London was a decade behind France and, between the
British intelligentsia and the rest, there was another decade at least.
Epstein, a New Yorker of Russian Jewish origins, stubbornly refused
to leave. His faith seemed vindicated when, shortly after that, he was
commissioned to carve life-size figures depicting the birth and death
of man for a building in the Strand. When the figures went on view the
opposition was even more violent than might have been predicted.
Only the intervention of such prominent artists as Rothenstein and
Augustus John prevented their immediate destruction.

Twenty-seven years later, in 1935, the figures were still there but, it
seemed, not for much longer. The South African government had
bought the building and was determined to have them down at last.
Kenneth Clark, and some other distinguished members of the art
world, were determined that they should stay, and the battle lines
were drawn. Who would defend Epstein against the charge that his
works were obscene and who would refuse to come to his defence?
The president of the Royal Academy, for one, refused to enter the
fray, whilst the news that the director of the National Gallery was
willing to do so made the newspaper headlines as far away as Durban.
The successful resolution of the issue, some months later, did not
obscure the dimensions of what was, Kenneth Clark could see, a
major problem.

Although an Englishman might have an almost daily exposure to
beautiful language, his visual surroundings were impoverished and

his experience of art limited to engravings of Highland cattle, Kenneth Clark wrote. Only those living in large cities could ever hope to see real art, in contrast to inhabitants of the smallest Italian towns who saw beautiful paintings whenever they entered their churches. In the past wealthy patrons had kept artists alive in Britain, but in recent decades the money had dried up, along with the interest, leaving only a very few to carry on a noble tradition.

The same problem pertained in public life. In the nineteenth century a provincial town council felt it must prove its seriousness of purpose by spending money on an art gallery or commissioning an artist, such as Ford Madox Brown, to paint decorations in its town hall, as Manchester did. But by 1922 a curator writing on the problems of provincial galleries found that most of the collections were mediocre, the galleries themselves overcrowded and indifferently run. Ten years later, as he travelled around Britain giving lectures, Kenneth Clark made the same discovery. In one gallery in Yorkshire he saw water trickling down walls on which valuable paintings were hanging. Other galleries were fire traps. Officials seemed more interested in displaying mediocre works than borrowing paintings from the National Gallery, although they were being made available to all comers.

Philistinism had carried the day, he wrote. Such melancholy conclusions always led him back to the most vexing problem of all, the indifference of the general public. People did not understand art, old or new, and did not want to understand it. Like their monarch, George V, they yearned to deface the unfamiliar as if it were, in some fashion, insulting them. And there were so few people left to carry on the work. Roger Fry, the man who had done more to educate British tastes than anyone else, had a severe fall in 1934 and died, shortly afterwards, of heart failure. The standard-bearer of that gallant and delusory faith that aesthetic pursuits mattered, was gone. Then Kenneth Clark received a letter from Helen Anrep, the woman with whom Fry shared the last years of his life. Fry, she wrote, believed that Kenneth Clark had a unique contribution to make. In many ways, Fry thought he had greater powers than he did himself. She begged Kenneth Clark to live up to Fry's faith in him.

Someone had to take up the cause. What an honour it would be, he said a few years later, to have his name linked with that of Roger Fry. To have been his pupil and friend had been a great privilege. How thrilling it would be if he could ever equal Fry's critical accomplishments. No wonder that Henry Tonks, an artist and professor at the

Slade School in London, wrote to the painter and author Douglas MacColl, 'Does Clark to you show signs of going Fry?'

Alice Clark's *objets de luxe* were clustered on end-tables at Sudbourne and dominated dressing-tables and mantelpieces wherever one looked. When Kenneth Clark himself began collecting, at the age of ten, he had no goal in mind except to buy pretty things. Whether it were furniture, china, sculpture, drawings or books hardly mattered. His reproductions of Augustus John's Dorelia, carried in his pocket or pinned up at Winchester, had become, by the time he reached Oxford, real paintings on the walls, and in Old Palace Place he had the imposing Tintoretto, a tiny Raphael and a Madonna by Bellini in jewelled hues. There came a further shift of interest once he realized that perfectly wonderful French Impressionist paintings could be bought in Paris if one knew where to look. In December 1935 he wrote to Jane from the Hotel Crillon, Place de la Concorde, to say how inexpensive everything was on the Left Bank. Marvellous Bonnards and Braques could be bought for £100 a time. He was about to succumb to an exquisite Maillol reclining figure that he wanted for the mantelpiece of her room.

On those triumphant Parisian forays he bought the fifty Cézanne watercolours for £5 each that he described in *Another Part of the Wood*. He bought four Cézanne oils from the famous dealer, Vollard, for somewhat more, Seurat's *Sous Bois* and his *Bec de Hoc*, and a study by Matisse, *Quai St Michel*, because no museum seemed to want it. (It cost something like £900 which seemed a lot of money to him then.) In those days when neither the Tate nor the National Gallery was in the running, he made his most precious find of all: *Baigneuse Blonde*, one of Renoir's ravishing nudes.

He made equally spectacular buys in England. In 1933 when Lord North's effects were for sale at Wroxton Abbey, he bought a handsome seventeenth-century painting, *The Saltonstall Family*, attributed to David Des Granges, for about £50. (The painting is now at the Tate.) An even more spectacular purchase was a Michelangelo drawing of the Virgin and Child which he bought in 1936, when all the experts were 'dismissing everything as not genuine', he said. The drawing came up for auction at a starting price of £500 and no one would bid. Kenneth Clark, convinced of its genuineness, could bear it no longer and offered £100. He got it.

One of the charges Berenson levelled against Kenneth Clark was that, if he bought and sold, it was considered his prerogative as a gentleman whereas, if Berenson himself did so, it was because he was a dealer. There is no doubt that Kenneth Clark was to treat some of his spectacular bargains as money in the bank, to be withdrawn as needed; he was too canny and shrewd to do otherwise. This was not his main motive. He followed his developing eye and was swept along in the enthusiasm of the moment. Once that had ended, the object ceased to exist for him. As a result, extremely valuable paintings – like the Tintoretto portrait, for instance – that once deserved a place of honour, might be progressively demoted and then sold for laughably little, even when they were worth something. When the Clarks sold Old Palace Place they included the two exquisite della Robbia reliefs that had been installed on either side of the fireplace and, it is said, when Kenneth Clark left the National Gallery he did not bother to take with him a sizeable personal collection of paintings and drawings. Because paintings were continually being hung and removed, or lent, or sold, it is almost impossible to say what was in the collection at any given moment. Grasping and letting go: he veered between the compulsiveness of the born collector and indifference.

The decline in patronage, Kenneth Clark wrote in the late 1930s, was a disaster for many reasons but its major consequence was that, during the last half century, the most important artists had withdrawn into a closed world in which they painted to please each other rather than communicate with an audience. Such artists needed the patronage of the emerging middle class but this did not exist yet. That could be attributed to the changing taste in decoration which, as it swept out everything ornate, Victorian and indigestibly overstuffed, had swept out art as well. Bright young things decorated with such understatement that there was hardly anything left to look at and certainly little scope for picture hanging. However, there were a few devoted collectors buying up modestly priced paintings and drawings and everything priced at, say, ten or twelve guineas was likely to be sold.

Such patrons bought after the fact. Kenneth Clark believed that the truly creative act of patronage required the commissioning of a work. He cited the great historical parallels, the royal patrons and others who, as the poet Poliziano did, for instance, for Botticelli's *Spring* and *Birth of Venus*, might suggest subjects and details. A really enlightened patron, one who could lead, guide and inspire, was as much practical philanthropist as popularizer. It was a point of view that would have been applauded as heartily by the Clarks of Paisley, those enlightened Victorian industrialists, as by Roger Fry.

To commission a portrait seemed the first step, since it presented the natural opportunity of influencing an artist in the way a patron thought he tactfully ought to go. He had tried this approach on Wilson Steer, who was considered, when Kenneth Clark was an adolescent, to be the best living British painter and the successor to Constable and Turner. Although Steer's reputation had been made with landscapes, Kenneth Clark had seen two or three beautiful portraits of his and decided that he should be encouraged in this direction. Steer painted Jane Clark's portrait: it was a disaster. Undeterred, Kenneth Clark commissioned Duncan Grant to paint her portrait, and Pavel Tchelitchev to paint Alan's, and chinaware from Grant and Vanessa Bell. Although none of these experiments lived up to his hopes, he persevered. His energetic interest was having its effect on artists, who quickly discovered an artist *manqué*, one whose intelligent questions and understanding of compositional problems revealed a perception and knowledge far beyond that of most collectors.

'I was enormously flattered to see my picture in your house,' a young artist, Frank Graham Bell, wrote. 'You can imagine how delightful it is to find people liking one's best pictures more than one's worst ones.' He was young, handsome and penniless, a South African who had sold enough paintings to finance a trip to London and rapidly ran out of money. Bell was, Kenneth Clark wrote later, the most learned and theoretical of a group of artists, which included William Coldstream and Victor Pasmore, who were making practical application of Fry's theories of pure colour. However, when Bell and Coldstream met Kenneth Clark in 1937, they had been driven from art by the need to earn a living. Would he, they asked, like to subsidize them?

It had been clear to Kenneth Clark for at least a decade that artists needed financial help. As early as 1929 he had conceived a scheme to organize exhibitions for young artists and was putting up most of the money. The idea was short-lived and when Bell and Coldstream appeared, Kenneth Clark agreed that something new might be done. They wanted guaranteed overdrafts; he responded with an alternative idea, a Trust Fund for Artists, from which they might draw a monthly stipend. It was something like £10 a month, the difference between starvation and survival. Perhaps those unobtrusively generous men, the Clarks of Paisley, had decreed that good deeds be done in secret, lest they be contaminated by the sin of pride. For decades only a few people knew about Kenneth Clark's fund.

Victor Pasmore who, in 1937, guided students at the Euston Road School of Painting along a path of polite realism, was another friend. Kenneth Clark had known him by reputation since 1930, when he bought the first of his paintings ever sold in an exhibition. He continued to admire and buy his work – Pasmore's nude at the Leicester Galleries was, he told Graham Bell in 1939, the best thing there – and helped him financially. Pasmore was exceptionally gifted but all the British artists had great promise, he believed. They were struggling to resist the pressures of the marketplace which practically guaranteed that, if they wanted to succeed commercially, young artists had to paint in a fashionable style and abandon their own ideas.

Among those evading the pull towards mediocrity was Graham Sutherland. Like Samuel Palmer, that poetic painter of pastoral landscape, Sutherland had begun as an etcher and engraver and painted little until 1935 when he began to attract attention for his highly individual vision. What made Graham Sutherland's work so important for Kenneth Clark was his ability to endow the natural world with a tantalizing symbolism. Bizarre and twisted shapes that Sutherland had found in hedges and sand dunes became charged with such heightened meaning in his canvases that, like him or not, one could not avoid being affected by his extremely personal view. His gift was to make him wealthy and widely imitated. However, when Sutherland first went to visit the director of the National Gallery at his Portland Place mansion some time in 1934, he was almost unknown. He was taken there by Oliver Simon, the well-known printer who edited an influential magazine on printing and typography called *Signature*. As it happened, Kenneth Clark had already seen Sutherland's work, a poster of the Great Globe of Swanage, commissioned by Shell Mex Limited. When he saw the gouaches Simon had brought, he was even more interested and made a purchase on the spot.

In those days Sutherland, who was teaching art, was as poor as the rest of his peers. He and his wife would have well understood the life Graham Bell was living: one room, almost no furniture, a single gas ring and meals of lentils and salad. Kathleen Sutherland recalled the days when they used to break a chocolate biscuit in half to have with their cups of tea. To be taken up by Kenneth and Jane Clark was flattering and unnerving. Graham Sutherland said, 'I was seeing the high life. Kenneth Clark had real charisma. I thought he was elegant, a Renaissance prince. But I was also frightened of him because he didn't suffer fools gladly.' After leaving an elegant formal dinner at Portland Place, Sutherland and his wife would 'give a belch and say, "That's better, now we can relax."'

Kenneth Clark bought heavily for his own collection and recommended that others do the same. When Gertrude Stein wrote asking him for his opinion about her latest discovery, Francis Rose, the latter replied diplomatically that he did not know the artist's work well enough to have an opinion about it. Did she, he countered, know the work of Graham Sutherland? Now there was a painter. From the very beginning, he told Sutherland, he was convinced that he was a genius.

Kathleen Sutherland said, 'Graham was a good teacher, but he had forty in his class and he was near a nervous breakdown. I went to see K at the National Gallery and told him, "I have made Graham give up teaching. Will you lend us some money?" Kenneth Clark replied, "No, I won't. It ruins a friendship". I started to interrupt, and he added, "But I will guarantee you an overdraft."' This happened just before the Second World War, according to Jane Clark's diary, and Kenneth Clark was as good as his word. He also lent the Sutherlands the down payment for the country house in Kent which they still owned when Sutherland died in February 1980.

Kenneth Clark, the great activator, was taking imaginative risks in that pre-war period, in the view of Sutherland. He was as attuned to sculpture as to painting, and when his father lay dying in the summer of 1932, dreamed of owning a house with its own sculpture gallery. He imagined a room with high ceilings, austere and unadorned, with mauve-grey walls and containing some unupholstered seats so that the contemplation of art would be invigorating rather than restful. As for its contents, he wanted some Greek and Egyptian pieces, a Maillol or two, perhaps an Eric Gill and even a Henry Moore.

When future historians try to fit Henry Moore into a scheme of British art they will find him most unyielding, Kenneth Clark noted. Already, in the aftermath of the great British art slump, the emergence of a powerful and fertile talent was being watched with awe. At Moore's first one-man exhibition, a group of drawings, held at the Dorothy Warren gallery in 1928, among those who bought for £1 apiece were the artists Henry Lamb, Augustus John and Jacob Epstein and the collector Kenneth Clark. He acquired a drawing of a green nude. Three years later Moore had another exhibition at the Leicester Galleries, a step up in terms of prestige. He sold £120 worth of work. By then he was teaching at the Royal College of Art. He remembers that his work was frequently being labelled 'Bolshevik', a catch-all term with which to condemn anyone thought to be challenging the conventional tastes. 'He's fearfully Bolshie' was the comment applied in some circles to Kenneth Clark as freely as to that upstart sculptor Henry Moore. Moore said, 'This was the atmosphere when Kenneth Clark came to London. The fact that the director of the National Gallery was willing to support artists, champion their cause, even give them money, made a tremendous difference to us.' Moore was the only artist who was also a close friend that the Clarks did not help with a direct grant. His work was already selling well enough to enable him to teach for two days a week, leaving the rest of his time free for sculpture.

However, Kenneth Clark helped in other ways. Over the next few years he bought some thirty drawings and half a dozen pieces of sculpture. He recommended the sculptor to gallery owners and spread the word whenever Henry Moore's works were showing in London. Sales were going much better than he ever expected, Moore wrote in 1939, thanks to the start Kenneth Clark had given the show. 'Altogether I'm very happy ... for after the pleasure of finding that the work is liked by the few whose appreciation one admires, & to have some sales as well, so to be able to go on working with a free mind – all makes Irina & I consider we're very lucky.'

That same year Kenneth Clark had another piece of good news for Moore. He had been made the buyer for the Contemporary Art Society (a non-profit organization established in 1910 to buy works that might not yet have found official approval). The Society was to buy a Henry Moore sculpture and the Tate Gallery board had voted to accept it. The work was a handsome *Reclining Figure*, sculpted in stone. After much inner deliberation the artist decided that £300 would be a fair price. Kenneth Clark agreed. The sculptor was delighted, because 'it might be a long time before I'm able to do another stone figure capable ... of standing up to the scale of the Tate's new sculpture gallery, & one which I'm as generally satisfied with as that one.'

For Kenneth Clark there was something innately appealing about this sculptor, son of a coalminer, remaining so steadfastly himself, asking little from life but the right to go on working, travelling with a battered suitcase or two, one containing a toilet kit and the other a suit and a raincoat. Even when Moore became immensely rich, he and his wife lived so frugally that the Clarks, if invited to visit, would not expect a meal and would stop for a sandwich lunch in their car before arriving.

Moore's belief in the best of all possible worlds was such that, John Russell noted, he 'is likely to give a characteristically equable and simplified account in which everybody comes out well'. That obstacles should so cheerfully melt when faced by Henry Moore would have seemed most engaging to his friend. That same buoyant outlook became a lifeline for Jane Clark. Moore said, 'K can sometimes put a glass screen between himself and someone he doesn't want to be with. No, never with me. It's probably a protection. Never with me. But Jane was so kind and warm-hearted and outgoing. She had the human touch.' During Jane's long final illness, when her husband felt wretchedly inadequate to help, Henry Moore telephoned every day, filling Jane's bedroom with his dogged optimism.

How much did Kenneth Clark influence Henry Moore as an artist? The former thought not at all. Henry Moore said, 'Not enough to change one's course, no – no. But one knows what an expert he is and one does take notice of people whose opinions one values.'

Henry Moore's letters of thanks were echoed in the letters of another painter. 'Your remarks about my show are particularly gratifying. As you must know, such shows are only made possible through the encouragement of you and one or two other people.' He was John Piper, who had trained as a solicitor and then, at the age of twenty-five, turned to art. He studied at the Royal College of Art, contributed art criticism to *The Nation*, and met Braque, Léger, Brancusi and Hélion in Paris. Under their influence he experimented with collage, embedding string and pieces of paper into abstract compositions. He went on to become one of the pioneers of abstract art in Britain, as well as a recorder of British architecture, writer and set designer. Like Bell, Piper talked as well as he painted, and since his second wife, Myfanwy Evans, edited an *avant-garde* quarterly which reviewed abstract painting and sculpture, the stage was set for an encounter in which aesthetic inclinations would once again lead to personal involvements. The Pipers were taken to meet the Clarks by the American sculptor Alexander ('Sandy') Calder and his wife Louisa, whom they had met in Paris.

Myfanwy Piper said, 'It was tea with housemaids about the place and the whole set-up was pretty grand. K was rather stately and very nice and I felt rather naughty going for him, but I did.' Her host soon made it clear that he was not much interested in abstraction, and, since her magazine, *Axis*, championed it, she bombarded him with arguments. Then they discovered their common love for the eighteenth/nineteenth-century landscape artist Joseph Mallord Turner. Roger Fry's dismissive references to that artist had always troubled Kenneth Clark and, in those days, when Turner was consistently denigrated, it was a relief to discover their shared outrage.

Aware that the Pipers were bringing up four young children, Kenneth Clark did everything he could to help financially. He arranged to have Piper hired by the Pilgrim Trust so as to sketch, along with other artists, buildings that might not survive the bombings to come. He recommended Piper to Queen Elizabeth, who commissioned him to paint a series of watercolours of Windsor Castle. Before long, Myfanwy Piper was inviting the Clarks to stay at their farmhouse of flint and brick near Henley-on-Thames, which they had rescued from near dereliction. They had painted the walls white and woodwork grey, placed immense bouquets of wild flowers everywhere, and hung Piper's exquisite early drawings over the mantelpiece. On that first of many visits, the host played jazz at the piano while one of the guests sang with gusto, in a vibrant tenor, 'If you were the only girl in the world' and 'Everybody calls me Teddy'. It was a side of Kenneth Clark that they never would have suspected.

Although the design of the 1930s – its postage stamps and posters, its textiles and toasters, its tube stations and telephones – had taken on a distinctive, unmistakable look, art and sculpture seemed to be in chaos. On the one hand were the voices of Bell, Coldstream and the like, declaring that art had lost touch with its public and that a radical return to realism was the only cure. On the other hand were artists like Ben Nicholson, son of the well-known Victorian woodcut artist Sir William Nicholson, who had followed an austere geometric path of abstraction derived from Cubism and the Dutch abstractionist Piet Mondrian. Painting and sculpture, he wrote, were simply ways to make contact with the Infinite and (thanks to the abstract movement) had now reached their profoundest moment.

Reviewers like Anthony Blunt chose to see, in Marxism, the cure for every aesthetic ill. Those New Realists, the Mexican painters Diego Rivera and José Orozco, had demonstrated the way to paint the human condition without compromising their aesthetic responsibility and, believed Blunt, 'profoundly to affect the emotions of the common man'. The great advantage of socialism was that it would selectively retain what was valuable in bourgeois culture and jettison the rest. The state, all controlling, enlightened and wise, would take over the role once played by the patron.

There is no doubt that Kenneth Clark was, at that time, sympathetic to socialist aims. It was evident, he wrote to his mother early in the Second World War, that socialism was the only solution. A centralized government would be bound to have flaws but to have profit as the only motive was even more dreadful. However, he was distrustful of totalitarianism in all its guises and thought it absurd for movements in art such as the New Realists to be identified with political beliefs. Whatever the future had in store, the likelihood that proletarian – or fascist – rulers would impose Cubism and Surrealism as the ruling aesthetic was too remote to be taken seriously, he wrote.

But, all that to one side, it was clear, he wrote in the *Listener* in 1935, that the Cubist aesthetic was severely limited and bound to reach a dead end. The pure vision being espoused would be the undoing of such artists since, without some contact with reality, they would be spiritually malnourished to the point of starvation.

Kenneth Clark made an oblique reference to the small band of high-brow art dealers and professors and those in middle life who were the chief supporters of such art. Herbert Read, the dauntless champion of advanced schools of modern painting, who happened to be forty-two years old, 'received this jagged splinter full in the eye', and launched his counter-attack. 'When, in the whole of history, has the finest culture of a period been, *at the time of its first creation*, anything but the affair of a small minority?' Read demanded in a subsequent issue of the *Listener*. 'The issue, for Mr Clark and for those who have been moved by his article, is clear: there are good artists today, and there are bad and indifferent artists. Without exception, I would claim, the good artists are in some degree "abstract" artists, and do not, in the present state of society, feel any compulsion to any other style.'

Read put forward the notion that art basically concerned itself with the life force, that energy that manifested itself in organic growth. Kenneth Clark leapt on the argument. That was exactly his point, he said, with a reference to the illustration Read had chosen, a carved white abstraction by Ben Nicholson. The more geometric and abstract the work, the less it would reflect that life-enhancing vitality they both agreed was essential, and the more sterile and dead it would become. He personally did not see any future for abstraction and thought a return to some form of representational art was essential – however long it took.

The stage, Eric Newton observed in the *Manchester Guardian*, seemed set for a spectacular fight. While the heavyweights retired to their corners, the spectators threw in a few taunts to urge them on-wards. 'Could Mr Herbert Read distinguish Mr Ben Nicholson's carved reliefs from similar ones prepared by any joiner?', one of the *Listener*'s readers wanted to know. The artist himself plaintively enquired of Kenneth Clark whether he really meant it when he wrote that many who enjoyed his work had done so for its decorative quali-ties rather than its high symbolism. Collins Baker, Kenneth Clark's immediate predecessor as Surveyor of the King's Pictures, was caus-tic. What was exasperating about Kenneth Clark, he wrote to D.S. MacColl, was not just his superior air, which called for a kick in the pants, but his way of seeming to know everything. The art critic Eric Newton, on the other hand, was sympathetic. The question was, could the artist communicate his intense vision about life's essential reality by means of geometrical forms? He plainly doubted it. Artists like Sutherland and Piper, privately reviewing their patron's com-ments about the sterility of abstraction, shook their heads and con-cluded that he was a conservative. For his part, Kenneth Clark was dismissing his pessimism as the result of an impacted wisdom tooth. However he must be more careful about labelling certain people as middle-aged.

The bell had rung for a new round but one of the contestants had already slipped through the ropes, too busy for more than a moment's reflection or contrition. He had gone off to Paris, where he began a typical day at the Orangerie at 8.50 a.m. At 10.20 a.m. he went to the Embassy. At 11.30 a.m. he saw dealers. After lunch with M. de Béhague he went to look at David Weil's collection, then returned to the Embassy. When he finally ended his day at 6.30 p.m. he was ready to sit down. Or he and Jane were on their way to Russia to see the Hermitage Collection. They planned to return by way of Berlin where he, with his beaky nose, was bound to be pounced on and beaten by the Gestapo, he told Berenson. Or he was in London where someone was after him every minute at the Gallery. People appeared until 7.50 p.m. and he was dining out at eight. Two more wonderful landscapes had been acquired, a glorious Constable and a memorable Rubens. He was negotiating for one of Ingres's most important portraits, that of Madame Moitessier. If to be busy were to be happy, he did not have a care in the world.

10 Top People

'he carried with him, perhaps in spite of
himself, an unsloughable air of high caste, of
constant contact with the nicest best people,
of impeccable upper-class taste'. –
JOHN FOWLES, *The Magus*

As Kenneth Clark saw it, a house should provide a tranquil atmosphere, allow one to move about it efficiently, and be a harmonious backdrop for their collection. On all three counts Portland Place, which they bought in 1934, had to be considered a failure. It was on a noisy London thoroughfare, it was too large for efficient living and stylistically uncongenial. Their growing collection of *objets d'art*, sculpture and painting cried out for subtlety, refinement, harmony, intimacy. Portland Place, with its vast reception rooms, painted ceilings, marble chimneypieces and Regency chandeliers, needed large, formal furniture to match its cumbrous dignity. It was not a house for an aesthete. It was just the house for a man in a public position who was expected to entertain as often and grandly as possible.

Those who visited Portland Place had memories of white walls and yellow silk curtains in the manner of Sibyl Colefax, the well-known hostess, who decorated houses as distinctively as she entertained. They recalled curtains designed by Duncan Grant in a free-flowing pattern depicting Apollo pursuing Daphne, executed in creamy pinks, terra-cotta, beige and brown. The daughter of a well-known harpist, Maria Korchinska, said that her mother talked for years about some satin curtains she had seen there, on which flowers were hand painted. But the main decorative influence on Portland Place was that of Marian Dorn, a talented textile and carpet designer, born in San Francisco, who came to England early in the 1920s with the artist E. McKnight Kauffer. Kauffer and Dorn were a formidable team and, along with the Sutherlands, Moores, Pipers and Andersons, became habitués of that handsome house that was to provide such a direct link with the people who mattered, those with the money to commission and the influence to foster careers.

Although the Clarks lived there on a far more imposing scale than they were ever to do again, it did not begin to match the munificent style of the senior Clarks. The disappearance, after the First World War, of the established and moneyed order brought its compensations. Society, for instance, was far less exclusive. One no longer expected to dine out in a white tie; a black one would do and on certain occasions one would be magnanimously instructed not to dress. One no longer needed to pay a footman to wait up for one's return late at night. Nowadays the man of the house was quite willing to let himself in with a latchkey, take off his own coat and mix himself a drink from the tray provided.

Nevertheless, the sheer size of Portland Place – three very large and two enormous reception rooms on the first floor alone – required a sizeable staff. There was a cook with two helpers in the kitchen, a butler, a parlour maid, a housemaid, a ladies' maid and a chauffeur. The staff slept on the top floor and had no set hours; they were always on call. They began at 6.30, because the main rooms had to be swept and dusted before the family appeared. They ate at noon so as to be ready to serve in the dining room at 1.30. This much-reduced staff would not be expected to deal with a large party without considerable extra help.

Nancy Bingham, 'the little B' as she was called, served as their social secretary for a time. She found the work exacting. Daily conferences with the cook were obligatory, along with a close scrutiny of bills from the butcher, the baker, the wine merchant, the vegetable and fruit shops, from Fortnum & Mason and Jackson's in Piccadilly. Since her employer required a constant supply of fresh flowers, these needed daily arrangement. Nancy Bingham answered letters, made phone calls and sent out invitations for dinner parties, involving many anguished decisions about the protocol of seating. On top of it all, 'Jane was always rushing in and out and asking me had I done something or other. She was very demanding.'

Mary Berenson, who had come for a visit, would have described their house, Kenneth Clark wrote to Berenson. He himself had little to add, since he usually went straight from the front door to his bedroom. However, he thought it looked quite agreeable. Alys Russell had tea with the Clarks and thought K was looking tired and 'official', with too much to do. By then he was complaining of interruptions whenever he sat down to write essays, speeches or letters: because there had been fourteen interruptions, one letter to Berenson had taken four days to write. When Jane was visiting the Comtesse de Béhague at Hyères in the south of France he wrote to say that he missed her. However, he was so rushed off his feet that, even if she had been home, he would have been too busy to see her.

He was afraid he would not be able to make his usual visit to her house in the south of France, he told Edith Wharton in 1937, because so many things had to be done. There were enormous preparations for the Coronation under way, involving new galleries, refurbishings and official meetings. He had a great deal of work to do on an important exhibition of British art in Paris. There was another major exhibition at the Tate to commemorate Constable's centenary. His book on Leonardo absolutely had to be finished by early summer. There was even more but just thinking about it gave him the despairing feeling of being in a wide-awake nightmare. Yet, as soon as he had a breathing space and no longer felt overwhelmed by obligation, he began to be uneasy. The fear that if he did not stop running he would become paralysed had become, by 1938, the fear that inactivity would lead him to 'the bottle'. That Christmas he told 'Ted' Kauffer that he was taking far too lively an interest in the next drink.

As Surveyor of the King's Pictures from 1934 to 1944, Kenneth Clark was in a front-row position to observe uninhibited royal behaviour and liked to regale his friends with anecdotes. He remembered seeing King George V, displaying a neatly turned calf clad in silk stockings and knee breeches, and waiting while 'old' Chamberlain attempted to walk in to dinner backwards so that he might not turn his back on his monarch. He also recalled that the irrepressible king, at a reception being given for the socialist Prime Minister of Australia, turned and said, 'See that fellow over there?' – meaning his guest. 'He's a socialist. Give him a good kick in the arse for me.' He was like that.

'The King took a great fancy to Jane and changed the "placement" at dinner in order to have her next to him. Strange that he should have been so intolerable with his own children; he was perfectly charming to me – gay and jolly and passionately interested in his subjects, whose every action he used to watch from the windows of his car.' Kenneth Clark added that the King was perfectly ignorant about art, although he liked to take complacent tours of the royal collections. 'See that?' he would say, indicating a handsome work. 'Joe

Duveen's offered me £50,000 for it. D'you think I should sell it?' 'Oh, no, sir,' Kenneth Clark would reply, not daring to add that the painting was not his to sell. Others in court circles were not much better informed. When Kenneth and Jane Clark were invited to the first dinner party given at Buckingham Palace by the new King George VI and Queen Elizabeth, Jane, who had forgotten to wear her tiara, found herself sitting beside Sir Hill Child. Her dinner partner wanted to know why the King's thirteenth-century painting by the Sienese master Duccio di Buoninsegna, with its decorative use of gold leaf, should be so valuable. Did so much gold put up the price?

Queen Mary was modestly interested in the Royal Collection and obviously relieved to find that her new Surveyor knew something about the Empire furniture she preferred. People invariably found her stiff and inarticulate, although she would declare that she was not shy at all and, less charmingly, that the British had backed the wrong horse in the First World War. Despite the transformation that appeared to take place after George V's death – Jane, invited to an exhibition of paintings by Sir Joshua Reynolds in the Park Lane mansion of their friend Sir Philip Sassoon, was struck by how young the Queen looked, wearing black velvet and pearls, her cheeks charmingly flushed – neither Clark felt as affectionately at ease with her as they had with her husband.

The Prince of Wales was a much more engaging figure. He seemed genuinely interested in social problems and less dogmatically opposed to a democratized monarchy than his father had been. After visiting him in a 'pleasant villa' near Ascot (probably the royal folly, Fort Belvedere, situated on land bordering Windsor Great Park, which the Prince of Wales had turned into a liveable house), and meeting his friend Mrs Simpson, they were even more enthusiastic. She had the buoyant kind of charm the Prince needed: 'She gayed him up and did him a ton of good,' Kenneth Clark said. It was, of course, the fault of the politicians that he had been forced to abdicate, and a great loss for the country. However, with his gift for seeing both sides of every issue, Kenneth Clark quite understood that it would not do to have a divorcée as Queen of England.

On Wednesday, 12 May 1937, the great day of the coronation of King George VI and Queen Elizabeth, they were awakened at 5 a.m. They ate a light breakfast and Jane was attired in a white court brocade dress, a tiara and a new white Schiaparelli long velvet cloak. When they arrived at the Abbey soon after 8 they found they had marvellous seats looking across to the High Altar, with an uninterrupted view of every moment of the ceremony. One would have to envisage productions of *Parsifal* and the *Golden Bough* as imagined by Reinhardt to appreciate properly the splendour and magnificence of that experience, Kenneth Clark wrote later. From the scene that immediately greeted their eyes, solid rows of peers and peeresses, like so many red and white carnations, on either side of a golden carpet, to a ceaseless procession of clergy, visiting royalty, yeomen of the guard and heralds, and then the actual entrance of the King and Queen – he had expected to be senseless from tiredness and an empty stomach by the end of the ceremony at 2.15 p.m. Instead, he could hardly believe it was over. When they reached the doors of Westminster Abbey it had begun to pour but as soon as the showers stopped they walked to a friend's house nearby. After a relaxing bottle of champagne, they were ready to take a taxi home.

As the servant of a new king Kenneth Clark found himself caught up once more in the stiff and interminable formalities that he disliked so much about his role. King George VI was as difficult to talk to as his mother. Janet Flanner described him as duty-bound by rank and work. Kenneth Clark turned with relief to the little Queen. His superficial impression, that she was not much better than the kind of person one met at a country house, and the King somewhat worse, changed quickly as he discovered that she had rare qualities, not the least of which were her sense and innate good taste. She and her husband wanted to get in touch with as many aspects of modern life as possible and were determined to start a collection of modern paintings.

Here was another natural pupil. He took up his role with zest. He persuaded Queen Elizabeth to commission artists and encouraged her in a heroically determined, ill-starred attempt to be painted by Augustus John. She endeared herself by buying a Wilson Steer painting of Lulworth Castle, landscapes by Duncan Grant and works by younger British artists. The Queen even allowed Kenneth Clark to indulge in his favourite pastime, hanging paintings. He improved the décor at Buckingham Palace and was particularly successful at Hampton Court, the palace on the Thames. His rearrangement of the pictures there was 'in the nature of a revelation', according to a newspaper report.

In March 1937 Kenneth Clark went to Philip Sassoon's house in

Park Lane to show Queen Elizabeth the Reynolds paintings. What a delightful person she was and how congenial and what a pity about her taste in clothes, he told Jane. Kenneth Clark was, in later years, to defend Queen Elizabeth's decision not to dress with too much dash with the comment that her instinct was sound. 'The Duchess of Kent could do it and was *mal vue* because of it.' A year later, after lunching with the Royal Family, he noted that the Queen was looking very trim, was wearing more fashionable clothes and drank only sherry in the morning.

He was a constant guest at Windsor Castle, which did not awe him in the least; 'very good grub', he commented. One was left free all day and had the use of a car. The castle did, however, have its drawbacks. Writing to Jane on handsome Windsor Castle stationery in the spring of 1939, Kenneth Clark explained that he had not telephoned because the only one available was in the footman's corridor and to attempt a conversation while they were standing around was too embarrassing. As was the norm, his room had nothing to recommend it but was doubtless an improvement over anything one could expect under communism. Visiting the castle in April 1938, he went for two long walks with the Queen. He was shocked to see how little she, and the King as well, did with their day: she never rose before 11. There were hardly any guests and the place was as dreary at night as it had been under King George v and Queen Mary. He and the Queen had at least spent one evening tasting country wines in one of the lodgekeeper's rooms. He liked her very much.

He might have been a little in love with her. Many of his generation felt the same way. When he talked about their romantic friendship in retrospect, he said that they saw as much of each other as they dared, adding that the King became unreasonably jealous and twice made scenes, once at Windsor Castle and again at Buckingham Palace. Perhaps Kenneth Clark was assuming more than was warranted from the Queen's lively interest in art and what another called her mild flirtatiousness, 'in a very proper romantic old-fashioned Valentine sort of way'. Her letters to Kenneth Clark, all about paintings, and written in an artless hand, have been burned, making the extent of their friendship impossible to assess. There is no question, however, of the royal regard in which both of the Clarks basked and the importance that was attached to K's opinions. Jane's diary notes that, after the Munich crisis and Chamberlain's confident declaration of Peace in Our Time, the Queen rang at lunchtime to ask what K thought.

Was the crisis really over? Jane commented approvingly on the Queen's sensible refusal to believe a man like Hitler.

Soon after the war began there was a magical evening when he was suddenly invited to dine *à quatre* with the Queen, the Duchess of Kent and an old friend, Malcolm Bullock. It was the Queen's first private party since the start of the war and one of those unforgettable evenings when one felt free to say anything that entered one's head – it was nearly midnight when he left. A funny thing had happened earlier that evening as he was dressing for dinner at Garlands Hotel, where he was staying. The head butler at Buckingham Palace had put through a call to find out what he would like to drink. He did not think the porter at Garlands would ever get over that.

Colette (called 'Celly' by her family), Colin and Alan lived at the top of Portland Place behind a green baize door. There was a nursery maid, Lam had returned as their nanny and they had a governess, Miss Newman (Newie). Almost from the day they were born the twins had distinctly different appearances. Colin had a narrow head, delicate features and a lively, impish stare. Colette was rounder-cheeked, darker-haired, with large bewildered eyes and a sweetly innocent, pouting mouth; her mother's mouth. They saw their parents every day at five, teatime. Colette played with her father's opera hat and a button on her mother's coat shaped like a mermaid. It was something to hold onto, that unexpected button, unique, strange and symbolic of this perfumed lady in expensive clothes whom one was taught to call mamma.

When the twins entered the room, identically dressed in white fur coats and bonnets, the ladies of the party would fall upon them with cries of admiration, their father wrote. Alan, the oldest, was much easier to resist. He seemed solitary and crabby. He wore glasses and was thin and gangling and people pushed him aside, including his mother.

Jane had wanted children but the physical act of giving birth had revolted her. She had not forgiven Alan for having had such a large head. Shortly after the birth of the twins, when Kitty Waterfield was expecting her first child, Jane came to tell her what agonies she had endured, rather gleefully, Mrs Waterfield thought. Kenneth Clark, however, confided his delight at the sight of his wife nursing the twins, one at each breast. The practical Alys Russell noticed Jane's air of fatigue and her slow recovery. Jane, Kenneth Clark concluded, was not a natural mother.

Shortly after the birth of the twins in 1932, the four-year-old Alan became ill of a 'mystifying distemper' which caused Owen Morshead, as the more experienced father, to wonder whether the illness did not disguise a childish distress at having been supplanted. Then, a year later, Alan came down with such a persistent fever and cough that his parents put him in hospital. The malady could not be diagnosed. Alan improved slowly and, by the end of March 1934, was playing with the penny-in-the-slot machines at Brighton along with the two little Balniel boys, although what had made him so ill remained a mystery.

Alan's first memories of his mother are fragmentary. In those days she seemed genuinely kind and thoughtful, rather like a wonderful fairy godmother one glimpsed at a tantalizing, dreamlike distance, because 'one hardly ever saw her and that was a pity'. He was scarcely aware that he had parents. Even Lam, who might have acted as a substitute mother, was very strict and not especially sympathetic, he said. His first memories are of 30 Portland Place, which he disliked very much. 'I hated the top floor. I was alone at night. I remember seeing reflections on the ceilings ... I can't remember when I was put to bed. Perhaps it was 6.30. I was terribly afraid of the dark.'

Alan thought London noisy and dirty, but remembered with delight a house on the north coast of Norfolk that his parents rented in the summer of 1935. It was there that he first got to know his father. They went for long walks and investigated abandoned boats. Colette thought that their father seemed more 'like an older brother' than a parent. He explored the beach with them, hiding in the sand dunes. 'I never remember him being angry or ticking us off,' she continued. 'He never talked down to us. It was always as if we were as intelligent as he was. The effect was to make you clever without realizing it.' She said, 'We adored him and never did anything to displease him.'

Alan was sent at first to Egerton House, a private day school in Cavendish Square. Then, in the summer of 1937, when he was nine, he was taken to his first term at a boarding school, St Cyprian's, at Eastbourne. It was, for his father, a gloomy experience. He was suddenly reminded all too clearly of the misery he had endured and felt enormous guilt to think he might be subjecting Alan to the same torments. However, Alan had a very pleasant dormitory with a view over the Downs and the school seemed a friendly, bustling place, with an easy-going atmosphere. Its teaching was said to be excellent. This was another reason for sending Alan, since his father was concerned about his lack of academic progress. And Alan took it so well, with a gentlemanly spirit that did his father proud, compared to the sorry-looking bunch of other newcomers. He left reassured.

Since he had hated it himself, why did Kenneth Clark send Alan away to school? In the first place, his memories of Wixenford, if not Winchester, had been happy. He fell back on the argument that it was a universal experience for children of the upper middle class and that Alan would have felt left out if he had not been sent. He also thought that such schools had improved vastly since his time. But the determining factor, for him, was that Alan had liked it there. Or so he told his parents at the time.

Despite his father's hopeful assertions, St Cyprian's was, Alan Clark recalled, a notoriously awful place. The bad food, absurd rules, tyrannical atmosphere and feeling of being imprisoned left a permanent scar. 'Luckily it caught fire in 1938 and we were all dispersed.' Why had he not told his parents how unhappy he was? 'It wouldn't have made any difference. They expected one to be unhappy,' he said with conviction.

Jane's reports to her husband, mother or friends about the children were always confident. Alan did not mind a bit going back to school even though he looked peaked. Alan was adorable, as usual, or looking fit and cheerful, she would tell her husband. She always added dutifully, even to herself, that her son was very much missed. Similarly, the twins were always playing together and in a good mood. Writing in the room below, she would add that she was judging from the noises they made. Owen Morshead's tactful suggestion that children learned at an early age to live up to their parents' expectations would have sounded far-fetched to the Clarks. Jane, in particular, had an idealistic view of motherhood and since her theories were untested by contact with real babies, she remained charmingly uninitiated. Catherine Porteous, for many years Kenneth Clark's indispensable assistant, recalled that Jane's way of amusing a baby was to give it a Fabergé box to play with, the kind from which a bird might pop out and sing, as though heedless of its fragility and those destructive small hands.

Jane's expansive fantasies and her concept of an idyllic family life in which she and her children played their flawless parts, were apparent in the birthday parties she gave. There would be the twins, adorably dressed, Alan wary, chin tucked under, perhaps in a kilt and buckled shoes, and rich people's children with their nannies, being ushered in by the butler. Presents would be heaped on everyone and Jane would sweep in, a little late, smiling, in sables or a fur coat with mermaid buttons. The perfect mother with her perfect children in the perfect house.

Jane dined at Buckingham Palace on Monday, 28 March 1938. Tiaras were not required so she wore her *robe déchirée* designed by Salvador Dali for Schiaparelli. It was a very informal and agreeable evening, she wrote in her diary. Three nights later she was back at Buckingham Palace, wearing her Schiaparelli white and silver lamé gown. Ruth Lee, wife of Lord Lee of Fareham, lent Jane her Queen Anne diamond brooch to wear. Those undergraduate years of draping upholstery brocade with safety pins had not been in vain. She had learned how to dress and, once married to a wealthy man, could give that impulse full rein. She chose Elsa Schiaparelli.

Jane was not quite tall enough to be an ideal model (she was 5′4″) but her proportions were pleasing and her curves minimal enough for the clothes of the 1920s and 1930s. Her choice of Schiaparelli stemmed, perhaps, from her awareness that the Italian-born Paris designer had exceptional artistic ability even in the ranks of the *hauts couturiers*. In this respect Jane was unlike her sober-minded mother, who wrote an article condemning fashionableness in clothes of the 1890s while she was still Dr E. Winifred Dickson. Jane's only concession to her mother's beliefs was to insist that her day clothes be cut high to the neck since, her mother wrote, one ran a serious risk if one left the upper part of the body exposed.

Although Jane seemed to believe that men liked becoming and picturesque clothes on their wives, rather than smart ones, her own preference for stylish daring is apparent in the clothes she chose. Sir Colin Anderson recalled that, in the 1930s, Jane owned a pair of trousers 'of emerald green velveteen with a row of large scarlet fly-buttons, not up the front, but creeping up behind, along the division between her buttocks'. On an Orient Line cruise to the Mediterranean she wore 'a silk day-dress made from a fabric printed all over as newsprint, with headings, illustrations, advertisements and stop-press column. It had not been done before, & was in itself quite acceptable. But it was complete only with its hat, of the same material, stiffened and folded into the shape of a child's paper hat.'

Jane's sartorial antics were much admired by her father. In

December 1935 he begged his 'Betty' to write soon and tell him what she wore, since that mattered to him almost more than anything else. Her husband took the same intense interest; his childhood pleasure in dressing up had metamorphosed into a preoccupation with every detail of his wife's costume, including her hair. That, often parted in the middle, was tightly curled around her ears and off her neck, giving that clean outline with a definite shape that he liked so much.

'Sandy' Calder designed jewellery for her and 'Ted' Kauffer her notepaper, as well as visiting-cards for both Clarks in which their Christian names were printed in flourishing black italic script and their surnames in plain, light grey capital letters. Meticulous attention to detail and flawless, expensive choices: there was absolutely nothing second-rate about her taste or judgement, her daughter observed. When Jane sent gifts they were the best money could buy: brandied peaches and chocolate oysters from Fortnum & Mason, or lavish boxes of the best Charbonnel & Walker chocolates.

Jane sent letters of invitation and flowers. She sent cards. She sent telegrams of welcome, commiseration and congratulation to friends, acquaintances, relatives, employees, friends of friends. They were spring cleaning and she had found some boxes of Christmas crackers she would send along for a birthday party, she wrote to her mother. Or she had found some ancient clothes (always an exaggeration, her brother Russell said), that she was sending and for which she did not want thanks as they were not worth it. She was so generous that she wanted to send the Duke and Duchess a present as thanks for a photograph, and had to be gently discouraged by a friend. People felt Jane had to be protected from herself, she was so impulsively, lavishly and endearingly generous.

One of the first hostesses to take up the Clarks was Lady Colefax, that astute spotter of young talent. She loudly proclaimed them her own discovery and was minutely interested in their social progress. They also saw that other great London hostess, Lady Cunard who was, by the time they met, 'looking frail and ill as the old do who are made up to the eyes', but who could still enliven the conversation with wit and epigrams. Or they were invited by Sir Philip Sassoon, to parties given with Oriental splendour in palatial mansions. Sir Henry ('Chips') Channon called Sassoon 'the strangest of sinister men'. People thought that, for a man with such evident taste in art, he decorated houses atrociously. Channon called Port Lympne, his house near Hythe in Kent, 'a triumph of beautiful bad taste and

Babylonian luxury, with terraces and flowery gardens, and jade-green pools and swimming-baths and rooms done up in silver and blue and orange'. It looked like a Spanish brothel. The Clarks also shuddered, but were so entranced by their host's engaging personality that it did not matter.

He was so kind. He plied them with invitations to his enormous parties where they met the rich and titled, including Sassoon's intimate friends the Prince of Wales, the Duke and Duchess of York and Queen Mary. He invited them for week-ends at Port Lympne where, some years before, another visitor, Lloyd George, had sung 'Cockles and Mussels' at the top of his voice. There Sassoon was at his best, talking perceptively about books and creating an atmosphere of ease and relaxation. He was desolate whenever they left. 'Welcome – *welcome* back –' he scribbled in pencil after one of their absences. 'We have missed you cruelly – I do hope you are both well & am longing to see you.' When the Clarks began looking for a country house, Sassoon offered them Bellevue on his Port Lympne estate. He thought it an ideal house and they agreed. Alan in particular came to prefer 'Bellers' to London, especially since Sassoon, a passionate advocate of British air power, and Under-Secretary of State for Air, took the children up on flights and would 'buzz' their outraged and horrified parents as they played golf.

For his own part, Kenneth Clark did not particularly like to entertain formally but felt that his position required it. He was, in any case, besieged with invitations, most of which had to be accepted for one reason or another. Then he must return the compliment. There were always visitors from abroad, many of whom had already entertained them, or trustees, or colleagues or various officials, Cabinet members and the like. It was common for him and Jane to be out almost every night of the month. Perhaps people were right in their comment that he backed into the limelight, as T.E. Lawrence had done. It is evident that Jane had no such ambivalence. She was plainly ambitious for him. She was bolder than he was, their friend Lady Gladwyn said. She seemed so confident and sure of herself in those days. She was his champion, always bringing him forward. She was launching him, but he wanted to be launched. She made him feel grand. Bryan Robertson, former head of the Whitechapel Gallery, observed, 'In their palmy Portland Place days she created the most perfect context a man could have, and made things very easy.'

They had everything: looks, charm and money. Hostesses queued up for them, Sir Trenchard Cox recalled. 'You couldn't not meet him about'; Kenneth Clark was everywhere. As royal favourites, they were courted, flattered and pursued. Journalists picked up the theme. The *Bystander*, noting that Kenneth and Jane Clark were among those at the opening of sculpture halls given by Lord Duveen to the Tate Gallery, called them 'that clever, attractive couple'. Edith Wharton wrote to say that Jane's description of their week-end in Paris had been so scintillating that it made her blink. Logan Pearsall-Smith asked, 'On your way to the great London parties where I hear of your glittering in diamonds night after night, couldn't you stop for dinner or at least for a moment – any night, for I never go out – at this hermit's cell in St Leonard's Terrace, where I dwell in solitude, thinking unworldly thoughts?'

Jane was a brilliant hostess. Like Lady Colefax, she had a gift for gathering an eclectic circle of British and foreign friends, courting young unknowns such as Coldstream, Sutherland and Moore as eagerly as she invited dukes and duchesses, Churchill and Chamberlain. She met the up-and-coming Cecil Beaton and was as delighted with him as she was with Noël Coward. She was not impressed by 'Willie' Maugham and took an instant dislike to that other prominent member of society, 'Chips' Channon.

They met Aldous and Maria Huxley through their friends Kauffer and Dorn and bought paintings from the artist, Tchelitchev, after hearing about him from Edith Sitwell. The latter stated that there was no one with whom Tchelitchev would rather discuss painting than Kenneth Clark and she was sure her friend now had a new respect for England. What did the Clarks think of the strange and interesting poems of Dylan Thomas, the boy she mentioned when they met at Sibyl Colefax's? Edith Sitwell was certain he would become a great poet.

They travelled in the grand world of the high intelligentsia, as well as of a very smart social set. Diplomats and politicians mingled with the prominent and promising: H.G. Wells, Raymond Mortimer, Peter Quennell, Cyril Connolly, Clive Bell, Duncan Grant, Vanessa Bell, Artur Rubinstein, Eddy Sackville-West, Kenneth Clark's friend at Oxford who played the piano so well and would become the fifth Baron Sackville, and that interesting young composer William Walton.

Colin Anderson and his wife Morna were among their closest friends. After they came down from Oxford the two men had lost contact but discovered each other again after the Andersons spotted Kenneth and Jane Clark pushing a pram beside the Round Pond in Kensington Gardens. The Andersons were duly invited to Portland Place: 'This was my first introduction to Jane and Morna's first encounter with either of them. She sat next to K at dinner and found him (or perhaps his conversational demands) so alarming that she declared on the way home that she would never go there again. However, I persisted.'

Sir Colin was a natural addition to that charmed inner circle, that setting, he wrote, for so many aesthetic experiences that would never otherwise have come his way. He commissioned artists such as Moore, Sutherland, Francis Bacon and Ceri Richards and assembled an art collection that rivalled the Clarks'. In his role as a director of the Orient Line, he broke new ground in the tasteful use of functional materials and designs for their liners. He served nobly on committees. He was always in the background, grateful for a friendship that endured, he wrote, because neither made any demands upon the other. Sir Colin's privately printed writings give, in their muted and delicate intensity, a hint of the literary talent that he might have become famous for.

Jane liked small lunches. She also gave dinners for sixteen select friends, often followed by large gatherings. Kenneth Clark remembered crowds trooping up the stairs. There were after-the-theatre parties presided over by a masterly parlourmaid called Murray, who 'drank a bit but not enough to fall down', Kenneth Clark said. They occasionally arranged musical *soirées*, although the host considered these difficult because some people would not stop talking and others smoked or snored. If they were living beyond their means, as he was beginning to believe, perhaps the time had come to sell 30 Portland Place. Apparently the other owners in their block had agreed to sell to a real-estate developer, who was going to tear everything down and put up an apartment building, with the Clarks as the only remaining obstacles. If they did so, he told Jane, they could buy a smaller house and entertain far less.

Jane's reply has been lost. However, the block of flats was never built and the Clarks did not move for another two years, suggesting that Jane was persuasively opposed. If they were living beyond their means, it was for a good cause. Nancy Bingham commented, 'The atmosphere around the house was that this was all being done for K's benefit.'

Jane was not a natural writer but did her best, in a pleasantly sprawl-ing hand, to keep a faithful record of travel plans, holidays, illnesses, houses, friends, dinners, hair appointments and clothes. The one enduring theme is her husband's activities.

K went to Kenwood. K was too tired to go to the Wimborne House concert. K had shown his Leonardo manuscript to Saxl of the Warburg, an expert on the subject, who thought it brilliant. He was revising it in London and he and the cook were making themselves bacon and eggs for supper. K lunched with W.G. Constable to hear his version of the Courtauld row. K went to see the Queen in Buck-ingham Palace and hung paintings with her until 1.15 p.m.

Jane listened to his speeches and passed a verdict, often laconically favourable, in her diary. She read his manuscripts. She was an extra pair of eyes in art galleries. When her husband was on a trip that did not include her, she answered his mail, postponing what she could and explaining when she could not. She often acted on his behalf. When the Crown Prince of Sweden, Gustavus Adolphus, asked the absent Kenneth Clark to bid on his behalf at Christie's, Jane took over. She went to the auction and wired her polite regrets that the painting had sold for more than the Crown Prince was prepared to pay.

Kenneth Clark had begun to rely on his wife's opinion at an early stage. While in Paris with Berenson he wrote a detailed outline for some seventeenth-century studies and sent it to her with a plea for a frank assessment. Once he joined the National Gallery, her influence on his daily decisions was pronounced, as can be seen by an exchange of letters between her and their friend David Balniel, when he was chairman of the Board of Trustees. She told Balniel that she was arranging for a special meeting of the trustees, had settled a matter involving an interfering restorer and had told Arthur (Lord Lee) that they would all be dining together the following Saturday night. The course of events was set down on paper with the uncompromising bluntness with which Jane tackled life. For her there were no Whistlerian ambiguities in delicate half-tones of grey, but only black and white, Beardsley-like certitudes.

Their friends were aware of the way Jane Clark protected her husband in those days. 'He was a young man but he didn't act like one,' Myfanwy Piper said. 'Before a public appearance he went to bed and had a boiled egg. Jane would then take over, answer the telephone and make excuses for him. At that stage she really nannied him.' Others also observed how well Jane defended her husband against the outside world, for instance, making guests leave so that he could go to bed. A good friend of Jane's described her fierce, unthinking loyalty: 'Jane would have hit anyone who criticized her darling. Her baby.'

'K thinks, K says ...' Burnet Pavitt, one of their friends, said, 'She used to talk as if he were the Universal Man. She worshipped him.' Jane observed, commented and advised. She was his twin, literally a projection of him at that period, her individual identity firmly fused into a composite 'we'. In those early days they stimulated each other. Whatever one took up the other would adopt with enthusiasm, according to a close friend.

Jane liked to stay in bed in the morning and, although she was habitually late, made great efforts to reform in order to please her punctual, early-rising husband. Like her mother she detested boats – Mrs Martin said she got 'sick on the quay before she boarded' – and had an even greater fear of heights, large dogs, plane rides; all those small dangers, unavoidable risks of ordinary life that her husband faced with exemplary calm. She tried gallantly to overcome those fears. He in turn tried to live up to her expectations. Jane was in the south of France, he told Pavel Tchelitchev, from whom he had just bought a painting of an apple tree. Perhaps he would be forgiven if he did not show the painter's letter to his wife, because she would be enraged to find that they had not paid him promptly. He would obey her wishes in little ways, like getting up from the table and leaving the room whenever he had one of his inexplicable fits of sneezing. 'Jane is quite right, they are disgusting,' he would say. And whenever Jane was ill, he was gentle and considerate. That was fairly often, since she suffered from nervous headaches, colds which could easily become influenza, and sinusitis, a chronic family complaint. In about 1935 she developed an infection of the posterior sinuses and, on her mother's recommendation, went to Bedford Russell, a Harley Street surgeon who was in charge of the throat department at St Bartholomew's Hospital. Russell's solution was to provide her with a fine spray to clear out the sinuses, applied with a syringe and bulb attachment. One of the first things her children remember about her is mamma's 'puffer'.

At the start of their marriage Jane had followed her husband at a discreet conversational distance. Now, however, she was speaking up. People found her remarks quick and sharp, with an ability to devastate the group. She had a 'maddening habit' of interrupting her husband just when he was saying something particularly interesting. A friend who met them at the start of the Second World War was astounded to discover that, at family meals, Jane and the children shouted Kenneth Clark down. She talked across him as if he were not there. Yet it was obvious that Jane genuinely admired her husband. If he were not at the table, she would have rung him up beforehand in order to quote his latest opinions in every other sentence.

Sir Colin Anderson described her as a 'vivid, buccaneering character', and her brother, Dr Russell Martin, thought she was closest in temperament to her mother's sister Edith, with the same Irish quicksilver quality. If her husband suppressed his emotions rigorously, Jane seemed at the mercy of whatever momentary impulse crossed her thoughts. Although ready to defend him from all the world, she expected him to live up to her own exacting standards of behaviour. For instance, whenever they entertained, Jane was the soul of gaiety and wit – her daughter noted that her mother never let down her guard in public – but once the room was empty and her husband collecting glasses and ashtrays, the post-mortem would begin. She would say, 'Why were you rude to so and so?' He: 'Was I?' She: 'Of course you were.' There were inquisitions and recriminations, which her husband bore as equably as he could. However, he was beginning to dread her moods, since one could never predict them. He found himself pacing up and down the street outside 30 Portland Place, trying to work up the courage to go inside.

Kenneth Clark thought of his wife as a very remarkable person, 'and in a sort of way I felt inferior to her. All the great social life before the war, especially in Portland Place, that was Jane's doing. Sir Winston one night and Mr Chamberlain two nights later, that was due to Jane!' He smacked the arm of his chair for emphasis. Jane's elegance and charm, her understanding of creative people and her affectionate concern for their welfare, her ability to set people at their ease, were what brought them their *renommée*. 'I was just tagging along.' Their daughter said that they were always known as 'Jane and K'.

Friends thought them the perfect couple. What a wonderful weekend they had spent at Bellevue, Kauffer wrote to Jane in 1938. It was one of the happiest times in his life. The house was charming, there were exciting things to look at and books to read, the children were enchanting and their hosts very lovable. They made, he said later, a rare duet. Others agreed. 'All and everything – what can I wish but that your fortunes shall be as happy as till now,' Sibyl Colefax wrote. '... [G]ood health and enjoyment – I needn't wish you love that you earn by all the lovely kindness you spread as you go ... it's so spontaneous that it's as delicious as sunshine.'

In contrast to his wife, Kenneth Clark loved the stuffy smell of trains and sniffed it with pleasure whenever they embarked on their visits to Edith Wharton in the south of France. In fact he was always happy on a train. He would set out with the usual good intentions and a bulging briefcase and find himself led astray by a detective novel and half a bottle of white Hermitage. It would be half a bottle, just as the ritual of the after-dinner cigar would be limited to a single delicious specimen. By nature he was as frugal as he was well organized; the days when he used to drop his clothes on the floor (at Winchester, some fag picked them up) had long gone. As at Oxford, his clothes were exquisitely neat – he favoured double-breasted pinstripe suits with a high cut, matching waistcoat, always buttoned. His ties alone showed distinction and, like the handkerchief in his breast pocket, might be displayed with slightly more dash than was exactly necessary.

His taste in food was as eclectic as his interest in wines. He tended to whistle under his breath, to rely on chocolate for quick energy and to take sleeping pills occasionally when exhausted. When he drank, he would toss back a Scotch before anyone else had begun on theirs, but then he did everything faster than other people.

Those he encountered were invariably impressed by the rapidity and clarity of his thought. 'One of the most remarkable men I ever met,' was a typical comment. People also remarked upon his air of absolute, impeccable breeding, perhaps traceable to the influence of his maternal grandmother and, arising from that, a natural command that seemed to stem from being rich and a Wykehamist. His *hauteur* verged on arrogance. Many, men in particular, found him cheerless, difficult to talk to and ill at ease. Sir Trenchard Cox said, 'He was the reverse of cosy because he was not at ease with himself.'

Women had less difficulty in seeing beneath the façade. Emerald Cunard, for instance, had come to know Kenneth Clark well enough to uncover the self-doubter and advised him not to be so diffident, or people would not respect him. Anne Olivier Popham, who knew William Coldstream and Graham Bell well at that period, thought that Kenneth Clark was at his best with those who were not repelled or silenced by his brusqueness, and were therefore able to break through the barrier. How warm and spontaneous he could be, at the right moment, lustily singing music-hall songs at the piano and telling his best and funniest stories. How remarkably he could talk at dinner parties, in the right company. What a gift he had for making others talk, so well that one felt one had never known them before. Hiram Winterbotham used to drive home from such dinners in ecstasy. There would be other evenings when Kenneth Clark drank rather too much, would stand on a chair, announce that he was Leonardo da Vinci and make a speech. The next day he would be likely to pass his companion of the evening before wordlessly on the street. His private reaction would have been, as he wrote to Jane, that he had monopolized the conversation once again and behaved rather badly. The person involved, however, might conclude that those who called Kenneth Clark arrogant were right.

For every friend they made in those halcyon days of the 'Great Clark Boom', as he termed it, they were making an equal number of enemies. For every Sibyl Colefax and Philip Sassoon there was someone on a London street or an office corridor who felt himself snubbed because Kenneth Clark was too absorbed in thought, or too embarrassed, to recognize him; some host whose pressing invitation had been declined unconvincingly; some celebrity for whom the doors of Portland Place had not opened.

As at Oxford, acquaintances received the impression that Jane was putting on an act. She spent money conspicuously. She flaunted their success. She dropped names. She seemed boastful about their houses, possessions, conquests. When she got into a 'boasting spell' she was likely to bring in the name of every grand person from the Queen downwards. It was fearfully embarrassing. A story made the rounds in London at that time that she had said, 'I simply must get another tiara; I've worn mine to Buckingham Palace so much that it's getting worn out.' Then there was the day that Professor Agnes Headlam-Morley, an old friend of Jane's from Oxford, went to Portland Place for a drink and was told, rather sharply, 'Don't finger the orchids, Agnes, the Kents are coming to lunch.'

If Jane disliked someone she did not take much trouble to hide it. It was said that 'Chips' Channon once complained that he was never invited to Portland Place and was told, too sweetly, by Jane, 'But Chips, we don't know anyone grand enough to have with you.'

In her attempt to present the right social façade and not let her husband down, Jane assumed a certain sophistication which, if it were not to seem arrogant, required a lightness of touch that she lacked. What she appeared to have was 'the pride of those who are not sure of their social position'. A friend remembered going to lunch at Portland Place and finding the house in turmoil because it had been robbed and all Jane's fur coats stolen. Jane remarked, 'We heard it all but couldn't be bothered to get up.' Then there was the time when the Clarks visited the Bond Street galleries of Colnaghi & Co. and stopped to look at a sentimental painting of a girl with a dead bird. The director, John James Byam Shaw, reminded Kenneth Clark that the painting had once belonged to him. Jane Clark said, 'Oh K, how *could* you own such an awful picture?' Her husband said, 'I rather liked it.'

The Clarks were too grand for their own good. They were being teased on that point by Logan Pearsall Smith and his sister Alys Russell. What Logan Pearsall Smith implied was what Kenneth and Jane Clark knew all too well; that there were many who wished them nothing but ill, who would be delighted to see them toppled from their dazzling eminence. A friend who knew them then remarked, 'They were bound together against a rather evil world. A mocking world.'

They were bound together, after ten years of marriage, by nostalgia for those early days when they had been so happy at the Chiostro di San Martino, in love with Italy and each other. From his vantage point that period of their lives had a dreamlike unreality, remote and idyllic. Would they ever return! Perhaps he no longer quite thought of Jane as half of his soul, but she was an indispensable part of his life nevertheless. Every separation served to drive the message home. À *bientôt*, he wrote. He was sure they would always be together.

11 The Giorgionesque

'. . . he who makes no mistakes does nothing'. –
D.S. MacColl

In four years as director of the National Gallery, from 1934 to 1938, Kenneth Clark bought paintings as often as limited funds (never more than £7,000 a year) would allow. By the spring of 1938 he had made some magnificent purchases. He had acquired, for £273, a rare Cima da Conegliano head of St Jerome. He had bought a first-rate Rubens, *The Watering Place*, a grand impressionistic landscape by Constable, *Hadleigh Castle*, an incomparable Rembrandt, *Saskia as Flora*, a glorious Ingres, *Portrait of Madame Moitessier*, and other notable works including Poussin's *Golden Calf* and four scenes from the Life of *St John the Baptist* by Giovanni di Paolo. There were some lesser acquisitions representing many schools, from the Italian primitives to French nineteenth-century artists, from Hogarth to the little-known Spanish painter Master Paulus. Altogether Kenneth Clark had bought fifty-three paintings, sometimes despite strong opposition.

Impressive though these acquisitions were, he had known when he took office that Parliament could not provide the handsome funds needed if the Gallery were to compete with the great American millionaire collectors. Like the museums in Boston, Philadelphia, New York and Washington, London's National Gallery needed a benefactor. Early in 1936 Kenneth Clark thought he had found one.

Calouste Sarkis Gulbenkian was, in his lifetime, famous for being a mystery. The art world knew that this wealthy Armenian was buying paintings, sculpture, jewellery and furniture with gratifying frequency. It was also known that, through tenacious business dealings, Gulbenkian had amassed a fortune in oil (by 1945, his income was estimated at £400,000 a year). His acquisitions from the Hermitage in 1928–30 – when the Russian government was so desperate for foreign currency that it sold some of its priceless possessions – were legendary. Yet details about his private life were unknown, his movements were stealthy, by nature he was suspicious, almost paranoid, and his possessiveness was a standing joke. He called his objects his 'children', his 'harem', and insisted that he wanted them to be burned on his funeral pyre, like Sardanapalus. Yet it was characteristic of him that he hid his beauties from prying eyes, including his own. His rare orchids were kept by a grower in London, his valuable birds installed on the terraces of the Parisian mansion he seldom visited, and the art objects he bought were often left indefinitely with the dealers who had sold them.

Gulbenkian's instincts were not simply acquisitive. He subscribed, the expert on Iranian art Arthur Upham Pope recalled, to the ancient Persian belief that great art made one feel 'young and strong and glad'. An aesthetic awareness, colouring every aspect of his daily life, so enchanted Kenneth Clark when he first visited Gulbenkian's mansion on the avenue d'Iéna just before Christmas 1935, that the collector was inspired to do something highly uncharacteristic: trust a stranger. Within months he had offered to loan a group of his choicest paintings that included two Monets, three Corots, four Guardis, a Degas, a Van Dyck, a Rubens (the famous *Portrait of Hélène Fourment*), two Rembrandts, *The Annunciation* by Dirk Bouts and *Cupid and the Graces* by Boucher. Only one painting was not of top quality, the Domenico Ghirlandaio *Portrait of a Young Woman*. Kenneth Clark thought it might even be a fake. It became, nevertheless, one of the most popular paintings on view.

When they met in Paris, Gulbenkian had hinted that he was looking for an heir, and in a few months he had returned to the subject. Kenneth Clark was not slow in prompting him. Why not leave his precious possessions to the National Gallery?

There were major hurdles to be overcome. Approval for an extension had to be obtained from the Office of Works, the Treasury and the Prime Minister. All agreed. A further objection was presented by the collector himself, who was determined not to pay the heavy British estate duties. To avoid this would mean a special Act of Parliament. Kenneth Clark worked for months and, early in 1938, told the trustees that matters were sufficiently resolved to make the bequest a certainty. The architect was at work on a Gulbenkian annex, the Office of Works ready to build and everything was going smoothly. Then Britain declared war on Germany and the whole scheme collapsed.

The reasons had to do with the elaborate precautions Gulbenkian had taken against such an eventuality. In a post-war memorandum to the National Gallery Kenneth Clark explained that Gulbenkian carried both a British and a Turkish passport. He was also the Iranian commercial attaché, his domicile was Paris and he was unwilling to leave even when France was about to collapse, for fear the Germans would seize his treasures. Although the Foreign Office knew all this it chose to classify Gulbenkian as an enemy alien. Years of patient work to entice an intensely suspicious man to present his work to the nation had been destroyed with a single stroke of masterful stupidity. Even more was involved, since one of the associate companies of the Iraq Petroleum Company, which paid Gulbenkian his immense yearly fortune, was the Anglo-Iranian, and a large number of these shares were held by the British Government. The Iraq Petroleum Company used Gulbenkian's classification as an enemy alien as an excuse to withhold his profits, and the collector was bound to jump to the obvious conclusion. In fact, Gulbenkian was deeply offended and never recovered. He was as attentive, friendly and courteous to Kenneth Clark as before, but the latter knew that all hope of a bequest was over.

It was obvious that Gulbenkian thought Kenneth Clark far too trusting, an innocent in a rapacious and treacherous world. Whenever he recommended a painting Gulbenkian would always check to make sure that his adviser did not have a private interest in the matter. Every one of his business dealings was continually being checked and rechecked and something of this intense lack of trust and suspiciousness – valuable assets, as it turned out – must have made itself felt. It was also axiomatic, as Kenneth Clark knew, that one was bound to buy a fake. Even Berenson had made calamitous errors in the first flush of his studies, having fallen in love with the portrait of a girl that had been in the collection of his mentor, Giovanni Morelli, but which the latter never allowed to be exhibited. Berenson grandly pronounced that the work was an early Leonardo and endured several mortifying years during which that claim was demolished and his own expertise brought into question.

Berenson had been young and relatively obscure. Kenneth Clark, however, was a prominent public servant buying for a national collection when, in the summer of 1937, he, too, mistook glitter for gold.

While on a trip to Vienna he had visited the apartment of an expert on Venetian sculpture named Salzer who showed him four small works. They had evidently been decorations on the case for a musical instrument and seemed, to Kenneth Clark, to breathe the unmistakable air of sixteenth-century Venetian art. More than that, he decided they must be lost works by Giorgione. He left, but the poetic images haunted his sleep. When the paintings were subsequently shown in London he presented them to his board of trustees. David Balniel wrote to say that he could think of nothing else except 'your Giorgiones', and added, 'Use every weapon you possess, brutal or persuasive, to force us to buy them.'

The four little paintings, mounted on a single square of grey felt, illustrated a poem by the Ferrarese court poet Tebaldo, written about 1495, telling of the unrequited love of a shepherd, Damon, for Amaryllis, and of his suicide. The delicate works, in a unifying palette of browns, brownish greens, pale blue and white, exude an air of poetic resignation. The foregrounds are all in darkness while the distant vistas – beckoning, pale blue hills and, in the final painting, an ocean fluttering with boats – suggest a tantalizing and inaccessible happiness. The theme is Giorgionesque, but the execution so far below the standard of that incomparable artist that it is difficult to see how Kenneth Clark could have been so deceived. Perhaps the plaintive longing of the subject-matter struck some deep vein of buried feeling. If so, those feelings would soon make themselves felt.

In recommending the purchase, Kenneth Clark had been careful to state that the works were probably not by Giorgione. The trustees must buy purely on the basis of intrinsic merit. Although he was careful not to commit himself publicly, he was emphatic in a letter to Edith Wharton, in which he unhesitatingly called the works Giorgiones. No doubt he said enough in private to reassure his trustees. They were convinced, but just to be on the safe side, insisted that he write an article in the *Burlington* making his opinion public. There was another problem. The paintings, at £14,000, cost more than the Gallery could afford. Sir Robert Witt, chairman of the National Art Collections Fund, offered to buy them for the nation. He stipulated, however, that for this price the paintings must be labelled Giorgiones. Kenneth Clark agreed.

The *Daily Telegraph* of 20 October 1937 announced that the 'Rarest of Old Masters', the National Gallery's new Giorgiones, had gone on public view. The director gave his 'spirit of Giorgione' argument to the press, but also stated that there was good reason to believe the works were actually by the master. Almost at once, some big guns were moved in to counter his argument. The paintings were certainly not by Giorgione, but by a minor Renaissance artist, Palma Vecchio.

The assertion came from Professor Tancred Borenius, the Finnish art historian who had been rejected as a candidate for the position of Surveyor of the King's Pictures three years before. He was almost twenty years older than Kenneth Clark, an expert on the Italian Renaissance, and had edited a new edition of the standard work on the subject by Crowe and Cavalcaselle, had lectured at the Slade School and had, for many years, been professor of art history at University College, London. As an older authority, to be passed over in favour of someone unknown would be reason enough to feel resentful. However, Borenius apparently suspected Kenneth Clark of engineering his defeat by blackening his name. Borenius seized on the attribution to Giorgione as a way of putting a rival in his place and restoring his own authority. He knew he was on firm ground.

Others agreed. Dr George M. Richter, a Giorgione scholar, con-ceded that the paintings were very close to Giorgione, but pro-nounced them the work of a Bergamasque painter, Andrea Previtali, and therefore worth a few hundred pounds instead of fourteen thousand. Borenius conceded to Richter and the criticism began to mount, notably in the pages of the *Daily Telegraph*. How could the Gallery have spent thousands on these panels when two authorities asserted they were worth a few hundred? As for Bernard Berenson, he told the American critic Royal Cortissoz that Kenneth Clark had bought 'four pretty nothings' done by a talented furniture painter.

During the uproar following Berenson's purported discovery of an early Leonardo it was rumoured that he had known the painting to be worthless but had recommended it to an American collector so as to make a handsome profit. In London the same kind of charge was being made against Kenneth Clark. He had been an intermediary in the sale and kept a handsome percentage. Borenius was telling every-one that when they knew the whole story they would be horrified.

The London art dealer J.J. Byam Shaw recalled going to a large reception in the Royal Academy and seeing Borenius at the top of the stairs waving a telegram and shouting that news from some unnamed expert conclusively proved that the paintings were not by Giorgione. Letters and articles followed from people Kenneth Clark had thought friendly and approving, and to be made the butt of so much public criticism was an unpleasant new experience, especially since he could not help conceding that Richter was right. It was disagreeable to go out for lunch and feel oneself the object of all eyes, see heads bending low, concealed smiles, and grow hot with humiliation. The controversy even caused a question in the House of Commons.

In the midst of it all, the problem of Sir Joseph Duveen presented itself. Duveen was now eligible for reappointment as a trustee and, despite his blatant conflict of interests, looked likely to get in. Several trustees, Evan Charteris, Lord D'Abernon and his friend Sir Philip Sassoon, were in favour; Kenneth Clark, along with his then chairman, Samuel Courtauld, was opposed. Kenneth Clark had seen at first hand just how Machiavellian Duveen could be. He came to believe that, whenever Duveen loudly proclaimed the worthlessness of a painting the Gallery was considering, it was because he wanted that painting for himself. There were several such examples, including a particular Italian Renaissance work which would have been a bargain at £3,500. Duveen successfully managed to convince the trustees that it was worthless and subsequently, quietly, bought it for himself.

Kenneth Clark did not trouble to hide his disapproval. When a group of friends came for Easter 1937, including Sassoon, he and Jane condemned the idea of having any dealer act as a trustee. He had cause to regret his outspokenness. Sir Philip was fanatically determined to have Duveen reappointed and rang Jane in a rage. She herself had received £25 worth of orchids from Duveen as a Christmas present and, refusing to be contaminated, gave them to the servants.

It seemed a wise tactic for Kenneth Clark to say no more. David Balniel was more than willing to take up the cause. With Courtauld, he went to see the Prime Minister, Neville Chamberlain, to argue against Duveen. Balniel wrote in mid December 1937 to say that the interview had been successful 'in so far as it was destructive. We put the case against Duveen, & he said, "You have completely convinced me."' Then in early January 1938 Kenneth Clark received a phone call from the Prime Minister's secretary bringing up the matter again. Sir Philip Sassoon and Evan Charteris had told the Prime Minister that the majority supported Duveen. Kenneth Clark suggested that each trustee be polled; the reverse was found to be the case. No one knew that Duveen was dying of cancer and it later caused Kenneth Clark much remorse. Nor did they know that their likeable friend Sir Philip Sassoon had only one more year to live. Fortunately this friendship was easily repaired. Shortly after his Duveen defeat,

Sassoon appeared at their house one evening after dinner as friendly as ever, and as if nothing had happened. K and Jane were charmed.

Sassoon seemed to have re-established his place in their lives. Neither was alarmed when, as they were about to sail for New York in the summer of 1939, he sent flowers to their cabin and a telegram saying, 'I don't expect to get better.' He appeared to be recovering from a mild case of flu. They never saw him again. He died on 3 June, two days before the Clarks were due to disembark from the *Normandie* on their return from New York. 'Chips' Channon provided a partial explanation. He noted that Sassoon, who was fanatically loyal to the Royal Family, had been in bed with a fever and streptococcal throat infection, but had arisen in the middle of his illness when summoned to spend a week-end at Windsor.

In the disastrous winter of 1937–38 there had come yet another blow.

Since his first day at the Gallery some four years before, Kenneth Clark had managed to stay on excellent terms with the trustees. He had, in fact, bent his energies so single-mindedly to that goal that he had overlooked another source of conflict which had, in the past, given his predecessors even more trouble: the National Gallery staff. The people he dealt with on a daily basis: the guards, caretakers, restorers, secretaries, publications staff and photographers, he knew and liked. Many others kept the gallery running and he gave their work little thought. He knew, for instance, that he was technically chief accounting officer, but the work had always been supervised by the keeper, his immediate subordinate Isherwood Kay, and he assumed it always would. He was therefore horrified to learn, early in 1937, that an accountant responsible for paying out the weekly wages had pilfered over £100 from the petty cash.

Kenneth Clark thought he might have to resign but this did not prove necessary. Nevertheless the London papers made the most of the story when the news leaked out in the summer of 1937. A committee of the Treasury concluded that a 'grave lack of supervision' was evident on the part of 'superior officers of the Gallery'. For his part, the director said that 'he had received no precise indications of the functions of an accounting officer and was led to believe that he was entitled to continue to rely upon the keeper for the effective discharge of those functions'.

It was a reasonable defence. It did, however, flout a British Civil Service tradition that the man in charge always assumes the blame, whether or not he is at fault. The incident also brought into sharp relief the painful issue of how much responsibility actually lay with the director. Either he was in charge or he was not. If he was, his immediate subordinates might have thought (with justice) that he should not have evaded his responsibility. He was not playing the game.

There were other reasons. While those who worked with him directly liked him enormously, those who only knew him superficially and met him on busy corridors, predictably found him aloof, stand-offish and cold. There is no doubt that he was far too successful, wealthy and well placed for others' peace of mind. As another friend pointed out, if one were a junior assistant working at the National Gallery and the self-appointed task of one's life was a study of Leonardo da Vinci, it would take years to see every painting and publish one's conclusions. Kenneth Clark, however, might decide to see a canvas in Cracow on Monday, be on a plane on Tuesday and back at his desk on Wednesday with three or four hundred photographs. 'If you are working on a modest salary,' that friend continued, 'you are not amiably disposed towards Kenneth Clark.' It is not surprising therefore that some people were not lenient in their judgements, vowing they would have 'nothing more' to do with him. The forcefulness of the condemnation was an indication of how much injured feeling ran beneath the surface at the Gallery. Some months later, that became painfully obvious.

David Balniel, Kenneth Clark's friend, had just been appointed as chairman of the Board of Trustees (in January 1938) when the keeper, Isherwood Kay, and assistant keeper, Martin Davies, came to see him. They said they wanted to leave the National Gallery. When Balniel asked why, Kay said that the director was determined to whittle down his own position and duties. He answered letters that the keeper had always handled. He gave orders to officials, which was the keeper's duty. He was generally untrustworthy. He would borrow books from the library and not sign them out, then forget to return them. He lost photographs. The staff felt they were not respected by the director. They had admired him at first, but now had no respect for his judgement or ability. The atmosphere at the Gallery was poisonous.

There was the matter of the Giorgiones. The pictures, Davies said, had been examined by the staff and no one was in favour. The director's response was that there seemed little chance that the paintings would be bought. As a result the staff did not prepare a case and were outflanked by the director at the crucial meeting of the Board of Trustees. Contrary to custom, the director had ordered the printing of the labels himself: despite the express wishes of the staff, he called the panels Giorgiones.

Kay brought up another grievance. He felt that the Gallery ought to become an institution of scholarship, and that publicity and popularizing should take second place. They might have a 'popularizer' for a boss but they, it was implied, were the real scholars, the ones on whom the Gallery's reputation depended. The director would be up for reappointment on 1 January 1939. They wanted him out.

Then, on 1 April 1937, Kenneth Clark entered Kay's office and, before he could speak, the latter lost his temper. He had discovered that the director had, without his knowledge, bought a stool for the restorer, price 27s. 6d. It was the last in a series of arrogant moves. The keeper, Kay said, was analogous to the permanent civil service official in a government department. The director was a political figurehead, an outsider. It was the keeper's duty to run the gallery and the director's job not to interfere.

Balniel replied carefully that Kay and Davies had misunderstood the changed nature of their duties. They had based their position on the Treasury minutes of 1852, giving the staff broad powers. It was explained to them that, as of 12 November 1934, the director had taken over.

Kay's feelings, on being held responsible for the embezzlement scandal on the one hand, and being told that the director was in charge on the other, may be imagined. There was nothing for him to do but capitulate and he did. For his part, the director saw no reason why the internal affairs of the Gallery should not run perfectly smoothly. There had been, perhaps, a lack of liaison in the past. This could be overcome by frequent consultations with the staff. He promised to hold weekly meetings. Some weeks after that the assistant keeper, Martin Davies, told the chairman that the atmosphere had improved markedly. The effort required from the director to bring this about may be guessed at from his remark (to his mother) that he would have liked to take a bite out of Mr Davies. Balniel, as ever, smoothed things over. It had been 'a nauseating episode', but it was behind them at last.

The trustees were charming at a meeting early in January and said to a man that the Giorgiones were an excellent purchase and very cheap. They would buy them all over again. This was gratifying, but then the Prime Minister came to see the paintings, liked them very much and told the director to pay no attention to the press. He was very nice, Jane's diary noted. But before that, in December 1937, Kenneth Clark had been given a hearty boost by an old friend, D.S. MacColl. It was particularly welcome. Christmas had been a nightmare. Reporters rang up every half hour for a week about the Giorgiones, Jane told Raymond Mortimer. Then a different set rang up independently about the Duveen row. People were either resigning, having hysterics or both. As for the *Daily Telegraph*, she wrote with a dark reference to Borenius's campaign, someone ought to stop it from being used by private individuals to pay off private grudges.

The *Daily Telegraph* did, at least, print a long letter from MacColl, allowing him to ramble on about attributions in general and the price in particular. Of course that was outrageous, but London was the Mecca of art dealers, and pictures, in their pilgrimage from outer cheapness, acquired merit by leaps and bounds as they approached the shrines of Bond Street. As for the director, he was the first tamer of the trustees since that turn-of-the-century figure, Sir Edward Poynter, and a joy to old hands like himself. Few would approve all his purchases, but everyone could agree with some of them. As the old adage said, no one was exempt from doubtful moves, since only he who did nothing made no mistakes.

In a letter of thanks to MacColl, Kenneth Clark said that he had no great ambition to stay on indefinitely at the National Gallery. However, the fact that certain people were after his arse made him determined not to budge. MacColl could tell his friends to lay off because he was going to be as tough as hell to get rid of. There was only one possible way to counter this uncharacteristic ferocity. Kenneth Clark certainly was a poor debater, MacColl wrote teasingly, though a better one than some. Both of them were a very arrogant, high-nosed pair, much too fortunate for their desserts but, he hoped, a little chastened by adversity in their 'Previtalisner' or other parts, however sustained by 'King Giorgionismus'.

There was a further reason for the incessant phone calls from the press that Christmas: Kenneth Clark was being knighted. Jane's diary shows that on 17 December they returned home from supper at the Savoy to find a letter from Chamberlain offering him a KCB (Knight Commander of the Most Honourable Order of the Bath).

Any other man would have seized on the honour, the mark of royal reassurance, as it were, with gratitude. Kenneth Clark's immediate response was to draft a letter of refusal. Before going to Ascot the next day Jane rang up David Balniel to ask his advice. Balniel answered that her husband absolutely must accept, for the sake of the Gallery if not for himself. That night they travelled down to 'Bellers' tired and depressed.

He was the youngest man to receive a KCB. Despite attacks over the cleaning of the Velazquez, the unpleasant matter of Duveen, the embezzlement, the Giorgiones and the rebellion of the staff, he still had friends in high places. As soon as the New Year's Honours List was published on 1 January 1938 the congratulatory telegrams and letters began to arrive. He doggedly tried to answer all those from friends; there were more than two hundred. How wonderful that it should come just then, to confound the 'pirate submarines', Morshead wrote exultantly. Only a man with a double cataract or both ears perfectly packed with fleas would not know he was a public benefactor, the painter Henry Lamb wrote. Jack Beddington, who was commissioning many of the leading artists of the 1930s, including Graham Sutherland, to design posters for Shell Mex, wrote that he was delighted because he felt that Kenneth Clark was doing more for the things nearest his heart than any other 'business gent' in England.

Logan Pearsall Smith had a few choice thoughts. 'I have always felt that a KCB was just the right distinction – the Garter is too gaudy, & the other orders I regard as dirt. A KCB can hold up his head in any company, undishonoured by a coronet.' Writing to a friend, Kenneth Clark said he thought his critics were running out of things to say about the Giorgiones at last. It was absolutely true that he had come to shudder at the mention of the word but just that day he had taken them off the walls because a restorer needed to look at them. To his astonishment they were as bewitching as ever. He was quite sure they had made no mistake.

A show of outer conviction and, buried beneath it, a poignant melancholy: these were symptoms of Kenneth Clark's mood in the summer of 1938 as he reached the age of thirty-five. The events of that year had caused as much inner turmoil as had the first performance of *Ghosts* in adolescence. Then, he had been convinced that he was doomed. Now, in mid life, the sense of being irretrievably set on the wrong course was symbolized by the image of being lost in a wood,

Another Part of the Wood, as he chose to name the first volume of his autobiography, which ends in 1939.

As happened in adolescence, old wounds were showing the extent to which they had failed to heal and old attitudes of mind the extent to which they had failed to evolve. To think of death in the prime of life is almost axiomatic and those whose creative possibilities are strongest are, perhaps, most poignantly aware of this. However, there is a hint that those who defend themselves most forcefully against a knowledge of their own hostile impulses are most likely to find themselves overwhelmed.

Other clues to the inner struggle can be seen in Kenneth Clark's letter to D.S. MacColl which, if only briefly, gave vent to the anger he felt and his fighting strength, when the chips were down. That he had sealed off whole aspects of his emotional life was becoming apparent to him. That same month he wrote to say how moved he had been by one of Berenson's letters. In an echo of his mother's distraught mood at the death of his father, he equated his own strangled emotional feelings with paralysis of a limb. Even if he could not show it he felt much fondness for him and not just respect, he wrote. Perhaps, as Dante wrote, at this moment of inner turmoil he was coming to himself.

Even though he felt despairingly convinced that he was not capable of writing, life was conspiring to persuade him otherwise. After three years of laborious work he had published his catalogue of drawings by Leonardo da Vinci at Windsor Castle (in 1935) and the rapturous reviews had encouraged him to undertake a book on Leonardo's development as an artist, which was almost finished. Leonardo was very much on his mind when, in December 1938, Berenson sent him his revised volume on the *Florentine Drawings*, finished at last. He looked at the revisions with mingled feelings. They were intimately connected with the whole of his life; with his early ambitions, his first apprenticeship, his high hopes and later regrets. Then the pupil himself published. Kenneth Clark's latest book on Leonardo was a triumph, Eric Newton wrote in the *Sunday Times*. His writing would 'set a new standard in art criticism in this country. His book does not fill a gap so much as reveal the existence of a hitherto unsuspected one.' Raymond Mortimer wrote in the *New Statesman and Nation*: 'I know of no one alive who writes better about painting than the Director of the National Gallery. He reminds us that it is possible to combine erudition with elegance; he is not interested merely in Old

Masters, he cares profoundly for Art; and the result is a book that will instruct the learned, and delight the rest of us.'

The book, Kenneth Clark told Berenson, had been much over-praised by his English friends because they were unused to books on painting being readable at all. Berenson replied with such enthusiasm that Kenneth Clark was overwhelmed. It was clear that he had not expected such an accolade and hardly knew how to respond. Then out it all came again, his private doubts about his writing talent, his fears that he had been advised to take up an administrative post because no one thought much of his abilities as a writer. Now, however, there was a new show of resolution. One sees him mentally squaring his shoulders, convinced of his next moves and eager to be on his way. There was a further rush of affection for Berenson as he realized they would not see each other again for several years (in fact, they did not meet until after the Second World War). He suddenly saw how many precious hours had been frittered away, he wrote, when he might have been spending them with people he really liked.

12 Black as our Loss

'Still falls the Rain –
Dark as the world of man, black as our loss –
Blind as the nineteen hundred and forty nails
Upon the Cross.' – EDITH SITWELL, 'Still Falls
the Rain'

As war became inevitable, Jane Clark faced the prospect with sturdy confidence. She did not for a moment doubt that Britain would win. She told K that she and her team had had a great victory when she was captain of the second hockey eleven at Malvern Ladies' College. They had actually beaten the first eleven by the force of their determination alone. This 'true grit' approach might manifest itself, during a dinner party conversation with an amateur gardener who feared the worst, as a little pep talk. He must think of the Nazis as a rank growth, Jane said, and stamp them out like weeds.

For her husband there were no consoling thoughts. It seemed to him that European civilization was crumbling and behind the façade lurked chaos, disintegration and disaster. He was also sure that Britain would never be the same and there would be no place for people like himself in the post-war world. What he had were the ability to be impartial and certain mental strengths but these frivolous qualities would be useless in the future. He supposed he could be dismissed as an intellectual lightweight but at least he had never lost his conviction of art's intrinsic worth – and now his world was collapsing like a pack of cards.

However, it was his duty to keep up a brave front however black the future looked. Typically, he was mulling over what would become of art once the war ended and had written an essay on the subject for *World Review*. He did not think anyone would be taken in by his optimistic conclusions. His mood was so bleak that action was his only salvation. At least he could take part in the war effort with an absolutely clear conscience because, for intellectuals like himself, it was a battle to the death.

Luckily there was an immediate problem to solve. The paintings at the National Gallery were in danger from the air raids considered inevitable and also, since the British expected to be invaded, from the Nazi fondness for plunder. It was said that Field Marshal Goering had already earmarked the *Rape of the Sabines* for his drawing-room. Kenneth Clark wrote ironically to Balniel that he was awaiting his orders from Berlin. The paintings had to be spirited away, and the sooner the better. During the Munich crisis, Kenneth Clark and Lord Lee worked out a meticulous plan to transport 2,000 paintings to three hiding-places, two of them in Wales. The paintings were on their way when 'Peace in Our Time' was declared and they all came back. Kenneth Clark, under no illusions, expected that the next crisis would occur in April 1939 (he was out by just three months; it came in August). Thanks to the dress rehearsal, he was confident he could cope.

On the evening of 24 August 1939 the code-word message was phoned to Lord Lee. He wrote, 'That same afternoon, up till the normal closing hour, the public were admitted at Trafalgar Square as usual and could see all the pictures hanging in their accustomed places. Then, the moment the doors closed, our respective teams "jumped to it" and by 10.30 the next morning the great vans were arriving.' Three days later almost 800 of the most valuable works had been removed and by Saturday 2 September, the day before war was declared, everything was gone.

Kenneth Clark reorganized his and Jane's private world with the same despatch. They had put Portland Place up for sale and he seemed distinctly relieved. He was heartily tired of so much formal entertaining. The children disliked the house and, what was more, to live there cost slightly more than he could afford. That could be fun for a time but might lead to disaster. They were moving to an apartment at 5 Gray's Inn Square, very charming and so quiet that he could work there peacefully. They would not even need a country house. The interiors were being refurbished by their favourite decorators, John Hill and Marian Dorn, and they were camping out in Portland Place amid walls of packing cases. He looked forward to a future of lively conversation, quiet evenings with books and the kind of relaxed entertaining that a large formal house had positively ruled out.

Jane had to leave London. Children in their thousands were being sent from the danger areas, accompanied by teachers and sometimes

mothers as well. They could no longer use 'Bellers', where they had
spent so many happy week-ends. Kent was out of bounds, since it was
thought that any invasion would hit the south-east coast first. They
therefore looked in the West Country and found a vacant middle-
sized Georgian house that had languished unsold. It was separated by
a road from the hamlet of Tetbury Upton, two miles from the small
town of Tetbury in Gloucestershire. It had many architectural
curiosities, including a salon, a vertical double cube, which took up
most of the centre of the house, leaving little bedroom space on the
second floor. There was a library for their enormous collection of
books, bedrooms for the children in a Victorian wing, and assorted
guest rooms and staff quarters. Since the owners had detested the
main house, preferring to live elsewhere on the grounds, it had fallen
into a picturesque state of decay. The garden was what Jane Austen
would have called 'a very small park', according to their neighbour,
Hiram Winterbotham. They rented Upton House for the duration.

Jane set off at the end of August by car with the three children. It
took hours to arrive. She lost her way repeatedly and had called every
AA man for miles, her husband heard. The last furniture was gone
from Portland Place but it would be months before they could move
into Upton House. There was dry rot in all the floors and he could not
think where Jane was going to store all their things. Meanwhile, she
and the children had found a comfortable inn, The Hare and Hounds,
in Westonbirt near Tetbury, and K moved to his club, the Travellers'
in Pall Mall. At first he was quite at ease. He had put up a little
drawing by Chassériau, there was a Maillol in his bedroom, and he
whiled away the evenings reading Matthew Arnold. However, after a
few days he had taken a dislike to the waiters and the food and had
repaired to Garlands Hotel in Suffolk Street. It was very cheap, only
10s. 6d. a night for a room with a washstand, a decent bed, and
breakfast as well, so that one did not mind its good-natured Dickens-
ian shabbiness. He was within easy walking distance of Trafalgar
Square and his room at the Gallery where, a few weeks later, he was
sitting listening to Maggie Teyte singing Debussy on the radio.

Life continued at the National Gallery even if its frames, with their
gaping holes, were witnesses to a general feeling of emptiness. The
first air raid warning had sounded, a melancholy fading wail like a dog
in the extremities of misery or agony. Like every other Londoner,
Kenneth Clark picked up his regulation gas mask and descended into
the shelters. He subsequently described the mingled feelings of

apprehension and elation that characterized those early weeks. By day Londoners coped with rationing and sandbags. By night, thanks to the blackout, they floundered about in 'the unaccustomed darkness of the streets, bumping into patrolling wardens or huddled strangers ... admiring the gigantic criss-crossing arms of the searchlights as they lit up the sudden silver bellies of the far balloons'.

Walking through the large, empty and ill-proportioned rooms of the National Gallery, Kenneth Clark was attacked by another wave of depression. The Gallery was out of action. Artists were out of work. Theatres were closed and actors on relief. Halls were annexed for the ARP and Fire Services. Just as things looked their worst, the famous pianist Dame Myra Hess came to see him. Like Jane Clark, Dame Myra had a shining and unspotted vision of victory in the midst of despair. She seemed like a messenger of hope to Kenneth Clark, who seized on her every word. She would like to give an occasional concert at the Gallery. Why not a lunchtime concert every day, he responded eagerly. A stage was set up, some chairs were found, and a few paintings not worth evacuating were rescued from the cellars. Dame Myra began her plan of action.

The first concert was unforgettable. People who had queued all along the north side of Trafalgar Square for a chance to get in, sat on the floor and stood in every corner. Myra Hess played Beethoven's *Appassionata* and then the piece that always seemed so personal to her, *Jesu, Joy of Man's Desiring*. As he watched the audience from behind a curtain he saw the faces of her listeners visibly lighten. Reassurance, Dame Myra had called it, but to him they looked like people who had been given back their reason for living. And so, in a way, had he.

He became impresario, stage manager and usher. He showed people to their seats. He managed queues. He sat beside Queen Elizabeth on the day that she, too, quietly came to a lunchtime concert. He even conducted a performance of Haydn's *Toy Symphony*. It was scored for two violins, double bass, keyboard, trumpet, drum, rattle, triangle, quail, cuckoo and nightingale warblers; and was performed by famous musicians. Kenneth Clark was much annoyed that the performers took it as a wonderful musical romp, instead of with proper seriousness. The audience loved it. For a moment the rather austere director of the National Gallery had become, the *Church Times* commented, 'an engaging and piquant figure'.

He was ready to serve on a minesweeper but had been told that he was on a short list of civil servants and should hold himself ready for an important appointment. Meanwhile he had been making week-end visits to Upton House and returning by train, often standing all the way, since it was too crowded even to sit on his suitcase. He was moving the paintings yet again, this time to abandoned slate quarries in Wales where they would remain for the rest of the war.

He had organized an exhibition to fill the empty rooms of the Gallery. The idea of showing contemporary art seemed an effortless way to promote worthy British artists and fill the Gallery, if not with masterpieces, at least with some lively paintings. If it were talked about, so much the better. It was. Two members of the Royal Academy complained that the paintings were 'just jokes by in-competent youngsters who don't know what they're playing at', and that Sir Kenneth was favouring artists he personally admired. He was trying to be a dictator of the arts. Kenneth Clark replied that he had not chosen the works himself and regretted some of the omissions. It was evident, however, that he liked the exhibition's experimental tone. So did many less hidebound viewers. The show, the *Oxford Mail* noted, was one of the most lively and stimulating to be seen in London.

That he was accused of being a dictator of British art – telling the public what to like – was an indication of the position he had achieved by 1940. If there was a radio discussion on art he was sure to be invited. When the Government formed a committee he was on it. As organizer of exhibitions he was first to be asked. 'Opening remarks' were becoming a distinct speciality. When there were refugee artists who had made their escape from Germany and elsewhere, their logical mentor was Kenneth Clark.

While he exhorted artists like Bell and Sutherland to continue working and ignore the war at all costs, he privately fretted about their fate. Letters from artists begging him to find them work arrived by every post. The situation was so desperate that a Committee for the Encouragement of Music and the Arts (CEMA) had been formed, backed by a modest grant from the Pilgrim Trust, in an attempt to create work for artists and the arts in a nation at war. CEMA, the forerunner of the Arts Council of Great Britain, had already organized twenty concerts by London symphony orchestras in indus-trial areas, set up other concerts in factories and asked for Sir Ken-neth's help in arranging for travelling exhibitions. This would help, but then his chance came to do more. The decision was made to enlist artists to record the war, as had been done very successfully during the First World War. He became the War Artists' Committee's first chairman. A number of 1914–18 war artists were young enough to be reappointed. To fill out their ranks he made as many radical choices as he dared. A magazine noted approvingly that the selections belonged to the progressive left wing of art rather than the conventional and academic right. To Kenneth Clark, the overriding concern was that artists should be paid to go on working. That, he told Kathy Sutherland, was the highest form of national service her husband could perform.

The Sutherlands were in acute financial difficulties. They planned to find tenants for their house and live like gypsies so as to make ends meet. There was their fear that Graham would be called up for active duty. Kenneth Clark promised he would personally prevent it. He sent a cheque for £50 and urged them to abandon their ridiculous idea of camping out and join Jane at Upton House. They accepted gratefully. Then Kenneth Clark made sure that Sutherland was appointed a civilian war artist in 1941.

In 1940 Henry Moore was in a similar predicament. His teaching job had come to an end and his little country house was, like that of the Sutherlands, in the danger zone. The Clarks urged the Moores to join them at Upton House. The invitation was accepted, but only for a short time. Moore 'couldn't be away from things', and returned to his studio in Hampstead. He could no longer sculpt because there was no chance of acquiring a handsome hunk of stone or the right tree trunk. To become a war artist seemed logical but did not appeal to him: he had joined up at the age of about nineteen in the First World War, had been gassed at Cambrai and was in hospital for three months afterwards. He said, 'I'd seen enough of war.'

Then one evening Moore was coming back from dinner at the Café Royal and was caught in an air raid. The buses had stopped running so he went into the Underground. He had heard that people were sleeping on the platforms but had never seen it. 'At Piccadilly women were undressing their children right there, while the trains came in and out. People had taken over and there was nothing they could do about it.' He got as far as Belsize Park and was not allowed to leave the station. Anti-aircraft guns had been set up on the outskirts of the city and 'all pandemonium was let loose'. So he stayed in the shelters, observing those sleepers lying helpless, deep in the earth, as if wrapped in winding sheets rather than blankets. Henry Moore filled a

sketchbook full of studies and gave it to the Clarks. Jane Clark hoped
she would live to see the day when the genius of Moore and Sutherland
was recognized. The sketches led to drawings. Four were bought by the
War Artists' Committee, and Moore was paid £50 to do others. Jane
commented that, once these were shown, K hoped to have Moore
made an official war artist, though it was an uphill struggle to convince
officialdom. She added an exclamation mark.

John Piper turned out to be the ideal recorder of bomb damage.
Graham Sutherland made semi-abstract and powerful studies of the
desolation following the bombing in South Wales and London, and
images of destruction in France caused by the RAF bombings of rocket
sites and railway yards. Epstein executed powerful portraits in bronze
and Paul Nash painted beautiful and moving records of the air battles.
Laura Knight painted the Nuremberg trial and Muirhead Bone made
delicate perspective drawings of the city of London, still smouldering
from the bombings. However, the tube shelter drawings were in a
category all their own, inspired works of art.

Those frivolous talents of intellectual energy and impartiality had
some value after all, if they could be put to a larger purpose. This belief
was strengthened by Jane's insistence that K was an important man
whose ideas had national significance. When Kenneth Clark expressed
doubts about joining a Board of Trade committee, his wife urged him
to consider the opportunities it presented for influencing post-war
design. The continual debate between the two voices (the one that
thought he ought to be writing and the one that said he ought to be
contributing) was stilled, for the time being, by the larger necessity of
war. When he was suddenly offered a position as head of the films
division in the chaotic Ministry of Information, he accepted at once,
even though he knew absolutely nothing about films and suspected he
had been appointed because he was supposed to know about 'pictures'. The previous head of films had done nothing and the staff was
completely disoriented, making the opportunities irresistible. He was
soon working ten-hour days and, by the end of January 1940, was
involved in producing twenty-five new documentaries and three short
films designed to show the British public the dire results of 'careless
talk'.

He had expected trouble from the film industry and it came quickly.
A number of them were insulted that the 'Assyrian rug experts' in
charge at the MOI had appointed him in the first place. They pounced on
gaffes major and minor – in one speech he incautiously referred to the

fate awaiting Jews and foreigners if the Germans won – and one trade newspaper pointedly asked whether the war was the moment to start teaching people their business. By then, however, thanks to the timely arrival of Sir John Reith as the new Minister of Information, Kenneth Clark was promoted out of films to a larger role as head of Home Publicity. The *New Statesman* commented that Kenneth Clark could 'begin the job of organizing a side of the work which has languished since the outbreak of the war'.

This was not to be the case. Kenneth Clark's second volume of autobiography describes the internecine struggles which led to his resignation from the MOI and return to the National Gallery, from which he had been given temporary leave. Despite his wife's conviction that he should have become a Member of Parliament because he would have ended up as Prime Minister, Kenneth Clark told Harold Nicolson that he was grateful to leave political life. He was unsuited to it. There is the further factor, that he was being required to convey a positive, inspiring, patriotic and heroic message at a moment when Britain seemed likely to lose the war.

Harold Nicolson, who was also working at the MOI on the home morale campaign, gives the clearest view of Kenneth Clark's life at that moment:

> I go into KC's room for something and there lying on his pillow with eyes upstaring is the most beautiful marble head. For the moment I assume that it is Greek until I look at the hair and lips which are clearly Canova. It is a bust of the Duc de Reichstadt which K had picked up in a junk shop. A tragic & lovely thing. I feel cheered by this. I do so admire K's infinite variety. He does not like being here really and wld be far happier going back to the Nat-Gallery and vaguely doing high-brow war service. Yet he works like a nigger here merely because he loathes Hitler so much.

The night Nicolson looked in on Kenneth Clark's room at the MOI, 8 November 1940, was the night the building sustained a direct hit. Among the hurdles to be surmounted by then was the day and night bombing of London, which had begun in earnest two months before, in September, in preparation for Hitler's invasion of Britain. From then on London was mercilessly attacked. An average of two hundred German bombers came over the city every night for fifty-seven nights in a row. 'At this time', Sir Winston Churchill wrote, 'we saw no end but the demolition of the whole Metropolis.'

The day before the blitz began, Jane took the 9.45 a.m. up from

Tetbury to spend the week-end at Gray's Inn Square. Eddy Sackville-West, K's music-loving friend from Oxford, now an author and critic, had become another of their permanent house guests. He and the children had seen her off and performed an impromptu ballet on the platform. The next day, Saturday 7 September, she and K went to Brighton, an hour's ride on the train, to open an exhibition. That done, they set off back to London. It was a pleasant walk to the Brighton station but they had not gone far when the air-raid siren sounded. The train left for London but, halfway there, pulled to a halt. Victoria Station had been hit and there was a time bomb on the line. So they took to the road and as they crossed the Thames at Chelsea Bridge beside Battersea Power Station, saw flames from fires in the East End lighting up the whole sky. They arrived at Gray's Inn Square and, after having a meal, walked out to look at the fires. They went to sleep in the middle of another air raid and, at about 2 a.m., a 500-pound bomb fell outside and blew out an adjoining flat. Jane told the Earl of Crawford that they were blown out of bed. They and their two servants, Stamp and Jessie, went down to the wine cellar and stayed there while the bombs rained down.

They all left the cellar with great relief at 5 a.m., imagining that the worst was over. The flat at least was intact. K and Jane slept until 9 o'clock and K went to the MOI after breakfast. They lunched with Cyril (Air Chief Marshal Sir Cyril Newall) at Buck's, where they ate with appetite. That evening they were dressing for dinner, trying to decide whether to dine at Claridge's or the Carlton, when another siren sounded. They ignored it until there was an enormous explosion outside their window and they rushed for the wine cellar. There they spent the night, smudged with dust from the blasts, taking swigs of Irish whisky while the bombs fell. The 'All Clear' finally sounded at 6 a.m. and they staggered back upstairs covered with dirt. What they encountered that morning was to become routine: gaping houses, still smouldering, an acrid smell of burning, the sound of shattered glass crunching underfoot and an indescribable pall of desolation. At such moments one thought obsessively of a bath but there was no water at all.

They had tried to treat the bombing as if it were a trifling annoyance but were forced to concede that they were under siege. That day Jane sent Stamp and Jessie to the country. She moved two beds and their best paintings and *objets d'art* into the MOI shelter where K would sleep. Somehow a taxi was found to take her the long way around to Paddington Station, where a refugee train was leaving for the West Country.

At Upton, Jane and the children were out of immediate danger but K was in the front lines. He sometimes went to a nearby restaurant with John Betjeman or Arthur Waley, but one had to dine at 7 sharp as the raids began at 8.15 and even he, with his love of spectacle, did not fancy the trip back through a hail of shrapnel, not to mention bombs. After dinner he worked in his dug-out and slept between 11 p.m. and 7 a.m. Most nights there was a tremendous racket but one could console oneself with the belief that one was hearing British guns. There were frequent daylight raids, some even more danger-ous. Just the day before a great many bombs fell on Howland Street, flattening it in an instant.

London was rather a mess. There had been terrible damage done to the docks, railway stations, power stations, Bond Street, Regent Street, Piccadilly, Kensington Palace ... the list went on and on. The number of handsome buildings that had been destroyed was heartbreaking. Jane dared not return to London and stayed at Upton House, fretting over the valuable furniture and paintings still at Gray's Inn. It seemed only a matter of time before the flat was demol-ished. She was determined to get to London and asked to borrow Lord Lee's car, but he refused. She agreed that it was too dangerous but could not help feeling discouraged. Then she had her first phone call from K for five days. He had just watched two German bombers crashing on Piccadilly in broad daylight and counted five Germans in parachutes. He was amazingly calm, even elated. He had a new crop of funny stories to tell her, he said.

The noisiest raid of the war so far came on Tuesday 8 October. The MOI was hit twice. K tore into the corridor and said it was remarkable how far one could run when one heard a really large bomb falling. Next day, Jane went up to London for fittings at Molyneux. While she was there the sirens went off again and she finished to the noise of bombs and gunfire. She and K walked to Claridge's for lunch, having decided to be machine-gunned drunk rather than sober. K was in the best of spirits and lunch was 'divine'.

By 11 October Jane was back at Upton House and convinced that something awful was about to happen to K. As soon as she woke up that morning she rang the MOI but he was nowhere to be found, so she spent her breakfast in tears. Now that the war was close at hand, their roles were reversed. She was convinced of imminent disaster whereas he was perfectly calm, even buoyant. He was volunteering to be a firewatcher at Westminster Abbey and would not be dissuaded, even though Jane was appalled, because, he argued, no one should be too important to be excluded from such duties. Besides, he seemed to lead a charmed life.

His closest call came on the night of 16 April 1941, the worst night of the blitz. He had been sleeping in a room in the Russell Hotel but, at about 3 a.m., decided the night was getting too noisy and he ought to move to the shelters. These, however, seemed unpleasantly full, so he walked back to the ground floor. Just then the hotel received a direct hit. Miraculously unhurt, he strolled into the street and discovered that the two top floors were on fire. He tried to go back up to his room but was barred: the roof had fallen in. So he walked to the MOI where he discovered a row of corpses, the victims of a direct hit on a house opposite. He spent the night helping the survivors and, next day, appeared at the MOI's policy committee meeting in a blue flannel coat and striped trousers. Everything else had been lost in the Russell Hotel fire.

Then came the news that Jane had feared. The Gray's Inn flat was badly damaged. Nineteen bombs had fallen on the square. When she visited the flat a month later she found it hanging drunkenly out over a void, with everything underneath it torn away. They had lost valuable furniture and paintings though not, as it turned out, one of the things K valued just as much, and which could not be found at first: his full court regalia. A few days later the suit – tails, knee-breeches and black silk stockings – was discovered hanging in a tree. The outfit was sent to be cleaned as a formality since there was nothing wrong with it.

Jane climbed the stairway to the old flat and went inside to look at the forlorn remains. Everything was filthy and wet and there was a Cézanne drawing under the bed. She was suddenly overcome with sadness. They had not liked living anywhere so much since San Martino.

The war changed Jane's life abruptly. Instead of being her husband's indispensable hostess, living on a luxurious scale, pampered, flattered and sought after, she had become an encumbrance, to be despatched into the country because of the children, who were her direct responsibility for the first time. All those languorous hours spent lunching with Churchill, and taking drives around London in taxi-cabs, something she loved to do, had ended. No more brilliant dinners at Buckingham

Palace when the rooms seemed to sway with jewels, no more ex-citement at Portland Place because the Kents, or King George VI and Queen Elizabeth, or Queen Mary, were coming to lunch, to confer the stamp of their gracious favour, the high watermark of her social success. No more tiaras in the royal box at the Opera, fittings at Schiaparelli, and trips to Bucharest, Vienna, Madrid, Paris, and Rome. It was over.

There was a further reason for her depression as she left Portland Place for a life of gloomy domesticity with three children in the depths of the countryside. Kenneth Clark was in love.

During the 1937–38 winter of crisis, when everything that could go wrong did, K had been sustained by Jane's fierce partisan love, but he had also had the loyal backing of a younger woman, someone he had known for several years. By the spring of 1938, just as K seemed to have surmounted the trials triumphantly, their marital relationship was under stress. Jane's diary gives only the obliquest of clues. Some-thing had altered, she wrote. Apparently it was not a change for the better because she was going to try to forget about it. Fortunately Lam appeared to spend the night and they could drop the subject.

K had told Jane of his feelings for the other woman. Jane, baffled and unsure of herself, tried to believe that the problem would resolve itself if she ignored it. For his part, K began to drop into his friend's small flat and leave tokens of his bower-bird's instincts: a Henry Moore drawing, a Siamese head, a Claude Rogers, a painting by Mary Kessell and his cigar boxes. In short, he had taken a mistress.

The closer their union became, the more it seemed to the lady in question that she needed his wife's blessing so as to be sure that, in loving K, she was not taking anything away from him. Jane, too, was determined to behave properly and seemed, to K, to be giving her tacit consent. It seemed the best of all possible situations. The wife was forebearing, the other woman honourable and the gentleman in the case free to wander with a clear conscience.

Jane was thirty-six in the autumn of 1938 and worried about getting older. Without being exactly ill, she was seldom really well. For her, daughter of a doctor, everything came to an immediate halt when illness threatened. The patient, whether husband or child, was en-titled to an immediate cessation of hostilities and the tenderest sym-pathy, coddling and much anxious hovering until the danger was past. As she treated her nearest and dearest, so Jane considered herself entitled to the same consideration, however minor the infection. She was particularly dependent on what the children called her 'puffer', Bedford Russell's prescription of a solution of ephedrine and co- caine. It was originally given for sinusitis but, for Jane, became a universal cure-all, to which she flew at the slightest symptom of dis- tress, physical or mental, although it did not always stop her bad headaches. Since her sinusitis was a chronic condition, it is possible that the prescription contained a strong dose of cocaine. Cocaine is known to deaden the nerve and taste buds and increase endurance so that the user can work for long periods without feeling hungry. It brings a temporary 'high' but depression can follow, along with headaches, and habitual use can lead to permanent damage to the pancreas. Cocaine also dilates the pupils. Morna Anderson remem- bered that, in the mornings, the pupils of Jane's eyes looked so enormous that one could not see the irises. Lady Anderson also recalled how dependent Jane was on her puffer. Once they were about to take a train to Northampton together when Jane discovered that K had forgotten to bring her puffer, 'and she gave him such a wigging...'.

After noting enigmatically that there was some marital discord, Jane had a long bout of what seemed like appendicitis. Mysterious pains came and went during the summer of 1938. In the early autumn she was ill with some kind of infection. She convalesced in bed at 'Bellers' during the Munich crisis, making lavender bags as she listened to Churchill's speeches. She was very pale and thin and tired easily. K told Berenson that he himself was better than ever 'and flourish like an old sinner'.

Jane's state of mind on that long journey from London with the children may be imagined. It was her duty to take them to safety yet, because of the crisis, she was obliged to leave the field clear for another woman. Colette remembers that car trip for another reason.

'It was my first rude awakening,' she said. 'I evidently behaved very badly in the car and my mother wasn't used to it. Actually I don't think I was so bad. And she was absolutely livid. She became an enemy for the next ten years. A major enemy.' It gave her, she said, 'an awful fright'. Once they had settled into The Hare and Hounds, the rows began in earnest. John and Myfanwy Piper, with four children of their own, thought that Jane was intolerant of normal behaviour and 'schoolmarmish'. Hiram Winterbotham, a constant visitor to Upton House, thought that Jane had obsessive ideas and that her children failed to conform. To Jane, Colette was a perversely difficult child; to Colette, her mother was a bully, someone who wanted total obedience to her will. Two women of forceful character had locked head on and no one in the family seemed able to intercede. Colin, who was made of different mettle, used to ask Colette why she did not weep, as he did, knowing that their mother would melt the moment she saw tears. Colette scorned such tactics. To her it was outrageous to be unjustly treated and then forced to capitulate.

'What was she like? Scathing, sarcastic, angry. Her fists would be clenched and her face distorted with rage. She'd say, "You are a spoilt, stupid, selfish girl and I wish you were dead." She was as bad as mad persons. The expression on her face ... I dreamed about my mother being angry until two or three years ago and so did Alan.'

What was so frightening to Jane's children was the suddenness of her rages, coupled with an unnerving ability to switch moods. She could be trembling with anger at one moment and then, a second later, when strangers entered the room, the quintessence of the gracious hostess; outside her family she never let down her guard. Colin once told John Sparrow, his father's friend from Winchester days, how many times his mother had lost her temper that day and Sparrow was dumbfounded. He said, 'I had no idea Jane was like that.' The only time Graham Sutherland caught a glimpse of this aspect of Jane was during their stay at Upton. He said that a shopkeeper came to the door asking to be paid for a bill he owed. Jane 'absolutely berated him' for not having paid it.

Alan Clark remembers the same unpleasant transformation once they left London and moved to Upton. His mother would have, he said, 'a screaming rage' if a raincoat were not hung up in the hall. 'The causes were trivial and forgotten. Anything would do to send her off.' She became the enemy and stayed that way. 'I flinched when she touched me.'

Colette said Alan would try to defend her, 'but he got into so much trouble that it was hardly worth it'. Her father said nothing. He would not, for instance, murmur that they should pay no attention. It was rather that he would be 'absolutely adorable' to them, and send them 'loving and sympathetic glances'. Colette remembers only one occasion when her father stood his ground, when they were on their way by train to a holiday in Wales.

My mother was with me and Alan and she sent papa on ahead to get seats. When he did she said they were bad and began to scream at him. That is the only time I remember him answering back. 'I have done my best,' he said, and walked away. Mother was very sobered. She had lost face in front of us and was embarrassed. I remember that she sat between us and we all sat there trembling together and she was terribly sweet. A quarter of an hour later, he came back, and she was adorable, as if nothing had happened.

Kenneth Clark says that he tried to stop Jane from being so 'beastly' to Alan, with remarks like 'Oh no, no, no, you mustn't.' Remembering that, his face flushed. Alan cannot recall having had anyone at all on his side. He said that he could not confide in his father: 'I might have tried, but there was a tacit understanding that "one didn't".' However, he was marvellous as a friend, 'and just occasionally you got a kind of intimacy ...'. Alan was not so much aware of being unhappy as frustrated, he said. However, an old family friend thought that Alan had been terrorized by his mother and that lasting damage had been done. Years later he had seen a grown-up Alan distraught when he had to speak to his mother on the telephone.

Colin escaped completely because he was, he explained, the favourite and so his mother was always making excuses for him and defending him. After a terrible scene his mother, trembling, would rush for her puffer. If that did not work she would have a stiff drink.

The children believed that their father suffered from their mother's outbursts because of the way he 'tiptoed' around her. A hint of the way he tried to deal with things is contained in a letter of apology he wrote to Jane in which he seemed abject yet obliquely on the defensive. It was true that he was an idiot, he wrote, although not as much of one as he used to be, and powerless to help, though not as bad as he looked, and indolent and slipshod. Nevertheless he realized that she was really angry with life in general and that was why he sometimes got it in the neck. He was her whipping boy in other words. A good friend of Jane's thought that Kenneth Clark was hopeless at dealing with her outbursts. 'He would react defensively instead of telling her to shut up.'

Things might have been worse. Colette commented that her father had enormous energy and great recuperative powers. 'I promise you he was very extroverted. He adored life and was always laughing and wanting to laugh.' Even though they thought he was weak for not defending them, they loved him dearly. He was one of them, in the same boat.

Whenever the children were not there, Jane was 'terribly happy' with K. 'She thought he was without flaw,' Colette said.

We never heard her say a word against him. When he wasn't there she always talked about him as a sacred figure and then she would be bloody to him the moment he walked into the hall. We were so sorry for him. We used to whisper, 'She was absolutely sweet while you were away.' She was always nicer to us when he wasn't there for us to adore and her to be jealous of.

What saved them all, Colette said, was being sent to boarding-school. The other factor was her father's love.

I do remember only two moments in my childhood when I knew perfect bliss and they were when we were with my father. He adored me and my mother knew it and we couldn't talk together or laugh together in a room when she came in, or she was in a rage. We practically had to meet secretly like lovers. Then she would come down to breakfast and we'd have a row every single breakfast. She was always in a bad temper. So we got her to have breakfast in bed, and that was bliss, but still we had to be careful because she couldn't bear to hear us laughing.

When the children were due home for the holidays, 'Mother cried for a week. It's not nearly so simple as it looks. She sent us wonderful clothes and wrote to us every other day. She was angelic when we were ill and would read to us for hours. She was terribly conscientious to do the right thing. She meant to be good.'

A perceptive observer of the Upton household provides a clue in his description of Jane's mother who, although in her seventies, was working as a volunteer doctor at a county mental hospital in Lancashire during the war. In contrast to Alice Clark, whom he found worldly and rather spoilt, Mrs Martin was an indomitable woman of great selflessness but a prickly saint who set herself, and others, extremely high standards. One morning, when he arrived at Upton House, he found Jane in tears. She had made the mistake of sending her mother an expensive box of chocolates, her favourite Charbonnel & Walker, and the gift had been returned with a stiff note about the appropriateness of such items in wartime. If Jane were treating her children as she had been brought up, with the same fierce perfectionism, she also suffered from guilt and remorse which expressed itself in indirect ways. She was dreadfully upset about a film she had seen about a battered child, she noted in her diary. She was ashamed of her reluctance to take care of her children. Something, she wrote, must be wrong with her maternal instincts.

These constant outbursts were the dominating aspect of family life.

Colette said, 'As a measure of how bad it was, I don't think we had one meal in a month when someone didn't leave the dining room in tears. Then I also remember my father saying to me, "What is going to help mamma?" and I answered, being a child, "Perhaps when the war ends?"'

Upton House was taking shape, thanks to the ministrations of Eddy Sackville-West, who had thrown himself into the work of restoration. The salon had been transformed by paint and paintings. They had borrowed a gramophone and a piano from Lord Crawford and Eddy played records or *études* on the piano, to Jane's great delight. The salon was the ideal place for chamber music and Eddy was helping Jane to organize a series of concerts in aid of the RAF benevolent fund. The Sutherlands were also gratefully living at Upton, after declaring their willingness to cook, keep house, do the gardening and look after the twins in return. There were other visitors, 'Bomber' Harris (Marshal of the Royal Air Force Sir Arthur Travers Harris, Commander-in-Chief of Bomber Command), and that interesting young politician, Anthony Eden, much quoted by Jane at parties. 'Anthony thinks', she would begin, and her guests would ask, 'Anthony who?' Lord Lee, by now an honorary uncle, lived just down the road. Life, for Jane, went on, perhaps not as grandly as at Portland Place, but with vestiges of the old splendour. One still dressed for dinner in black tie. Once Churchill popularized the siren suit, a one-piece outfit resembling factory overalls, Hiram Winterbotham took it up and wore it to dinner despite Jane's vehement objections.

The Sutherlands remember their charming suite on the top floor: a bedroom, studio and bathroom. Breakfast was sent up and the Sutherlands lunched and dined with whoever was in residence. Kathy Sutherland protested that she could not live at Upton because she lacked the right wardrobe, and Jane had gaily answered, 'We'll all have coupons [for clothes rationing] and we'll all be in the same boat', but Kathy noticed that she was always dressed exquisitely in Schiaparelli creations and never wore the same costume twice. Whenever Jane was there the Sutherlands were nobly wined and dined. However, Jane periodically went to London, leaving Alice Clark in charge. She was 'a very puritanical and stiff old lady who gave us water and herrings'. Mrs Clark was also disapproving on the subject of drink, although the Sutherlands knew that she kept a bottle of gin beside her bed. She also did not trouble to hide her lifelong dislike of artists. 'She was always thinking that Graham led a dissolute life and asking him when he was going to join up.'

Then there was the terrible time, during one of Jane's absences, when Eddy Sackville-West uncovered an 'Aladdin's cave' of pre-war delicacies and complained about the spartan diet being imposed upon them by Mrs Clark. Jane felt obliged to suggest that Eddy should go. He responded with tears and a nose-bleed. He said he would commit suicide if he had to leave. He had been happy at Upton for the first time in his life. Jane felt sick at intervals and had ferocious headaches. Meanwhile, London was being bombed.

There was another confidant to relieve the tedium of life at Upton, the composer William Walton. While at Oxford Walton had become a close friend of the writer and aesthete Sacheverell Sitwell. When he left, the eccentric, talented Sitwell family – Sacheverell, the poet Edith and writer Osbert – gave him a home in their Chelsea house for the next fifteen years. Subsequently Walton was taken up by the society hostess Alice Wimborne, a great music lover, who provided him with a room in which to compose and eventually left him a house and substantial income in her will. By then Walton had achieved remarkable recognition for his compositions. First there was his work *Façade*, written to accompany some satirical poems by Edith Sitwell, then a viola concerto and *Belshazzar's Feast*, an oratorio for chorus, orchestra and two brass bands. When he was commissioned to write the *Crown Imperial March* for the coronation of King George VI in 1937, William Walton had arrived.

'Willie', as she called him, was constantly at Upton, taking Jane to lunch and listening patiently to her harangues about the plumbers and workmen and children and staff. She, in turn, was beginning to keep the same notes about his daily doings and artistic aspirations – he was then working on the music for a film version of Shaw's *Major Barbara* – that she had about K at Portland Place. Then one day Willie declared his love for her. How serious was he? How interested was she? That night she dined alone with K and realized how much she loved him. She rang Willie next morning and must have told him just how lucky she felt because he reacted with an outburst. Jane was more confused than ever.

Kenneth Clark began to emerge as a film personality early in the war years. In a film called *Listen to Britain*, he had a cameo role as a listener at a Myra Hess concert, seated beside a radiant and winsome Queen Elizabeth. In *Out of Chaos* he took on the larger task of introducing a film about the work of war artists. His aplomb, standing beside a magnificent desk and a statue of a Madonna and Child, was remarkable. In a few bold clear strokes he sketched in the outlines. The profile was more youthful, the voice pitched a trifle higher, but it was otherwise the Kenneth Clark millions of viewers would come to know, exquisitely dressed, and with that way of squaring his shoulders slightly before plunging into an assertion, and running his tongue rapidly across his teeth, oddly self-revelatory mannerisms which are, on camera, the essence of successful self-projection.

The moment the Ministry of Information was behind him he began to fill his time with 'delectable' alternatives. Besides appearing in wartime films he was lecturing with such marked success that, at the end of one appearance, the audience stood up and cheered. He was organizing exhibitions and launched a scheme to put the old masters back on view one at a time. The public, starved for the sight of beauty, bombarded him with letters nominating their favourites and came in such numbers that the temporary exhibit became one of London's most popular activities of the war. He broadcast on the BBC on such themes as *Art and Life*, demonstrating his ability to talk rapidly and persuasively, in terms the average listener could understand. He joined the BBC's popular *Brains Trust*, and the *Sunday Dispatch* dubbed him 'gentle in appearance, but clear and forceful in his views'. He published a sequel to a short book on details of paintings at the National Gallery that, to his surprise, received such comments as, 'if anything, more exciting than the first'. He returned to an early interest, Leon Battista Alberti, a model humanist, fabulously proficient in mathematics, music and physical exercises, and skilled as a painter. Kenneth Clark's fancy might have been taken by the thought that, when ill, Alberti had been cured by a beautiful landscape. He persevered, but was unable to write the book he had hoped for; a few lectures were the only result.

He returned with vigour to the 'letters' column of *The Times*, where he conducted a new battle in defence of the highbrow. Out of this came a 3,000-word pamphlet which now exists only as a reference in Jane's diary. Its intriguing title was, 'To Hell with Materialism: An Aesthetic for Democracy'. He was writing about the English romantic poets and landscape painting and, Jane's diary for 1940 noted, planned to write a book on the subject of the nude as soon as possible.

He was running as fast as ever and, on the occasions when he was invited to stay overnight with Colin and Morna Anderson at Gerrards Cross, would scrupulously tell Jane that he was taking the 'other woman'. Jane felt sure it was wrong but did not want to make a fuss.

Dealing with the 'other woman' preoccupied Jane at this time and, as usual, she reacted rather than acted. If the lady made a scene because she felt herself neglected whenever Jane was in town, Jane would urge K to ring her up and comfort her. Next day she would cheerfully record that there had been an improvement. Yet whenever it was clear that the other had been consulted first – about a piece of writing, or a planned job move, usurping Jane's role as Number One wife – Jane was infuriated. She would then note placidly that she had gone to lunch with K and given him a wigging. She could not help musing about K's new relationship and their present predicament. They had been so happy in Italy, surrounded as they were by beauty, and with no one else in their lives. The theme filled her mind. In the summer of 1941 she noted that K had published an article without first showing it to her. It seemed as if their life together had ended.

Some time after that K asked Jane how to end his relationship with the other woman without hurting her. Jane, much mollified, thought of some tactful words. Still K continued to see her, and Jane to be privately unhappy, falling back on Willie. That same summer she discovered an old letter from K's lady friend and read it. If letters like this had come to K then their marriage must really be on the rocks. Just at that moment K walked through the door. She had to believe that it was over, he said. They had tried to make things work but the experiment had been a disaster. The only thing that still concerned him was how to break things off without making his friend utterly miserable. His voice carried complete conviction.

The 'other woman episode' was over. Jane should have been relieved and happy but was still tormented. After one bad night, a telegram and letter came from K but they failed to lift her spirits. She was so tired and depressed that she would never be able to enjoy life again. That she should be so miserable was doing the children an injustice, she wrote, artlessly revealing the process by which she, when angry, vented her anger on others and then looked for someone to blame. K was in the best of moods but she was perpetually sad nowadays. Had Jane Clark known the reason for her husband's buoyant mood, she would have been unhappier still. By then he had met Mary Kessell.

13 'Green Grow the Rashes, O'

'The sweetest hours that e'er I spend,
Are spent among the lasses, O.' –
ROBERT BURNS

When Kenneth Clark first met her, Mary Kessell was an unknown artist eleven years his junior. She was born in Ealing, on the western outskirts of London, in 1914, one of fraternal, rather than identical, twin girls. Her parents had Mary's aptitudes tested as a child and were told she was a born artist. At the age of sixteen she was sent to Clapham Art School for three years. She then won a scholarship to the Central School of Arts and Crafts, the most important training centre for artists at that time, and was there for four more years. In 1937, as she came to the end of her studies, Mary Kessell began to specialize in illustration. Her teacher recommended her as illustrator for a humorous poem by Sir Osbert Sitwell, *Mrs Kimber*. Then she was hired by Jack Beddington, that enlightened patron of art, and while at Shell Mex came to know the poet John Betjeman and some of Beddington's coterie, including Kauffer and Sutherland. In December 1937 she was one of a group of artists invited to tea at Portland Place.

Two years later came her first big opportunity when she was hired to illustrate *The Dictionary of Love*, a work by an anonymous eighteenth-century French writer being edited by Theodore Besterman, an expert on Voltaire. Some time afterwards she sent Kenneth Clark a shy letter asking whether she might show him her original drawings for the book. Kenneth Clark subsequently wrote some kind words about them. To have his written testimonial was a real coup, but it was in vain. The book was about to be published when, in one of the early raids on London, all the type was destroyed.

Mary Kessell had an extraordinarily retentive visual memory. If, for example, she saw a man working in a field, she would recall every detail of the scene long afterwards, the clothes he wore, the colour of his skin and the way he wielded his spade. Her bold, powerful sketches, full of condensed imagery, showed the strong influence of Rouault, but without his crudeness; she was always a delicate observer. Then, when she began to paint in 1938, her work showed a new aspect. Fragile, barely defined shapes were floated across landscapes so tenuous that they looked, one critic said, as if a moth had painted them. Such poetic reverberations were not surprising since Mary Kessell read verse constantly. She liked the mystics and seventeenth-century poets, Donne, Marvell and Milton. The Bible, Greek mythology and translations of Chinese poetry were other influences upon her severely restrained style. One writer observed that her art portrayed a tranquil and serene vision of life, overcast by a small cloud of sadness.

She was strikingly beautiful. In common with Jane, she had clearly defined features with wide cheekbones and lustrous eyes, but she was more classically lovely and, since she wore her abundant hair in bizarre styles of her own invention, inevitably attracted attention. She was equally nonconformist in her dress. She liked hand-made, swirling capes and wore trousers long before that became the uniform for the young. On a trip to Italy she once went in a monk's outfit and, when curious Italians followed her on the street, was reduced to tears. To express her taste unconventionally, even eccentrically, had less to do with self-display than an instinctive and original talent.

Mary Kessell was, it was said, very much influenced by her parents' religious beliefs, their vegetarianism, their faith in natural healing and their gentleness with animals. These she loved passionately, but then, Mary Kessell always championed the helpless and suffering, from whatever branch of the animal kingdom. She was warmly affectionate and without the least social guile. She was, however, growing to adulthood at the start of the Second World War, when the future for any artist looked bleak, let alone one just starting her career. By then she must have heard how helpful K could be if he liked an artist's work. He liked Mary Kessell's subtle compositions very much indeed, and thought her talent was exceptional.

At the start their friendship was that of patron for a bright new talent. She was part of a group, at parties with the Sutherlands, Pipers and Moores, someone to be mentioned in Jane's dutiful record of teas, dinners and after-theatre *soirées*. By Christmas 1940, when K was declaring his disenchantment with the 'other woman', Mary had moved to Bath where she was working on drawings, among them sketches of the adorable children who belonged to a family running the Chinese laundry. There was a betraying note of warmth in her insistence that he must somehow get enough petrol to come to Bath. She also mentioned some wonderful memories of London, unforgettable ones.

That they should fall in love was almost inevitable. Early in 1941 K bought a quaint, small white house, Capo di Monte, on the edge of Hampstead Heath, which had associations with Mrs Siddons, the famous actress, and they met often, taking long walks in the snow on the heath. Mary was everything he had found so attractive about Jane: spontaneously affectionate, warm and impulsive, but without Jane's artificialities and pretensions. Unlike Jane, Mary made no demands. She seemed happy with him and just as happy alone with her work. Since Jane was away there were few constraints. She was adorable, irresistible.

Being a twin herself, Mary was entranced by Colette and Colin. Colette remembers meeting her just after the move to Capo.

> My father said, 'I have got a sweet lady coming to see you. She's not like the kind of ladies you are used to,' he said, making apologies for her. She certainly wasn't. I remember her velvet skirts and white embroidered blouses and the gypsy earrings she used to wear, her hair in a scarf. She had a sweet and beautiful voice, a very special voice. I remember her sitting on the stairs and hugging us and thinking, 'Is this what he meant?' She was incredibly warm and terribly funny. She was totally interested in one and one confided in her and told her everything. Col and I worshipped her.

The meagre emotional rations meted out by Kenneth Clark's mother were having their delayed effect. He was aware, he said, of having been very much neglected by her. If he had been angry at such short shrift, he had ceased to feel it.

Unmet needs for affection can, however, become indiscriminate. No one can fill the emptiness which is perceived as ravenously destructive. Had Kenneth Clark ever caught a glimpse of the power of this longing he would have been appalled. For the most part he kept it well hidden. What he did experience was his own need in mirror image, in the seductive and beckoning glances of women. There is no doubt that women found him startlingly intelligent, handsome and charming, and he was in a position of power. No wonder they fell.

Why K should need to experiment at this period is another question. There was the apparent fact that he was separated from Jane for the first time, after fifteen years of marriage. Furthermore, he had never undergone any of the normal testing of young adults. In meeting and marrying (almost) the first woman he met, he had disregarded an important intermediate stage, the merits of which he was discovering. His first affair coincides with that period, in the summer of 1938, when he was questioning the whole direction of his life. There was the further factor that, during the war years, the usual mores were suspended if not dispensed with entirely. People who would never have met, let alone fallen in love, were throwing caution to the winds before it was too late.

K needed and wanted to be loved. Yet, as has been noted, the person who has been emotionally deprived in childhood is not well equipped to deal with close relationships. To him, the longed-for love brings with it a terrible price. One has lost one's unique individuality and, as has been seen, such a person has an insecure sense of himself to start with. Much as he longs for the bliss of fusion, he has equal reason to fear it. What is desired and feared presents an impossible dilemma: he must be close enough to feel loved, yet far enough away not to be sucked into an emotional maelstrom.

Here, then, was the crux of the problem with Jane. She gave him the fierce loyalty and protective warmth that he needed, but her price was the submerging of their single identities into a joint 'we' in which her needs loomed largest. The slightest deviation from her exacting standards brought about her retaliation and some severe psychic rebuffs. To protect that inner fortress he had determined to maintain against all attack, he did something very characteristic. He walked away.

He saw it as self-defence. She was, he said later, sexually inexperienced, almost puritanically so, and very easily shocked. He called her 'desperately innocent'. Perhaps it was after the birth of the twins that she began to withdraw sexually. She did not make him feel loved.

The dictates of circumstance placed emotional safeguards on his relationship with Mary. As long as he was safely married there was little danger of his becoming dangerously committed to Mary. As long as he had Mary, he could keep Jane, with her imperious demands and smothering love, at bay. He loved Jane and never meant to leave her. He was merely placing the necessary psychic distance between them; he always protected himself from women by women, John Piper remarked. And, if he felt remorse, he could console himself with the thought that Jane had Willie Walton — an association equally without peril, since Willie had his own more or less permanent attachment. It worked so well that, for years, Mary Kessell was the beloved friend of the family that she wanted to be. She even went on holidays with them in Wales. On such occasions, Jane might go out to dinner with Willie while K went out with Mary. Mary came to family celebrations. She took the children on outings. She was always at their big parties although, it was noted, she did not like to circulate; she wanted to sit in a corner with K and talk about art, music, poetry, life. It worked because Jane silently acquiesced. 'It is almost impossible to know how much the other person knows, but I think she knew a great deal,' he said.

Although K never considered leaving Jane, Mary clearly believed that one day he would. In her happiest moments she would beg him not to worry about her, reassure him of his generosity and goodness to her, and reiterate her conviction that life had fated them to be together. Moments such as the Bank Holiday Monday when, under a hot sun, he gave her a rose and told her how happy he was, were all the proof she needed. She loved him as a man and needed him as a patron. He filled both roles as well as he humanly could. At other times, less sure of his love, she would write disjointed, painful letters. She was paying a high price for his love: an extremely lonely life. When he had to cancel their plans for tea or a drink, she was desolate. She would go walking on the heath in the snow and think of their first walk the year they fell in love, the times they had gone out together, meeting his friends, or had read books together and listened to music. She wanted proof that she was still part of his life. She did not want to be a door at the end of an alley, a shameful secret. To be abandoned by him made her feel as bereft as a widow. Why hadn't she been invited to dinner since the previous Christmas? Why weren't the children coming to visit? At such moments she would be certain that Jane had somehow entered the secret part of his psyche that no one should enter and was destroying him. Mary thought that Jane did not love him, but she would never leave him. He need not panic, because he could have it all, if he was daring enough. If he would only have the courage.

Perhaps Mary chose to ignore the effect that a long relationship (it lasted for fourteen years) was bound to have on Jane. Colette remembers saying heatedly, when her mother was angry, 'There are three people in the world I love: Col, Father and Mary —' and immediately realizing what a blunder she had made. Jane must have thought that Mary had stolen not only her husband's affections, but even those of her children. Colette used to visit Mary in secret but, just the same, Jane always knew and would say accusingly, 'I know where you've been. You've been to see Mary Kessell.' Then the Clarks moved from their tiny house to a large imposing mansion, Upper Terrace House, close by, and Mary moved to a small house in Mount Square a stone's throw away. Jane knew perfectly well what was happening and would have been inhuman not to resent it.

The moves took place just as the war was ending. To have his mistress literally at his doorstep, almost another member of the family, was as much of a public statement as he dared to make and Mary knew it. Mary Kessell was K's steadfast love during the 1940s but far from being the only one. The enchantment he had felt from the age of eleven had returned in force. Everywhere he looked, entrancing creatures appeared with magical smiles and dazzling glances.

There was, for instance, Joan Moore, whose ability to talk with bewitching animation is referred to by James Lees-Milne in his diary of the war years, *Ancestral Voices*. She was the wife of Garrett Moore, later the Earl of Drogheda, a man Lees-Milne described as 'tall, thin, willowy, sharp-featured, distinguished and patrician. A poetic and romantic-looking man', and she was an accomplished pianist. When K saw her playing the clavichord in the drawing-room of the interior designer Marian Dorn, he was immediately intrigued. For her part, she wrote him letters confiding her delight in Serge Aksakhov's book *Years of Childhood*. She listened raptly to his lectures. She commented on his radio appearances, teasingly considered herself his pupil and thought he was the most amazing person she had ever met. It was a friendship without peril since both, from the first, skirted deeper waters.

There were other loving friendships; with 'E', who might ring on a busy Monday to confide her marital troubles, and send him postcards illustrated with eighteenth-century paintings of lovers meeting; with an architect, who debated ideas with him, listened to his lectures and would sometimes need to be fortified with a drink before she could tell him just how good he was. There was a young artist with whom he discussed Constable and Turner, and who confided her dream of founding an art gallery in the town in which she had been born. There were transient admirations, for people like the writer Rosamond Lehmann whom he thought, when they first met, the most beautiful woman he had ever seen. Many of the women to whom he was attracted either had liaisons or were married, as if part of their allure lay in his success in deflecting their interest from a rival onto himself.

There were lovely, serene, smiling women whom one might admire mutely from afar, or not so mutely, as it turned out: to her astonishment, he made a passionate declaration of love to Morna Anderson. There were tender friendships with women like Vivien Leigh and Irene Worth – he had fallen for actresses ever since childhood. There was Myfanwy Piper, the writer and editor, who knew she could write grumbling letters letting off steam about her round of cooking, housework, and child care, and find a sympathetic ear. She wrote worried letters about his being too thin and tried to cheer him whenever he seemed depressed with the advice that he should not be too self-sacrificing. Her cool-eyed comments about his own work, made with all the detachment of a fine critical intelligence, must have been particularly welcome since she had a strong belief in his literary powers and, still more, his poetic approach to art. Hers was the ideal friendship, tactful, stimulating and undemanding. She was concerned, almost motherly, and always there.

The man who needed love badly was finding it in the most unexpected places. It must have seemed like the sweetest of all balm for old wounds; welcome redress for those bad old years of isolation and self-denial. He had evolved a method, that of compartmentalizing his life – 'egg-boxing', one friend called it – that worked remarkably well. For a time he rented a flat at 44 Dover Street, and there love letters could be sent and visits made quietly and unobtrusively. He was so successful, in fact, at keeping the private K safely removed from the public image that many of his ladies earnestly believed they were the only ones and then, when this became impossible, that they were the most important ones – he never could resist telling them what they wanted to hear. And, if a woman were not too demanding, he might stay distantly loving indefinitely. However, not everyone was prepared to take him as lightly as Joan Moore, as sensibly as Morna Anderson or as patiently as Mary Kessell.

One such dangerous episode came just after the Second World War, when he received an invitation to visit the Melbourne Gallery in Australia and give his advice, all expenses paid. By chance, one of the Orient Line ships, the *Orcades*, was making its maiden voyage to Australia just then and the Andersons were to be passengers. The three of them – Jane, as has been noted, hated travelling by sea –

embarked on this delightful trip. Then, as luck would have it, Colin became ill. He and Morna disembarked en route and returned to England. K was left to continue the journey alone.

By the time he came to write about that fateful trip to Australia, all K could remember was the brazenness of the women passengers. It was, even thirty years later, a memory painful enough to put him on the defensive. In fact, he had been very glad of the company of an Australian friend of Morna's, Barbara Desborough, who was returning to Australia to live with her English husband and children. Sir Colin Anderson described her as an intriguing but also rather infuriating woman with red hair and freckles. Apparently she did not relish the thought of life in Australia and poured out her troubles to K's sympathetic ear on long morning walks. He tried to cheer her up and was rewarded by seeing her turn a hopeful smile in his direction.

A relationship begun largely out of sympathy and propinquity rapidly took the kind of turn he rightly dreaded. By October 1949 the lady was back in London, having left her husband and children. She was preparing for a divorce and announced her intention of devoting herself to K. But, as far as he was concerned, Jane only needed to tell him how happy and lucky she was for a rush of warmth to engulf him. He would then turn back in her direction, contrite and promising to reform. That should have ended things, but the lady was made of sterner stuff. The Andersons had bought a five-storey mansion in Hampstead, Admiral's House, on a hill directly overlooking Upper Terrace House, and Mrs Desborough was seeking to be invited to lunch. This, Morna Anderson believed, was because of the excellent strategic advantages their house afforded as a look-out point. K appealed for help and, Lady Anderson said uncomfortably, 'We defended him from her.'

The refusal of one lady to take him lightly was equalled by the determination of yet another. She was a few years his junior, and on the edge of his world like so many women whose interests in art, poetry, literature and music led them to take dispiriting jobs as secretaries and research assistants. Their paths crossed often in those years, first at the Ministry of Information, where she met him in corridors, then at the National Gallery. Like his other admirers she was dazzled by his learning and charmed by the fact that, unlike some clever men, he did not make one feel foolish. By turns artless and tentative, her letters became bolder as she realized he would take her 'scoldings' without demur. So she lectured him about art. She gave him earnest advice about his private life. She tried to bring him to God.

She must have seemed charmingly skittish, admiring and volatile, by turns the scolding aunt and contrite little girl. Her admiration must have seemed flattering and her friendship unforced. She seemed perfectly content with a *rendez-vous* by the lions at the entrance to the British Museum, with a beer in a local pub, with a half-hour interval of tea and cakes. If they did not meet she simply sent her love gift-wrapped in long letters which he, judiciously, asked to be sent to his club.

When, however, he tried to break things off, she fought like a drowning creature. There was something claustrophobic about her conviction that she was going insane and would do violence to herself or him unless he would see her. Abject pleas were interspersed with extremely detailed descriptions of his shortcomings. He had struck her a mortal blow. Women always suffered more in love, it was their fate. However, since they had both sinned, they must make restitution to God. This time the man could not get off scot free. He had taken and he must pay.

He seemed paralysed by her stranglehold on his life. Months after she had apparently accepted the inevitable she was still trying to re-establish the relationship and asking for money. She had discovered his secret: that the clinging of a frantically determined woman was his private proof of worth. She knew the price he was willing to pay for such reassurance.

In his autobiography, Kenneth Clark made several references to his mother's singular inability to laugh, indeed express any feelings. That dampening aspect of her character, as someone closed off from the world in a room of her own choosing, pervades his memoirs. Others described her as 'a cold fish', 'stuffy', 'cold and sexually inhibited', 'small and flinty', or parsimonious and prudish. In later years Kenneth Clark went to some pains to aver that his mother became much more human and likeable after his father died.

He recalled that they took her to Venice and on cruises on the Orient Line steamers around the Mediterranean. Once away, 'she bucked up a good deal, became very flushed and talked amusingly and intelligently'. They took her to Capri to meet Gracie Fields, then married to the comedian Monty Banks. The two ladies sat talking in the back seat of a car. Suddenly it took off without Banks and he, in a panic, jumped onto the back mudguard. Seeing a sweaty face peering through the rear window, Mrs Clark exclaimed, 'Can't anyone tell that man we don't want to buy anything?'

'My mother comes off very badly in my autobiography,' he said. 'She was intelligent and had good sense. She never moved fast; she never agitated herself. She was absolutely calm and steady.' Even if she showed little interest in his activities and would not discuss the past, it was a relief to have her so approachable, relatively speaking, and a human contact was developing between them for the first time. His letters attest to this. While they are dutiful – he enquires solicitously about her health and politely tells her how much he enjoyed his last visit – a confiding tone creeps into the later letters which is absent from the earlier ones, particularly with respect to his ambitions.

He described his and Jane's social life. A week of dinner-parties included one with the Sitwells that was a complete flop and a second with less demanding friends that went well. He discussed family plans, holidays, illnesses, and gave his mother full reports on the children. Alan was doing so well at Eton that he was in no rush to leave for Oxford. He certainly was not repeating his father's pattern; K could not wait to leave Winchester. Alan seemed better than he had ever been, full of energy and wit. As for Colin, he had been lonely at Eton to begin with but, with Alan's help, was making a circle of friends. If only his mother could see Colin in his Etons and top hat. He looked adorable. K added that he had been organizing a store of furniture that his mother would not need for the time being and had been looking at pictures of himself in an old stereoscope. What a dear little fellow he had been, after all.

As the war drew to a close he had made up his mind to take the decisive step which had caused him so much anguish in 1938. He would definitely leave the National Gallery and concentrate on writing. What he really wanted to do, he told his mother, was become Slade Professor of Fine Arts at Oxford and really make something of the position for the first time since Ruskin. Typically, he had already sketched out a year's-worth of lectures in his mind, which would deal with the art of humanism, though he had no idea whether he would be offered the job. They turned down Roger Fry, he reflected ruefully.

The family took two badly needed holidays in Portugal and, returning from the second in the autumn of 1946, were met at the airport with the news that his mother had had a bad fall at the age of seventy-nine. Her hip was broken and she had hit her head so severely that she was in a daze. She might not even have known he was there. She was perhaps dying, but he was committed to leave the country. He was to open the first important exhibition of English painting to be sent to America since 1938. He put off his departure as long as he could and then, after receiving the best obtainable advice – that his mother would live until his return – left in October. Jane stayed with her and sent him reassuring bulletins.

The moment he returned he went straight to Alice's bedside. His mother was physically no better but she recognized him at last. He said, 'I have known so many cases of this, it's awfully hard to know why. On the last day her mind became absolutely clear and we had an awfully sweet talk. She talked about my father's early life and also about death. Then she said, "Now the time has come when we must part."' She went into a coma and never spoke again. He paused. 'That's a good way to die, isn't it?'

Did he still miss her? 'Very much indeed.' He could not bring himself to say more.

14 Art Completes

'Art completes what nature cannot bring
to a finish.' – ARISTOTLE

That remote Welsh landscape about which he would dream repeatedly had yielded its treasures. Soon after the war ended fifty masterpieces by Rembrandt, Vermeer, Titian, El Greco and Rubens were back in two rooms of the National Gallery, and more were to come. If colours seemed a trifle brighter than they had six years before, viewers must have thought that a trick of memory had made them forget just how vivid the paintings were, not suspecting that the director had arranged to have the necessary cleaning done during those years of exile. One furore over a Velazquez had been enough.

Now they were hanging in a battered building (the west side of the National Gallery had been badly damaged by bombs) in a grimy, war-scarred city in which luxuriant growths of purple milkwort and willow-herb were beginning to bloom on empty sites strewn with rubble and broken glass. The black-out had ended. So had the final trauma of flying bombs which, following the saturation bombings, struck at random. Despite their frequency one's chances of being hurt were sufficiently remote for Londoners to become inured. People gambled on their ability to make split-second decisions and sometimes lost.

Kenneth Clark was waiting in a bus queue one day in broad daylight, when he heard the familiar sound of a flying bomb. It was growing closer and closer; suddenly it stopped. He dashed across the street and threw himself to the ground in front of a doorway – the only one who did. After the explosion, when he dared to look up, he saw that the bus queue had been decimated.

His reflexes were still in working order. Now, at a time when he might have rested on his laurels, he handed in his resignation. Had it not been for the war, he would probably have left the National Gallery much sooner. He confided to the director of the Tate Gallery,

John Rothenstein, and his wife Elizabeth, that he was tired of the innumerable committee meetings, the lack of money and staff, the petty squabbles and lingering animosities of life at the Gallery. He had been longing to devote himself to writing ever since the publication of his book on Leonardo's development as an artist; now was the moment. There is no doubt that he had become an extremely important and influential figure. His power to give energetic, elegant, often profound expression to his ideas, his social connections, his enthusiastic commitment to all of the arts, made him something of an 'elder statesman' at a relatively early age, Rothenstein noted. He was 'one of the phenomena of the period between the wars'. The Sunday *Observer* called him the 'uncrowned king' of the modern art world.

Finding the proper landscape in which one might entice a new idea to appear was constantly on his mind at that period. It seemed to be Tuscany, because there he would catch sight of a concept so tenuous that he could barely grasp it. Did Jane remember how he wept on the way to Siena because he thought he had lost a concept irretrievably? He would make his homage to Athena, that deity of pre-Hellenic remoteness who was patron of the arts and the personification of wisdom; Athena, with eyes as grey as the silvery green-grey leaves of the olive tree which was her symbol.

Athena was kind. Up at Casa al Dono, the summer house in the hills above Florence at Vallombrosa where Bernard Berenson and Nicky Mariano spent their summers, he was writing seven times more in one day than he did in London. This amazing achievement was not accomplished without a certain cost to himself. Italians had the fixed notion that their summers were so sweltering that drastic remedies were called for. So they fled to mountain chalets that were freezingly cold and where they never saw a ray of sunlight. There they happily puttered about in winter coats and sat around fires drinking tea. This was hardly his idea of summer but he had been brain-washed and uncomplainingly put on layers of sweaters, he told Morna Anderson.

In the city below, by contrast, it was wonderfully scorching. How glorious it was to be back in Florence, he wrote to Jane at home in London in the autumn of 1949. Perugia always turned out to be a disappointment. As for Cortona, with its tomb chambers and massive Etruscan walls of flaking limestone, that was too gloomy for enjoyment. Arezzo, by contrast, did not even pretend to be worth seeing. Florence, however, had it all. It was everything to have precious mornings free to work in I Tatti, to be fussed over by old servants, to have the luxury of a 50,000-volume library and, when the host was in residence, to go on wonderful walks over the hills. In these post-war years I Tatti had become his spiritual home and – without doubt – Berenson played the role of the ideal father, the one he ought to have had. Small wonder that when he proposed writing a book about Berenson and his circle in the winter of 1951, Berenson gave his delighted approval. For one reason or another the project was postponed and then, three years later, to his surprise, Kenneth Clark learned that Berenson was cooperating with another writer, Sylvia Sprigge, who later published *Berenson*. Although he assured B.B. that their books would not conflict, he seems to have decided that they would and abandoned the idea some time afterwards.

A few months after he had settled into private life, intending to travel and write, the opportunity appeared that he had hoped for. However, this new appointment, as Slade Professor of Fine Arts at the University of Oxford (which he took in December 1946, a year after leaving the National Gallery), could act as a spur to writing rather than an obstacle. Lectures could become books and vice versa; it would have appealed to his sense of economy and the need for the most efficient use of one's time. The appointment conferred great distinction and required little effort since, by tradition, the Slade Professor only gave five or six lectures a year. The professorship had been founded by Sir Henry Acland with John Ruskin, who was its first holder. The connection meant a good deal to Kenneth Clark because, from the time he began to work on *The Gothic Revival*, Ruskin had been the predominant influence on his thought.

The extent to which Kenneth Clark tried to be a worthy successor to Ruskin can be discerned from his inaugural lecture, on the subject of Ruskin at Oxford, delivered a few days after his mother's death. Ruskin's belief that no one could pretend to know about art unless he or she practised it, would have been obvious to Kenneth Clark. Ruskin's conviction that an art lover's first duty was to the work of his times would also have been self-evident to his pupil, even though it flew in the face of the contemporary notion that art history must concern itself with the past.

Ruskin's supposedly outdated aesthetic beliefs were worthy of study even though many of them had almost become heresies. In contrast with one contemporary art movement, Ruskin did not believe that art was ever mere imitation. Two elements were necessary to transform a visual impression into a work of art: an artist's love for his object and his ability to impose a superior kind of order upon it. By extension, he rejected abstract and geometric forms. These, he thought, should be organic, following his conviction that nature must be the life-spirit of art. Ruskin and Fry both believed that the most fatal defect an artist could have was to be more interested in displaying his skill than in conveying an idea.

It was perhaps more difficult to accept Ruskin's moralistic position that the best art was fundamentally good and that great art actually demonstrated an epoch's social and political virtue. The fallacies of such an argument were obvious, Kenneth Clark said. Yet we had only to look at the mechanical paintings being churned out early in the nineteenth century to see the worth of Ruskin's belief that a painting could not be considered a masterpiece unless it was making some kind of valuable statement about the human condition. If Ruskin could not look at an ugly lamp-post without drawing a moral message, perhaps we should take his cue. There was a great deal to be said for raising the general level of public awareness, which was abysmally materialistic, whether inside an art museum or outside it on the street, and on whatever pretext, Kenneth Clark thought.

Writing later about Ruskin, in an introduction to Ruskin's autobiography, *Praeterita* (published in the summer of 1949), Kenneth Clark noted that at least three great English critics – Hazlitt, Ruskin and Roger Fry – had all come from philistine, puritanical homes and had been set on their aesthetic pilgrimages by the lack of beauty in their everyday surroundings. To that list Kenneth Clark might have added his own name. In addition to his birthright, he had inherited the same radiant artistic sensibility. He could have said, as easily as Ruskin did of a building he was drawing in Verona, 'I should like to eat it up touch by touch.' For Kenneth Clark as for Ruskin, art was a substance which nourished the bloodstream and, it should be added, both had the gift of kindling the appetite of their audiences.

Kenneth Clark set about, in Ruskin's words, 'making our English youth care somewhat for the Arts'. He decided that his students could easily be interested in the art of their own time, but that they would need a certain perspective if they were to unravel its puzzles. Such a perspective could be provided by lectures on landscape painting because that was the chief artistic creation of the nineteenth century. Once he had warmed to the subject, his ideas fell into easy categories: the Landscape of Symbols, the Landscape of Fact, the

Landscape of Fantasy, the Ideal Landscape and so on. A book seemed the natural sequel. The subject of landscape painting appeared to arise spontaneously but it had its origins two decades before, when he was living in Italy. Perhaps he had been influenced by Berenson's ability to see paintings in terms of the natural world.

The lectures were duly given and the book prepared, but the title was difficult to arrive at. Kenneth Clark balked at his publisher's suggestion that he call it 'Landscape Painting'. He wanted something much more tentative, such as 'Thoughts on Landscape Painting', because he feared that the book lacked depth and that his chapters still sounded too much like lectures. Whenever Berenson saw a landscape it made him think of a painting and perhaps this is the origin of the title Kenneth Clark finally chose: *Landscape into Art*. When the book appeared in the autumn of 1949, reviewers called it 'one of the most interesting and important books on a general subject in art to appear for a long time'. The writer was praised for his wide-ranging knowledge, his ability to draw inferences from apparently unrelated facts, his gift for exposition and, above all, his love and contagious enjoyment of art. The book was beautifully ordered and composed and singularly persuasive, Herbert Read wrote. 'Kenneth Clark is a writer who expresses a fastidious sensibility in a precise prose. That precision is made possible, of course, by a forceful intelligence.'

Read made a reference to the Clarkian approach: 'separate aspects of the human spirit reflected in the medium of landscape painting'. Ruskin's belief that a masterpiece must reflect the human condition had been transposed by Kenneth Clark, consciously or unconsciously, into a study of what art had to reveal about human thought and aspiration. This ability to place abstract concepts in an understandable framework perhaps accounted for his astonishing success at Oxford. Classes of twenty-five expanded by leaps and bounds until there were audiences of five hundred, many of them ex-servicemen, responding to their professor's magical ability to bring a boring subject to life. The *Spectator* noted that Sir Kenneth Clark's lectures had become so crowded that they had to be held in the Town Hall.

It was an enormous triumph but it was hardly unexpected. For several years people had been making note of the spell-binding way in which Kenneth Clark talked about art. Attending one lecture in 1943, on the influence of Greek art on British architecture, a perceptive listener wrote, 'K must be the most brilliant of lecturers – superhuman learning worn with ease, diction perfect – because he makes me concentrate as though I were immersed in a book.' If his students thought him the best lecturer in Britain, it was a popular verdict.

Typically, he made light of his success; it was a freak gift, he said. Lecturing was so easy that there must be something wrong with it. In retrospect it had ruined his style since it had encouraged him to ignore the careful examination of every issue that would have turned him into a real scholar. On the other hand, in order to write learned articles one had to feel that points of contention mattered, and he did not. That comment was made decades later, but it parallels his remark in 1947, to Clive Bell, that pedantry was a useless bore. One of life's great pleasures, the delight of composing sentences, was equalled for him by the challenge of transforming stodgy facts into delectations for the mind and imagination, of communicating his own rapture, and of making people think. The child who had talked to himself, at long last, had the audience he deserved.

No matter what subject he approached in that halcyon period immediately after the Second World War, whether it were the conflict between Classic and Romantic art, or Ingres, Delacroix, Giorgione, Titian or Rembrandt, seemed transformed by the alchemy of his velvet pen. Ideas that had been barely visible were, thanks to Athena, arriving in such profusion, so fully formed and in such organized sequence that committing them to paper was a joy. He seemed, at that period, as incapable of a still-born concept as he was of a graceless phrase.

He turned from a series of lectures on Rembrandt to a book on Piero della Francesca commissioned by Dr Bela Horovitz, the enterprising director of the Phaidon Press. Piero had been neglected by critics for centuries but had been rediscovered at the end of the nineteenth century by Berenson and others, and praised in the twentieth by Aldous Huxley and the Italian art historian Roberto Longhi. However, a full-length study of the master had not been attempted. Kenneth Clark decided to tackle it.

Little was known about Piero except that he was born in the tiny town of Borgo San Sepolcro in Umbria and died there, a very old man and perhaps blind, at the close of the fifteenth century. The mathematical perfection of his forms and the sense of interval which gave a timeless and serene air to his works, qualities long ignored, could be appreciated at their full value by a generation brought up on Cubism and the intellectual rigour of Cézanne. The artistic legacy Piero left behind, particularly the fresco cycle in the choir of San Francesco at

Arezzo, depicting the story of the True Cross, was incomparable. To study it Kenneth Clark made I Tatti his base in the autumn of 1949. The moment he saw Piero's work he was assaulted by so many ideas that they made his head swim. He began to work rapidly and with confidence. His patron at the Phaidon Press spared no expense in commissioning photographs of exemplary clarity and fidelity and the resulting book was hailed as a masterpiece. Kenneth Clark had, one critic declared, transported his readers to a plane from which all that was trivial dropped away. Another writer commented that there were two kinds of books about art, those providing information and those providing facts interpreted by imagination. Kenneth Clark's book belonged to the second category. 'It is accurate, factual, shrewd, ingenious and imaginative ... Sir Kenneth Clark makes a habit of expressing quite difficult abstract conceptions in mellifluous sentences composed of simple words.' Add to these qualities 'the faculty of clarity, formidable erudition and a fastidious eye, and no man of our time is better qualified to discuss so great a painter'. In the *Sunday Times*, Raymond Mortimer wrote,

> To be outstanding alike in devotion to the arts, in public spirit, in intellectual power and in practical ability: so rare – so unfair – a combination of excellences may well fill the rest of us ... with an envious dismay. Nor can we console ourselves with detecting any shallowness beneath this Keynesian versatility ... Can we at least pretend not to notice that, on top of everything else, he is a dab at actual writing? No, we cannot.

An author is either brought to a halt or launched by such praise; Kenneth Clark belonged to the latter group. His term as Slade Professor was expiring (he served again in 1961–62) and the next step seemed to be a great book – *the* great book. As luck would have it, an idea had been germinating in his mind since 1940. It was the subject of the nude.

He launched himself on his ambitious subject in the summer of 1951. It was to appear first as a series of lectures at the National Gallery in Washington, but since he had had so much difficulty in transforming the spoken word into the written one for *Landscape into Art*, he decided to work first for the page and 'colloquialize' the result. As a method it was vastly superior, but the subject itself proved so sprawling and full of vast implications that he struggled with it for the next two or three years, while staying at I Tatti and while working at the round table in the summer dining-room of a friend, Barbie Agar, or at the Wentworth Hotel in Aldeburgh, another favourite writing retreat. It cost him an enormous effort and, at first, he had no idea whether *The Nude* had succeeded or not, even though the success of his lecture series on the subject at the National Gallery of Art in Washington (1953) should have reassured him. Then the advance reports came in on the book's publication in 1956 and they were glowing. Lionel Trilling believed that the book would, in all likelihood, have an enduring effect on modern taste. Sir John Rothenstein praised the author's vivid and graceful prose, capable of evoking in a single sentence contrasting worlds of thought and feeling. Francis Henry Taylor, in the *New York Times*, called *The Nude* the simple and beautiful statement of a writer whose command of language was rivalled only by the breadth of his curiosity and the sharpness of his visual memory. No living writer, Dame Edith Sitwell wrote, cleared and focussed the vision of the reader more completely. Kenneth Clark put it best when he remarked that, where art history was concerned, a careful analysis only took one so far. At the point of impasse the critic-analyst would have to abandon scholarship and take a flight of the imagination – become a creator. There is no doubt that in *The Nude* Kenneth Clark brilliantly met his own test.

While writing *The Nude*, Kenneth Clark had what seems to have been a moment of divine inspiration. He had been working in his hotel room in Aldeburgh and had just finished a passage on Rubens when he realized that he was shaking and had to walk along the sea-front to calm himself. Perhaps it was the examination of such inspired works as Rubens's *Venus and Area*, or *Three Graces*, that had produced in him a sudden vivid awareness of the mysterious origins of creation. Perhaps it was the moment of true inner vision described by Walter Pater and John Ruskin, or what Bernard Berenson meant when he spoke of 'IT-ness', an insight into the mystery of existence.

After Somerset Maugham read a copy of his lecture, 'Moments of Vision' (given at Oxford in 1954, following this experience), he wrote to say how such an experience resembled the flashes of illumination experienced by the Spanish mystics. Inspiration and spiritual illumination: perhaps they were interchangeable ideas. As Kenneth Clark walked unsteadily along the sea-front at Aldeburgh, his bafflement was complete. If one accepted the idea of inspiration, one would have to believe in a source. However he, though an admirer of the church, was no convert. Such tricks of the mind could be explained as transparent wish-fulfilments. Or could they? At about this time he began having some other strange experiences which he believed were mystical in origin. In his autobiography he describes one that took place in the Church of San Lorenzo while he was staying at I Tatti. These feelings eventually subsided but that they happened at all was a mystery. In *The Nude*, as in all his later writings, Kenneth Clark asserted that great art could only be understood in terms of a divine source of inspiration. Such paintings were acts of adoration and proof of celestial joy.

15 Ministering to the Arts

'This fury for the sight of new things, with which
we are now infected and afflicted, though partly
the result of everything being made a matter of
trade, is yet more the consequence of our thirst
for dramatic instead of classic work.' –
JOHN RUSKIN, *Ruskin Today*

As an example of ideal form it would be difficult to surpass the painting
Auguste Renoir made of his young wife at Sorrento. The simple
sensuality of the nude, her pearly flesh in delicate contrast to the
Mediterranean, captivated Kenneth Clark. The work never lost its
precious qualities for him and, after he and Jane moved from their
cramped little jewel of a house, Capo di Monte, to Upper Terrace
House, the spacious mansion in Hampstead, the *Baigneuse Blonde*
was given pride of place over the fireplace.

That a famous Renoir hung in the drawing-room seemed to sym-
bolize life at Upper Terrace House for those who visited it in the
post-war years. To be invited there, according to several rhapsodic
reports, was to enter another world. One went through a yellow door in
a wall to find a red-bricked mansion standing in an island of its own
grounds, surrounded by a beautifully kept garden.

> Now on the step, with hand held out to greet us, is an elegant and eminent
> young man ... He is only forty-one, but already he has packed such a
> wealth of work and study into his life that in another two or three years he
> hopes to be able to retire and to record, for the benefit of posterity, the sum
> total of his experience.

The Clarks are depicted strolling in the garden or having tea in the
oval drawing-room, panelled in pale, unpolished pine, furnished with
Regency satinwood and decorated with dull gold satin curtains (designed by Marian Dorn) with their motif of autumn leaves. Or he might
be seen working at his Empire desk in the library, panelled with
sweet-smelling cedar wood, or posing in the small, charming dining-
room, his hand lightly touching its Deepdene Regency table designed

by Thomas Hope, his beloved Turner on the wall behind him. Or he is seen crossing the large stone hall, with its decor of green, black and white, furnished with a bust of Agrippa in Egyptian granite beside a precious jade Maori ceremonial sword given to his father during a visit to New Zealand.

Despite Kenneth Clark's protestations to a nobleman who wanted to bring a group to tour the house, that there was hardly anything worth a visitor's time, people came so insistently that the garden was made a public attraction. When his publisher, John Murray, was about to visit to talk about illustrations for a revised edition of *Landscape into Art*, Kenneth Clark said that the garden would be open to the public that day. Would he please buy a ticket, in order to make the gardener happy? He would get his shilling back.

Once the London blitz ended, Jane Clark turned Upton House over to state farm workers known as Land Girls, abandoning her role of housekeeper with relief. She wanted wartime work and took on the job of collecting paintings and commissioning murals for British Restaurants, government cafeterias established, early in the war, to supplement the meagre rations of workers with inexpensive food. Then she organized a meeting place, called the Churchill Club, for American troops in England, and took charge of its cultural programmes. If, during the 'other woman' episode, Jane had believed that her part in K's life was over, it was clear by the end of the war that she had resumed her old importance. When he joined a committee to decide the post-war future of Covent Garden Opera House (now the Royal Opera House), K sent Jane the minutes of the first meetings and asked her to put them in her files. He sent her copies of proposals for exhibitions he oversaw as chairman of the art panel for CEMA, about to become the Arts Council of Great Britain, and asked for her comments. That she had an important role is verified by a secretary of Kenneth Clark's in later years, Gill Ross. Mrs Ross noted that Jane Clark read everything her husband wrote and that he would often appear in the morning saying, 'Jane thinks it's too long or this or that is wrong', and would alter it.

Jane Clark's life as a society lady began at 9.30 a.m. when she dictated letters before going to see the gardener. She planned menus and did the ordering twice a week. Small formal dinners (the dining-room only held eight) called forth her talent for improvisation. She might use plates from a different dinner service for each course: grey Sèvres for the oysters, blue Chantilly for the dessert and so on. The wine glasses were sixteenth- and seventeenth-century Italian; the knives and forks, instead of the solid silver one might expect, had prettily decorated china handles. 'We dine out one night a week on the staff's night off,' she told a journalist. 'When we have a late supper party the butler likes to see us started, then we wait on ourselves. We never keep him up late, and when the guests have gone I clear away, for I myself should hate being faced with the debris in the morning.'

Her menu for buffet suppers might consist of a hot soup, cold meats and a salad, served with appropriate wines. One of her favourite cocktail-party snacks was home-made cream cheese made from goat's milk, spread on hot cheese biscuits. For their two biggest parties, for from one to two hundred guests, given in the summer, a marquee would be erected on the lawn and all the doors of Upper Terrace House's ground-floor rooms thrown open. No matter how many times a guest came to visit there would always be something new to see because paintings were habitually rotated. Jane told a journalist about one dinner party in Portland Place before the war when Prime Minister Chamberlain, on her right, asked her about a painting over the dining-room fireplace. Jane was seated with her back to it and, without turning around, airily explained that it was a portrait of herself, painted by Duncan Grant. From the Prime Minister's mortified expression she realized, all too late, that the painting had just been replaced with a nude by Bonnard.

If, before the war, Jane had limited herself to the role of 'other half', she now began to take on public duties. She started by opening church bazaars and speaking at school prize-givings and then joined national committees, such as those for the opera and ballet at Sadler's Wells. Her biggest role, however, was as president of the Incorporated Society of London Fashion Designers, the official organization for the leaders of British *haute couture*. As such, she presided at all official functions, attended the shows, opened exhibitions and gave large cocktail parties. It was a role she continued to execute impeccably. A writer commented, 'It is one of the tests of a smart woman that she can look well in black. With flashing ear-rings, immaculate dark hair, perfect make-up . . . she is elegance itself.'

One finds many photographs of her, perhaps seated beside the wife of the French Ambassador, Madame Massigli, inspecting with a severe eye the latest court costume from Hartnell, or fingering woollens from Yorkshire in the company of the young Queen Elizabeth. She posed for *Vogue* on the staircase of Upper Terrace House, and discussed her clothes choices with the *News Chronicle*. The national press followed her activities assiduously and sent photographers the day she made a deep curtsy outside Claridge's to welcome the Queen and Princess Margaret to a fashion show staged by the Society of London Fashion Designers for the Coronation Year. Although she was wearing the tightest of hobble skirts, she curtsied to the floor. Such obeisance, going far beyond that strictly required by protocol, led to much bemused comment by columnists and a wicked cartoon by Osbert Lancaster.

Her greatest moment of triumph came in 1953, when the family was obliged to move out of Upper Terrace House so that television cameras could be set up, its thirty-foot drawing-room transformed into a *salon* and the bedrooms into dressing-rooms for a royal fashion show. Black and maroon Daimlers drew up at the entrance, discharging the Queen Mother in a star sapphire silk dress, matching hat with pink feathers, and Princess Margaret in a yellow pleated dress and mink coat. Police were stationed at every road leading to the house and behind every Henry Moore statue lurked a detective, guarding the dresses, the £¼ million-worth of jewels (mostly diamonds) adorning forty mannequins and, last but not least, the paintings, sculptures and *bibelots*. A diarist for a London newspaper proclaimed that Upper Terrace House was becoming famous for its 'successful and brilliant occasions'.

Then, without warning, Jane Clark retired as president of the Society of London Fashion Designers. She explained that they were moving from Hampstead to a castle in Kent and that her time would be taken up in supervising repairs and alterations, as well as arranging a London apartment in Albany. What appeared to be a too-scrupulous sense of obligation hid other reasons. For some years Jane had been in poor health.

She had been too ill to join the family on a visit to Portugal in 1947 and K returned from an ecstatically happy time alone with the children to find her improving but in poor spirits. She was continually succumbing to bouts of flu or various mysterious ailments. Judging from Kenneth Clark's letters to Berenson, all it took was an uninterrupted bout of family life – presumably children home for the holidays – to set her off on another round of illness. The trouble was, he wrote in the autumn of 1951, that she needed a major operation (perhaps a reference to her attack of appendicitis before the Second World War) and would never be healthy without it. The operation was performed in 1951 just before Christmas and seemed more drastic than anticipated. For five days she was seriously ill.

The following summer she seemed to have recovered, although she
grew tired and depressed easily. Then she returned for a second
operation. It was hard to take, particularly since she had seemed
much better, well enough to take a holiday. Jane, however, accepted
the news with stoicism. She seemed to expect the worst from life.
Kenneth Clark could not help seeing her as a tragic figure, although
he was quick to add that she had, of course, no reason for her
despairing view. But he reflected that continually to feel tense and
unwell was enough of a reason for anyone.

When K left for a visit to Casa al Dono in the autumn of 1949, Mary
Kessell seemed on the brink of marrying Theodore Besterman, her
old editor from the *Dictionary of Love* days. He felt that this was his
cue to fade out of her life but, when the marriage did not take place,
resumed his old role. Both of them knew the artist Derek Hill and
since the latter had taken up a lengthy residence in the *villino* on the
grounds of i Tatti, Mary was invited to stay there. Somehow or other,
one of Mary's visits to i Tatti coincided with a visit by K. Jane
found out and, Derek Hill said, she always believed that he had
arranged for the coincidence, although he had not. She would not
speak to him for twenty years.

For some time Jane had been engaged in another of her ambivalent
friendships, in this case with the brilliant French Ambassador, René
Massigli. The Ambassador recalled that he and his wife met the
Clarks on the eve of war and became close friends once he was posted
to London in 1945. A love of art was his personal vice, he said: in
addition, he was attracted by Kenneth Clark's intelligence, open-
mindedness and *joie de vivre* and his wife's thoughtfulness and
charm. As for Jane, he had the impression that, although genuinely
admiring her husband, she had decided to retain a certain independence. Massigli was impenetrably diplomatic about the extent of
their friendship, apart from saying that he was devoted to her.
Asked whether he thought Jane was happy in her marriage, he hesitated and did not reply.

Then in October 1953, K broke off his long relationship with Mary
Kessell. Mary was seriously, hopelessly in love. She longed to be
married. He, however, felt painfully torn. He loved Mary, but to
marry her was out of the question. He said:

I never thought of her as that sort of girl at all. To me she was an art school girl; one who would have lots of love affairs and take it all as part of the life she led. I am bound to say that Jane didn't grumble or fuss but in the end she did feel badly about it and it was clear that I had to give Mary up. This is when I behaved terribly badly. I wrote to Mary and said that our relationship had got to end and then I did a bunk.

Mary Kessell was agonized, although she tried to accept his decision, wish him God speed and not to mind that she was being completely cut out of his life for, as he also said, 'I left and never saw her again. I said to Jane I wouldn't and I didn't.' She eventually married but not until after several severe and painful years, made harder for her by the completeness of the break. Colette Clark recalled that, some time afterwards, a friend came to the house and, in surprise at not finding Mary, asked innocently, 'Whatever has happened to Mary Kessell?' The remark was followed by a 'deathly hush'. Her name was never mentioned again. In the years to come Jane might be heard to make barbed comments about women who broke up marriages.

In *The Other Half*, Kenneth Clark's second volume of autobiography, he described his first view of Saltwood and the chance visit which led him to discover that it was for sale. Not only was it an enchanting castle but it seemed to offer the perfect solution for their marriage. Instead of Hampstead, with its constant reminders of Mary, Saltwood provided a diverting interest for Jane, a better library, a dreamlike atmosphere, a new start. Jane was rapturous. Diana Menuhin remembered Jane's gay announcement at Aldeburgh in 1953 that they had bought a castle, in much too grand a voice. It reminded her of the quip about Gertrude Lawrence, who came sweeping into Beatrice Lillie's dressing-room to declare, 'I've just taken a house in Berkeley Square', at which the comedienne retorted: 'Put it back at once!'

For Kenneth Clark, living in the country had much to recommend it. London had become too costly and fast-paced. He could no longer write there, reading at leisure was out of the question and there was no chance of getting to a park. Working in a bank could hardly be worse. He was depending upon a change of scene to shake him out of his melancholic mood but nothing was happening. Instead, he felt physically and mentally exhausted, hounded by too much to do and no time in which to do it. He was months late on promised manuscripts. His watchword ought to be lackadaisical and remiss, he wrote. Additional evidence that he was going through a difficult time is contained in a letter to a friend, Sir Alec Martin, dated the end of October, just as he was ending his fourteen-year relationship with Mary. He was sorry not to have accepted Sir Alec's invitation so far to visit his new home, but lately he had hardly been able to drag himself around. There are references to continual bouts of self-disgust and something approaching despair at his weakness and inadequacy where others were concerned. He made promises he did not keep. He did not measure up, he wrote. He was a fake, a phoney, a cheat.

The spring brought its compensations. He had chosen a quiet distant room for his study that overlooked the old walls, the moat and a valley winding down to the English Channel. Certain moments, when the sun was going down and the trees were fringed with silver, wine and purple, or delicately outlined in gold, were almost magically beautiful. Before long he had given his new home a nickname, 'Salters', a sure sign that he was settling in, and was organizing his library in one of the buildings on the edge of the courtyard that had been the Archbishop's hall of audience. Whenever he was at 'Salters' all thoughts of London seemed absurd. Yet he knew that he needed a new challenge as much as any alcoholic did his liquor. He had been offered the chairmanship of the Arts Council, then the nearest British equivalent to the continental post of Minister of Fine Arts, and had accepted.

The way in which government might patronize the arts had been one of Kenneth Clark's major concerns ever since he joined the arts panel of CEMA. The gap left by the decline of patronage had to be filled somehow and if the middle classes could not, or would not, provide the funds, the government must. But if the state were to direct public taste then the time had come to ask what creative patronage actually was. Diaghilev, for instance, gave modern art a magnificent showcase by commissioning musicians, poets and painters to work on his Russian ballet and had an incalculable influence. But Diaghilev was a genius, in the centre of a group of brilliant men and women who kept a vortex of ideas swirling around them. The idea that a governmental committee might be able to reproduce the same atmosphere seemed almost farcical. However, the larger problem, as he saw it, was that the arts would always have a minority appeal (he did not anticipate, at that point, the vast crowds that would be attracted to a museum's great exhibitions), whereas democratic societies were bound to be concerned with quantity rather than quality, with middle-brow taste rather than the standards of the intelligentsia. Kenneth Clark was particularly emphatic about the basic, anti-egalitarian nature of art. To assert, as Lenin did, that a work of art had to be understood by the average man to have any value, was a travesty. To assert, as was becoming popular, that masterpieces could be assessed in terms of their functional utility, or good design, was equally outrageous. Someone had to talk about fable, ceremony, passion and mystery, qualities that even primitive man knew could be found in art. Someone had to say that such qualities were worth having.

However, the extent to which the state could or should patronize the arts became the least of his problems once he became Arts Council chairman in the summer of 1953. In its nine or ten years of existence the Council had established an excellent reputation for its judicious support of the nation's art museums, ballet and opera companies, theatres and orchestras. It had not attempted to do much more, in the way of creative patronage, than organize exhibitions and assemble a modest collection of art, and it seemed unlikely that it ever would, because of the desperate shortage of money. Theoretical considerations seemed beside the point if the Arts Council's yearly grant were to be whittled down to the vanishing point. When Kenneth Clark took over as chairman that seemed just about to happen.

The Arts Council was then housed at 4 St James's Square, and its drawing-room used for recitals, meetings, auditions and exhibitions. The building's elegant colonnaded halls, panelled walls, chandeliers and paved terraces (ideal for displaying sculpture) fulfilled expectations, but the job was disappointing on all counts. Kenneth Clark discovered that he had taken on the role of figurehead. Previous occupants of the position hardly ever appeared and the real work was being done by the Secretary General, a flamboyant Welshman, Sir William Emrys Williams, who wrote the reports, directed policy and appointed staff. Although Kenneth Clark does not say so, the implication is that Williams took steps to ensure that his chairman would not meddle in Arts Council affairs. He decreed, for instance, that Kenneth Clark did not need a secretary. He would be brought whatever correspondence it was thought safe to show him. A younger Kenneth Clark would have taken about two months' worth of such frustration and then left. Surprisingly, he lasted seven years. Having an excuse to go to London and an office there were too important to him. In addition, he enjoyed being in the chair at board meetings as well as being an office of last resort for members of the staff and their grievances; he would apply glasses of sherry and soothing words. He was so clearly anxious to be useful that others were impressed. Joanna Drew, who was a junior member of the art department during his chairmanship, recalled that, unlike other chairmen, Sir Kenneth appeared promptly every day. Unlike his predecessors, who wanted everything prepared for them, without any bother, he always said, 'I like to be bothered.' When exhibitions were being hung in the drawing room he wandered through and would give impromptu lectures to a delighted group on the subject of art.

He was being wasted there and he knew it. An appreciator, an advocate, a persuasive voice – these were his natural roles. His gifts of speaking and writing, his wide cultural erudition, his easy manner and *entrée* into the 'right' circles made him exceptional, unrivalled, as a propagandist for British art. To these qualities might have been added an ability to communicate on a broad human level that his role as chairman of the Arts Council barely tapped. Then, a year later, he was invited to become chairman of the new Independent Television Authority, for a three-year term (August 1954–57).

A great deal was made of the fact that the new chairman did not own a television set. Furthermore, 'many educationists and intellectuals were in full cry against the coming horror that would, they thought, debase national taste. That Sir Kenneth should become its architect must have seemed to many in their donnish world a gross betrayal.' Soon after his appointment he walked into the dining-room of the Athenaeum and was astonished to hear some booing noises. It seemed hardly possible that a man who had forcefully argued for the aristocracy of art, and for the life of the spirit in an era of crass materialism, should be willing to sanction – at any price – the trivialization of art to sell toothpaste.

During the debate leading to the Television Act, Kenneth Clark had been ambivalent. It was obvious that commercial television would produce its share of rubbish but the BBC had become monopolistic and hidebound and needed the challenge. Sir Robert Fraser, who became Kenneth Clark's director general, liked to press home the message that commercial television was the medium for the masses. However, in choosing to see the problem in black and white terms – with the BBC playing its establishment role as *The Times*, versus commercial television as, say, the *Daily Mirror* – Fraser and Clark were using a misleading metaphor. One could equally well argue that only a non-profit, independent institution such as the BBC was likely, at least potentially, to respond to a wide spectrum of minority tastes since, in commercial terms, the only needs which counted were those of the majority.

Although the political licence allowed to the new commercial television tycoons, called 'programme contractors', was curtailed by the ITA, there was no way to prevent a handful of powerful men from exercising a vast social and cultural influence. They decided which programme would be seen when, arranging for the worst to be shown at peak viewing times and vice versa. To no one's surprise, they proved to be unenthusiastic about experimentation. They were instantly alert, however, to television's insidious ability to convey through images, ways of life and associations of ideas, a culture of crass materialism. That Kenneth Clark might be ushering in a powerful force with far-reaching consequences (Maurice Bowra quipped, 'All television corrupts and absolute television corrupts absolutely') must have been far from his thoughts when he took office in 1954. To him the position was a heady antidote to the Arts Council: a delicious opportunity to think, act, organize, influence.

On his first day there, he took the 8.50 a.m. train up from Folkestone. From 11 until 12.30 p.m. he met with the Postmaster General. He lunched with his new staff until 2 p.m. and then went to a meeting that lasted until 4.30. There was a press conference with eighty-five reporters and photographers, followed by an hour-long meeting with the chairman of the BBC and another press conference. He had no idea what he had said to all those reporters or what they would write about him. He had to organize staff, offices, make policy decisions – from the ground up. What a stroke of unanticipated good luck, he wrote.

The first day set the pace, which was relentless. He and Fraser were responsible for the choice of the first four programme contractors and had to tell them, since television was a vastly expensive undertaking, that they must be prepared to put down at least £3 million – far more than any of them were willing to invest at that time. Along with Fraser he was also setting up the first news programme and battling his way through mountains of papers. There were hostile columns and the inevitable letters to the editor to be dealt with, and the pressures of so much work were having their delayed effects. Sometimes he brought the car to London, driving short trips that he preferred to make by train, and felt the resulting fatigue at night, when he dreamed of a road continually unwinding before him. One impossible Tuesday began with difficult meetings followed by a visit to a radio show that was so dreadful he wanted to weep, or rage, for sheer embarrassment. The day ended with another press conference and reporters draped about on chairs – he steeled himself, but they were surprisingly kindly. In the middle of the night he became convinced that he had said too much, recalling, with a start, that he had mildly criticized the BBC's extravagant ways. He foresaw headlines and could hardly eat breakfast, but his fears were groundless.

There were battles on more than one front. At the end of a rough week Jane listened to his complaints and said it was probably all his fault, that the ITA were officious Civil Servants getting themselves into muddles. He did not get a wink of sleep after that and the thought that Jane must be looking enviously at the fun he was having, did not help. To be embattled at the office was one matter but to be attacked at home was more than he could bear. He could not help thinking of Ibsen, he wrote.

The result of moving from London was, whether by accident or design, to allow him to lead distinctly separate lives. Saltwood stood for the family: Jane, children and dogs, visits of friends, the routine of family life. London symbolized his intellectual life (since, in his dual role as chairman of the ITA and the Arts Council, he might be living there four days a week), the world of decisions, meetings, speeches, public appearances. They had taken a flat in Albany, B5, and this, as 44 Dover Street had done, provided a retreat and an escape, an inner sanctum. He could now place an actual distance between himself and the needs of a demanding wife.

At first Jane Clark was completely entranced by her castle. Once she realized, however, how much her share of his life had dwindled, she resented it. Arriving home on Friday nights, for K, then became as bad as arriving home any day of the week at Upper Terrace House. In those days one of his Hampstead neighbours noted that he would park his Bentley, lock its door and stand on the pavement inspecting himself with a mirror which he carried in his pocket, comb his hair carefully and survey the results before going into the house. He needed to put his best face on things because he never knew what avalanche of grievances would descend upon his shoulders the minute he turned the key in the lock. On one terrible occasion when he assumed that two dinner invitations in London included her, Jane cancelled everything at Saltwood, ordered a new dress, made hair and facial appointments – then learned that she had not been invited. Sometimes the thought of going home was unendurable.

The core of the problem was that his other half had no interests of her own. He was her whole world and although that had its advantages it also made life very difficult. Frustrated and angry, Jane seemed to act, as she had at Upton House, as if she had been left with the drudgery while he had all the fun. So after a perfectly happy day she might fly into a rage over his lack of responsibility and unwillingness to deal with problems, designed to make him feel as guilty as possible. He had convinced himself that she needed an outlet for her frustrations and that he should not take it personally. However, he wrote, he could not sleep that night.

When Kenneth Clark and Janet Stone both became godparents to the Pipers' younger daughter, Myfanwy Piper described Janet Stone to K as Elizabethan in her distinctive good looks. K privately decided that her period ought to have been pre-Renaissance. He frequently thought of her when he was walking around the moat and looking across it towards the castle. He would be almost in tears if the day ever came when he could see her against such a background, because she was so much a part of Gothic England. That, he wrote, was one more way of declaring his love. Myfanwy Piper's prediction that they would like each other had been spectacularly accurate.

As his affair with Mary Kessell was ending Kenneth Clark received a letter from Janet Stone saying that she was coming to London. Her husband, Reynolds Stone, was a wood engraver of delicate miniature evocations of pastoral life in the manner of Thomas Bewick. Stone also became known for his mysterious, disturbing and enchanted visions of childhood, used for book illustrations. Janet was a descendant of Elizabeth Fry, the Quaker philanthropist, and daughter of the Bishop of Lichfield. When she met K she was attempting to revive her early career as a soprano and recitalist and was making frequent trips to London for singing lessons. When her husband objected to her being away from home on tours she turned to photography, becoming an accomplished portraitist. A few months before the Clarks moved to Saltwood, the Stones and their four children moved to a large, romantic vicarage in what Janet Stone called 'dear, darkest' Dorset.

There were some polite exchanges. She had suggested that they meet one day in July and he wrote that this seemed difficult as he had an official luncheon and then an invitation to the Buckingham Palace garden party. It was the dullest event of the season but he had always been told that attendance records were kept and absenteeism was frowned upon. The friendship warmed slowly and, early in October, he was averring that he did not deserve to have an admirer. He looked upon her as a beautiful friend, one with whom he felt an immediate rapport. If life were otherwise, he said, he would be falling head over heels in love with her. As it was he felt as if he were swimming about in a fish bowl, signalling frantically from behind his barrier.

Several months after that, in February 1954, he was discussing what Henry James would have called their plight. There could be no mistaking what had taken place. Whatever the future might hold he agreed with her that nothing could disturb their immediate and instinctive rapport. They wanted to meet often and Janet was prepared to fit her London dates in with his. However, he was continually worried that she would come to London and he would not be able to see her because of some unavoidable emergency. Or he would fret if he could not manage a daily letter, something she insisted upon, since he would be bound to disappoint her occasionally, then be agonized because she must be spending a miserable morning on his account. When she wrote, convinced that he no longer loved her, he panicked. However inadequate an object he was for her love, he was wholeheartedly in love with her.

As for telephone calls, he had grown aware, while they lived at Upper Terrace House, of the fact that all his private calls were being listened to by Jane – an echo of the days when his parents used to open his letters. Amazingly, he endured it without protest; perhaps he felt he owed it to her. At Saltwood it was not so easy for his phone calls to be tapped but the habit of years was difficult to break. This would explain what might seem like his stiff and formal manner. The figure of Jane – autocratic, unpredictable, demanding, always to be considered first – loomed over them both. He would plan a delicious evening with Janet only to have his plans wrecked by Jane's sudden decision to come up to London. There were many such crises and he was always convinced that Janet would give up on him – but she never did.

What was her allure for him? Evidence that he felt himself to have been a failure in his private life is not hard to find. It was allied to the

feeling that he was ageing, and not with grace. He was mortified by
the signs he saw in his face of insensitivity, selfishness and lax
behaviour. Almost nothing was left of the ardent young aesthete,
whereas her face retained the wonderful qualities that he valued. Her
worth seemed closely connected to her ability to dispel the clouds of
despondency that surrounded him. He always felt revived after their
meetings, he wrote. She wrapped him in the enveloping warmth of
her love. She defended him against the world.

In the autumn of 1979, just after Reynolds Stone died, his wife was
still living in the Old Rectory in a small village two and a half miles
from the sea. The house, literally in the shadow of a small church, was
absolutely silent, except for the animated cawing of rooks and an
occasional gull. It was an old stone house, enchantingly littered with
the clutter of generations: an old owl in a glass case, *primitif* paintings of children in pantaloons, china birds on china logs, threadbare
oriental carpets, thick walls, shuttered windows and thousands of
books. In the red damask sitting-room, with its striped red wallpaper,
a high-backed sofa stood before a wood fire and, in the dining-room,
four white candles in white china holders were placed on a lazy Susan
so that the light danced above one's head around the room.

   Her marriage, she said, had been a happy one and she was devoted
to her husband, but he never wanted to leave the house. She did not
seem to feel imprisoned by his affection, but certainly isolated.
Having K in her world was a 'lifeline'. Being so adored by him made
her marriage far happier, because everyone else seemed more adorable. Although they met at least once a month, basically what they
had was a correspondence. She did not think the relationship would
have lasted as long if he had seen her every day. Just as she found his
affection sustaining, so she believed that knowing her made it
possible for him to continue in his marriage. Early in their friendship
he told her that he felt duty bound to remain with Jane, but if he were
free, would she marry him? She replied that she would not. She felt
even more obligated to her husband by bonds of love. He would
always come first in her life. Loving Reynolds, she was in love with K.
It is interesting to speculate how much the two men she chose were in
the thrall of their childhoods.

The new television era was ushered in with ceremony in London's
Guildhall in September 1955. A film of the occasion shows Jane quite

far down at the banqueting table, her hair parted in the centre, gesturing prettily to her partner (a distinguished and balding gentleman wearing a riband across his chest) while her eyes never ceased their flickering and flirtatious search over the scene in front of her. Her husband, at the head of the table, was leaning against a high, leather-backed chair, his hands crossed. From time to time he stole a look at his watch. At the age of fifty-two he looked slightly heavier around the chin and there was a hint of a slackening waistline, but his hair was still dark and, wearing a white tie, with five medals pinned to his left breast pocket, he looked extremely distinguished. When he stood up to speak it was to talk about the fact that television had been controlled, to that moment, by a public corporation. That weapon was now being placed in the hands of companies who were hardly controlled at all. In a phrase that was much quoted, he called the formation of the ITA an attempt to solve one of the chief problems of democracy: how to combine a maximum of freedom with an ultimate direction.

The voice was crisp and the delivery, as usual, full of confidence. His hands, however, were in a strange state. They crossed on his chest, uncrossed, joined below the waist, went to his sides and crossed again. Then they began to knead his upper arms. It was as if they were fighting to go up to his head in a gesture of despair and as if he were battling to keep them in their place, squaring his shoulders each time. The reason for this flurry of embarrassed movement can be deduced from letters he wrote afterwards. He told Berenson that the opening had left him feeling as if he had constructed a handsome building that was being lived in by barbarians. That might have been inevitable from the start, given the 'disgustingly low' standards of public taste. Still, there was nothing wrong with the edifice he had built and inhabiting it might improve their manners. In short, the humiliation of being obliged to defend the indefensible was becoming increasingly difficult to endure. There was an obvious solution, but before he resigned, Kenneth Clark decided to put up a fight.

He reminded the Postmaster General that when he and other members of the ITA had been appointed they were told that they had a responsibility to maintain quality and balance in the programming. As much as £750,000 a year might be made available for this from public funds. However, the 1955 autumn budget had ushered in an era of financial retrenchment. Assisting commercial television, however deserved, was politically impossible.

The following year Kenneth Clark asked for £515,000 to develop quality programmes – less than the maximum but far more than a token sum. The reply came while he was on a lecture tour of India. The sum of £100,000 was all the government could offer. Since the chairman was away, the ITA's four programme contractors answered for him. The ITA, they said, would never accept such a paltry sum. Bernard Sendall, the official historian for the ITA, commented later, '[T]he companies' statement . . . can only be described as arrogant and uncouth.' The blunder more or less confirmed Kenneth Clark's decision that the situation was hopeless. In *The Other Half* he implies that he was not asked to take a second term, but it is clear that he was not willing to be reappointed. By way of compensation he was now free to make public his distaste for its lack of standards. Four years later he testified at a government enquiry that the ITA could have done much more to keep up standards if it had tried. Exactly how much control was required would have to depend on the view taken of public taste. Reading statistics was bound to bring one to the cynical conclusion that one could hardly go low enough although, occasionally, good programmes could be successful with the masses. However, if American television was any guide, he thought more government control was the only way to stop the headlong plunge.

Since he dreaded the *Angst* which always seemed to descend upon him the moment he stopped running, Kenneth Clark was casting about for his private addiction, as he called it – a new job. He was still nominally working at the Arts Council, and accepted an invitation to write a series of articles on master works by Titian, Leonardo, Velazquez and Delacroix for the *Sunday Times*. Then, two months after the crushing disappointment at the ITA and his private decision to leave, a reaction set in. Whenever he bent down, or sneezed, or picked up heavy objects, he experienced an acute headache. A specialist advised him to enter a hospital for tests, a step he deeply distrusted on the theory that experts in white coats might be tempted to use drastic methods. The headaches continued for months and he began to see a connection between their appearance and nervous tension, since a week-end off seemed to cure them. He was almost tempted to think it was evidence of a neurosis, although this, of course, could not be the case, since he had never experienced such things. But it was said that even the most normal kinds of people, i.e. Army brass and football players were not immune, he wrote, so there was no reason why he should be an exception.

Life continued to provide headaches of its own. One week-end in the summer of 1957 there were dozens of people at every meal who stayed on uninvited until he could hardly bear it, he told Janet. Each group meant a new tour of the battlements, which was pleasant up to a point, but he finally ached to sit down. The inevitable result, on Monday, was that the cook gave notice. The gardener was ill, their charlady at Albany away for two months, both secretaries gone and there were piles of letters to be answered by hand. Occasionally, by some miracle, he and Jane would find themselves alone, rattling around the old stone walls like two shrivelled peas in a mammoth pod. They worked in the garden and kept the dogs company.

The domestic atmosphere, as usual, was unpredictable, owing to Jane's fondness for dramatic confrontations, he wrote. All it took was her conviction that he and the boys had done something wrong and he could be sure of hysterical recriminations and some sleepless nights. There were other evenings, such as the dinner-party for the J.B. Priestleys, when Jane would talk some nonsense or other and he would not know where to look. Since the family was used to it no one bothered to contradict her, but their guests must have thought her odd. Jane was becoming genuinely peculiar, he decided.

As for himself, he was tolerably happy. He was using a new pen in the hope that its novelty would conceal from him the desperate state of his handwriting. Sometimes he felt marvellously well, just as he used to do. At other times he would catch sight of himself in a full-length mirror and make the unpleasant discovery that he had grown old, paunchy and grey. Even this did not really matter, he told Janet. He actually had only two ambitions left: to slim down his waistline and perfect the loops on his 'e's.

16 Another Side of the Alde

Graham Sutherland: 'I said to John Sparrow
once, "I don't really know K." He replied,
"None of us do."'

Among those visiting Saltwood at that time was a woman director of a
local gallery who had persuaded Kenneth Clark to open an exhibition. Jane was annoyed. She protested that if her husband frittered
away his time in such a fashion he would never write books. The lady
thought that was a fine idea as he had already overdone it. Jane, her
husband noted, had the grace to giggle.

He was, an influential magazine observed, still six men in search of
a character, restlessly seeking out new worlds as he, with equal
abruptness, relinquished others. He seemed impelled to accept every
challenge, whether it were making opening remarks, writing lectures,
introductions or serving on yet another committee (the British
Museum, the Victoria and Albert, the Conseil Artistique des Musées
Nationaux) while, at the same time, fretting that he was squandering
energies that should be concentrated on a single important subject.
Yet he believed that, if he did nothing except work on a book, he
would stagnate. The trick seemed to be to find a balance, that delicate
state which would allow time for serious study, while giving his
gnawing need for action an outlet; an elusive equilibrium that was
always just beyond his grasp. No sooner did he make a stern inner
resolve not to accept anything else than he would find himself being
hounded by a publisher for an overdue manuscript, such as an introduction to a book on Walter Pater. He would sit down to work in a
turmoil, even though one simply could not rush such a project. Then,
quivering with exasperation he would throw Pater's masterpiece, his
book on the Renaissance, across the room.

There was a further claim on his time. The night his term as
Chairman of the ITA expired he was asked to appear as the star of a
new series, '*Is Art Necessary?*', by one of the programme contractors.
He had failed in his attempt to wrest money from the government

for just such a project. Here was his chance to show how it could be done.

As he envisaged it, each programme would begin from a single idea, such as the element of illustration in painting, or the inherent absurdity of opera, or the significance of gesture, and enlarge upon the theme by means of interviews, film clips, paintings, photographs and so on: worthwhile and comparatively unfamiliar subject-matter, described in terms the average viewer could understand. He had moments of wondering whether he could make such an idea work, and intermittent panic. After one sleepless night, and in a state of exhaustion, he suddenly realized how far behind he was on all of his projects and lay awake trying to write articles and broadcasts in his head. A month later the first film was finished and he viewed himself pontificating on pottery and aesthetics with mingled feelings. His wild lunges from one side of his prison cell to the other (as he characterized his life to Janet Stone) were being brought to a halt by the tedious process of making a film. Had he realized just how time-consuming it was, he never would have begun, he told her.

The first programme in the series was a failure. Jane was upset about that, but then she was used to easy victories. He had yet to learn, he wrote, that a programme had to be scripted down to the very last word and, furthermore, that what people wanted was information and not speculative ideas. His contract was very nearly cancelled but, two months later, he had his first success. After four months, the discovery that television could do what he believed it might was so exhilarating that he was urging friends to buy television sets and not condemn the medium prematurely. To Berenson he confided that television appealed to the latent ham in him, while providing the intellectual challenge of presenting complex subjects simply. Television provided the immediacy he craved, the sense of accomplishment, and undreamed-of possibilities to educate and influence. Television, with its rapid pace, cornucopia of images, its urgency and scope, intimacy and distance, seemed made for him and he for it. Angus Wilson called him 'the great television star' and wrote of another series, three lectures on Michelangelo, that these were the best things he had done. A newspaper columnist put the reaction of the man in the street with emphatic succinctness: 'Do we want more of Sir Kenneth Clark? The answer is: Yes,' he wrote in the *Daily Sketch*. 'He makes adults of us all.'

As Kenneth Clark said, his wife was used to success; so, for that matter, was he. He was not, however, prepared for the avalanche of attention he was receiving as a result of his regular television appearances – eventually he made almost a hundred films. Wherever he went he was being lionized. At every dinner he was seated beside his hostess and obliged to force down gargantuan helpings. In Paris, he wrote, the red carpet was rolled out and his colleagues acted as if he were a star, which was baffling, as they had always ignored him before. After having given a reasonably good lecture he was inundated with so many flowers that he reeled under their weight, just like Maria Callas. To appear sweet and unspoiled despite all this acclaim was becoming difficult. He wrote that it had given him far too good an opinion of himself, but no doubt it would all end shortly. Nothing, however, affected him as much as the day he stopped to buy some daffodils from a street vendor. As the man wrapped up the flowers he ventured to say how much he enjoyed his customer's programme on art, and so did the other flower sellers at Covent Garden. Shades of Henry Higgins! It confirmed the value of television and made him feel that it was all worth while.

Was art necessary? People seemed to think so, thanks to his efforts, and from the most unlikely walks of life. Was modern art necessary? If Kenneth Clark had been caught in an unguarded moment he would probably have said that it was not. Ever since his prediction in 1935 that modern art would arrive at a dead end, he had not changed his views. Yet, in defiance of probability, the new vogue had swept all before it and with it all vestiges of representational art. The more abstractionism triumphed, and the more freedom the artist felt to paint or sculpt without reference to the aesthetic of the past, the more art itself seemed to be floundering in uncertainty. What was art nowadays? In one of his most important essays, 'The Value of Art in an Expanding World', Kenneth Clark wrote that nobody knew. The critics, on whom one might have relied for guidance, seemed as baffled as anyone else to judge from the paradoxes and ambiguities that passed for analysis nowadays. And if one turned to the art historians one discovered that they had totally washed their hands of the whole problem. Their neat resolution of the dilemma was to study paintings as if they were historical artefacts, divorced from any consideration of the work's actual value. If pressed, art historians took the position that absolute values did not exist. There was, in other words, no such thing as a masterpiece but only a transient vogue.

The overwhelming success of abstract art was bound to leave Kenneth Clark in an uncomfortable position. As director of the National Gallery he had rapidly built the reputation for being the champion of modern art. He had persistently taken what looked, to his critics, like a radical position in the artists he chose to champion. Yet his original aversion to Picasso – much tempered in later years – was an indication of his natural taste, which was towards art that had its roots in the great classical traditions of the past, however modified and transmuted by the contemporary artist's vision. He had never warmed to abstraction and never would. However, his was becoming almost the only dissenting voice. With something of a shock he realized that he must be looking hopelessly outdated and old-fashioned. Was it indeed his own inability to get the point? Sometimes he thought this must be true. And yet he was constantly being asked to open exhibitions and explain modern art, if not enthuse about it. He must either retire from the field or come up with some explanation for his persistent inner belief that abstraction – what he called 'The Blot and the Diagram' – must eventually reach an impasse.

In 'The Value of Art in an Expanding World', Kenneth Clark observed that great movements in art had invariably coincided, historically, with periods in which the society that nurtured such phenomena harboured workable assumptions about the universe. The Florentine artists of the Renaissance, for instance, made use of Euclidean geometry in designing their compositions. Once the fact that the earth was round had become generally accepted, the pictorial vanishing point began to be placed outside the edge of the painting's frame. Whatever most people around him thought gave the artist the almost religious certainty he needed. The more secure society's belief in an ordered universe, the more solid and broadly based the aesthetic upon which the artist built his imaginary world.

Contrast this enviable state of affairs with the contemporary discovery that there were no borders whatsoever to the dimensions of the universe, whatever end of the telescope was used in attempting to explore it. As J.B.S. Haldane once said, 'My own suspicion is that the universe is not only queerer than we suppose, but queerer than we can suppose.' This discovery, that the universe was a vast riddle inside an enigma, was bound to have a profound effect upon artists. We had, he wrote, direct evidence that this was exactly what happened. The great Russian abstractionist Wassily Kandinsky wrote,

'The crumbling of the atom was to my soul like the crumbling of the whole world. Everything became uncertain, tottering, weak. I would not have been surprised if a stone had dissolved in the air in front of me and become invisible.' Kandinsky made that observation in 1918 and that same year Kasimir Malevich painted a white square on a white ground. For such artists it seemed essential to return to basics: to truth in feeling, pure construction, pure relationships; an inner purification, perhaps, but one which expressed itself in the language of the inner landscape.

The more abstract and personalized art became, the more it dealt with the highly obscure and arcane symbols of the human unconscious, the less likely it was to convey a comprehensible message. It was almost a dream vision, full of meaning to one with the hidden key, but as ambiguous as automatic writing to anyone else. At the same time the yardsticks by which such art might have been assessed had been abandoned. If all that counted was the purity of the artist's intent then everything had equal value and an equal claim to fame, although the bewildered viewer, confronting one muddy, stained and blotted canvas after another, might be forgiven for wondering aloud whose leg was being pulled.

Kenneth Clark continued to predict that abstractionism would reach a dead end. In the first place he held the debatable opinion that the unconscious was soon drained of inspiration. More plausibly, he argued that one stained and blotted canvas looked pretty much like another and that the patience of the viewers would soon be exhausted as spots danced before their eyes. Finally, the 'intuitive blot', as he called it, contained the seeds of its own disappearance. No one could argue with the contention that all great art had been about something. It had a message, even if that message could not be put into words but only stated symbolically, by means of colours and images. It dealt with large universal truths and it must convey that message to have a lasting impact. When he made that observation, in 1958, it seemed that art would have to wait a long time (he thought it would not come during his lifetime, but he was wrong) before some new aesthetic arose that was strong enough to require expression through art rather than through the language of the computer.

Every avenue he explored led back to the necessity of defining an aesthetic and, in the late 1950s and early 1960s he devoted considerable energy to that end. If great art were the means of communicating some immortal truth then Walter Pater must be right in his belief that

Kenneth Clark filming early in World War II.

The best lecturer in Britain.

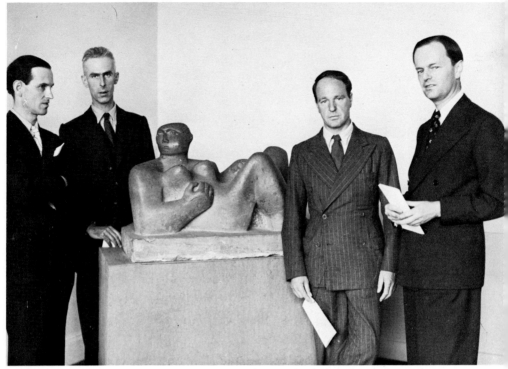

Graham Sutherland, John Piper, Henry Moore and Kenneth Clark with a nude by Moore.

Jane with Alan at Upton House.

A picnic at Eton with Alan and Colin Clark (*at left*), Jane Clark (*in background, raising a glass*), Kenneth Clark (*centre*), and the future Earl of Crawford, Lord Balniel (*right foreground*), with Lady Balniel and their son Rupert (*in white tie*).

Kenneth Clark described this photograph as 'Being told off by Jane'.

Mary Kessell.

Sir William Walton.

Lady Clark with Princess Margaret.

The Clarks at Saltwood Castle.

The Queen Mother plants a tree at Saltwood Castle.

Jane Clark on location during the filming of *Civilisation*.

Kenneth Clark speaking after receiving a medal for distinguished service to education in art at the National Gallery of Art, Washington.

Kenneth Clark with his second wife, Nolwen, in the grounds of Saltwood Castle.

Kenneth Clark at work in his favourite
chair at The Garden House.

Kenneth Clark in the grounds of
Sudbourne.

art achieved this effect by a union of form and matter, and the closer the union, the more perfect the work of art. The flaw in the reasoning of Fry and his followers was, he believed, that it concentrated only on form. A later school of art historians concerned itself entirely with subjects, and could have reached its conclusions without ever examining an original work. Little had been done to analyse what Pater called 'that complex faculty for which every thought and feeling is twin-born with its sensible analogue or symbol'. Yet it was the absolute crux of the matter. If one could somehow define it, one would be making a major contribution to contemporary thought.

In the summer of 1961, as he was preparing for a return engagement as Slade Professor at Oxford and while he worked on his lecture series, he and Jane went to Aldeburgh to visit the artist Mary Potter, the divorced wife of the humorist Stephen Potter. As had become the rule, these lectures would act as the groundwork for his next book. Almost immediately he ran into difficulties.

The problem, 'to pierce the mystery' of 'form and matter in their union and identity', as Pater phrased it, proved frustratingly difficult. To avoid vague general statements he had decided to take examples and study their historical evolution. He did, however, need some solid evidence upon which to build his theses and aesthetic experiences hardly filled the bill. He decided therefore to concentrate on what he called motives, recurring images throughout the history of art, such as the Virgin and Child.

He worked on the problem steadily. The idea seemed an inspired one from a distance, but the more he tried to refine and develop it, the more frustratingly out of focus it became. He was, however, committed to give a series of lectures and so he persevered despite the vast difficulties of the theme. Lectures were given and the title of a book – *The Recurring Image* – decided upon. He hammered away at the idea for years before abandoning the attempt with a grateful sigh in 1970. While *Motives* produced some brilliant insights he had set himself an impossible task. The mystery of the fusion of form and matter remained as impossible to define as the precise moment when sleep overtakes us, for, as he also wrote, when faced with trying to express the inexpressible, all that the critic could finally do was confess his own inadequacy.

Tuscany was one of those landscapes in which a new idea could be trusted to appear; another was Aldeburgh. He did not know why.

He had somehow come to the conclusion that the atmosphere cleared his mind and sharpened his focus and, whenever he had a particularly exacting writing task, there he would wend his way. Sometimes they stayed with Mary Potter, whose company he always found so restful and undemanding; sometimes at the Wentworth, that rambling, comfortable family hotel on the front where one met everyone. He would drive his car up to the heath and write, with an occasional pensive glance over the dashboard, or stroll along the beach, searching among the pebbles for words and ideas as he had once looked for pieces of amber. Aldeburgh had been, after all, one of the romantic outposts of his childhood, the other side of the Alde, and the Suffolk countryside, with its heaths and woods, its sandpits and oak trees, had become his inner landscape.

Another reason for communing with the delicate music of the Suffolk coast had to do with his friend, the composer Benjamin Britten. When Britten was organizing the first of his celebrated festivals of music and art at Aldeburgh he invited Kenneth Clark to lecture. In the years to come there were many such orations, on William Blake, Jean François Millet, Samuel Palmer, Edith Sitwell and others. During those great Aldeburgh days of Kathleen Ferrier, Sviatoslav Richter and Mstislav Rostropovich, the evenings were filled with music, such as a performance of *Noye's Fludde*, which he watched in tears. Days were spent walking on the golf course or visiting his grandmother's house, still standing beside a dreary thirteenth-century castle keep, with a splendid view over the marshes, in the village of Orford. After taking Janet Stone there, he was sure she understood, he wrote, why it still filled his dreams. He remembered, as a child, having tea in the boat-house as a special birthday treat, and the white sails that filled the horizon. As always, he followed the road meandering down to the sea.

He had once disliked the Riviera intensely, he told Ben Britten, but now enjoyed their annual visit to Somerset Maugham and his companion, the sprightly Alan Searle, at their luxurious villa on Cap Ferrat. It was wonderful to be there since he was left undisturbed by his host during the day, which meant he could write. The only difficulty was to time their departure carefully so as to leave the moment they had run out of new stories. K and Jane would move on to Menton, where they stayed at the Hôtel des Anglais. The rooms had not changed one iota since Queen Victoria's time and reminded him of Matisse's interiors: all pinks and scarlets, with a glimpse of a blue sky and sea behind the palm and banana trees. Unfortunately the rooms were very noisy, which was just as well, otherwise he would have stayed there for ever, he wrote. He would sit on the beach writing to the sound of the waves, lulled into thinking he had conquered *Motives* at last. While at Menton they usually visited Graham and Kathy Sutherland in La Villa Blanche, the Mediterranean counterpart to their white house in Kent, overlooking the town. He and his wife were well heeled nowadays, as was Henry Moore. It was inspiring to see the way the sculptor's extraordinary works seemed to have an organic relationship with the strip of meadow he had set aside for them at Much Hadham. Moore had built on a handsome room and bought a Cézanne painting. His three old friends were certainly in clover. The third, John Piper, had just had an exhibition of his paintings in London. The preview was crowded with socialites straight from the pages of the *Queen*. Myfanwy looked radiant and her husband slightly discomfited – all the works had already been sold.

Graham Sutherland, who had refused countless requests from the rich and famous, was preparing to paint his portrait. K had the idea that he looked better in a hat, so he sat in the garden wearing his old green one at an angle, and a green pullover, while the painter made preliminary sketches. Some months later the hat was discarded and Sutherland was trying for a full face or profile. K enjoyed the sittings. It was an honour to be painted by Sutherland at all, he told the artist. Other sketches and some small preparatory paintings were made but Sutherland was dissatisfied. His subject's expressions were too evanescent to be grasped and he had been put off his stride by the hat as well as, one guesses, by his sitter's influential role in his own life. Not only did K's expressions tend to flicker but, one assumes, it was difficult for an artist to make up his mind which inner man the sitter unconsciously wanted to see portrayed. Even an artist as delicately sensitive to nuance as Derek Hill, who painted almost every famous figure in Europe, and tried two portraits of Kenneth Clark, could not come to grips with the mercurial figure beneath the characteristic impassivity. Cecil Beaton perhaps did better, having touched a chord of wistful melancholy with his portrait, taken in the living-room of The Garden House, Kenneth Clark's final home, with his beloved Turner in the background. Another photographer, Janet Stone, did as well with a profile portrait in which she chose to emphasize the calm and confident K. However, when this solution was adopted by Graham Sutherland, although there were 'great politenesses all round', as Sutherland said, he could tell from Jane's reaction that K had not really liked his painting. This was true. K decided that the portrait made him look haughty and belligerent. When, some time later, he sent Janet Stone an early photograph of himself, taken as he was choosing between a career as an artist or art historian, he complained that his expression already showed signs of the callous insensitiveness he thought Sutherland had portrayed.

During the winter months he worked in the panelled room at the top of the central tower. The room was warm and sunny and ideally situated, since his library was close by. He called it Montaigne's Tower and said he would like to die in it. Even in the brown days of early winter when everything was oozing, when there was no light and blues looked black, Saltwood had its own charm, and when it snowed the castle's beauty was too much for his descriptive powers.

When spring came and the gardener brought bouquets of lilies-of-the-valley to fill his room with fragrance he was in ecstasy, 'like some latter-day saint'. At such times he woke very early and went for walks beside the sea, taking the dogs under the cliffs at Folkestone and into that deserted resort atmosphere of shuttered cafés and solitary paths which, in his mind's eye, became transformed into Chinese paintings. Or he would finish cutting back the rosemary and forking up the nettles that were choking the moat. Eradicating them took as much patience as fishing, and when he had extracted a root six feet long he felt as triumphant as if he had just landed a salmon.

As at Upper Terrace House he felt it his disagreeable duty to conduct regular tours of the castle. One of the very worst involved taking fifty boys from a private school in Canterbury around. They were wheezing and snuffling with colds, chilly, and reeking with an indefinable odour of school that brought back some miserable memories. Guests were a different matter, particularly if they were people like Sidney Nolan, the Australian painter, the young Caryl and John Hubbard, friends of Colette's whom K and Jane had appropriated, or the actress Irene Worth, or Laurence Olivier and Vivien Leigh, or Yehudi and Diana Menuhin. They were all asked often, for lunches, dinners and the week-end. There were visits from the poet Edith Sitwell, a woman of great gifts, he believed, although she had grown decidedly eccentric by 1961. There was the writer E.M. Forster, so old that he was always half asleep, but very benevolent. There was Victor Pasmore, who brought one of his most exquisite paintings as a gift and then spent four hours arguing about aesthetics.

Such visits might bring forth such revelations as the discovery by
Caryl Hubbard and Irene Worth that the yellow room was haunted by
voices and the sound of bells at five in the morning. In fact, K heard
them himself. There were periodic visits from people he liked to term
bigwigs, who discussed politics incessantly and buried themselves
behind newspapers while he stole away to write. There were, as
before, visits from those he called 'The Royals', including the Queen
Mother. On perhaps the most glorious occasion of all, his old friend
came to plant a tree, looking the picture of confidence and charm,
while her hosts stood with their hands clasped behind their backs, stiff
with pleasure. She was an exception, but K could not help confessing
that, as a general rule, he was happy to see people leave. He was
teased about that because once a late-departing guest had gone to the
bathroom and, emerging, overheard his host saying to the dog, 'Isn't
it wonderful, they've all gone!'

The high point of the year should have been Christmas. From the
time the children were little there were endless presents for everyone,
games, gargantuan gustatory celebrations – all the fun of Christmas
that K had been denied as a child. A family tradition had been established of inviting a few close friends, usually Maurice Bowra, John
Sparrow, E.M. Forster and Irene Worth. It should have been pure
delight. He dreaded it. *En route* from Paris, speaking of his misery at
the thought of returning home, he referred to his tearful state whenever Christmas approached. Perhaps K and Jane both felt under a too
scrupulous obligation to be perfect hosts, or perhaps those days when
all mankind expected to be at its happiest made him aware of a
submerged melancholy. At any rate, his assessment of the Christmas
house party was invariably negative. Bowra had kept up a continual
barrage of chatter, demanding to be listened to from breakfast until
midnight. Other guests complained that the water was too cold.
Obviously they were having such a miserable time that he supposed
no one would want to return. Yet they had tried so hard to make
everyone comfortable, he wrote. As usual, he dismissed the problem
with a gesture of defeat.

By January 1959 the fact that he spent long week-ends at Saltwood
and the rest of his time away was becoming a major issue between K
and Jane. She hated living at Saltwood alone, yet she seemed incapable of going anywhere else. In March 1960 he wrote that getting
ready for a visit to see Colin had thrown her into a frenzy: she seemed

unable to do anything by herself. It was awkward, because he longed to travel to inaccessible places and was convinced that she could neither travel nor be left. In fact, it was clear to Forster that Jane might reach a stage when she could not leave the house, or allow him to leave, for more than an hour. She had not ventured outside the garden at 'Salters' for four or five years.

Would she stay down, or would she come up to London? Jane's panicky dependence and anxious clinging, however genuinely felt and painful for her, had its devious usefulness. Nothing could be better calculated to appeal to her husband's need to be needed than her insistence that she absolutely had to follow him everywhere. Nothing could keep him better in check because she could always claim that it was his fault she was unhappy. If he did not want to have her with him, he could not love her. He would be bound to protest, however miserably, that of course he wanted her company – and then she would have won. She knew he would not dare to tell the truth and, in fact, his feelings about Jane were always painfully ambiguous. Much as he longed for freedom, he expected restraint – he professed to believe that his mother had never let his father out of her sight – even, perhaps, required it, since to have escaped unscathed would have unleashed his sense of guilt. He was also capable of lightning switches of mood. Once, when he was explaining to Janet Stone that he could not come to London after all, he added that he was really happy at home, as well as in his work, and that he did not intend to relinquish such happiness or see it threatened.

Having made such a declaration, he was just as likely to state that he was becoming utterly bored by the work at the Arts Council. He would then debate whether he really ought not to resign, not from laziness, but because of the hopelessness of the task. It was an exercise in frustration, like trying to bring back the use of canals. Yet, perversely, once the time actually came to leave the Arts Council he was melancholic. Having an office in London had provided him with a tiny outpost of independence and now that escape route was gone. There were fewer and fewer reasons to leave his ailing companion and the chances of his getting free for a day seemed infinitesimal. He grew despairing. In an unconscious echo of his father's favourite remark, he called himself an old dog for such a hard road.

He longed to be 'let off' for a night or so, but of course that was quite impossible because, apart from anything else, Jane was genuinely dependent upon him. He began to complain of a buzzing in his head and headaches, of feeling unworthy and gross, and of deadly bouts of depression. When he actually found himself in Madrid, free to wander through the Prado, he was too upset to enjoy himself and, he wrote, suffering from persecution mania. In the middle of the Velazquez room, he found himself in tears. The fact was that he had gone down hill in every way and ought to be left to die in a ditch. But he must not let himself get into such a state. One of the views about himself to which he clung throughout his life was that he was an ordinary, well-balanced individual, and his emotional life almost boringly without incident. This opinion was likely to surface at moments of stress.

If he were reassuring himself, he seemed unaware of it.

Colette had 'come out' at a lavish garden party in which the Duchess of Kent danced with Lucien Freud; she then read history at Lady Margaret Hall, where she became the senior scholar. Alan had married, had two children and was turning into a first-class writer. Colin, after national service as a pilot in the RAF, was launched upon a theatrical career and would shortly marry Violette Verdy, the French prima ballerina. Although all three lived some distance away they came home often, which should have made Jane happy but did not. There were still great battles with Colette; complaints, from Jane, that her daughter was insulting and did not love her. As for Alan, he invited a friend to a party for Colin whom Jane particularly disliked. Jane reacted by devoting a disproportionate amount of time to this particular person, and then insisting that he had ruined her evening. She telephoned her son Alan to berate him about his friend. He, in turn, fuelled by a sense of ancient grievances, retaliated with vigour. The result was tears for Jane and some miserable nights for her husband. K felt unable to intervene, since he would be bound to point out that Alan's belligerence was the logical result of his mother's unjust attacks on him a decade before.

Things were far different with Colin but not necessarily better since his mother refused to believe that he was ever in the wrong, and that brought its own problems. Inevitably a visit from him threw her into a panic of anticipation. For his part, Colin found the burden of being loved a heavy one. On the rare occasions when family reunions went well, K was overcome with relief. No one suddenly ill, or dissolved in tears – it was practically a record. Even though Bowra had arrived a day early, which would normally have enraged Jane, she was too drunk to make a fuss, a distinct advantage from K's point of view. There were passing references to Jane's being 'in bad form' and, in September 1960, to the fact that her doctor had warmly recommended a tranquillizer. A month later all was going well, however. The only cloud on the horizon was that Jane was hitting the bottle much sooner in the day. K feared he would have to tackle her on the subject, although he was worried about making her guilty and on the defensive. If drinking were her attempt at self-cure, to allay the nervous tension, the trick would be to know when the cure became worse than the disease.

Ever since the early days of their marriage Jane had rushed to her 'puffer', the cocaine solution which had been prescribed for sinusitis but which came to be used to calm her nervous headaches and anger. For at least a decade she was utterly dependent on it. Kenneth Clark remembered that, when he went to have the prescription filled, the chemist in Wimpole Street 'used to look at it and shake his head', but said nothing. Some time afterwards, in 1946, Jane's doctor, Bedford Russell, was taken to court. A woman patient of his had committed suicide with a drug overdose and it was discovered that she had left her doctor £25,000. The executor of the will sued for the recovery of £10,000 which the lady had already given Bedford Russell. The surgeon returned the money and, the coroner having ruled on a verdict of suicide, no criminal liability attached to Russell. It was then, Kenneth Clark said, that he enquired into the nature of his wife's prescription and found that it contained an addictive dose of cocaine. A few months after discontinuing the dose, Jane turned to alcohol. This version is questioned by their son Colin, who believed that his mother was still using her puffer some years after the court case because, he said, the same cure was prescribed for him when he was training as a pilot in 1951. The concoction produced a strong tranquillizing effect and made objects look unreal. The exact moment when, as her husband said, Jane's cure became worse than the disease, would be impossible to pinpoint. Colette and Colin agree that their mother was using alcohol for relief for years before they actually became aware of it in about 1954, coincidentally the period when Kenneth Clark was ending his relationship with Mary Kessell, had just met Janet Stone and was moving to Saltwood. Colette remembered that her mother would become sleepy after dinner, very 'woozy', and she finally voiced her bewilderment. Colin said, 'My

dear, she's drunk.' Since the subject of drunkenness was as taboo in
the family as homosexuality, Colette could hardly believe her ears.
But then, when she became ill with virus pneumonia at about the age
of twenty-two, and was being read to by her mother while she lay in
bed, she remembered hoping that her mother was sober enough to
read.

There was a bar behind a door in the library. If one entered the
room hastily one sometimes heard the 'clink and clank' of a cupboard
door being shut. Then Jane became wilier. She was known to keep
gin in a beautiful set of painted bottles in her bathroom. Violette
Verdy remembered occasions when Jane, just about to sit down for
dinner, would rise on the pretext of going upstairs for her glasses. Her
husband would jump up faster, saying hastily, 'Oh no, my dear, I'll
get them.' Jane drank gin, sherry, anything. She would begin in the
morning with two to four Martinis, followed by a beaker of neat
whisky, then go out to lunch unaided. K confided to Colette that he
realized the extent of her mother's problem when he discovered that
she could drink two or three mammoth Martinis before dinner without effect.

As has been noted, a sober Jane dominated the meals by talking
without pause and interrupting her husband continually. Alcohol
caused a personality change. The first drink would make her calm, a
second even calmer, childlike and childish. Slowly K took over as
principal conversationalist and, Colette noted, Jane was too bleary-
eyed to object. Similarly, if Jane were easily shocked, jealous and
vengeful when sober, she was the soul of fuzzy benevolence after
several drinks. There was, Violette Verdy added, an Ophelia-like
quality to her state, appealing and poignant, that made one want to
rush to her defence. At such times she might scrawl wavering, semi-
coherent messages of love to her husband, thanking him for his goodness to her, telling him how much she adored him and how lucky she
was.

K made repeated attempts to suggest to Jane that she was too dependent upon alcohol and was always rebuffed. Then Colin had the
inspired idea of taking his mother to an expert hypnotist with the
hope that she might be cured. It seemed a slender chance, but there
was an immediate improvement. K wrote that Jane was having her
best days in England (she was always much better abroad) and he was
daring to hope. For several months the improvement was marked;

then Jane slid slowly downhill. She discovered, according to Colin, the real purpose of the visits and refused to see the hypnotist again. On the rare occasions when a guest appeared whom she particularly wanted to see – her dear friend William Walton, for instance – she would be particularly well, but once that friend had left, she would lose all interest in life. K found it deeply discouraging to watch her going through every stage from about noon onwards, particularly when the castle was full of guests. The two grandsons often stayed, and although they welcomed the visits, the small children were too much for Jane, who gave vent to her exasperation by attacking her husband. K was sure that it was a sort of therapy for her but, just the same, it ruined his day.

Natalie Barney, an American aphorist, liked to observe that growing old involved a series of deprivations, things one had to give up, and marriage must have seemed a great deal like that for Jane. From their earliest days when her husband called her a part of himself, asking what good it was to see a Giorgione when only half of him felt it and declared that the thought of her made him breathless, she had perceived a gradual cooling of his ardour into something more dutiful, seemingly, than heartfelt. Instead of the endless reassurances she needed, she was being doled out some meagre fare. Interestingly, Jane's list of ancient grievances (what Colette called 'Mamma's bruises'), ones she regularly voiced, included the complaint that her husband had only given her a bag of peppermints on their honeymoon, choosing to forget how much had been lavished upon her since. To her, marital love was something owed and, insecure as she was, every happy moment her husband spent with another woman felt like a theft; she was even jealous of her own daughter. He had, she must have felt, let her down.

Even so she knew in their days at Portland Place how necessary she was. One has to believe that her role was, after all, compensatory. As long as it was abundantly clear that she was the real draw, she could fulfil her life through his. He might be cleverer, but she had all the human qualities: grace, charm, warmth, generosity and poise, the lure of a forceful personality – knowing this, she could be at her most magnanimous. However, after the war, he needed her less. As he gained in stature and assurance, becoming more and more absorbed in his work, Jane became less the true centre, relegated to the sidelines and without much to show for it, although she put up a brave front.

Feeling threatened but not knowing why, she panicked. Somehow she must force him to face her distress, her feeling of being wronged.

But her tendency to blame others (she once said it was her husband's fault if she raged at the children, because he had made her unhappy) was bound to put him on the defensive. He was in the complicated position of not being able to believe he was properly loved unless unusual demands were being placed upon him. Yet (as he knew) he was hypersensitive to them; he wrote that, like Cézanne, he could not stand the feeling that someone *a jeté le grappin là-dessus**. A fast sprint had been his way of solving this problem since the early days when he feared paralysis: a physical and psychic distance. Violette Verdy recalled that, when at a crisis point in her marriage with Colin, she pleaded for help from her father-in-law, he invited her to meet him at Overton's – 'in a public place', she said, 'to make sure that I didn't abandon myself to hysterical tears'. She realized that she had asked for help from the wrong person. Alan Clark thought that his father would either refuse to acknowledge that anything was wrong, or capitulate in tears and say that everything was his fault, and that was just as difficult to deal with.

In a sense Jane had followed her mother's pattern, playing the part of the supportive, dutiful and self-sacrificing partner. She had tried to become the flawless lady of fashion her husband seemed to want, and when this failed to bring the expected rewards, she became daddy's spoiled and demanding little girl. In depending upon him, she kept him chained, as his father had, by links forged from obligation and her ability to evoke in him what his friends called an 'icy, frantic despair'. If he was never able to prevail, since Jane was a master at making him feel guilty, neither did he ever really lose; his evasive tactics saw to that. Their relationship was an intricate interdependency, a stalemate. She could not take the risk of offering him emotional freedom, nor he the anxiety involved in taking it.

That K was somehow implicated in Jane's need for alcohol is clear from independent observers. Catherine Porteous, who became his indispensable assistant in London, thought her employer believed that his wife would have been 'dead in three weeks' without him:

> When she flew to New York alone, he was in a great stew, wanting the travel agent to take her to the airport. Jane was perfectly able to get on the plane herself and did it without a drop. He was always worried about leaving her, but she was actually much better when he wasn't there. She

* had taken a stranglehold (colloq.)

didn't get so drunk ... K took over so much that there was no role left for her. He made her feel like a child.

Another member of the household confirmed the observation that, when alone, Jane drank far less and coped far better with life. However, whenever K returned, he might be seen next morning on his way to his wife's room with her first drink of the day in his hand. Whether she needed it or not, she was not likely to turn it down.

17 Civilisation

'He asked the Duke what is necessary in ruling a
kingdom; the Duke replied: *essere umano* – "to
be human."' – KENNETH CLARK, *Civilisation*

It is difficult to believe that Kenneth Clark scored his years of greatest
triumph at a time of severe personal stress. Publicly, he seemed to be
achieving that rare feat for an ageing writer in the modern world:
increasing accomplishment and renown. Privately, he felt himself on
the verge of collapse, a prisoner with every exit blocked. Yet the more
he felt enslaved by his poor invalid, the more hounded by her demands,
the more his spirit rebelled. At such moments he would send Janet
Stone a long discourse on the error of doing what one conceived to be
one's duty. Such efforts were doomed to fail, which showed that they
were against the life force. Although he might ridicule in himself what
he called a monstrous egotism, characteristically finding it necessary to
belittle his strengths, he had a saving grace, one that he recognized.
Somehow he had managed to keep his essential self intact, and,
somehow, his love of art still shone with the same lustre, along with his
zest for a new project. What a selfish monster he was, in the wrong
again, because he could not cure himself of those moments when work
was all that mattered.

When one considers that Kenneth Clark would eventually call the
period of filming *Civilisation*, the television series he began at the age
of sixty-four, the happiest years of his life, it is surprising that his first
reactions were distinctly lukewarm. As it transpired, however, such
misgivings were well founded. The idea took shape in the early
summer of 1966, when David Attenborough, head of BBC-2, found
himself seated beside Kenneth Clark at lunch. Discovering that the
latter's contract with the rival channel, ITV, had run out, Attenborough
casually suggested a series on the history of art. Kenneth Clark found
himself inspired to jot down a dozen titles for possible programmes.
No one was calling it *Civilisation*.

Several lunches later Michael Gill, one of the BBC's top producers, a veteran of some ninety films, who had just finished a highly acclaimed portrait of the British artist Francis Bacon, was included in the discussions. Gill's impressions were not favourable. 'I didn't like what I had seen of Kenneth Clark on television. He seemed stiff and pompous', Gill said. The biggest problem from his point of view was, however, that Clark's previous programmes had been essentially televised lectures. The speaker pontificated while the cameras rolled. That would not do at all. What Gill wanted was a series conceived in visual terms, in which text would, in the final analysis, be subservient to the image. That meant a directorial upper hand.

Gill's misgivings were confirmed at their subsequent meetings. 'We didn't get on at all,' he said. 'Kenneth Clark realized that I would not do what he expected, but he had never been in the charge of a director before. Furthermore, he hadn't the faintest idea how to go about writing such films.' Then Kenneth Clark wrote to the BBC saying that he thought Gill would be happier working with a younger man. All seemed lost, but Humphrey Burton, head of the BBC's music and arts section, would not concede defeat. He persuaded Kenneth Clark to attend a filming of Gill's *Francis Bacon*. To everyone's great surprise and relief, Kenneth Clark really liked it. It was, however, he said later, somewhat late in life for him to undertake this experiment: 'I may be a great disappointment to you.' Gill countered: 'If you will write these programmes as essays, I will turn them into films.'

Kenneth Clark began writing in the autumn of 1966, then invited Gill to his Albany flat. He had, he said, found the perfect way to start. Gill brought a few BBC executives along. Kenneth Clark, plainly dismayed, began to declaim. He had chosen the Pont des Arts, Paris, for his opening location and was quoting Ruskin. It was a book, Gill decided, not a film. Then Clark introduced the prow of a Viking ship coming up the Seine. How, Gill wondered aloud, was he going to shoot that? In the middle of an embarrassed silence, the double doors separating the living-room from the bedroom were flung open and Jane appeared. She took a few unsteady steps forward. 'Wish one of you is from the BBC?' she enquired loudly. The reply came hurriedly that everyone there was from the BBC. 'I don't care what you are called. Wish one of you is in charge?' she demanded, trying to light a cigarette and dropping it. After they left, David Attenborough remarked, 'This is not going to be easy.'

Jane was determined that K should not make *Civilisation*. There was no doubt that she did not want him to spend so much time away from her. She knew he was worried about the amount of work involved and, his theoretical retirement age being seventy, there were only a few years left for all the books he would rather be working upon. There is the additional likelihood that Jane did not approve of the proposed collaboration. It would have seemed to her as if the playwright, having written the script and been offered the leading role, were being made subordinate to a director, and not a particularly malleable one at that. As always when she sensed that her husband was hesitating, she put his case with her free-wheeling bluntness. Even after the first scripts had been written and the first filming completed, Jane was still making her contempt for the project, and its organizers, crystal clear. Gill and his co-producer, Peter Montagnon, recalled one painful luncheon when they and their team had gone to Saltwood for some filming. Lady Clark announced loudly that the Queen Mother had lunched there the week before and left a handsome tip for the servants. In short, the price of lunch for the BBC team was to be £20. Not a man there could come up with that much in cash. Would a cheque be acceptable, Peter Montagnon enquired. Kenneth Clark, backing up his wife, said, 'Yes that's all right.' Lady Clark added, 'You'd better be careful, K. It might bounce.'

That terrible lunch marked the nadir of the Clark–Gill collaboration. That the series was ever made has to be credited to Gill's ability to persuade Kenneth Clark that his ideas could be realized. The concept was made more difficult by the fact that there were no precedents. 'This sort of essay had to move through geographical sequences if it were to have visual continuity,' Gill explained. It had to be a seamless blend of ideas, movement, colour, sound and image. It has to seem inevitable and it had to be a pioneering work in film. There were numerous false starts and endless sessions in which drafts were cut up, sometimes in mid paragraph, and reassembled into a pattern that would give structure to a sequence of images. The two men were still frostily polite, but the gap was narrowing. After a few months of filming the turning-point came one evening when Kenneth Clark went to see the editing of an early sequence, and entirely agreed with Gill about the sequences that should be dropped. His director realized that he not only had an intuitive understanding of film but was learning its grammar with lightning speed. His sense of structure was impeccable and his patience, as he wrote and rewrote, truly admirable. What looked unforced on camera might be the result of dozens of reshapings as one draft after another was tried and

discarded. It was the height of artifice but the principal actor made it
look offhand and unforced, almost cosy. As they began to sense that
their ideas were succeeding, a remarkable rapport developed
between Gill and Clark. What should the series be called? Kenneth
Clark thought it should be something modest, akin to the title eventually used by the Japanese: *Some Aspects of Western European
Civilisation*. Gill disagreed; it had to be *Civilisation*. Kenneth Clark
meekly assented.

Kenneth Clark had seen some of the Florence and Rome rushes by
August 1967 and found them somewhat stiff and 'lectury'. The paintings, however, were stunning, especially the fresco by Raphael, *Par-
nassus*, in the Pope's private library in the Vatican. He had made a
sequence inside the Greenwich Observatory where, he was to say,
'one breathes the atmosphere of humanized science'. He had also
filmed in Michel de Montaigne's tower, that haven of refuge for the
famous French essayist whose love for the classics was equalled by his
detachment. Forced into isolation by the wars of religion, Montaigne
retreated into an introspection that, Kenneth Clark believed, really
marked the end of the heroic spirit of the Renaissance.

Perilous introspection and melancholy versus the world of action:
it was clear which of the two he preferred. He positively beamed with
delight at being released from his own tower. What a pleasure, he
exulted early in 1967, to be in contact with such stimulating people.
The enthusiasm of Gill was contagious, since he adored making films
and thought of nothing else, but they were all like that. Peter Montagnon, for instance, another director on the series (Anne Turner was
the third), who was a genius at organizing, had arranged shooting
schedules so masterfully that, when Kenneth Clark appeared, the
crew was ready and he did not have to waste hours cooling his heels.
This was important since, despite Jane's fear of flying, hatred of boats
and terror while a passenger in cars going faster than forty miles an
hour, she was coming along. K was again embarking on something
new. He needed her and she knew it.

Once K had made up his mind to like *Civilisation*, Jane charmed
everyone whom she had previously been at such pains to antagonize.
Gill found her enormously helpful as a mouthpiece for her husband's
unspoken feelings. For instance, when they shot Michelangelo's
David in the Accademia the ratio of man to huge statue was so
unbalanced that drastic measures were called for. A platform was

improvised, a pyramid of crates, and Kenneth Clark mounted man-fully. Jane took in the situation at a glance and then went to Michael Gill. 'K's not happy up there,' she said solemnly. Gill commented, 'She was flawed and difficult, but she was also extremely acute and amazingly helpful to him.' Jane watched patiently for hours. She made intelligent suggestions. She went far past her bedtime uncom-plainingly and was always ready to take decisive action. Once when the Swiss Guards were unwilling to let them in to the Sistine Chapel for a filming session, Jane, Gill recalled, was all for getting out of the car and clobbering them.

By the autumn of 1967 Kenneth Clark was in Holland filming Rembrandt, a pivotal sequence, and trying not to eat too much. This was difficult since the food was not only plentiful but superb and people were offended if one did not leave a clean plate. He arose from every meal feeling like a blimp. Just the same it was refreshing to be pampered like an infant, instead of playing nurse for an even greater infant.

After a concentrated two weeks of filming in Italy early in 1968, he returned convinced that he had seen more works of art than he had done for years. He gave a prayer of thanks that his responses were, if anything, more acute than ever. The only problem had been that the sun had been very hot and the churches very cold, so that one either staggered about in a coat or sneezed and froze in the transept. He could not decide which he liked best, Assisi or Urbino – sacred or profane love – and certainly did his best performance at Assisi, although unfortunately a fly got into the lens during one very long 'take'. He wanted to use the resulting film and say that the blur the viewers could see was Brother Fly, and that they should not adjust their sets.

The ducal palace of Urbino, creation of the first duke, Federigo da Montefeltro, was unlike any other palace – the most ravishing inter-ior in the world. It was marvellous to spend four days there, instead of the usual twenty-four hours, and to run in and out at whim. The whole building was permeated with the character of that first Duke, that courageously cultivated and evolved being. To be human: that was the spirit that pervaded Urbino.

Kenneth Clark's normal round of activity had been sharply curtailed by *Civilisation*'s demands, though he had squeezed in some commit-tee meetings and made speeches at Aldeburgh and in Holland to honour Henry Moore. He was making tedious revisions to his book on Piero, having finished some necessary work on the outdated 1939 edition of *Leonardo da Vinci*. As consultant he had the leading young Leonardo scholar, Carlo Pedretti. He also had Margaret Slythe.

When they met in 1966, Mrs Slythe was writing a thesis on book illustration and establishing herself as a librarian, researcher and antiquarian. The suggestion was made that she might help organize Kenneth Clark's library. She and her husband Vincent were invited to see the size of the problem: 20,000 books in no particular order, plus hundreds of others still in packing cases. Mrs Slythe remembers that her future employer said, as her husband picked up a delicately beautiful object, 'Take care of that glass, it's four hundred years old.' He replied carefully, 'I'd like to point out that it's cracked already.'

Despite this guarded start, they liked each other. She compared him to a 'jaunty punter at Kempton Park' and he, amused, sent her a copy of his new book, *Rembrandt and the Italian Renaissance*. Soon she was insisting that he needed an indispensable assistant, a Nicky Mariano, referring to Bernard Berenson's consummate secretary and *amour*. He, with exemplary adroitness, was agreeing with her while turning her down. Still, he was inviting her to lectures and to tea in B5 Albany, and thought she might help on his Leonardo revisions. They could sit on opposite sides of a large desk, checking the hundreds of entries. He thought it might be 'necessary to sit on the same side occasionally'.

At one of those first meetings he asked her to accompany him to a lecture and keep him awake since it was taking place after lunch, during the hour in which he had, since the war years, taken a nap. 'I hardly knew him and didn't know where to touch him, i.e., should I prod him on the knee and say "Wake up?"' she said. Or they went to exhibitions, where he gave her lessons in procedure: 'He, "We are standing here looking at this horrendous picture because the artist is over there. Now we can move on."' As she came to know him, she discovered a double image. 'For instance, whenever we went to Windsor Castle library to work, we would have a lot of fun in the car. Then as he got to the castle he'd put on his Po face, as I called it, and no one could have penetrated that. Once inside he would revert back to his fun-loving, bottom-pinching self.' He was an exhilarating person to be with because there was nothing he could not do. He actually ran in those days. She would accompany him back from Wheeler's, his favourite restaurant, to B5 Albany and find herself racing beside him. She would protest. He would apologize and slow down but, within minutes, he was off again. He made her feel that wherever the action was, that was where he was; and that was what she wanted.

Both of them, it was clear, enjoyed the challenge of concurrent relationships. While accepting that for herself, she had not realized the complexity of K's involvements until the fateful, inevitable day when she discovered a love letter. Even though he went to enormous lengths to reassure her, she could not help feeling badly treated – 'It's appalling to say so, but I wasn't grand enough for him.' Nevertheless, she remained a loyal friend all his life, as well as Jane's defender. As for Jane, 'K was so jumpy and protective while we were at Windsor. He'd ring up six or seven times to see if she were still on her feet. No one actually said the words that mamma needed treatment. Only very close to the end did he ever mention her drinking at all. It seemed important to K that some semblance of domestic dignity be maintained.' And, despite their correct public stance – no letters mailed to Saltwood, strict decorum at all times – Jane was bound to find out, and of course she resented it.

> She was appalling to me. She'd come in where I was working and say, 'You've overstepped the mark this time', in a triumphant, condemning way, and I understood. She hated that it wasn't *her* – all those times coming back from Windsor with our eyes shining. Then she'd lash out for ten minutes, saying, 'Well of course it's too much for K, carrying all those boxes of books around', and then she'd get over it.

There is no doubt that K found the attentions of an intelligent, attractive woman thirty years his junior hard to resist. He could not bring himself to throw away her letters, which lay around dangerously. He was calling her his obsession, telling her she should hover over his bed and catch his thoughts as he lay awake. He provided an unconscious clue to his state of mind when he wrote that he had feared his emotions were deadened, and it was paradise to know that his feelings and senses were still in working order. How he wished he had received such letters thirty years earlier, when he needed them badly, and was still capable of responding. Even so, perhaps she did not realize how complicated old people's lives could become, the ancient intermeshings and the hidden complications. It was too late for him to sunder the ties, but the very thought of seeing her made him feel giddy.

The problem was, he told Margaret, that television programmes could not involve her as much as would a book. Thank heavens he was finally reaching the end of writing scripts, and some of them had turned out well. There was still an enormous amount of filming to be done. In the autumn of 1968 he returned to Paris in search of a suitably terrifying prison setting with which to illustrate Beethoven's *Fidelio* and found it at Vincennes. Thence to Malmaison, where he sat at the very desk at which Napoleon wrote his Code. They went on to the Château de Ferney, Voltaire's country house outside Geneva, where it rained steadily, destroying all hope of filming in the garden. As for Rousseau's island on the lake of Bienne, that was exactly as he had described it, a miniature world, almost unchanged. Kenneth Clark spoke his piece in a little rowing-boat, exactly like the one in which Rousseau had drifted about the lake. That was followed by a simple, rustic feast in the old Hospice, now a farm. They went up into the high Jura Alps for a film sequence on Turner and found a splendid, Turneresque valley. Alas, a plane ruined the best shot, and afterwards the light lost some of its magic. The hazards of film making were, in fact, formidable. Once their cameraman was attacked by swans. On another occasion all sound was rendered impossible by a repeating gun that was scaring birds away from a nearby vineyard. In Paris, just as they were about to film, a barge sailed into the picture and ruined the effect.

Sometimes, however, chance conspired to their spectacular advantage. Back up in the mountains, the whole line of the Alps, from Mont Blanc to the Matterhorn, was suddenly revealed rising above the clouds, just as Ruskin had seen it. While cowbells clattered, Kenneth Clark began to recite a piece in which he discussed Turner and Goethe as well as the study of clouds. He was standing with his back to the scenery and, just as he arrived at the word clouds, he saw the crew break into smiles. As if on cue, the whole landscape was erased by a giant cloud which, seconds later, had enveloped him as well. It was a magnificent piece of luck.

By Christmas, he was worn out from the effort and went to Ischia to recuperate at the invitation of Sir William Walton. He could not begin to describe to Margaret what it meant to go to sleep that night without having to be concerned about the next day's schedule. It was marvellous to think that two years' work was over at last, and yet he could not suppress a feeling of flatness, even grief, as he came to the end of such blissful happiness. It was back to Montaigne's Tower for him, or was it? Perhaps he should begin his autobiography.

When the idea for *Civilisation* was first mooted, Kenneth Clark had just finished work on a lecture for Oxford University about the end of the High Renaissance (1520–35). The abrupt decline of Florentine painting was difficult to explain. The conditions of patronage were unchanged and the political situation no more menacing than it had been two decades before. To explain the decline, he believed one must look at the subsequent life histories of the artists themselves which showed, he wrote, a failure of nerve.

Botticelli, for instance, that exquisite sensualist and poet of beautiful line, painted, later in life, scenes from the life of St Zenobius which, to Kenneth Clark, were almost violent renunciations of the beauty he had once celebrated. Even in the confident masterpieces of Leonardo and Michelangelo one could not escape the uneasy feeling that mankind felt overwhelmed by fate. An increasing self-doubt or actual neurosis had brought the most glorious of all moments in the Renaissance to an end. Only Raphael, with his superb self-confidence and even temperament, had escaped being tainted by the general malaise.

In *Civilisation*, although Kenneth Clark's scope was encyclopaedic, his view was personal. Although civilization might seem solidly based in mankind's extraordinary mental and spiritual powers, the fall of the Roman Empire showed that it was vulnerable. Fear was its enemy: fear of wars, invasion, plague or famine that made action futile. To that one must add, he thought, emotion, which he saw as wholly destructive. The psyche, with all its 'false turnings and dissolving perspectives', was a labyrinth; entering it, one left all hope behind. A successful civilization looked not inward but outward, lest it destroy its own confidence in its capabilities. Similar fears could be discerned in our own era, despite the achievements of engineering and science and the advances made by humanitarianism. These had to be weighed against the loss of religious faith, the sense of purposelessness and the spectre of nuclear annihilation.

'Things fall apart; the centre cannot hold,' he wrote, quoting W.B. Yeats. 'The trouble with our present civilisation [Kenneth Clark implied] was that we have lost touch with our spiritual roots, our sense of the human scale, our sense of man's proper place in the frame of nature.' It was an elegy for a vanished past. Behind it, however, one might glimpse a flare of rebellion. Like Balzac, one ought to defy the conventional wisdom and uphold beliefs 'that have been repudiated by the liveliest intellects' of one's time, showing

one's unalterable opposition to the forces threatening one's humanity. In retrospect, *Civilisation*'s pessimistic assessment and the small
hope offered by its creator are easy to see. Yet when the series was
shown in Britain and the US in 1969 and 1970 almost no one noticed.

In the first place there was the herculean amount of energy expen-
ded: 80,000 miles travelled, eleven countries visited, 130 locations
used, £130,000 spent (then a record), and enough feet of film shot to
make six feature-length films. Sheer prodigal energy is no guarantor
of quality but in this case it was equalled by the exhilarating breadth
of knowledge and insight demonstrated by Kenneth Clark. 'Lord
Clark has used his masterly knowledge and understanding of the
arts of Western civilisation to describe and appraise its creative
achievements. He opens his knowledge, like a window through which
his viewer-listener ... can catch a vision of the whole gamut of life in
the Western world', the *Times Literary Supplement* wrote. The
Burlington Magazine commented that 'the *Civilisation* series ...
represents the mature response to things that matter of a man who is
perceptive, sensitive and wise'. It was a testimony to man's genius,
Sylvia Clayton observed in the *Daily Telegraph*. 'It is this underlying
faith in humanity together with a profound respect for work of genius
that has made the series for me the most enjoyable ever produced on
television.' The series 'was in itself a contribution to civilisation', J.B.
Priestley wrote. Kenneth Clark had brought it off so triumphantly
because he combined sense with sensibility, courage with enterprise,
wide knowledge with tact and charm. Most of all there was his
passionate love of art, apparent in every phrase. It was easy to see the
series as he characterized it, 'an expression of gratitude for all the life-
giving experiences I have enjoyed in the last fifty years'. It was a work
of art.

Since to examine one's own nature, he said, was to discover
nothing positive but only shameful faults, Kenneth Clark was bound
to see the history of art and ideas from his own bias, and believe that
self-confidence depended upon a deliberate avoidance of inner
knowledge. Yet confidence based on accomplishment rather than an
intrinsic sense of worth was a fragile flower and, sensing it, he
despaired. What he never knew about himself was his tenacity and
courage, at its very best in his worst moments. He was pulling through
by the skin of his teeth – interestingly, that was the title of his first programme – and the message was not lost on his audience. What he also
did not anticipate, after baring his ideas, opinions and conclusions,

along with the very human and lovable qualities of mind and heart that he possessed, was that the response would be so overwhelming. *Essere umano*: it was his truest goal. There is no doubt that *Civilisation* was not just a landmark in the use of television, but a personal watershed.

Typically, he foresaw a hostile reaction, but since he never read newspapers it did not matter. He could not help seeing, however, that the early episodes looked superb in colour and were, at moments, even moving. He had already been asked to turn the series into a book and, after hesitating (Jane was again opposed), decided to do it. By the time the fifth episode had been shown, letters were arriving along with requests for interviews and he was being praised and flattered everywhere. If there were occasional criticisms from some members of the intelligentsia, these were drowned out in the clamorous approval – or Jane took care of it. At a BBC party following a preview of the series at the National Film Theatre, Jane was observed talking to a film producer. Suddenly she swung at him with her bag. Kenneth Clark was across the room and had her into the lift in about ten seconds saying, as he passed Margaret Slythe, 'See you back at Albany.' Jane had understood the producer to say that her husband had given a pedantic and rigid performance and that his ideas were outdated. So, she said, she punched him.

By the early summer of 1969, with all of the programmes viewed, he was working on proofs of the book and trying to answer forty or fifty letters a day. Some of them were very touching. A friend wrote to say that the films had restored his courage, after a year of disasters. Nine would-be suicides wrote that they now had a reason to go on living. He began to feel a wretched fraud and, when the stream of letters became an avalanche, found himself in tears. Soon there was a further reason to regret his new eminence: a life peerage.

He had tried his very best to decline, he told Margaret Slythe, but the Prime Minister was even cleverer at insisting than he was at evading it. As a result there were two hundred more letters to be answered, just as he was getting to the end of 600 *Civilisation* letters. He could not understand the appeal of the series unless it were due to a journalist's sense of timing.

When the films were shown at New York University in the autumn of 1969 he went there for six personal appearances during which he did what he called his 'Danny Kaye' act and accepted an honorary degree. The most daunting aspects of his schedule, which began at 9 a.m. and ended at midnight, were the receptions. Successive waves of people bore down upon him and by the time he had phrased a new response with the right combination of thankfulness and humility he was fairly well exhausted. That was bad enough but the next visit to America a year later was unbelievable. By then, *Civilisation* had been shown on national television, the book was a best-seller (it sold a million copies in the US alone) and he was famous. He had not even left London airport before being accosted by three separate Americans as guards were inspecting their luggage. Americans, he observed, thought of their momentary heroes in terms of a gigantic buffet. After the favourite had been poked, shoved and butted about there was likely to be nothing left of him but some pathetic shreds of lettuce. He had accepted an invitation to open an exhibition at the Metropolitan Museum of Art, which was not a success. In addition, it poured with rain and he had forgotten his umbrella. He staggered, dripping, into Bloomingdale's and asked the way to the umbrella counter. He was immediately recognized. Finding the right department, he was told that to sell Lord Clark an umbrella would be an honour. What a stroke of luck, the salesman continued. He had just come on temporarily from the glove department. Well, K told Jane, one could not help being touched. As for the Metropolitan, he could hardly move for crowds of young people, but that was far more fun than being by himself.

In Washington he was presented with a handsome medal at the National Gallery of Art. In *The Other Half* he described how he prepared to enter the gallery by the main door but was warned that he might be mobbed. He found himself in an enormous auditorium, walking the length of the room, while hundreds of people stood up and roared their approval, waving their arms and trying to touch him. It was a long walk to the podium and half way there, he burst into tears. He had felt, he wrote, like a doctor called to the scene of a disaster, who was being inundated with desperate pleas for help from those affected. But he was not a doctor, let alone a prophet of hope. To keep despair at bay, all he had were some meaningless clichés. That his audience chose to see him in the triumphant affirmative, as the repository of enduring values, was a cruel irony and he dared not disabuse them. He was an utter fraud.

What had happened? In *Of Love and Lust*, Theodor Reik recalled that the famous writer Anatole France, a modest man, took a trip to

North Africa during which he was celebrated and revered as a god. In one town in particular young girls stood on both sides of a staircase, wearing sashes on which the names of the author's books stood out in relief. France had to mount the steps between them. Halfway up, he wept. Such mingled feelings had their origins in an old daydream of being appreciated and loved that had never been fulfilled. The verdict was usually accepted with resignation. If one were not appreciated, it must be because one did not deserve it. So that when the great day actually dawned, the happiness felt like redemption, akin to being pardoned for one's sins. However, past feelings of unworthiness were bound to rise to the surface, making one feel one did not deserve to be loved.

How horrifying it was, Kenneth Clark wrote, that in America he really had been worshipped like a god. Now, because of a large grant, copies of his films were being sent all over the country. It was astonishing and how he wished it had never happened to him. The only thing he could do while he was there was offer a silent prayer that God would forgive him. He did not know why, but he was grateful just the same. He must, he decided, go into a retreat.

18 Other Parts of the Wood

*'Black spirits among the grey, all like a mist
between me and the green woods.' –*
JOHN RUSKIN

He had been appointed Chancellor of York University and a Peer of the Realm. He had been given yet another mark of its favour from the British Crown, the Order of Merit. He received an honorary doctorate in literature from Oxford University, and other honours, from academic institutions on both sides of the Atlantic, followed in profusion. People would not leave him alone but expected him to write introductions to their books, talk about deceased celebrities and go to farewell parties. As an 'authority', he was expected to make 'pronouncements' on increasingly tenuous grounds. He managed, courteously, to decline an invitation to write an appreciation on the occasion of Picasso's ninetieth birthday. When the same editor at the *New York Times*, Herbert Mitgang, asked for his opinion on the Watergate scandals, his refusal was less graceful.

However, what could be considered his crowning moment of recognition came in the early summer of 1970. He was invited by Winchester College to be received *Ad Portas* (at the gates). This ceremony, by which his old public school honoured the famous, went back to the seventeenth century when presiding Bishops of Winchester were formally greeted on their arrival. In those days it had been a point of pride to respond in Latin and though, in recent times, even such famous people as George V and Queen Elizabeth II had resorted to English, Kenneth Clark was not going to let tradition down.

When, at the end of Short Half, members of the school wandered around Meads and lit candles of farewell in those little Gothic niches called 'temples', how often, he wondered, did they think of their futures and their accomplishments once they left the delusive security of Winchester's walls? He himself had had no such thoughts while at school. His career there was undistinguished and he saw no bright future for himself nor, he thought, did his contemporaries. One man alone, Montague John Rendall, that great Victorian eccentric, might not have been too surprised by developments. His old headmaster understood that the ones who profited most from Winchester's teachings were not necessarily those who conformed most successfully while there. The reference to his unhappiness was typically oblique.

He might have burst into tears, as when he had walked the length of the auditorium in Washington. He might at least, as his friend David Knowles thought, have derived some bleak satisfactions from the revenges of time, when he thought of his own miserable school days. He merely found it depressing. Despite the wonderful beauty of the place all he could think of, he told Janet Stone, was what poor use he had made of his time there and what a little creep he had been, probably still was. The speech in Latin had fallen flat and he had not even moderately enjoyed the honour, let alone felt pride in his accomplishment. Perhaps he was past caring.

He was growing old and tired and there was too much to do. One of the great unresolved issues was making arrangements for his and Jane's old age. He had always imagined that when he retired they would move to Florence. The dreamlike vision returned to him when, a decade after his old master's death, he went there to narrate a documentary about Bernard Berenson for BBC-TV in the autumn of 1970. It was wonderful to be at I Tatti again and the affection of the old servants, who treated him like an heir, was touching. But, despite a momentary nostalgia, he did not really want to end his days in Tuscany. He hardly wanted to leave the grounds of Saltwood. So he decided to give the castle to his elder son and build a new house in what was the kitchen garden, with a clear view across a sunken field to the battlements, the turrets and the ancient grey stones. An architect was hired – John King, a friend of Mrs Slythe's – to design a new house with three wings leading from a central hall, on the model of Saltwood. King would have preferred a two-storey building which would echo the castle's turrets, constructed of the same grey stone, but Jane insisted on a single floor and K on a white-boarded exterior which, he thought, could be used with rather the same fenestration as in Japanese architecture.

When a model was brought to the castle for inspection in the autumn of 1969 K pronounced it exactly what they had been hoping for and even Jane, although awash in her private sea, was perfectly delighted. However, when the time to leave his panelled room, and Saltwood, drew nearer, he became saddened beyond words. By

March 1971, he detested the new house, called it the Motel, and refused to go there. The thought of leaving 'Salters', with its wonderful, lavish use of space, and its crazily placed rooms, for the mathematical predictability of the three boxes, he wrote (referring to the three wings), was almost more than he could endure. He began to pack, numb with sadness.

It was curious to see which paintings and *objets d'art* would work in the Motel (it was eventually named The Garden House) and which would not. Nothing too emphatic could be hung and if he had owned a Van Gogh he would have had to sell it. The fifteenth-century Italians were lost on its walls but, naturally enough, the Henry Moores made a marvellous statement in the hall, and there were the melancholic beauty of Robin Ironside's portrait of Colette in the guest bedroom, the splendour of the Turner in the drawing-room, and the delicate charm of Jack Yeats's painting of a rose in a washbasin, that looked enchanting in Jane's bathroom. He had to concede that the views from the windows were splendid and that most of his collection looked better in the new house because, in Saltwood, there simply had not been enough natural light for the Constables, Renoirs and Pasmores.

The actual signing-over of Saltwood on his sixty-eighth birthday, a gay and sentimental affair, was celebrated with champagne. It tasted so delicious that he drank a great deal, became very talkative and told stories like an old lion. Now that he was actually living in the house he really liked it. It was exactly what he wanted and that, his London assistant Catherine Porteous would say, cut him down to size.

The gift was celebrated with champagne rather than a good bottle of wine because, ever since his operation, red wine had tasted like ink. Early in 1971 he had discovered that, as he expected, his gall-bladder was full of stones. However it seemed vitally important to postpone an operation until Jane, immersed in laundry and linens, and tactfully watched by their indispensable factotum, Leonard Lindley, could be left in the comparative security of the one-floor Motel. He went into hospital with perfect calm, even gaiety, but was disturbed, when he returned, at Jane's state of mind. For the first night or two alone she thought she had seen people peering in at the windows. It was very worrying.

He was also concerned about his shortcomings as a correspondent, particularly where Janet Stone was concerned. What might serve as a kind of letter to her was his latest writing project: his autobiography. When he had been asked to contribute an essay to a volume in celebration of Benjamin Britten's fiftieth birthday, he had begun by thinking back to his memories of Aldeburgh and ended by writing a lyrical evocation of his childhood. The essay, *The Other Side of the Alde*, was charmingly illustrated with some exquisite drawings by Reynolds Stone, printed by the Stones at Litton Cheney and published by Warren Editions, but the memories it had released kept multiplying. He began to record them on a plane trip to Palm Beach, continued in Washington in 1971 and convalesced from his gall bladder operation with more memories. The more he wrote the more the book's character changed. His original plan had been to write essays on various aspects of his life, but he had ended up writing more about himself than he planned. Then he tried to introduce a succession of portraits of people who had influenced him and that made him wonder whether the book's detachment was becoming too marked. On the whole it was not a bad form for an autobiography, since the thought of self-analysis was too daunting. He made a similar comment to the novelist Rosamond Lehmann after the book's publication. Several of his friends wondered why he had not looked deeper but he lacked the ability. Or rather, whenever he tried, the vision was so appalling that he did not dare to examine it.

His title, *Another Part of the Wood*, is, interestingly, also the title used by the British novelist Beryl Bainbridge for a work which appeared in 1968. The coincidence seems to have been genuine but there are some interesting overtones. Wales, the country in which Kenneth Clark spent many wartime months, and about which he dreamed in old age, was the setting for Bainbridge's novel. For her it was a more or less allegorical wood, on which curtains were raised or dropped as the dramatic moment required, to reveal one set of characters after another following the tangled thread of their lives. For Bainbridge, the title seemed an obvious choice; for Clark, a puzzling one. It was certainly meant to be read symbolically but the text gave no clues.

Kenneth Clark tried to remedy the omission in the preface to his second volume. He explained that he had conflated the stage directions of *A Midsummer Night's Dream* with that passage in Dante's *Inferno* beginning, 'I found myself in a dark wood.' He was also thinking of the remark, 'We're not out of the wood yet.' Since his first volume ended with the outbreak of the Second World War it seemed a reasonable explanation. Yet he had used those same lines from Dante decades before when, on the occasion of his thirty-fifth birthday in 1938, a year before *Another Part of the Wood* ends, he complained of being lost in a dark wood. If that same phrase floated to the surface just as he was pondering the themes of a lifetime one must ask why he still felt, like Dante, as if he were looking back helplessly at the past and fearfully towards the future? The clues were there. Jane, he wrote in 1962, seemed much better but he did not pretend that they were out of the wood. Twelve years later he was still using the phrase to Juliette Huxley, wife of Sir Julian: they were not, he wrote, out of the wood yet.

'Oh, but it was so public!', a friend said. 'At Covent Garden one could see her swaying in her box. It was dreadful.' Jill Day Lewis, widow of the poet, saw Jane being picked up off the pavement outside the Arts Council. Michael Gill's most vivid memory was of leaving a sober Jane at the entrance of S. Maria Maggiore in Rome while he and Kenneth Clark went up to the belfry. When they came down fifteen minutes later Jane was so unsteady that she was reeling. An art critic remembered the 'clump and thumpety' of Kenneth Clark coming up the stairs at Saltwood with Jane on her hands and knees, crawling up behind him.

At one French Embassy party one of the guests, Lady Gladwyn, saw Jane sink to the floor. Kenneth Clark, there with Colette, said, 'Mamma's fallen down', and they were laughing to hide their embarrassment, but Lady Gladwyn realized that something was wrong. She took Jane by the arms and propped her up on a chair. As she did so Kenneth Clark gave her an eloquent look of thanks. The French Ambassador's wife said, 'I can understand people getting drunk at a party, but to arrive that way!' Jane was said to have fallen down at more embassies than any other woman in London. Tumbling, K called it.

If Jane felt that her husband had let her down in their marriage, by accident or design she was turning the tables. Her first fall appears to have come in the summer of 1954, just after his relationship with Janet Stone began, when she broke an arm. Over the next few years there were many 'tumbles'. Just before a trip he was planning to Liverpool she fell and broke two ribs. In the summer of 1966, on returning from another trip, he was greeted by the news that Jane had fallen in the garden and cut her head on the corner of a marble table.

It was the fourth accident at night, others have led to a broken rib, a twisted ankle and a broken wrist. It showed how dangerous it was for him to leave her. Since four members of the Royal Family were coming and could not be put off Jane made a brave showing, though her enormous black eye was covered with sticking plaster. That was the week Jane discovered a phone bill in which a suspicious number of calls were found to have been made to Litton Cheney in Dorset and perhaps it was only a coincidence that she seemed particularly drunk. She passed out on her bathroom floor and it was no easy matter to drag her into bed. He begged Janet not to mention it to anyone.

In December 1967, a week before Christmas, Jane had a really terrible accident. She crashed down the steep stone steps between the hall and dining room and was knocked out. He, being upstairs, did not discover her for half an hour. Again, he begged his confidante to tell no one. The following summer Jane broke bones in both feet. He did not know how she had done it. In 1970, there was another nasty fall down the same stone steps in which she cut her chin badly and damaged her right hand.

Jane's falls from grace, as his letters indicated, were a private matter. Their friends were astounded that K would never convey, by the flicker of an eyelash, that anything was amiss. To keep the outside world at arm's length had become so ingrained that, although perfectly aware of his troubles, his friends – the Andersons and Pipers for instance – knew the subject was taboo. It was part of K's inner code to keep the secret because, as he wrote, 'I believe in courtesy, the ritual by which we avoid hurting other people's feelings by satisfying our own egos.' And if Jane, who had tried so hard to keep up appearances, should be destroying their image before everyone, if she should be deliberately injuring herself, like Zelda Fitzgerald enraged at Scott, nothing would come of it as long as he, like grandmother McArthur, refused to react.

Yet everyone knew. Colin Clark, in particular, wondered why his father continued to take his mother to one social event after another. That, however, might be explained by K's comment (to Janet Stone) that Jane had been so outraged when he had attended two parties for art historians without her, that he could never exclude her again. Similarly, on the occasions when he was pressed to explain why Jane drank, and he replied that she liked it, it would seem lame unless one knew that he had tried to help her find a cure and that she had emphatically rejected it. Colin had advised him against a confrontation.

In fact, even to mention her drinking caused such an outburst that K shrank from the ordeal. Colette commented, 'She never admitted she was a drunk. Never admitted anything, my mother.' This could have unfortunate repercussions as when, on a trip to Newcastle in August 1963, Jane had a violent attack of abdominal pain, nausea and vomiting on the train and had to be taken off. To avoid a row, K did not mention her alcoholic intake and her doctors were at a loss to account for the verdict: pancreatitis. As a continual invalid Jane oppressed him and made him feel trapped. On the other hand, there was much to be said for the fact that, once immersed in her private world, she was too woozily benevolent to make trouble. Colette remembered her father commenting that it was a 'toss-up' between Mamma in her rages, or Mamma drunk, and in some ways he preferred her drunk. That should have settled it, but the unanswered questions were always somewhere under the surface. Rosemary Gordon, the wife of the producer Peter Montagnon, who was a Jungian analyst, recalled that Kenneth Clark had referred, with his usual delicate obliqueness, to the coincidence between the behaviour of his father and his wife, and wondered what might explain it. Leonard Lindley was given yet another indication of the questions pursuing his employer one day when he picked him up at the station. Lindley reported that Lady Clark had been in fine fettle during Lord Clark's absence, and had not 'touched a drop'. K looked at him searchingly: 'You mean it's my fault then?' he asked.

His attempts to 'jolly' Jane along and affect a normal life continued. So did the obstacles. As at 'Salters', Jane could not be left alone. She never watched television or read a book. Instead she seemed in a brown study, or talked endlessly on the phone, or worried about the right Christmas present for each servant. She was very forgetful. Although Reynolds and Janet Stone had already seen The Garden House, Jane insisted they had not, and would not listen to arguments. It made the pretence of normal life hard to sustain. Guests continued to arrive. When Yehudi Menuhin and his wife came to stay there was Jane, sporting an enormous black eye, obviously tipsy but determined to take care of them. On a second visit some years later they all had lunch and Jane, much the worse for wear, went off for her afternoon nap. The violinist was about to perform and his wife had assumed that Mr Lindley would be there to prepare the thermos of herb tea that her husband always took to a performance to have in the interval with nuts and honey. However, it was Lindley's afternoon off. Mrs Menuhin heard noises in the kitchen and found Jane there, somehow still standing, staggering around trying to make the tea.

One series of films, on six pioneers of modern art (Manet, Cézanne, Monet, Seurat, Rousseau and Munch) had been made with his son Colin as director. It was followed by fifteen educational television programmes about the Classic-Romantic period, also with Colin. He was hard at work writing and filming. Mornings were spent making one film from 9.30 to 12.45, and afternoons in rehearsals for the next. Jane was passing out most evenings and it was quite a job to get her into bed. He had taken her to one of the best doctors in Britain, who took the view that she needed confidence and reassurance. Jane interpreted this as meaning that there was nothing wrong with her physically and that she was free to continue her heavy drinking.

There were three taxing weeks ahead before his next trip to America in the spring of 1972. He had two long lectures to write and a third to concoct, his translator was coming to prepare a French version of *Civilisation*, and there were endless pointless parties connected with the opening of an exhibition. As he struggled onwards Jane came down with flu. As soon as she recoverd she celebrated by going on a colossal binge, so that she could hardly stand or make herself understood. He did not know how it would all end.

Nevertheless he was determined to take Jane with him to Washington and the University of Virginia, where he was to give an address on Jefferson, although he did not see how they would get there. She was falling down all day. He himself had a small collapse from sheer exhaustion, could not eat or think and was having terrifying retinal images of Kandinskys in front of his eyes. When he went to lie down, Jane was enraged and had hysterics all evening. Obviously he could not afford the luxury of falling ill.

The American trip was more successful than he had dared to hope and he returned to a full schedule of lectures, dinners, meetings and films. He was preparing a television programme about the rape of Bath, that extraordinary eighteenth-century town in Somerset that had survived the Industrial Revolution and German bombs only to be torn down by the city fathers in their wisdom. The script almost wrote itself and Jane was in wonderful shape. A minor attack of cystitis caused her to stop drinking and she amazed him by being coherent, cheerful and completely adorable for two days. She even sat through a performance of the uncut *Don Carlos*, five solid hours without a murmur, and that was more than he could say for himself.

Such happy times, when Jane was clear-witted, able to travel, almost her old self, were followed by the predictable lapses. There must have been another bottle in the back room, he wrote, after they had attended a neighbour's cocktail party during which she did her by-now famous act. In fact she lay on the ground in the middle of a circle of cars and gave departing guests no end of trouble. He finally got her home and by the time they arrived she was almost recovered and remembered nothing. If asked how she felt, she would invariably reply that she was in fine form and perfectly content. Since she seemed unruffled by the episode, he could not help thinking, in a detached sort of way, what a marvellous shot it would have made for a film.

Alan was concerned that his father was destroying his creative powers out of a mistaken sense of duty. K, however, thought they were dead anyway. As a writer he was something of a con artist, but he had to say that he made an excellent male nurse. Around Christmas 1972 they both had flu and ended up in the same nursing-home in Folkestone. Jane's letter to Sir Colin Anderson was nostalgic about the Christmas they had spent in Jersey in 1969. They had stayed on the large estate bought by Morna's father, that sloped down to an immense sandy bay facing due south. There they had walked all day in the hot sun. Could they not repeat that wonderful experience one more time, Jane asked, before some of them were dead?

Among the friends on the fringe of their lives were Edward and Nolwen Rice. Edward Rice was a wealthy and influential cattle and sheep farmer, at one time owner of a 5,000-acre estate in Til-manstone, Kent, and Dane Court, a twelve-bedroom mansion dating from the eighteenth century, standing on sixty-five acres. His wife Nolwen also farmed at Parfondeval, a smaller property in Normandy that had been in de Janzé hands for over three hundred years. Her father, Frédéric Jacques François, Comte de Janzé, was a writer, occasional lecturer for the Vatican and chairman of the local county council.

Nolwen, who was born in 1922, hardly remembers living with her parents. They separated when she was four and a year later, in 1927, the Paris and London press were full of reports of an extraordinary shooting incident that took place at the Gard du Nord. Raymond de Trafford, a gambler, alcoholic and 'fine desperado' as Evelyn Waugh would describe him when they met in Kenya in 1931, was about to leave for England. Nolwen's American mother, born Alice Silverthorne of Chicago, now the Comtesse de Janzé, entered de Trafford's first-class compartment and fired a gun at him. She then turned the gun on herself. Since it was obviously a crime of passion, and the principals in the case were well placed, public interest was intense. The Comtesse de Janzé would give no explanation, murmuring 'It is my secret' from her hospital bed. As soon as she was well enough she was imprisoned in the infamous gaol of St Lazare, in the cell once occupied by Mata Hari. She was tried, given a suspended sentence of six months in prison and fined the French equivalent of 16s. 6d. At the trial Raymond de Trafford testified on her behalf and, a few years later, the couple married and went to farm in Kenya. The marriage lasted for three months. Apparently de Trafford's shortcomings were too much to take at close quarters, even among the startlingly casual set of English émigrés with whom Alice romped in Kenya. Nolwen's mother never really recovered from the effect of her self-inflicted wounds which required eleven operations. She eventually committed suicide.

Nolwen and her younger sister Paola spent six months of every year at Parfondeval in the care of their Irish grandmother, née Moya Hennessy, daughter of the Irish-American painter William John Hennessy, and the remainder in Paris with their American great-aunt, Mrs Frank Edwin May. Nolwen dearly loved the parents she seldom saw. A visit from either of these handsome and vital people, both first-rate *raconteurs*, was a major event in her life. But she was perhaps closer to her father and was inconsolable when he died; she was only eleven years old. Then, at the age of seventeen, she lost her mother and grandmother in the same year.

Nolwen was educated at home, attending a musical academy in Paris. She took lessons at the Art Institute of Chicago, graduated from Sarah Lawrence College in 1944 and served in Free French field hospitals in the Normandy campaign, Alsace and Germany. In 1948 she married Lionel Armand-Delille, a captain in the French army, landowner and farmer, who had also inherited a beautiful old property, a mediaeval castle near Chartres named Maillebois. They had a son, Frédéric, and a daughter, Angélique. The marriage failed and Nolwen married Edward Rice in 1962.

The Rices and Clarks had friends in common, including the writers Peter Quennell and Cyril Connolly, but did not meet until the success of *Civilisation* prompted Edward Rice to write a fan letter. They exchanged visits and it was soon apparent that Nolwen and K shared the same dilemma. For the last years of his life Edward Rice was an invalid, suffering from cancer, and Nolwen would wake up in the morning to find her pillow drenched with tears. She remembered a lunch at The Garden House, attended by the Andersons. Jane was still standing, but barely. After lunch Edward became ill. They got him to the bathroom, where he was violently sick. Nolwen remembered the strong feeling of sympathy that came from her host. That more was involved than simply a sense of shared fate Jane, for all her befuddled state, seemed to know. She thought, she told K, that he was almost in love with Nolwen. It would be easy to see why K would be attracted to this clever, witty woman with her dragon-fly movements, her gay little comments and her habit of wrinkling up her nose at something too funny for words before opening her mouth in a large, silent guffaw. Nolwen was unconstrained and free, gypsy-like almost, in the way she racketed through life.

Jane continued no better, in fact slightly worse, and K left her alone for his annual trip to America in May 1973. He telephoned daily from New York to her hospital bed, where she was recovering from cystitis and haemorrhoids. While there she was clear and crisp, but once back at The Garden House she had been submerged and incomprehensible. On his return there was more to do than ever in the way of lectures. There was also an essay to write on Henry Moore's drawings, chosen from five hundred photographs, the hardest work he had done since his Leonardo studies. He was also committed to make a film on Egypt with Colin and Michael Gill called *In the Beginning* and preparations were under way for a lunch at the Café Royal to celebrate his seventieth birthday. Most of the old friends would be there, including the Menuhins, Dame Margot Fonteyn and her husband Dr Roberto Arias, Mr and Mrs J.B. Priestley, Sir Colin Anderson, Irene Worth, John Sparrow, Mary Potter, Lady Margaret Douglas-Home, Brinsley Ford, Burnet Pavitt, John and Myfanwy Piper and Janet Stone. There were some omissions, K wrote by way of apology to Margaret Slythe, who was not invited to the party. He had become fairly apprehensive about the affair. Still it would not quite be the gathering of ten girl friends that Margaret thought he ought to have had. He did not think he would have exactly enjoyed that, either.

Given Jane's handicaps, the decision to take her on a tour of the eastern Mediterranean in the autumn of 1973 seemed ill-advised. There would be the tiring sight-seeing trips, the terrifying views from heights, the drives around serpentine bends at dangerous speeds above five miles an hour, the crowded buses, strange faces, loud voices, early-morning starts, the delays. The decision can only be seen in terms of Jane's unwillingness to let him go alone and his conviction that she could not be left.

In the case of this invitation to lead a group of Americans on a Smithsonian Institution cruise, the advantages seemed narrowly to outweigh the drawbacks. He knew from experience that she drank far less on holiday. He hoped she would enjoy sitting peacefully on deck and disembarking at intervals to see beautiful things. He was excited by the challenge of lecturing on Sumerian, Greek, Egyptian and Islamic art, even if the information so stimulated his imagination that he stayed awake all night. But there were some ominous signs of distress from Jane. She had become very shaky, as she always did just before a journey.

They were to meet the cruise at Athens and flew to Greece a few days before. Jane was even strong enough to climb up the Acropolis, although she had to be almost carried down. All seemed well until the terrible moment when she was unable to climb the stairs leading to the wall paintings from Santorin and his heart sank. He was even gloomier once they went aboard the *Argonaut*. The cruise had all been a horrible mistake, he told Janet Stone. The moment they saw their cabin Jane, already upset by having had to endure a bus trip and all those loud American voices, burst into tears. She went on crying for another twelve hours and was barely keeping herself in check by large doses of medicine. He found the ship most tolerable. It was true that some of the passengers were trying but they were, after all, *mon cher publique*, and he their sage, even if this image was rapidly being destroyed.

Jane seemed to be recovering. She enjoyed the sightseeing, and all was going well until they anchored off Palermo and the boat was hit by a tidal wave. In *The Other Half*, Kenneth Clark described the narrow escape of the passengers, wearing only the clothes they had on, and Jane's composure and fortitude in the difficult days that followed. She seemed to survive wonderfully well. However, once at home, she had so little grasp of reality that she was asking him when the ship would reach harbour. He was very depressed, but went on working because he did not see what else he could do. They went to visit friends at Oxford and, on their way home, stayed at Albany. He was cooking some pasta and Jane was on the phone. Suddenly she fell to the floor. She had had a stroke and the whole of her left side was paralysed.

As K realized, Jane's stroke was a turning-point in their lives. His fragile remaining hope that somehow she would return to normal – even if he did not know how that could happen – had been destroyed. Nevertheless he tried very much to act as if normality was within their grasp. His detailed description of the stroke in *The Other Half*, and particularly Jane's hairbreadth escape from death once she was back home, showed just how much energy and determination he had invested in her recovery. And, for some time afterwards, her improvement confounded the best medical opinion. Two months after her stroke she had talked to Henry Moore on the telephone, if incoherently. Helped by a platoon of Scottish nurses, she could be dragged as far as K's room and sat on the window seat beside his chair. Having done nothing for months but concentrate his energies upon her, he began to feel safe enough to make cautious forays back into his world. He was adding the finishing touches to the last part of his autobiography, the start of the war. It was such a dreary time for them both. He could see from Jane's diaries how often she had been ill – already. He had begun a book review, there was a trip to London to attend a British Museum meeting.... As for Jane, she was well enough to dictate a letter to Morna and Colin Anderson. She apologized for not writing personally, explaining that she had not yet recovered the use of her arm. They also had had terrible disasters in their lives and would understand what it meant to have a stroke. She had not yet learned to walk but felt perfectly healthy and hoped to be back to normal in a month, she wrote. It was the 19th of February 1974.

19 The Last of the Roses

'Then glut thy sorrow on a morning rose.' –
JOHN KEATS, Ode on Melancholy

On an end table beside the white upholstered chair on which he always sat to write, one might find a telephone and his glasses case, along with a marble egg of beautifully variegated browns, beiges and rust, matches, scissors for opening letters, paper clips and a brown button. There was also a medallion presented by the National Gallery of Art in Washington on the day of the long walk up to the podium. It was engraved, 'For distinguished service to education in Art: Lord Clark, CH, KCB.'

His chair was placed beside a large, rather conventional picture window overlooking a terrace, something of a suntrap, where peacocks from the castle were wont to make their appearance, preening in their resplendent blues and greens. Muted repetitions of this plumage might be found inside, the angular modernity of The Garden House having been much tamed by lavish use of William Morris wallpapers with their softening arabesques and contrapuntal curves. There was, however, no such wallpaper pattern in the living-room. K had appropriated this room as his working space, even though a room led off it that had been designed as his private study, with an adjoining room for office equipment and files. He liked to sit surrounded by his beautiful sculptures and porcelains, many of them arranged upon an enormous square book cabinet of table height, that took up the centre of the room. A capacious sofa, covered in a William Morris print, stood at right angles to the fireplace and over it hung a Degas of a woman bathing. If the subject of the Degas arose, K would say, 'I look upon it with some distress because this is where my *Baigneuse Blonde* ought to have been.' The Renoir had been sold to help the children financially and was now in Turin, owned by Agnelli. 'If that were hanging then this house would have been something.'

Jane had a beautiful bedroom, large, rectangular, with a handsome window at the far end providing a spectacular view of the castle beyond the lawns and fields and the valley winding down to the sea. K kept his clothes there, but slept in an adjoining dressing-room. Although it was narrow, and his single bed cramped, he seemed content since the window afforded an excellent view over the front of the house, with its sweeping drive, and whoever might be approaching. There he woke early and undisturbed and might begin writing before breakfast. He would have tea and a boiled egg at 7.15 a.m. and at 8.15 would insist on going for the post himself. He took in a tray to Jane at about 8.30. By 9.30 he would be dressed and ready for Elizabeth Johnston, the faithful secretary who managed all his business affairs and typed his manuscripts. From 9.30 until 10.15 was set aside for dictating letters and from then on he was ready to write. Since to get the structure of his thought wrong distressed him greatly, he would not begin until he had made a careful plan. Even so, there was usually a great deal of crossing out and additional material to be added in balloons in the wide margins. If temporarily stuck he would go for a walk and end up talking the next paragraph aloud.

Punctually at noon he would look at his watch and announce that it was time for a drink. At one time he had consumed as much as a bottle of Scotch a day, but in these years he limited himself to a single stiff whisky, dispatched with alacrity. Until lunch (between 1 and 1.15 p.m.) there was more writing of a less demanding nature, perhaps an appreciation of a famous person lately dead. People invited for lunch were not expected to appear a second before 12.45, even though they might have driven from the other end of the country, or he would say 'Dammit, here they are !' Once they had been welcomed, there was every kind of aperitif to offer but he could not be bothered. The main point was the meal, and a fast one at that.

If, for instance, one were a guest at a restaurant with K, as Margaret Slythe described it, he was likely to order the same menu for everyone. 'Now, what are we going to have ?' he would say, and then answer his own question: 'I think we'll have some avocados and the sole, and we'd like a drink. And we will have the wine in a bucket, and we will have the bucket off the table.' Once finished, he would announce, 'The potatoes were quite the best things of that,' in a loud voice. At home, the guests would have to be really important to be served coffee. Once, when the painter John Ward and his wife came to lunch, Mrs Slythe said, Mr Lindley produced a magnificent leg of English lamb and K cut everyone a single tiny slice. His guests were not encouraged to ask for more. On another occasion an American composer who had been served a truly superb English trifle, was asked by his host in a terribly casual sort of way whether he would like a second helping, and eagerly assented. 'Go ahead!' his host said tartly. 'Take the lot.' After lunch guests were expected to depart promptly. 'He terrified me when he was in that mood,' Margaret Slythe said. 'He was like a train shunting us through the station. But if guests didn't come, he would say very sadly, "No one comes here now."'

After lunch week-end guests were expected to take a snooze along with their host. As a rule, however, he did not sleep, but read a bit, or daydreamed. He kept a small supply of sweets and chocolates – invariably After Eights – in a drawer beside his bed for the moment when he arose. Then there might be more work, or another walk, the ritual of the afternoon tea and finally the evening drink. As long as Jane was alive he ate almost nothing at night and would be quite content, before an early bedtime, to watch television while smoking a single beautiful cigar. He particularly enjoyed snippets of rugby and football and would shout 'Well done!' If there were an opera to watch, he would smile with delight as the overture began and start to conduct.

The routine of work, walks, guests, lunches and trips to B5 Albany somehow continued once there was an invalid in the house along with a 24-hour staff of nurses, who had to be accommodated, since Jane could never be left alone. When she began to make a rapid improvement he optimistically believed, as she did, that she would soon be walking again. After three heroic efforts to get back on her feet, and three failures, she was inconsolable, howling as if possessed. But then Jane under stress had been showing unsettling symptoms ever since the time, during his operation in 1971, when she had seen strange people outside the window. The question of evil seemed to obsess her. She insisted to their friend David Knowles that it disproved the existence of God. If K's own religious faith had not asserted itself so far with any real conviction, he had always believed that, if one accepted that human beings could be inspired, one had to concede a divine source for that inspiration. That Jane should be capable of damning God and wishing that He could have a stroke, shocked him profoundly. There was no way, he discovered, to dissuade her from such awful blasphemy. He had, however, hit upon an explanation, one Jane accepted, that a demonic force had invaded the house, and that they must be very quiet until it departed. Thank heavens it calmed her. Who could tell? It might even be true.

Throughout her illness, Jane never stopped drinking nor K his anxious hovering. Although he seemed to thrive on interruptions – he would have leapt up and down continually, without the excuse of checking on Jane – the demands she made upon him were, at times, excessive. She would not let him sit down; he must change her position, or her pillows, or telephone the doctor for a new medicine. He would rack his brains for ways to divert her, as if she were a monstrously spoiled child to be pacified at all costs, and count himself lucky if she would submit to one side of a gramophone record, or half an hour of hearing him read Boswell. Periodically she would accuse him of talking to his lady friends on the phone and insist that her own extension never be switched off, presumably so that she could eavesdrop on his calls, as she had done for years. Periodically, too, she would make him watch television beyond his bedtime, on the pretext of needing his company, expressly to torment him. At such moments he would note that her devilish mood had seemed overdue for a return. Other days would find Jane in tears at her own selfishness and insisting, between sobs, that K take a holiday away from her. The complexities of their interdependence were, if anything, more profound than ever. While describing to Janet, in almost daily letters and telephone calls, how hounded he was by Jane, and absolutely at his wits' end – and there is no doubt that pacifying Jane filled every waking hour – he rebuffed any attempt from her or anyone else to suggest that he should ignore Jane for her own good and his, on occasion. His daily progress reports reveal that there was still a vital area of his life on which she did not impinge, and in which she supported and sustained him as she had always done: his writing. That was important enough to require sacrifices, even from her. And, since she was so weak, he continued to dominate on the home front.

As they observed the drama that was playing itself out at The Garden House, some old friends were deeply disturbed at the strain imposed on someone who was himself physically frail. Derek Hill, the artist, voiced these feelings when he said that, 'Whatever pain he may have caused, it was a martyrdom for him.' Others, among them Sir Cecil Beaton, Henry Moore, Burnet Pavitt, Catherine Porteous and Margaret Slythe, retained their admiration for Jane throughout her final illness. They saw her as a charismatic figure of great warmth and charm, and commented on her way of attaching people to her.

'To give you an idea of her thoughtfulness,' Mrs Porteous said, 'my husband once missed a performance at Covent Garden because of a bad bout of pneumonia. A month afterwards, Jane handed me an envelope. "Darling, I have got two tickets to the Gala for you because you had that disappointment."' Another friend thought Jane was deliberately sacrificing herself so that K could go on feeling in charge, while remaining ever prepared to stiffen his resolve if she thought that were needed, since she had uncompromising ideas of right and wrong. She had a 'marvellous, blazing integrity'. She was incorruptible, except by drink.

After so many physical and emotional storms, it was a great relief to have Jane in a mood of benevolent resignation occasionally, even if she were weaker. At such moments they might sit together in the garden admiring the Saltwood roses. These had always been their passion; now they seemed lovelier and more fragile than ever. At about this time he commissioned Reynolds Stone to design a new motif for his notepaper. It was a white rose on a black ground, encircled by delicate leaves and the words, intertwined: 'The Last Rose of Summer'. Jane would sit quietly, admiring the flowers, drinking a Martini and listening to an essay K was preparing for a lecture (later a book) on Botticelli's drawings to illustrate Dante's *Divine Comedy*. Whenever she was in these moods K would find himself with a fresh burst of energy, in the grip of another subject and marvelling that it was still possible to feel the joy of discovery. In the evening, writing to Janet Stone, he would comment that they had experienced a nearly perfect day.

For a few pathetic months after Jane found a new healer (she had already consulted two others) she was buoyed up with hope. How wonderful it would be if he could heal them both, she wrote to Beaton. K watched the inevitable process of euphoria, temporary improvement, and raging despair, with sad detachment. Then, to take Jane's mind off her disappointments, he moved her to an expensive, excellently run hotel in Eastbourne, where she spent most of her time in their sitting-room or dozing, while he worked. He had become obsessed with the idea of writing a second volume of autobiography and it took up all his spare time; he thought it was probably a form of withdrawal. Jane's health continued to fluctuate. There had been so many crises, when the best medical opinion predicted that she could not go on living, that he was not too alarmed when a new set of nurses insisted she was close to death. She seemed to have nothing more serious than skin blisters. Then, a few days later, one of the nurses came to say that she did not want to alarm him, but the skin of Lady Clark's back had come off on her hand. It was pemphigus, a severe inflammatory disease. Jane was immediately moved to a London hospital for massive doses of cortisone and he took refuge in Albany.

The doctor had warned him that cortisone treatments would make Jane euphoric. This turned out to be an understatement. She was now absolutely convinced that she was going to Australia to get married, she hoped to their mutual friend Brinsley Ford. Since to have a conversation with her was somewhat fatiguing, he wrote, he hoped she would become less 'wacky', although the doctor did not hold out much hope. It would be the final blow if she had to enter a mental hospital. Once Jane's euphoria subsided she was left weaker than before, and could only nod her head or shake it. The strange thing was that, in hospital, she said every day how happy she was. If only she could die in that state, he told Nolwen, sure of a sympathetic response, since her husband, Edward Rice, had recently died.

By 10 October 1976 he had reached the last chapter of his autobiography. Jane was quite peaceful and sleeping most of the day, then going to bed at an early hour. When he was hard at work he had been grateful but now, for some reason, he seemed to have lost all intellectual energy and felt lonely, almost deserted. He had been having strange and vivid dreams. These were really, he told Janet Stone, the only incidents in his life. His lecture on Botticelli's Dante drawings was being published, and he had sketched an outline for a new book, titled *What is a Masterpiece?* As for the autobiography, that was in its final stage of revision, comfortably lazy work. He was thinking of calling it *The Other Half*, a title that had jaunty nautical associations for him, since in those circles it meant 'have another drink', he told Nolwen. If it were a *double entendre*, a reference to his 'other half' and her predilections, he seemed artlessly unaware of it.

Jane had a clear presentiment that she was going to die for about a week. In mid November she talked about death with her friends and managed to write beautiful letters to all the family. Just the same, when the actual moment arrived, he was caught off guard. On Friday 12 November he told Janet that they had had a bad day, with so many worries and distractions in the morning that he had become quite jittery. Fortunately dear Burnet Pavitt came to luncheon and calmed him down. As for Jane, she was back to her incoherent, tearful and dreadfully exacting self. However, just before she went to sleep, she calmly announced that she would not be alive the next day. That was certainly a new statement, coming from her.

The next afternoon, when Margaret Slythe appeared at The Garden House, she was greeted by the news that Jane had not yet awoken. Margaret replied, 'My God, I don't like the sound of that.' Jane was breathing perfectly normally but she seemed in a strange kind of limbo. They started work as usual but K was clearly uneasy. He kept going in to look at her. Margaret said, 'Do you think we ought to wake her up?' K replied, 'I'll leave it until teatime.' They managed to do some work on a lecture, Margaret searching through the files for the right references. He went off for his usual nap but could not sleep. There was a kind of nervous calm about him. Then, at about 6 o'clock, when they sat down for a drink, she again wanted to know what he was going to do. He consulted with the nurse and decided to do nothing. Margaret left. At 10 o'clock on Sunday morning, 14 November, K rang to say that Jane had died four hours before without ever awakening. There were Armistice Day services and he thought he might as well go.

On Sunday evening K telephoned Margaret. He was buoyed up, almost happy. What a relief it was. The children had been marvellous. She went to see him next morning and stayed for lunch. K went for his usual nap and, when he awoke, she sat on the edge of his bed and asked what she could do. Nothing to be done, he said. She asked, 'What about flowers for the funeral on Wednesday?' Miss Johnston had made all the arrangements. Might she come to the funeral, she asked. 'Of course.' So she went to the village of Hythe to place her own order with the florist and found there was none from Lord Clark, but only one from his staff. Margaret conveyed the news. K was grateful to have her take over and place an order on his behalf.

There was the further complication of a card to accompany the bouquet, requiring his signature. She went back to the house. 'Oh, my dear!' he said. They spent twenty minutes looking for the right card. None of them was suitable. Finally they found a really beautiful one. He looked at her and said, 'What do I write?', and she realized, for the first time, what a bad way he was in. She almost had to 'programme' him back to bed, she said. He suddenly realized that he owed her money for the flowers, dug in his pocket, and brought out two one-pound notes.

He felt a terrible sense of emptiness and desolation, he told 'darling Nolwen' in mid November, but he would not give in. He was making plans for London with abandon: meetings, lunches and dinners, and long *tête-à-têtes* with Janet Stone. He had accepted an invitation from the Andersons to visit them in Jersey and he and Celly were going to stay with 'little Edith', the sister of Sir Frederick Ashton, now married, who had treated him so kindly in 1939 when Jane was being so awful. Mary Potter was coming to London and he was, as usual, going to Aldeburgh to stay with her. All of this activity was designed, he confessed to Sir Colin Anderson, to keep himself from brooding about his solitary state. He could manage the day in fine fettle until the late afternoon. By then all thought of work was finished, everyone had left – Mr Lindley only worked half days – and he felt depressed and desperate for company. Margaret Slythe came as often as she could during those critical hours from 5.30 to 7.30 and he would be invited to supper at the castle with Alan and his wife, 'little Jane' as he called her, and sometimes call upon a lady friend who lived in Hythe.

Early in the New Year he went to Basel to see the great Isenheim altar in Colmar and spent a long day looking at pictures. It was thirty years since he had last been there. He was glad to say that his range of response had deepened. In those days there were artists he could not even look at; now he loved them. He paid a short visit to New York, where he was given a gold medal by the Mayor and made a freeman of the city. He could not find that any benefit accrued from this. Free taxis would have been more useful, he commented to Lady Anderson. He went on to Washington where he stayed with a widow he had hoped to console and care for. However, his hostess didn't wake until 11 a.m. and took a good nap after lunch. It was very restful and a bit deflating. He saw his old friends and made dozens of new ones. Strangers accosted him on the street, striking up conversations about everything from Munch to billiards. As for remarriage, one of his Washington friends, after giving him lunch, asked whether he was considering it. He replied, in spring 1977, rather emphatically in the negative. The ladies he might have chosen were already married, he said. He looked pensive.

To say that he was not considering marriage was hardly the case. He had discussed it with Mary Potter, whose company he found so restful and undemanding, as she revealed shortly before her death. She loved him dearly but, perhaps, did not feel well enough to embark on a closer relationship. There were other indications that he was determined to marry someone, so much so that he managed to convince a couple of his dearest friends that he must mean them. He told one of them, whose own husband did not have much longer to live, that he had fallen in love with her all over again. Really in love, the first time since Jane. A different friend had a wedding ring designed and sent him the bill. Perhaps this was the person who, he said, had threatened suicide if he would not marry her. He was half convinced that she meant it. There was no doubt that he had made a mess of things and felt enormously ashamed, he wrote to Nolwen. This did not prevent the shock waves of anger and outrage on several fronts when he announced, in the summer of 1977, that his mind was made up. He and Nolwen de Janzé-Rice were going to be married.

During that year of widowhood his health was in a precarious state. Years of nursing Jane had taken their toll: while staying in New York, he had had an attack of paralysis that could have been a stroke, and could not climb out of his bath, and he now began to experience other uncomfortable symptoms. His knees were troubling him – he could no longer rise from a chair without an involuntary exclamation – but, like other reminders that his body was not as tirelessly able to do his will as before, he ignored these signs, as if such lapses were an inexcusable form of weakness. So when his memory began failing him he was loudly indignant, as if enough protest would make it see reason. His intake of alcohol increased at around the time of Jane's death, but he never seemed to see the connection between polishing off several stiff drinks and a good bottle of wine at lunch and dinner, and the blankness that would descend shortly thereafter. He wrote at some length about the declining quality of his writing on the boat back to England, after having proposed to Nolwen and been accepted. He must really apply his mind to his studies. This was the only thing, apart from their love, that mattered to him. He intended to return to the Italian Renaissance in the hope that strict attention to detail would bring him back to himself. What he must never attempt again was the awful *Is Art Necessary?* kind of writing. Despite his physical symptoms, and those days when he shuffled rather than walked, so much seemed to depend upon his mood. Returning from Parfondeval, he was absolutely buoyed up and filled with renewed confidence and strength. All his various physical symptoms vanished and that showed, he told Margaret, that they were imaginary.

After his marriage to Nolwen in November 1977 K had never seemed so genial and convivial, so easily aroused to laughter and praise, or so clear-minded. The weather was perfection in the autumn of 1978, a cloudless sky, a warm sun, there were banks of flowers everywhere, and he sat on the brick terrace outside his living-room, talking about the way his father drew rabbits from hats, singing snatches of old music-hall songs, telling jokes with a faultless Scottish brogue, clearly revelling in his recollections of his parents and the house he loved best, Sudbourne. His attitude towards his mother and father was, however, ambivalent. While freely conceding that he felt neglected by them – a real admission, coming from him – he would not permit his listener the natural assumption that their attitude cast a certain pall over his childhood. Similarly, when the subject of his old governess, Miss Frankish, came up, along with her refusal to allow him a night light and her hasty departure, the words, 'the moment I got shot of her' were hardly out of his mouth before he bristled at the suggestion that he had wanted to see her go. 'I was never horrid to anyone,' he said. His reactions to having his biography written were equally mixed. On the one hand he thought the book might discuss aspects of his life that he had been unable to mention in his autobiography. On the other hand he resisted the idea that there might be more to an issue than whatever conclusions he had made about it. There was nothing underneath his surface, nothing, he said, waving his hand. However vexatious his biographer might find this news, he suggested in his courteous way that the verdict must be accepted.

He called himself 'persnickety'. Speaking of dreams, he said that he had recurrent ones and that missing trains was one of them. 'I only once missed a train, just once and I remember thinking, "There's a dream come true."' Recalling that incident seemed to annoy him. 'I can't face that grass growing up among these bricks,' he said, referring to his terrace. 'Will you pull it up? It's truly revolting.' The deed accomplished, he became benevolent once more. 'I feel all Mr Wordsworth felt about daisies,' he said. 'I feel elated that life is not over.'

At The Garden House, life went on exactly as before. The main meal, invariably a satisfying Edwardian roast or joint, was followed by a sumptuous dessert and K seemed amiably disposed to let his guests eat their fill, unlike former times. In fact, he grumbled, in a jaunty way, about his expanding waistline. Dishes were presented by Mr

Lindley, brown-suited, always pleasant, who would smile and say 'All right?' as he always did before carefully closing the kitchen door. K sat, as he always did, at the head of the table and Nolwen at the foot. Miss Johnston appeared when she always did, other helpers came and went, and by mid afternoon the breakfast trays, covered with their cloths, were prepared and waiting in the kitchen for the next morning. Nolwen thought the household needed several reforms, yet there was great resistance to the idea of a dishwasher, or having the upholstery cleaned, and when she succeeded in having a freezer installed, it upset the whole household. Nolwen also thought things could have been managed more efficiently; one day when she went into K's bedroom, she found him polishing his own shoes.

K thought that Nolwen was scandalized by his insistence that the house be filled with flowers, winter and summer. However, it was his sole extravagance, he said. One noted that he made small economies, like refusing to throw away whatever was left unconsumed of a guest's Scotch. He would replace it carefully in the whisky cabinet that was attached to the wall behind his chair. He also tended to reclaim old file folders and re-use envelopes and stationery left over from Saltwood Castle. Just, however, as one thought one had him pinned, he would come up with an expansive and extravagant gesture. At teatime one day, when there was either water or tea in his saucer, he grandly emptied it onto the carpet. Finding a matchbox empty when he needed a light, he would be likely to hurl it across the room. On learning that one of the rooms, in the library wing of the castle, had been locked and the key mislaid, he drew himself up and announced, 'Then we must change all the locks!' Nolwen, in a panic at the very thought of such an undertaking, had a hard time dissuading him.

It was agreed that they should divide their time between the two houses. In Kent, Nolwen would be K's guest and in Parfondeval he would be hers. This seemed like an equable arrangement and the only remaining issue seemed to be how much time would be spent where. K, plainly set upon returning to work, would be helpless without his large, well-stocked reference library. On the other hand, as a farmer, Nolwen plainly needed to be on the scene at crucial moments. What should he do? he asked. The reply was the obvious one that they should sometimes go their separate ways. By a marginal shift of expression, something K did with consummate skill, he was able to convey the idea that, although it was too soon to contemplate such a drastic step, he thought it might eventually work. For her part Nolwen confided that she would be willing to leave K by himself were it not for those treacherous hours between 5.30 and 7.30 p.m. There was also the worry that he might end up imbibing more than was good for him.

It seemed like an impasse, one bound up with the way K felt about his work at the time. That he was having continuing doubts about its merits seemed apparent. Margaret Slythe noted that, although he was 'writing himself off' he reacted angrily and defensively if anyone else did. He was also being heard to remark that no writer had produced anything of value beyond the age of seventy-five, and he had just passed that birthday. Nevertheless he had a list always at hand of the projects he was about to tackle next.

At Parfondeval in the autumn of 1979, K was walking with a cane. He had not written as much as he would like. 'I am lazy.' In the same breath he added that there had not been a writer who had continued at his age. He was no longer capable of concentrated effort and his memory was just about gone. He was giving a lecture on Turner at Petworth House in Sussex that would probably be his last. He was turning down invitations daily but accepted this one so that he could show the famous eighteenth-century mansion to Nolwen. Nolwen herself was hard to find. True, the house was narrow, being built, in the French manner, to the width of a single room, but it was on several floors and the hostess fleet of foot. K said, 'As soon as you think you have pinned her down she has vanished again.' Nolwen had taken over the driving and was charmingly insistent upon it. He was baffled and hurt. 'Why can't I? I've been driving for sixty years,' he complained, not to her, but to anyone else who would listen. He was prepared to take charge at Parfondeval but, as usual when he was receiving spirited opposition, he seemed wandering and ineffectual, merely getting in the way. Nolwen: 'K, don't cut all the bread darling.' He (defensively): 'I am only cutting up one', piqued to have to leave two other *flûtes* out of the breadbox because they could not be made to fit. He would accompany her to visit her dressmaker, in a tidy little white house surrounded by identical neighbours, all fenced, and with barking dogs in the gardens. While Nolwen went inside he would wait in the car. If she took too long he would get out and wave a newspaper to see how many of the dogs could be made to bark. To succeed in enraging every one gave him huge satisfaction.

Nolwen was making plans to leave the château and move into a pavilion on the estate, and was supervising extensive renovations. He did not tell her, he said, but, 'I shan't live to see it'. Meanwhile she was taking charge of his smoking, alcoholic intake and his menus – 'Oh, *can* I have sausages?' he exclaimed one evening with rapture – and worrying about his dental problems. He had broken one of his front teeth and kept worrying it with his tongue. The effect was disconcerting, as if he were holding back, or toying, with a comment. His health was Nolwen's constant preoccupation. Shortly after their marriage, K needed an immediate operation on his prostate. The doctor told Nolwen some time later that he had a developing heart condition. He suffered from arteriosclerosis and the beginnings of Parkinson's disease, which would account for his occasional shuffling and the visible tremor in his handwriting. She decided to keep all of this a secret from him, along with the medical advice that, for his own safety, her husband should no longer be allowed to drive. However, the sense that he might not live for long gave her much anguish. At about that time she said, 'I'll take him on any terms.'

By now one could never quite predict which mood K would be in, and when. The old K, exquisitely lucid and eloquent, would assert itself at the most unexpected moments. One evening at Parfondeval, seated in a room decorated with Chinoiserie wallpaper of fantastical scenes in beige and rose, the magical beauty of the surroundings seemed to act on him like a tonic. Suddenly he began speaking of the wallpaper's parallels with the work of Hieronymus Bosch. It seemed unbelievable that the fifteenth-century artist could have invented such scenes, and in fact he had not, K said. They were part of the mythology of the secret sect to which Bosch belonged. He then began to relate some of Bosch's themes to the dream-created visions surrounding him, with such a poetry of improvisation that one hardly dared breathe for fear of shattering the beauty of the moment.

At other times the K one knew would be submerged, replaced by someone who was benign and stumbling, as if in limbo. After lunch one day, when it was mentioned that Margaret Slythe was coming to visit, he said, 'Who, dear? Princess Margaret?' He could be comically forgetful. At Parfondeval one evening he entered the dining-room with Colin and Morna Anderson and another guest – Nolwen was still in the kitchen – and surveyed the scene. Obviously, he must do the *placement*. 'I'll sit here,' he said, indicating the head of the table, where Nolwen always sat. 'Now you sit here,' waving his guest to his left, 'Morna you sit on my right and Colin you sit there.' He stopped, puzzled. He added, 'But I thought there were five of us?'

As has been noted, Jane's illness did not prevent Kenneth Clark from accomplishing an enormous amount of work. The first volume of his autobiography, *Another Part of the Wood*, was a bestseller. John Russell, the art critic, spoke for the majority view when he wrote that the book was intensely enjoyable, provocative and quietly moving. Others found it full of amusing stories, bewitching, urbane, or ironic – there seemed no end to the diversity of reactions and the paradoxical nature of the passages singled out for censure or praise, Kenneth Clark wrote. It was a formidable success, coming as it did on the heels of *Civilisation* and another highly-praised book, *The Romantic Rebellion* (1973). This was a series of essays, developed from a television programme, on the theme of romantic versus classic art. It made a handsome book and was praised for its discrimination and sympathetic insights.

In this final decade he was returning to the themes of a lifetime. He liked to recall that, when he presented Berenson with his entrancing book on Piero della Francesca, the inimitable B.B. made the tongue-in-cheek comment that 'Rembrandt is the only artist you really understand.' As K also said, he had been studying Rembrandt's drawings and etchings since childhood, and perhaps his most deeply felt book, based on the Wrightsman lectures he gave at the New York University Institute of Fine Arts in 1964, was *Rembrandt and the Italian Renaissance*. So in 1976, when things looked their bleakest, it was understandable that Kenneth Clark should launch himself into a series of television programmes about Rembrandt which would also become a book. *An Introduction to Rembrandt* (1978) was perhaps his last completely successful book. A study of the relationship between men and the animal kingdom (*Animals and Men*), though beautifully produced and respectfully received when it was published in 1977, seemed to lack something of the master's usual verve and lucid depth of insight. *Moments of Vision*, a collection of lectures and essays, published in 1981, received mixed reviews, as did *What is a Masterpiece?* in 1980. His book, *Feminine Beauty*, also published in 1980, was generally dismissed as being superficial. As for *The Other Half*, his second volume of autobiography, he had been in two minds about it and his misgivings were well founded. Although he had abandoned the project with the comment that he would have to leave out too much, he later took it up again. He confined himself to a description of travels, friends and work, ending with a short account of Jane's death. Reviewers sensed a hint of punishing tensions behind the smooth urbanity. Christopher Booker wrote, 'As the picture of a man who to the end has never dared face up to "the other half" of himself this is a spine-chilling book.' Kenneth Clark was very glad, he told Mrs Menuhin at a literary luncheon in honour of the book late in 1977, that she had enjoyed volume one. 'This was nothing like it.' The conviction that his mind had lost its edge was responsible, finally, for his decision not to attempt a new study but confine himself to the routine editing and revision of lectures and essays. For a man of his delicate sensibilities it was a sad dilemma. What he had achieved would have more than satisfied most people, but he needed the constant stimulus, as well as the reassurance, of being in the public eye. Still, what he wrote had to be good – his pride would refuse to allow the publication of anything but his best, and that meant he could not go on writing. Yet if he no longer had some new raft to buoy him up, as Rembrandt had done during the worst part of Jane's illness, he had lost a large part of his reason for living.

In the days when he still wanted to write about everything, when he had to weigh the pros and cons severely if he were not to be led astray by one glittering idea after another, he was considering a few of the most tempting ones. On the one hand, he deliberated in May 1960, he had always wanted to write books about Rodin and Ingres and Delacroix and Turner and Raphael. On the other hand he thought he might investigate the contrasts between Northern and Mediterranean art and had found a felicitous title straight out of Ruskin, 'Agora and Tanglewood'. Or it might be rather exciting to take the period from 1415 to 1435 in Florentine art and consider it as a journal – but that might not do justice to his ability to see large themes and the interrelatedness of apparently disparate elements – his philosophical gift. In short, for every proposition there was a refutation, save for the theme, *The Art of Humanism*. That possibility had intrigued him since the days when, in *Landscape into Art*, he had explored the physical sources of art and then, with *The Nude*, the historical influences of the human body on artistic expression. Now he was ready to define the more amorphous and pervasive influences of the mind, character and moral sense. He had sketched out a sequence of chapters, ending the book with an epilogue on Rembrandt and the

humanist Renaissance. However, once he learned of his reappointment as Slade Professor of Fine Art (1961–62) he switched to what he
mistakenly believed to be the easier theme of *Motives*. Since *The Art
of Humanism* was his last great challenge, the book he never managed to write, perhaps it is not surprising that he chose the title for his
final collection of essays, published posthumously, in the autumn of
1983. If, for Kenneth Clark, that subject had poignant associations, if
it was bound up with all that might have been and everything he was
relinquishing, it would be characteristic of him to keep his secret.

During the final two years of his life he was still managing to struggle
between Kent and Normandy although the stays at Parfondeval
became more and more lengthy. A degenerating hip was giving him
great difficulty in walking and there were bouts of diverticulitis and
septicaemia, as well as the usual colds and fevers to which he was
prone. His death came on 21 May 1983. He had been ill for a week
with a severe digestive complaint and running a high fever. As soon as
he seemed slightly better the doctor ordered a stay in a Hythe nursing
home. On the evening of his arrival he got up in the middle of the
night to go to the bathroom. As his mother had before him, he fell
and broke his hip. Like her, he was seventy-nine years old.
Immediate surgery was necessary. The operation seemed a success
but, a few days later, his heart began to fail him. He asked for a priest
and, according to Nolwen, after receiving the Eucharist, lost con-
sciousness in the presence of his wife and son Alan, and died in the
night. He is buried in the graveyard of the parish church at Saltwood
beside the castle.

Kenneth Clark had asked for a priest because, to the amazement of
his friends, he had become a Catholic. The news emerged obliquely
during a lengthy memorial service at St James's Piccadilly in the
autumn of 1983. It was a very grand affair, attended by members of
the intellectual and cultural élite as well as representatives of the
Queen, Queen Mother and Princess Margaret, who braved a deluge
of rain and packed the church. Among them was the architectural
historian, biographer and diarist James Lees-Milne. He wrote, 'At
the very end of the service an Irish Roman Catholic priest, whom I
had noticed officiating ... gave a second address ... He claimed that
a week before he died K asked for him, made his confession, received
the Sacraments and so was received into the Church of Rome ... The
priest said, "This great man then said to me, 'Thank you, Father!

You have done for me what I have long been wanting',," or words to
this effect.' The news, which had not been made public in typical
Clarkian deference to others' opinions, caused a considerable stir,
despite Lady Clark's explanation that her late husband's religious
commitment was of long standing. James Lees-Milne could hardly
believe his ears. Sir William (Tony) Keswick, K's old friend from
Winchester days, stoutly refused to think that he ever desired to 'take
the veil', as he termed it. The whole idea was completely against K's
nature, he wrote.

If, in those last years, Kenneth Clark had felt torn between conflicting loves, it is clear that his longing for Saltwood finally became par-
amount, despite the charms of Normandy. He told many of his friends
with tears in his eyes that he never wanted to leave it. As it happened,
most of 1983 was spent at The Garden House. A trip back to France
had to be postponed constantly because of his fluctuating health.
However there was a wedding coming up that summer and he had to
get well enough to travel to Parfondeval for the big family celebration,
but his health did not improve. He spent his days in bed, sometimes
listening to the radio or watching television, or trying to read. He
occasionally hobbled to the kitchen for meals, wearing a dressing-
gown and supported by sticks. He penned brief notes in a shaky hand.
However, Nolwen dealt with most of the correspondence, as she did
with his banking, business affairs and the myriad daily details of the
household. She nursed him with loving care and was constantly at his
side. On one occasion, however, about two months before he died, she
was away for a week-end. That Saturday morning Mr Lindley was in
the kitchen when he heard a noise. He turned around and got the shock
of his life; Lord Clark was in the doorway, dressed and standing.

Those with long enough memories will recall what a stir Kenneth Clark
caused as the youngest director of the National Gallery ever appointed
and what a force he was for constructive change. He became a patron at
a pivotal moment, championing those artists who were forging a
British reply to the pre-eminence of Paris. Forceful, authoritative and
well-placed, he was in an ideal position to help gain an international
status for all of the arts in Britain and made energetic use of it.

Others will remember the part he played in the safe removal,
during the war, of great works of art, the precious lunchtime concerts,
his influence in bringing about enlightened government support and
his emergence as the most brilliant lecturer in Britain. Some will

see him as an innovator, particularly in his middle years, when he was moving from one post to the next, restlessly seeking out the newest challenge, the latest demonstration of a pressing need, organizing, influencing, and uncovering possibilities that others had not appreciated. In many ways he had a sculptor's vision and he liked to remark that if he had been given the opportunity to sculpt in adolescence he might have done nothing else.

Civilisation's reviewers to the contrary, Kenneth Clark was not an urbane aesthete who was having an overnight success but someone who had spent his entire life bridging the gap between the vast incomprehension of the general public and the refined taste of the few. One has to see him as the Ruskin of his generation, as dedicated as Roger Fry to the thesis that ordinary people could be raised to a state of high excitement by the right teacher. Surely, no one has ever bettered Kenneth Clark in the art of exposition. Anyone who listened long enough was bound to see the world through his eyes and, as he once wrote, discover that one's living-room had been painted by Vermeer or find, in the crumbling logs of a fire, the echo of Titian's *Entombment*.

His lasting accomplishments are his beautiful and singular books: *Leonardo da Vinci*, *Landscape Into Art*, *Piero della Francesca*, *The Nude*, and *Rembrandt and the Italian Renaissance*. These works are not only praised for the scholarly breadth of their analogies and their unerring taste, intuition, and judgement, but the poetic beauty of their language. Kenneth Clark was always a confident aesthete and he brought his clarity and insight to bear on a prose style that was, for all its impressionistic sparkle, composed with the utmost care. His words, the *Burlington Magazine* wrote, took on a 'resonance that seems to make art and life touch closely'. He would have considered that his greatest compliment.

If one can see Kenneth Clark as a man who spectacularly fulfilled his promise (an art critic wrote, 'He had been dealt a marvellous hand and played it superbly'), what cast a long shadow on his life was – in Oscar Wilde's words – the gulf he perceived between art and the sordid perils of his actual existence. For one whose instinctive urge was towards unity and wholeness – his drive for self-expression was indomitable – the contrast was acute. This unresolved issue continued to colour his view of himself and accounts for the pessimism of many of his conclusions and the failed hopes of his old age.

Yet, given his Edwardian code of behaviour and the feeling,

ingrained by adulthood, that self-examination was gross conceit and that emotional problems were a shameful weakness to be corrected by a stiffening of the backbone, it is difficult to see how he could have extricated himself. From childhood he carried a heavy load of guilt and obligation, and his solution to his wife's drinking problem was to shoulder her burden, numbed and helpless. If, for him, the psyche was a treacherous labyrinth into which one ventured at one's peril, nevertheless the K of old age was far more approachable, tolerant and endearing than he had been as a frigid and frightened young man. After Jane died, that gentle and affectionate mood was closer to the surface than before. Although he felt that inner unity would always be beyond his grasp, he never stopped trying to bring life closer to the harmonious vision he had seen so clearly in art.

In the autumn of 1979 Kenneth Clark drove to the tiny village of Orford in Suffolk, near his father's former estate. His grandmother's house still stood, although hidden by a high wall, beside a castle that belonged to the National Trust. There was quite a good crafts shop in the village and the village hall, where he had made his first speech at the age of ten, was still standing. What was the speech about? 'On the war, I think.' The colour of the stones of the local church was charming and there were two rather nice paintings inside in the style of Bernini. However, it was a Sunday morning, with a service in progress. He would not go in.

He peered through the windows of the local pub. No sign of life. He said, 'It comes over me that the pubs here don't open until twelve on Sundays. It would be a proud day for Orford if they did.' So he went down to the dock beside the river Alde and looked out over the sedge-coloured waters, the ashen sky, the mottled greens of the dune beyond. In this subdued and forlorn setting he had felt a thrill of aesthetic feeling. As Landor had said, 'Nature I loved, and next to Nature, Art.'

It was here too that the Sudbourne party came for their infamous shoots of hares, those pathetic screaming animals. What could have possessed his father, an otherwise humane man? 'Ah!' He raised his hands in defeat. 'Habit and convention.' Now he was driving along a country road, following the course of the Alde. The road twisted and turned, threading through hedgerows. Each time he took the road he swore he would never do it again. On the other hand, to catch a glimpse of fields and poppies in bloom was very pleasant. Off to the right was the road one took down to the river, and there he had been painted at the age of seven or eight, paddling in a sandy cove. He would not go down it this time. At each crossroad he sounded his horn with the right Toad-of-Toad-Hall panache. 'I hoot a great deal because Jane loved it,' he explained. 'She used to say, "Hoot, hoot!"'

Arriving at Sudbourne he proceeded to make the tour as if it were still his, which in a sense it was. He surveyed the immaculate sweep of lawn where the house once stood, confronting each avenue in turn. Here were the stables, that was the game larder, in which the day's shoot once hung, and there was the estate's electrical generating plant. He was very fond of the machinist and used to spend a lot of time in the man's company, staring at his toy engines. It was fascinating to discover what he remembered and what he had forgotten. When he first returned, after the war, he was greatly disturbed to see the decay, the roses run wild, the greenhouse in ruins. Now, however, it did not trouble him. If one wanted to know why he kept returning to the small town of Aldeburgh, to Orford, the Iken and this empty sweep of lawn, the answer was that he did not know.

So much woodland had grown up since his father's time. That would not have been tolerated. It all had to be kept as meadowland for the shoot. To look at all the thistles and brambles that had once been meticulously kept grounds – well, it made one feel quite sick. Such an estate took an immense staff, of course, and vast amounts of money. At about the time his father sold Sudbourne he had lost much through foolish investments, 'the silly old cuckoo'. But then he reflected that he was rather glad not to have inherited a vast fortune. It would have been an embarrassment. As it was he had been left comfortably off, independent.

No, his father never gave himself airs or acted the squire. He was an adorable character, easy and direct. His mother was much more formal but then she never met anyone if she could help it. His father's love for her never wavered. The first thing he would say was, 'How do you think Alice is looking?' As for his grandmother in Orford, she never made a fuss about his father's drinking the way his mother had. She looked after him angelically.

How terrible it was that, with all his great gifts, his father had wasted his life. One could not quite say the same about Jane, because she would be perfectly fine whenever they went abroad. When at home she did drink rather too much but she was no trouble. He would simply carry her off to bed. Poor darling, it was awful. He could not blame himself because he was absolutely sweet to her and looked after her like an angel. But, he was asked, what could have driven her to such a state? He looked hounded, about to burst into tears. 'I'll tell you when I get out of here,' he said, looking around him wildly. 'I have too many things pressing around me here.'

The woods reminded him perhaps of that labyrinthine stand of small oaks, ferns and bracken that he had discovered while on a lecture tour of Ireland in 1962. That day he had gone exploring far up the glen, his only companions an elderly greyhound and an intelligent labrador. He had not felt the slightest sadness or loneliness on that walk. In fact, he had been happy, immersed in memories of his youth. So one watched him walking away, contemplatively, a solitary figure, dissolving into an impenetrable distance, out of the frame.

Acknowledgements

I would like to make clear that this book is not, and was never intended to be, an 'authorized' biography, if by that one means a biography that is read and approved before publication by the subject or his literary heirs. Although, as I have said elsewhere, the late Kenneth Clark was enthusiastic about having me work on the project and co-operated fully during its preparation, his written permission to quote directly from his letters, diaries and writings was never obtained. It is an unavoidable omission, but one I much regret.

However, Lord Clark did allow me unrestricted access to his files and personal correspondence. He answered endless lists of questions by mail and granted countless interviews. Lady Clark was similarly generous with her time and interest. She was the kindest and most considerate of hostesses at Parfondeval, her estate in Normandy, and at The Garden House in Saltwood, Kent. I would also like to thank her for making available to me Lord Clark's letters to her, as well as hers to him, and for her suggestions and comments. My thanks also go to Alan, Colette and Colin Clark, for their readiness to be interviewed, to Colin Clark for a photograph of his father's drawing of his mother in his possession, and particularly to Alan Clark for showing me the whereabouts of an important collection of letters whose existence I did not suspect. I would also like to thank him for bringing to my attention a perceptive review by Christopher Booker of his father's second volume of autobiography, *The Other Half*.

My thanks also go to Mrs Reynolds Stone, who entertained me in the Old Rectory, her enchanting house in Dorset, and allowed me to study the more than 1,500 letters from Lord Clark to her from 1954 onwards. It is an extraordinary correspondence and indispensable to any student of Lord Clark's life. I am similarly indebted to Mrs Vincent Slythe, for her continued generosity, hospitality and patience in answering my tiresome questions, as well as her major role in helping me to document Kenneth Clark's Winchester years. Mrs Ruth Taylor, who is superbly gifted as a researcher and interviewer, gave me indispensable help for tasks that often required a pronounced talent for diplomacy. She helped me with interviews in London and elsewhere, burrowed through files, borrowed letters, made telephone calls and pursued numerous promising leads which often ended in disappointment. She even managed to wring a fresh memory or two from my subject about his school days, circumventing his desire to repeat his own description of that period in his autobiography, sometimes word for word. She made an important contribution to this book and I am deeply indebted to her. I am also grateful indeed for the help I received from Kate Miller, who invariably answered my questions in a prompt and enlightening way.

Numerous friends and associates of Lord Clark in Britain, the United States and France, allowed themselves to be interviewed. My warm thanks go to Janet Adam-Smith; Sir Geoffrey Agnew; the late Sir Colin and Lady Anderson; Sir Isaiah Berlin; David Blackburn; Christopher Booker; Mrs Humphrey Brooke; the late Lord Butler of Saffron Walden; John James Byam Shaw; the late David Carritt; Sir Hugh Casson; Sir Trenchard Cox; Edward Croft-Murray; Mrs Cecil Day-Lewis (Jill Balcon); Lady Margaret Douglas-Home; the Earl and Countess of Drogheda; Tom Eckersley; Brinsley Ford; Michael Gill; Lady Gladwyn; Mary Glasgow; Rosemary Gordon; Cecil Gould; Prof. John Hale; Mr and Mrs Hamish Hamilton; Prof. Agnes Headlam-Morley; Derek Hill; John Hill; Dr Richard Howland; Mr and Mrs John Hubbard; René Huyghe; Lord James; Prof. Elliott Jaques; Sir William and Lady Keswick; Dame Alix Kilroy (Lady Meynell); John King; James Lees-Milne; Dr Donald Leinster-Mackay; Michael Levey; Drs Russell and Margaret Martin; Dr Rae Martin; Ambassador René Massigli; Mrs Diana Menuhin; Peter Montagnon; Dr Charles Morgan; Henry Moore; John ('Jock') Murray; Sir Karl Parker; Burnet Pavitt; Prof. Carlo Pedretti; Mary, Countess of Pembroke; Mr and Mrs John Piper; Mrs Robin Porteous; the late Mary Potter; Peter Quennell; Dame Marie Rambert; Sir James Richards; Bryan Robertson; Helen Roeder; Jill Ross; Vera Russell; Anya Sainsbury; Bernard Sendall; John Sparrow; the late Graham Sutherland and Mrs Kathleen Sutherland; Nancy Thomas; Mrs Jean Townsend; Hugh Trevor-Roper (Lord Dacre);

Ann Turner; Violette Verdy; Mr and Mrs Gordon Waterfield; Sir Francis Watson; Sir Huw Wheldon; and Gabriel White.

To those who were willing to let me borrow letters I am particularly indebted. Besides Mrs Stone and Mrs Slythe, I would like to thank Dr Russell Martin, brother of the late Lady Jane Clark, and his wife, Dr Margaret Martin, for their indispensable help in establishing the family history of Lady Clark, and for letting me examine family correspondence. They discovered several letters from Kenneth Clark to his mother-in-law which were particularly valuable for my pur-poses and also found photographs which they generously lent. I would also like to thank Dr Craig Smyth of I Tatti, Dr Fiorella Superbi and Dr Cecil Anrep for their efforts in making available copies of Kenneth Clark's letters to Bernard and Mary Berenson for this study. I should further like to thank James A. Sharaf, general counsel of Harvard University and Ronald Goldfarb, for their help in bringing this about. These letters, which begin in 1926, are the only extensive record I found documenting the pre-war life of Kenneth and Jane Clark. Mrs Barbara Halpern, Mary Berenson's literary heir, was extremely generous in making available to me whatever references to the Clarks she had found in her own collection of family letters and diaries. Mrs Thelma Cazalet Keir kindly lent *The Coats Story*, a privately printed memoir of the Coats family by David Keir, which includes the best description of the Clark family history that I found. Hugo Vickers, the biographer of Cecil Beaton, courteously provided copies of Kenneth and Jane Clark's letters to his subject, as did Roger Berthoud, the biographer of Graham Sutherland. The late Sir Colin Anderson took a particularly warm interest in my work, contributing what amounted to essay answers to my questions and providing copies of Kenneth Clark's letters to him and his wife. Paul Hyslop kindly made a search in the archives of the late Raymond Mortimer for similar letters. Sir Henry Moore generously provided what letters he found of Kenneth Clark to himself, and the Earl of Crawford made available the extensive correspondence between Kenneth Clark and his father. Michael Colefax, son of Lady Sibyl Colefax, provided further letters as did James Lees-Milne and Donald MacClelland. Nigel Nicolson kindly gave permission for his father's unpublished diaries to be read for references to the Clarks.

Innumerable people answered my questions with sometimes ex-tensive accounts of their friendship with the Clarks. Hiram Winterbotham, who was almost a member of the family circle during the war years, gave a lengthy and illuminating account of that friendship. The loan of a list of Trinity College, Oxford, 1922 graduates, from Louis B. Warren, led to letters of enquiry and some fascinating replies from Kenneth Clark's contemporaries. They included: Phyllis Bishop, wife of the late Dr P.M.F. Bishop; Rev. Gerald Streatfield; Christopher Smith; Michael Lubbock; Rev. Prof. N.W. Porteous; Dr H.R.J. Donald; Rev. Br. Francis Tyndale-Biscoe; C.H. Jaques; W.T. Gairdner; Michael Maclagen; Rev. J.C.V. Wilkes; C.B. Lace; His Honour Judge Douglas C.L. Potter; C.G. Eastwood; Rev. Wilfrid Tribe; C.P.M. Green; and Mrs M.A. Macdonald. Mark Baker, archivist of Wellington College, also helped with information.

The curator of Wiccamica at Winchester College, J.P. Sabben-Clare, was immensely helpful, as was the archivist, Dr R.D.H. Custance. Actual essays on their experiences at the school were contributed by Reg Snell and Dr C.I.C. Bosanquet. The latter lent a valuable collection of books about Winchester and its traditions. Sir William Keswick gave a vivid account of his experiences, and G.R. Mitchell answered my questions with detailed and enlightening comments. Other help was provided by Judge Harold William Paton, Richard M. Deanesly, Sir Alexander Sim and John Sparrow. Tracking down Kenneth Clark's experiences at his preparatory school, Wixenford, turned out to be a more difficult task. Preliminary help was provided by J.H. Dodd, secretary for the Incorporated Association of Preparatory Schools and Miss A.J.E. Arrowsmith, county archivist for the Royal County of Berkshire. My letter of enquiry, published by the *Wokingham News*, was answered by James Watson-Smith with the information that the school still existed in Wokingham under the name of Ludgrove. Dr D.P. Leinster-Mackay of the department of education, University of West Australia, who is author of the first history of the English preparatory school, kindly furnished invaluable additional information about the school's history. The present Headmaster, Gerald Barber, gave further help in a conversation with Mrs Taylor and provided booklets with photographs of the school in Lord Clark's time.

The following libraries, archives and universities made material available for this study:

John Rylands University Library of Manchester, Glenise A. Matheson, Keeper of Manuscripts: correspondence between Lord Clark and the Earl of Crawford.

Glasgow University Library, Kate Donnelly and N.R. Thorp, special collections: D.S. MacColl Collection.

New York Public Library, Donald Anderle, associate director for special collections: Lord Clark to E. Sackville-West, Leonard Clark and Herbert Mitgang.

Royal Archives, the Librarian of Windsor Castle, Robin Mackworth-Young: a letter of Lord Clark's.

The Pierpont Morgan Library, New York, Herbert Cahoon, curator: Lord Clark's letters to E. McKnight Kauffer, Cyril Connolly, Jose Garcia Villa and from Edith Sitwell to Lord Clark.

King's College Library, Cambridge, Dr Michael A. Halls, modern archivist: Lord Clark's letters to Rosamond Lehmann, Clive Bell, Vanessa Bell, T.S. Eliot, E.M. Forster, Margery Fry and J.M. Keynes.

Benjamin Britten Estate, Aldeburgh, Rosamond Strode, secretary: Lord Clark's letters to Benjamin Britten.

Washington State University, Terry Abraham, manuscript-archives librarian: letters of Sir Maurice Bowra, John Sparrow and Kenneth Clark in the Salter/Sitwell papers.

Library of Congress, David Wigdor, specialist in twentieth-century political history: the David Finley papers.

Houghton Library, Harvard University: Lord Clark's letters to Sir William Rothenstein.

Washington University in St Louis, Timothy D. Murray, curator of manuscripts: an exchange between Kenneth Clark and Erica Marx.

Vassar College, Frances Goudy, special collections librarian: a letter from Lord Clark to William K. Rose.

Beinecke Rare Book and Manuscript Library, Yale University, Lisa Browar, assistant to the curator, collection of American literature: letters of Kenneth and Jane Clark to Doris I. Farquhar, Gertrude Stein and Edith Wharton.

Wadham College, Oxford, J.D. Gurney, librarian: five letters from Kenneth and Jane Clark to Sir Maurice Bowra.

Yale University Library, Robert O. Anthony, adviser to the Walter Lippmann papers: Kenneth Clark to Walter Lippmann.

Humanities Research Center, University of Texas, Ellen S. Dunlap, research librarian: Kenneth and Jane Clark's letters to Edith Sitwell, Pavel Tchelitchev, Mary Hutchinson, Peter Owen, Parker Tyler, Denton Welch and others.

My thanks are due to those who gave information, help and advice:

Dr R.S. Rowntree; Anne Olivier Bell; Frank Herrmann; Prof. Lord McGregor of Durris; Pamela Diamand; Martha M. Smith; James Fox; Dr Bruce Laughton; Sir Ellis Waterhouse; William Gaunt; John Ward; Mrs Andrew C. Ritchie; C.H.V. Sutherland; the Lord Caccia; Kinta Beevor; Eleanor Dwight; V.S. Maxwell; George Rylands; Francis King; D.L. Corcoran; Prof. Francis Haskell; Penelope Betjeman; Rt. Hon. Lord Glendevon; J.B. Priestley; Elizabeth Arnold; Edward Ardizzone; Sir Alfred Beit; Prof. Christopher Brooke; Basil Gray; A.R.A. Hobson; the late Raymond Mortimer; Iris Murdoch; Angus Wilson; Elinor Anderson-Bell; the Lord Kinross; Bjorn Kornerup; Henrietta Partridge; Sir John Rothenstein, Quentin Bell; Charles Osborne; W.S. Hardcastle; Edward Money; R.C. Pulford, deputy secretary-general of the Arts Council of Great Britain; G.B.N. Hartog; John Pearson; Mark Haworth-Booth; John Richardson; Alan McHenry; and Prof. Jean Hamburger.

Miss Elizabeth Johnston, Kenneth Clark's invaluable secretary at Saltwood, never lost her patience despite my endless calls upon it, and Mrs Catherine Porteous, his assistant in London, was particularly generous of her time, advice and hospitality. Mr and Mrs Leonard Lindley gave me ample opportunity to observe just how vital a role they played at The Garden House, and some magnificent examples of their cooking. Particular gratitude is due my agent, Murray Pollinger, who represented me during some difficult negotiations with great tact and finesse. I would also like to thank my London editors, John Curtis and Alex MacCormick, and to add a special word of thanks for the patience, support and sympathetic understanding of my New York editor, Jennifer Josephy. Only one person, however, really knows what writing this book involved. To him I owe its successful realization, with infinite love and gratitude.

MERYLE SECREST

Notes

Abbreviations used

APW   Kenneth Clark, *Another Part of the Wood* (London: John Murray, 1974)

TOH   Kenneth Clark, *The Other Half* (New York: Harper & Row, 1977)

JD   Diaries of Jane Clark

KCJ   Letters from Kenneth to Jane Clark

KCS   Letters from Kenneth Clark to Mrs Reynolds (Janet) Stone

KCM   Letters from Kenneth Clark to Mrs Vincent (Margaret) Slythe

KCB   Letters from Kenneth Clark to Bernard Berenson

KCMB   Letters from Kenneth Clark to Mary Berenson

Chapter One   Young Man Running

1   'Happy and Glorious': Owen Morshead to KC, 22 Dec. 1933.

1   'many middle-aged men': Peter Quennell, *A London Letter*, March 1934.

2   'sharp-beaked, dark, bird-eyed': *Manchester Daily Express*, 23 June 1938.

2   'People of my generation': interview with Sir Geoffrey Agnew.

2   his dearest ambition: referred to in a letter from Owen Morshead to KC, 11 June 1932.

2   a taste for Old Masters would prejudice their sales: Kenneth Clark, *The Idea of a Great Gallery*, Specialty Press, Melbourne, 1949.

3   'a pure scholar': Hesketh Hubbard, *A 100 Years of British Painting* (London: Longmans Green, 1951), p. 243.

3   'sheer incapacity': Alan Clark (ed.), *A Good Innings: The Private Papers of Viscount Lee of Fareham* (London: John Murray, 1974), p. 321.

3   'neither to be asked nor expected': C.J. Holmes, *Self and Partners* (London, Constable, 1936), p. 320.

3   'ineradicable spirit of faction': *A Good Innings*, p. 6.

3   'Hydra headed, Medusa haired'; Lord Balniel to Lord Lee, 23 Sept. 1941.

3   'there must be something queer': *Self and Partners*, p. 320.

4   would not mind a hornet's nest: Philip Wilson Steer to Henry Tonks, 9 Sept. 1933, Glasgow University Library.

4   had he known the truth: *APW*, p. 209.

4   'Many people would envy': *Manchester Daily Express*, op. cit.

4   wrote to his mother-in-law: KC to Dr Martin, 7 July 1938.

4   to write about art: KCB, 22 Aug. 1938.

4   it was ridiculously easy: ibid.

4   detested the National Gallery: KC to Alice Clark, 5 Feb. 1940.

5   human nature can best be studied in a state of conflict: Erik H. Erikson, *Young Man Luther* (New York: Norton, 1962), p. 16.

5   Elliott Jaques, *Work, Creativity and Social Justice* (London: Heinemann, 1970), p. 16.

Chapter Two   The Clarks of Paisley

6   The wealthy style: described in Simon Newell-Smith (ed.), *Edwardian England, 1901–1914* (London: Oxford University Press, 1964), p. 152.

8   'determined to marry her': interview with KC.

8   Ages of Kenneth and Alice Clark at marriage established by a family tree in the Clark family possession.

9   The library floor collapsed: *TOH*, p. 70.

9   Alice adored her husband: KC to author, 22 Oct. 1980.

9   Children banished to boarding schools: *APW*, p. 33.

9   'he liked tarts': interview with KC.

10 Father only worked for two years: *APW*, p. 1.

10 Entranced by billiards and snooker: *APW*, p. 5.

10 Learning to ride: *APW*, p. 9.

10 Origins of the Clark family business obtained from David Keir, *The Coats Story*, privately printed, 1964.

11 told to go to hell: *APW*, p. 27.

13 'He thought to himself . . .', interview with KC.

14 Had claimed everyone else: *APW*, p. 2.

Chapter Three   Keeping Secrets

15 Quotation from Rosamond Lehmann, *The Swan in the Evening* (New York: Harcourt Brace, 1967), p. 52.

15 he would never master the art: *APW*, p. 6.

16 The Golliwog example: *APW*, p. 6.

16 'a hook in the bathroom door.': Jonathan Garnier Ruffer, *The Big Shots* (New York: Arco, 1977), p. 95.

17 Description of the shoot: *APW*, p. 14–17.

18 seated near her husband: KC to author, 22 Oct. 1980.

19 Information about the Sudbourne Stud Farm from the *Ipswich Evening Star*, 22 Aug. 1951.

20 Diet of the Edwardian child: Marghanita Laski, *Edwardian England, 1901–1914* (London: Oxford University Press, 1964), p. 205.

21 'Wonderful meals': interview, *New York Times*, 3 May 1978.

21 George Bernard Shaw, *Man and Superman*, Act I.

21 Kenneth Mackenzie Clark's drinking problems: based on interviews with KC, letters and an account in *APW*.

23 'We must be clear': Thomas J. Cottle, *Children's Secrets* (New York: Anchor/Doubleday, 1980), p. 191.

24 closed-off and on the defensive: *APW*, p. 29.

24 'One stands alone': *Children's Secrets*, p. 84.

24 the pressure of fearful expectations: Bruno Bettelheim, *Truants from Life* (Glencoe: Free Press, 1955), pp. 33–4.

24 Left to do battle alone: *APW*, p. 8.

Chapter Four   Moments of Vision

25 Quotation from Oscar Wilde, 'The Critic as Artist', part I (*Nineteenth Century*, 1890).

25 Sir Richard Wallace: described by Kenneth Clark in a speech, 'Collectors and Collecting', given to the Royal Scottish Academy, 16 Nov. 1978.

26 to have a drawing accepted by Punch: KCM, 16 July 1967.

26 The admirable qualities of Charles Keene: Kenneth Clark, *Drawings by Charles Keene* (London: Arts Council, 1952).

26 Disastrous choices of Kenneth Mackenzie Clark: *APW*, p. 46.

26 'Don't spend your money': interview with KC.

26 How to look at pictures: described by Kenneth Clark in *Looking at Pictures* (New York: Holt, Rinehart and Winston, 1960), p. 17.

27 as if designed by Titian: ibid. A mystical experience of art: 'Moments of Vision', Romanes Lecture, 11 May 1954.

28 'absolutely worthless, irresponsible people': *Sunday Times Magazine*, 6 Oct. 1974.

29 Cézanne was inexhaustible: *APW*, p. 51.

30 His parents did not want him: KC to author.

30 His courage in danger: interview with Sir William Keswick.

31 Kenneth Clark's memories of Wixenford: interview with Ruth Taylor, 9 Dec. 1980, and in *APW*.

31 The annoyance of children: KC to author, 27 Dec. 1981.

32 'She made my life': interview with KC.

Chapter Five   Winchester

33 Quotation from John Betjeman, *Summoned by Bells*.

34 'self-conscious about it and competitive': Harold Nicolson, *Good Behaviour* (London: Constable, 1955), p. 232.

34 Rise of the *nouveau riche*: described by Jonathan Gathorne-Hardy in *The Old School Tie* (New York: Viking, 1977), p. 183.

34 This and other information about Kenneth Clark's progress at Winchester is taken from the Winchester College archives.

35 furtive, sideways looks: Reginald Snell to author, Oct. 1980.

35 a vague sense of having done wrong: *The Old School Tie*, p. 224.

35 'One stands alone': Thomas J. Cottle, *Children's Secrets* (New York: Anchor/ Doubleday, 1980), p. 84.

36 'what a Wykehamist is thinking': Anthony Sampson, *Anatomy of Britain Today* (London: Hodder & Stoughton, 1965), p. 202.

36 Winchester's traditions: Christopher Dilke, *Dr Moberly's Mint-Mark* (London: Heinemann, 1965).

36 Derivation of the word 'toys': *Winchester College Notions* (Winchester: P. & G. Wells, 1901).

36 'deprived us of our childhood': Reginald Snell to author, Oct. 1980.

37 'six hard cutting strokes': ibid.

37 'A beating by the Headmaster': ibid.

37 'I contemplated . . . suicide': Graham Mitchell to author, 2 June 1980.

38 'All intellectuals complain': *Sunday Times Magazine*, 6 Oct. 1974.

38 'I was never beaten': interview with KC.

38 Kenneth Clark struck him as arrogant: letter to author, 13 June 1980.

38 'I lay low': interview with author.

38 'Our horrid little housemaster': interview with Sir William Keswick.

39 'We looked at each other': interview with Sir William Keswick.

39 'a photograph of your mum': ibid.

39 Biographical material on Montague Rendall from *Rendall of Winchester*.

40 a moving letter: ibid, p. 57.

40 Conceives ambition to work for Berenson: *APW*, p. 76.

40 Goes to see art master: *APW*, p. 56.

40 'ended up running the class': interview with author.

40 Gives lecture on art: *The Wykehamist*, No. 605, 18 May 1921.

41 They sat in the Warden's Garden: *APW*, p. 59.

41 'Some of us had to translate': Graham Mitchell to author, 2 June 1980.

42 'absolutely amazed': interview with KC.

42 No talent for art: ibid.

42 A scholarship to Oxford: *APW*, p. 84.

43 A gamesman was left alone: Leonard Woolf, *Sowing: An Autobiography of the Years 1880–1904* (New York: Harcourt Brace, 1960).

43 Collapsed after a run: *APW*, p. 67.

43 'At that period': C.I.C. Bosanquet, *Recollections of Winchester College, 1916–1922*.

44 'We spent our whole time': interview with Sir William Keswick.

44 'I remember another occasion': ibid.

44 'My attitude towards him': Graham Mitchell to author, 2 June 1980.

44 'the kind of boy': Reginald Snell to author.

45   '"not really our sort"': ibid.
45   'jolly, friendly man': interview with Sir Colin Anderson.
45   'He was a very cross old man': interview with Sir William Keswick.
45   'I never thought I would live': interview with KC.
45   'overwhelmed with an horrible melancholia': quoted by W. Jackson Bate in *Samuel Johnson* (New York: Harcourt Brace, 1977), p. 118.
45   'in the hope that it could shake him': ibid.
45   'Oh Lord, enable me': ibid.
46   'Chivvied and harried': *The Old School Tie*, p. 223.

Chapter Six   Ghosts

47   Quotations from Henrik Ibsen, *Ghosts*.
47   Fainted at a performance: *APW*, p. 82.
47   Overwhelmed by memories of family life: Nolwen Clark to author, 18 Dec. 1981.
48   Normality of parents crucial: Thomas J. Cottle, *Children's Secrets* (New York: Anchor/Doubleday, 1980), pp. 190–1.
48   Violent feelings of hatred: Melanie Klein, *The Psychoanalysis of Children* (New York: Delta, 1975), p. 189.
49   Berenson less intimidating than own father: Barbara Strachey and Jayne Samuels (eds), *Mary Berenson* (London: Gollancz, 1983), p. 262.
50   Planning to become a historian: *APW*, p. 93.
50   Tutor unsatisfactory: *APW*, p. 103.
51   'We, as a college': Peter Green to author, 8 Aug. 1980.
51   'Most of us were paid for': Douglas C.L. Potter to author, 17 Aug. 1980.
51   'Curzonian superiority': Peter Quennell to author, 23 Nov. 1979.
51   'To me, much younger': Letter to author, 30 Sept. 1980.
51   Learned but chilly: David Knowles to KC, 22 July 1973.
51   Thought he was much older: Peter Green to author, 12 Aug. 1980.
51   Precocious learning: Christopher Eastwood to author, 6 Aug. 1980.
52   'a bit of a Philistine': Dr N.W. Porteous to author, 17 Sept. 1980.
52   'an immense admiration': Christopher Smith to author, 22 Oct. 1980.
52   'muddy as any other oaf': Sir Colin Anderson, *Three Score Years and Ten* (London: privately printed, 1974), p. 11.
52   Leicester Gallery bargains: *APW*, p. 78–9.
53   'cocooned in a civilization': *Sunday Times Magazine*, 6 Oct. 1974.
53   'ordinary rather negative good taste': Christopher Eastwood to author, 6 Aug. 1980.
53   'You're hopeless! Don't you like anything?': letter to author, 22 Aug. 1980.
53   'There was one occasion': Brian Pye-Smith to author, 15 Aug. 1980.
54   the kind of man one could pinch: David Pryce-Jones (ed.), *Cyril Connolly, Journal and Memoir* (London: Collins, 1983), p. 59.

54 'If disobliging jokes' – slandered ... as a matter of course: ibid, p. 65.

54 laughed them to scorn: *APW*, p. 100.

54 'He's a most brilliant young scholar': interview with Sir Trenchard Cox.

55 his exclusive preserve: *APW*, p. 104.

55 'wonderfully generous': interview with Edward Croft-Murray.

55 Ashmolean holdings: David Piper, *The Treasures of Oxford* (London: Paddington Press, 1977).

55 Dangers of the artist's life: *APW*, p. 53.

55 'desperately ambitious': interview with Gabriel White.

56 'hoped to enter politics': Dr N.W. Porteous to author, 17 Sept. 1980.

56 'driving you into the business': Maurice Bowra to KC, 3 Aug. 1925.

56 'no prestige whatsoever': Mary Berenson to Alys Russell, 12 Jan. 1926.

56 the best possible education: *APW*, pp. 105–6.

57 Influence of Roger Fry: Kenneth Clark (ed.), *Last Lectures by Roger Fry* (New York: Macmillan, 1939) and *APW*, pp. 109–10 and 200–201.

58 not clever enough: *APW*, p. 119.

59 Bell again came to the rescue: *APW*, p. 108.

59 preferred others to publish: interview with Sir Francis Watson.

59 Theory of permanent adolescence: *Cyril Connolly, Journal and Memoir*, p. 9.

59 charms of womanliness: *APW*, p. 36.

59 seemed to think a match; KCS, 8 June 1977, and to author, 18 Aug. 1981.

60 'Undergraduettes lived in purdah': Evelyn Waugh, *A Little Learning* (Boston: Little, Brown, 1964), p. 168.

60 He was bowled over: *APW*, p. 121.

60 Information about Jane Martin, her parents and siblings obtained from interviews with and letters from Dr and Mrs Russell Martin and letters in the Martin family possession.

61 'all her brilliant brain work': Dr Mary Guiscom to Dr Russell Martin, 28 March 1944.

62 'was fond of her father': interview with KC.

62 'Once more I must repeat': undated, Robert to Jane Martin (Martin family papers).

62 'I hardly ever saw her smile': interview with KC.

62 'feckless and boastful': ibid.

62 'an incredible old fake': ibid.

63 'a horrible school': ibid.

63 'extremely glamorous senior': ibid.

64 would rumple her bed: Evelyn Sharp to author, 2 May 1980.

64 'You must cut him': interview with Lady Meynell.

64 'before she met K': ibid.

64 'something of a Bohemian': interview with Gordon Waterfield.

65 shoved Jane into a cupboard: *APW*, p. 122.

65 she launched herself: interview with KC.

66 'very straightforwardly and properly': Gordon Waterfield to author, 24 March 1978.

66 'one terrible occasion': interview with Gordon Waterfield.

66 'she looked so terrible': interview with KC.

Chapter Seven   I Tatti

67   Quotation from Barbara Strachey and Jayne Samuels (eds), *Mary Berenson* (London: Gollancz, 1983), letter to her family, 10 Nov. 1926, p. 262.

67   would have to be a 'Jap': Bernard Berenson to Frank Jewett Mather, 14 Jan. 1925.

68   Invited to become Berenson's assistant: *APW*, p. 128.

69   His parents horrified: KCMB, 10 Oct. 1925.

69   an attack of jaundice: *APW*, p. 120.

69   a secret vice: KCMB, 20 Jan. 1926.

69   'a very remarkable youth': Mary Berenson to Alys Russell, 5 Jan. 1926.

69   'but it is a lie': ibid., 12 Jan. 1926.

70   'sitting with the B.B.s': 8 Jan. 1926.

70   'a very pretty epistolary gift': Logan Pearsall Smith to KC, 13 Feb. 1926.

70   stimulating mentor: KC to Dr Martin, 15 May 1927 (Martin family papers).

70   Parents should be misled: Mary Berenson to KC, 30 Jan. 1926.

71   A discourse on Ruskin: KCMB, 14 Feb. 1926.

71   Bringing a chauffeur: KCMB, 31 March 1926.

71   Discovery of a Rembrandt: KCMB, 14 Sept. 1926.

71   'under the Settignano tree': Mary Berenson to Alys Russell, 29 Dec. 1926.

71   a well-heeled suitor: Interview with Kitty Waterfield.

71   an unscrupulous fortune hunter: KCJ, undated.

72   'He is the keenest': Mary Berenson to Alys Russell, 11 Nov. 1926.

72   no wedding dress, ... no champagne: KCMB, 11 Jan. 1927.

72   'I still feel very polite': interview with Alix Kilroy.

72   'he is really stingy': Mary Berenson to Alys Russell, 2 Jan. 1927.

72   'the Upper Hand': ibid., 26 Jan. 1927.

73   wonderfully picturesque: KCMB, 8 Feb. 1927.

73   Berenson's rudeness to Jane: *APW*, pp. 168–9.

73   Ambition to become a connoisseur: *APW*, p. 151.

73   Jane's talent for connoisseurship: interviews with KC.

73   Decision to give up book on the Gothic Revival: *APW*, p. 172.

74   Seeing the Giorgione in the sunlight: KCJ, 8 Sept. 1927.

74   Dreadful paintings for sale: KCJ, 10 Nov. 1927.

75   An evening out with Nicky Mariano: KCJ, 8 Sept. 1927.

75   Journey home to London: KCMB, 8 March 1928.

75   Birth of Alan Clark: KCMB, 14 April 1928.

75   Labour was prolonged and painful: Maurice Bowra to KC, 20 June 1932.

76   The publishers were kind: KMCB, 14 April 1928.

76   Avoided lengthy analyses: interview with author.

77   His digs too half-hearted: *The Gothic Revival* (London: John Murray, 1962), p. 2.

77   exploring ... London: Alys Russell to Mary Berenson, 28 Nov. 1928.

77   Content with heavy mahogany: KCMB, 15 June 1928.

77   'nursing little Alan': Alys Russell to Mary Berenson, 16 May 1928.

78   Italian works a bargain: KCB, 20 May 1928.

78   never revealed his association: ibid.

78 nothing for 'us': KCB, 15 March 1929.
78 'loathed the pettifogging': Mary Berenson to Alys Russell, 9 Feb. 1929.
79 devote his gift for scholarship: Berenson to KC, May 1929.
79 'ungenerous, self-centred': Mary Berenson to Alys Russell, 9 Feb. 1929.
80 Influence of Felix Warburg: *APW*, p. 189.
80 Declined Berenson's suggestion: KCB, June 1929.
80 Descriptions of Old Palace Place based upon *APW*, advertisement, *The Times* of London, 4 July 1931, p. 24, and interviews with KC, John Hill, Dr Russell Martin and Edward Croft-Murray.
82 'putting on such a pose': interview with Alix Kilroy.
82 'putting on an act': interview with Kitty Waterfield.
82 An empty lecture hall: KCB, 4 June 1931.
82 Worked non-stop: ibid.
83 The Italian Exhibition: *APW*, p. 137.
83 a complete disaster: *APW*, p. 182.
84 Art world antagonisms: *APW*, p. 178.
84 Edinburgh University offer rejected: KCB, 30 Dec. 1930.
85 astonished to be offered the job: KCB, 4 June 1931.
85 Berenson disapproves: Berenson to KC, 26 June 1931.
85 No ambition to administrate: *APW*, p. 198.
85 National Gallery his ambition: Owen Morshead to KC, 11 June 1932.
85 His name was on their lips: Alice Clark to KC, 6 July 1931.
86 'a delightful white Italian villa': Alys Russell to Mary Berenson, 12 Oct. 1931.
86 Shotover Cleve no prize: KCB, n.d.
86 Jane's rebellious attitude: C.F. Bell to KC, 22 June 1931.
86 'looking frightfully smart': interview with Edward Croft-Murray.
86 Jane writes to D.S. MacColl: undated.
86 'third picture on the right': interview with Kitty Waterfield.
86 'we want to hear what Clive Bell': interview with author.
86 'I was very hurt': interview with Isaiah Berlin.
86 'he'd make a sign to her': interview with author.
87 'Don't talk about Norman Shaw': *Sunday Times Magazine*, 6 Oct. 1974.
87 'a manual of evasive': Janet Flanner, *London Was Yesterday* (New York: Viking Press, 1975), p. 7.
87 'a cosy sensation': Alan Pryce-Jones in the *Listener* 1 March 1951, p. 345.
87 a clever young assistant: KCB, 16 Aug. 1931.
87 a bargain figure: KC to author, 22 Oct. 1980.
87 'the most soaring fantasy': C.F. Bell to Kenneth Clark, 22 June 1931.
88 Bell turns against Clark: interview with Sir Francis Watson.
88 Fry's illness: KCB, 31 Jan. 1932.
88 Jane in an accident: ibid.
88 Born on 9 October 1932: Not on 9 April, as in *APW*, p. 201.
88 His father would recover: KCJ, 18 Aug. 1932.
89 He might take up art: KCJ, 17 Aug. 1932.
89 An unused limb: *APW*, p. 202.
89 Mother's operation: on 29 October 1932.

Chapter Eight   Getting Things Done

90 A battered, dirty office: C.J. Holmes, *Self and Partners* (London, Constable, 1936), p. 318.

90 Impressions of his room: KC to author, 4 June 1980.

90 Day started well: KC's diary, 1 Jan. 1934.

91 Bargain expected by Lord Lee: inteviews with KC.

91 'That's all right': Helen Roeder interviewed by Ruth Taylor, 11 July 1980.

91 'the first great English collector': *Country Life*, 29 Sept. 1934.

91 The Tate's obstructive role: *APW*, p. 78.

91 Hangs Manet and Cézanne: *London Evening News*, 5 March 1934.

91 The most exclusive institution: *Observer*, 4 March 1934, p. 16.

92 Art before football: *Country Life*, 28 April 1934.

92 No spikes on the job: KCB, 5 Feb. 1934.

93 Pros and cons weighed: KC to Lord Balniel, 16 March 1939.

93 The Gallery had no money: ibid., 30 March 1939.

93 Praise for the director: Sir Philip Sassoon to KC, 1 Jan. 1935.

93 a professional entertainer: KCB, 5 Feb. 1934.

93 a new broom: *Sphere*, 17 Sept. 1934.

93 'Never, in any country': *Manchester Evening News*, 15 Feb. 1934.

93 Russian gift: KCB, 26 Feb. 1933.

93 had gone to his head: KCB, undated.

94 every atom of energy: KCB, 27 Feb. 1934.

94 entertained friends for dinner: KC to Clive Bell, 22 Jan. 1934.

94 Glorious nights and mornings after: KC's diary, 9 and 16 Jan. 1934.

94 Art collection of the British crown: Sir Oliver Millar, Surveyor of the Queen's Pictures, *New York Times*, 19 Feb. 1981.

94 Kenneth Clark withdrew: Owen Morshead to KC, 11 June 1932.

95 Tancred Borenius as candidate: *APW*, p. 236.

95 Did not buy good examples: KC to Sir Vincent Baddeley, 10 Nov. 1952.

95 Visit of George V and Queen Mary described in KC's diary, 25 March 1934.

95 no necessity for further honours: KCB, 15 June 1934.

95 KC on the National Gallery: *Johannesburg Star*, 26 Jan. 1935.

96 felt bound to see everyone: ibid.

96 a heroic attempt: Edith Wharton to KC, 2 Jan. 1935.

96 looking for antiques: ibid., 8 Feb. 1935.

96 Purchase opposed: KCB, 14 Oct. 1934.

96 vogue for Surrealism: *Antique Collector*, Dec. 1934.

96 Price of the Sassettas for Duveen: Colin Simpson in the *Sunday Times*, 3 Feb. 1980, p. 13.

96 Duveen's profit on paper: ibid.

97 had been reworked: KC to author, Jan. 1981.

97 Mackay had never paid for the paintings: *APW*, p. 228.

97 carry him out feet first: Sir Philip Sassoon to KC, undated, c. 12 Jan. 1935.

97 Heavily retouched: *Sunday Times*, op. cit.

97 Extent of restorations described: *National Gallery Technical Bulletin*, Sept. 1977, p. 3.

97 the Duveen gloss: *Sunday Times*, op. cit.
97 crassness of the restoration: ibid.
97 nothing would give him more pleasure: Berenson to KC, 21 Oct. 1934.
97 Request for an article: KCB, 14 Oct. 1934.
98 Berenson declines: Berenson to KC, 21 Oct. 1934.
98 Cleaning of paintings: *Observer*, 27 Dec. 1936.
98 a picture must be dark brown: Kenneth Clark, 'The Aesthetics of Restoration', 1938, pp. 382–403.
98 Cleaning of *Bacchus and Ariadne*: *Daily Telegraph*, 11 Dec. 1934.
99 enchanted by the transformation: KC in the *New York Herald Tribune*, 20 Dec. 1936.
99 nothing had been damaged: Dr A.P. Laurier in ibid.
99 no reason ... to obscure ... a wonderful painting: Arthur de Casseres, *Daily Telegraph*, 29 Dec. 1936.
99 transformed into a masterpiece: E.M. Konstam, *Daily Telegraph*, 24 Dec. 1936.
100 Paintings were not being tampered with: 'The Aesthetics of Restoration', op. cit.
100 He was a bad ally: KC to Allan Gwynne-Jones, 26 Feb. 1947.

Chapter Nine   Fearfully Bolshie

101 Quotation: Roger Fry, 'Saying of the Week', *Observer*, 22 April 1934.
101 Epstein advised to move to Paris: William Rothenstein, *Of Men and Memories*, vol. 2 (New York, Tudor, n.d.), p. 87.
101 a decade behind France: Robert Graves and Alan Hodge, *The Long Weekend* (New York, Macmillan, 1941), p. 181.
101 Epstein defended: letter to *The Times*, 10 May 1935.
101 British attitude towards art: Kenneth Clark, 'Art for the People', *Listener*, 23 Sept. 1939, p. 999.
102 State of provincial galleries: Hesketh Hubbard, *A 100 Years of British Painting* (London: Longmans Green, 1951), p. 247, and Kenneth Clark, 'Art, the State and You', *Manchester Evening News*, 11 Feb. 1938.
102 A privilege to have been Fry's pupil: KC to D.S. MacColl, 4 Dec. 1937, Letter C170 MacColl Collection, Glasgow University.
103 'Does Clark to you': letter T332, ibid., n.d.
103 Art prices in Paris: KCJ, Dec. 1935.
103 Acquisition of the Des Granges and Michelangelo drawing: interview with KC.
104 Della Robbia reliefs abandoned: interview with Sir Colin Anderson.
104 Paintings abandoned at the National Gallery: Max Deliss, picture restorer, quoted by Ruth Taylor.
104 Kenneth Clark on the decline of patronage: 'Art for the People', op. cit.
105 Steer's portrait of Jane Clark: *APW*, p. 187.
105 Duncan Grant commissions: KC to Duncan Grant, undated.

105 'I was ... flattered': Graham Bell to KC, undated.

105 Trust Fund for Artists: Anne Olivier Bell to author, 22 March 1980.

106 Pasmore's nude the best: KC to Graham Bell, *c.* Sept. 1939.

106 Graham Sutherland friendship: interview with Graham and Kathy Sutherland.

107 'I was seeing': ibid.

107 'give a belch': ibid.

107 Praises Sutherland: KC to Gertrude Stein, 5 Jan. 1939.

107 convinced that he was a genius: KC to Graham Sutherland, 12 June 1953.

107 'Graham was a good teacher': interview with Kathy Sutherland.

107 Just before the Second World War: 31 Dec. 1938.

107 Description of sculpture gallery: KCJ, 17 July 1932.

107 Henry Moore unyielding: Kenneth Clark, 'Apologia of an Art Historian', *University of Edinburgh Journal*, Summer 1951, p. 234.

108 'This was the atmosphere': interviews with Henry Moore.

108 He bought 30 drawings: Dennis Farr, *English Art* (London: Oxford University Press, 1978), p. 363.

108 Sales were better, 'Altogether I'm very happy': Henry Moore to KC, 22 Feb. 1939.

108 £300 a fair price, 'it might be a long time': Henry Moore to KC, 26 March 1939.

109 Frugality of Henry and Irina Moore: interview with KC.

109 'a characteristically equable': John Russell, *Henry Moore* (New York: Putnam, 1968), p. 40.

109 'Your remarks about my show': John Piper to KC, 14 March 1940.

109 Their relationship with Kenneth Clark described to author by John and Myfanwy Piper.

110 Painting and the Infinite: *Thirties* (London: Arts Council of Great Britain, 1979), p. 35.

110 Marxism the cure: George Steiner on Anthony Blunt in *New Yorker*, 8 Dec. 1980, p. 161.

111 Sympathetic to socialism: KC to Alice Clark, 5 Feb. 1940.

111 Outlook for art: Kenneth Clark, 'The Future of Painting', *Listener*, 2 Oct. 1935.

111 'received this jagged splinter': Eric Newton, *Manchester Guardian*, 1 Nov. 1935.

111 'When, in the whole of history': Herbert Read, *Listener*, 16 Oct. 1935.

112 No future for abstraction: Kenneth Clark, *Listener*, 23 Oct. 1935.

112 The stage was set: Eric Newton, *Manchester Guardian*, 1 Nov. 1935.

112 'Could Mr Herbert Read distinguish': *Listener*, 23 Oct. 1935.

112 a kick in the pants: Collins Baker to D.S. MacColl, 7 Jan. 1936.

112 Geometrical forms inadequate: Eric Newton, *Manchester Guardian*, op. cit.

112 more careful about labelling: KC to Eric Newton, 2 Nov. 1935.

112 ready to sit down: KCJ, 10 Nov. 1935.

112 Trip to Russia described: KCB, 3 Sept. 1935.

112 Day in London described: KCJ, no date.

113 Negotiating for Ingres portrait: KC to Sir Gerald Kelly, 19 Dec. 1935.

Chapter Ten   Top People

114   The ideal house described: KCJ, 31 Oct. 1939.

114   Hand-painted satin curtains: interview with Mrs Humphrey Brooke.

115   Role of social secretary described: interview with Nancy Bingham.

115   Mary Berenson would have described the house: KCB, no date.

115   looked tired and 'official': Alys Russell to Mary Berenson, 29 Jan. 1936.

116   A letter took four days: KCB, 20 June 1935.

116   Too busy to see his wife: KCJ, 2 March 1937.

116   He could not come to the Riviera: KC to Edith Wharton, 3 Feb. 1937.

116   Too interested in a drink: KC to E. McKnight Kauffer, 29 Dec. 1938.

116   Anecdotes from his role as Surveyor: interviews with KC.

117   Did so much gold put up the price?: JD, 15 March 1937.

117   Queen Mary's furniture preference: KC to Owen Morshead, 26 July 1934.

117   'how young the Queen looked: JD, 8 Feb. 1937.

117   'She gayed him up': interview with KC.

117   Coronation described by Kenneth Clark in letters to Edith Wharton (6 June 1937) and Dr Martin (15 May 1937).

118   interminable formalities: KC to Edith Wharton, 1 May 1937.

118   A duty-bound King: Janet Flanner, *London Was Yesterday* (New York: Viking, 1975), p. 72.

118   Royalty's merits assessed: KC to Edith Wharton, 1 May 1937.

118   Queen's objectives praised: ibid., 11 June 1937.

118   Anxious to start a collection: JD, 2 Dec. 1937.

118   'in the nature of a revelation': *Christian Science Monitor*, 20 July 1938.

119   a pity about her ... clothes: KCJ, 2 March 1937.

119   'The Duchess of Kent could do it': interview with KC.

119   The Queen looked trim: JD, 16 March 1938.

119   'very good grub': interview with KC.

119   Advantages of life at Windsor Castle: KC to author, 4 June 1980.

119   an improvement over communism: KCJ, 14 April 1939.

119   tasting country wines: JD, 14 April 1938.

119   Many of his generation: interview with Sir William Keswick.

119   Relationship with Queen Elizabeth: interviews with KC.

119   'old-fashioned Valentine': *Chips: The Diaries of Sir Henry Channon* (London: Weidenfeld & Nicolson, 1967), p. 52.

119   the Queen rang: KC to author, 15 Dec. 1980.

120   The Queen had good sense: JD, 1 Oct. 1938.

120   Dinner with the Queen: KC to Alice Clark, undated, c. Oct. 1939.

120   Earliest memories of Colette Clark: interviews with author.

120   Ladies fell on the twins: *APW*, p. 257.

120   Alan not attractive: interviews with KC.

120   Jane described her agonies: interview with Kitty Waterfield.

121   Alan's illness discussed: Owen Morshead to KC, 1 Jan. 1933; Edith Wharton to KC, 21 Jan. 1934; KC to Berenson, 23 March 1934.

121   Earliest memories of Alan Clark: interviews with author.

122 Reasons for sending Alan to school: KC to Dr Martin, 15 May 1937; to author, 29 March 1980.

122 Alan did not mind: JD, 23 Jan. 1938.

122 Alan was adorable: Jane Clark to KC from Portland Place, no date.

122 her son was very much missed: Jane Clark to Edith Wharton, summer 1937.

122 judging from the noises: Jane Clark to KC, no date.

122 Jane an inexperienced mother: interview with Catherine Porteous.

123 Children's birthday parties described: interview with Lady Anderson.

123 Men liked becoming clothes: Jane Clark, quoted in the *London Star*, 1 April 1952.

123 'a row of large scarlet fly-buttons', 'a silk day-dress': Sir Colin Anderson to author, 10 Sept. 1979.

124 Her clothes mattered most: Robert Martin to Jane Clark, 6 Dec. 1935.

124 Her judgement first-rate: interview with Colette Clark.

124 She had to be discouraged: Owen Morshead to Jane Clark, 7 Jan. 1936.

124 Sibyl Colefax's championing of the Clarks: *APW*, p. 214.

124 'looking frail and ill': James Lees-Milne, *Ancestral Voices* (New York: Scribner, 1975), p. 168.

124 'the strangest of sinister men': *Chips, The Diaries of Sir Henry Channon*, p. 7.

124 'a triumph of beautiful bad taste': ibid.

125 Sassoon at his best at home: KC to Edith Wharton, no date.

125 'We have missed you cruelly': Sir Philip Sassoon to KC, no date.

125 Sassoon would 'buzz' the Clarks: *APW*, p. 257.

125 Out almost every night: KC to D.S. MacColl, 4 Dec. 1937.

125 She was ambitious for him: interview with Gabriel White.

125 She was bolder than he: interview with Lady Gladwyn.

125 She seemed so confident: interview with Nancy Thomas.

125 She was his champion: interview with Lady Gladwyn.

125 She was launching him: interview with Michael Levey.

125 She made him feel grand: interview with Margaret Slythe.

125 'In their palmy Portland Place days': interview with Bryan Robertson.

125 Hostesses queued up for them: interview with Sir Trenchard Cox.

126 'that clever, attractive couple': *Bystander*, 7 July 1937.

126 it made her blink: Edith Wharton to KC, 14 July 1934.

126 'glittering in diamonds': Logan Pearsall Smith to KC, 8 Feb. 1931.

126 a brilliant hostess: interview with Sir Colin Anderson.

126 She was sure her friend: Dame Edith Sitwell to KC, 10 Jan. 1937.

126 the grand world of the high intelligentsia: interview with Sir Trenchard Cox.

127 'she would never go there': Sir Colin Anderson to author, 10 Nov. 1979.

127 so many aesthetic experiences: ibid., 30 May 1980.

127 neither made any demands: ibid.

127 'not enough to fall down': interview with KC.

127 living beyond their means: KCJ, 28 Feb. 1937.

127 'The atmosphere around the house': interview with Nancy Bingham.

128 Extracts from Jane Clark's diaries, 1937–39.

128 a frank assessment: KCJ, *c*. Nov. 1927.

128 settled a matter ... restorer: Jane Clark to Lord Crawford, April 1940.

128   'he didn't act like one': interview with Myfanwy Piper.
129   making guests leave: interview with Bryan Robertson.
129   'the Universal Man': interview with Burnet Pavitt.
129   'sick on the quay': interview with Dr Russell Martin.
129   Enraged that he had not paid: KC to Pavel Tchelitchev, 26 Feb. 1937.
129   'they are disgusting': interview with KC.
129   Jane's sinusitis problems and the Bedford Russell solution: interviews with Colette and Kenneth Clark.
130   'maddening habit': James Lees-Milne to author, 21 June 1980.
130   'vivid, buccaneering character': interview with Sir Colin Anderson.
130   The Jane Clark post-mortem: described in interview with Margaret Slythe.
130   pacing up and down: interview with Nolwen Clark.
130   'I felt inferior to her', 'I was just tagging along': interview with KC.
130   A wonderful time at Bellevue: E. McKnight Kauffer to Jane Clark, 22 April 1938.
131   'All and everything': Sibyl Colefax to Kenneth and Jane Clark, no date.
131   loved the stuffy smell of trains: KCJ, 22 Feb. 1935.
131   led astray by a detective novel: KCJ, 21 Sept. 1939.
131   Difficult and ill at ease: interview with Cecil Gould.
131   'the reverse of cosy': interview with Sir Trenchard Cox.
131   people would not respect him: James Lees-Milne, *Prophesying Peace* (New York: Scribner, 1977), p. 44.
132   pass his companion ... on the street: interview with Mrs John Murray.
132   behaved rather badly: KCJ, 22 Feb. 1935.
132   Jane's spells of boasting: KCS, 28 May 1958.
132   'it's getting worn out': related in interview with Sir Colin Anderson.
132   'Don't finger the orchids': related in interview with Sir Isaiah Berlin.
132   'But Chips, we don't know': *Sunday Times Magazine*, 6 Oct. 1974.
133   'Oh K, how *could* you': related by J.J. Byam Shaw, interviewed by Ruth Taylor.
133   being teased ... by Logan: KCB, 10–14 June 1934.
133   indispensable part of his life: KCB, 15 Sept. 1939.

Chapter Eleven   The Giorgionesque

134   Quotation: D.S. MacColl in *Daily Telegraph*, 4 Jan. 1938.
134   Purchases for National Gallery: Kenneth Clark in *The Times*, 8 April 1938.
134   Biographical information about Gulbenkian from: *APW*; *Collectors and Collecting*; a speech by Kenneth Clark to the Royal Scottish Academy, 16 November 1978; and an article on Gulbenkian in the *Smithsonian Magazine*, July 1980.
135   'young and strong and glad': *Smithsonian Magazine*, op. cit.
135   Reasons for collapse of Gulbenkian negotiations: Kenneth Clark, Confidential Memo to the Board of Trustees of the National Gallery, no date.
136   Berenson bought a fake: Meryle Secrest, *Being Bernard Berenson* (New

York: Holt, Rinehart, 1979), pp. 205–6.

137-8 Kenneth Clark first sees Giorgiones: *APW*, p. 263.

137   Provenance of Giorgiones: established in a letter from Dr George M. Richter
       to the *Daily Telegraph*, 26 Jan. 1938.

137   'Use every weapon': Lord Balniel to KC, n.d.

137   probably not by Giorgione: KCB, *c*. October 1937.

137   unhesitatingly called the works Giorgiones: KC to Edith Wharton, 11 July
       1937.

137   the paintings must be labelled Giorgiones: *APW*, p. 263.

138   Paintings by Palma Vecchio: Tancred Borenius, letter to *The Times*, 21 Oct.
       1937.

138   Borenius's suspicions: interview with KC.

138   The work of Previtali: Dr George M. Richter, *Burlington Magazine*, January
       1938, pp. 33–4.

138   The paintings were worthless: Berenson to Royal Cortissoz, 12 Dec. 1937.

138   had kept a handsome percentage: KC to Sir Gerald Kelly, 14 Jan. 1938.

138   People would find the truth horrifying: Borenius, as quoted by KC in interview
       with author.

138   Borenius waving a telegram: J.J. Byam Shaw, interviewed by Ruth Taylor.

139   The painting Duveen dismissed and later bought: interview with KC.

139   A dealer as trustee condemned: JD, 24 March 1937.

139   Sassoon rang in a rage: JD, 30 Dec. 1937.

139   Duveen sent flowers: JD, 23 Dec. 1937.

139   Chamberlain is persuaded: this account differs from that given in *APW*,
       pp. 265–6 and is taken from letters from Lord Balniel to KC, 20 Dec. and
       31 Dec. 1937; and from entries in JD of the same period.

139   Sassoon reappears and is friendly: JD, 5 Feb. 1938.

140   'grave lack of supervision': *Daily Express*, 21 July 1937.

140   'entitled to continue to rely': *Manchester Daily Despatch*, 21 July 1937.

141   'If you are working': interview with Bryan Robertson.

141   'nothing more' to do with him: Sir Ellis Waterhouse to author, 11 March 1980.

141   Staff rebellion: This account differs from that given in *APW*, p. 262, and
       derives from Memoranda written by Lord Balniel (30 March and 1 April 1938)
       and a National Gallery Memorandum, *c*. 4 April 1938.

142   he would have liked to ... bite: KC to Alice Clark, 5 Feb. 1940.

143   The paintings were cheap: JD, 11 Jan. 1938.

143   The Prime Minister was very nice: JD, 28 Jan. 1938.

143   Reporters rang up every half hour: Jane Clark to Raymond Mortimer, n.d.,
       c. 1 Jan. 1938.

143   D.S. MacColl defends Giorgione purchase: letter to the *Daily Telegraph*,
       4 Jan. 1938.

143   tell his friends to lay off: KC to D.S. MacColl, n.d., *c*. 4 Jan. 1938.

143   arrogant, high-nosed pair: D.S. MacColl to KC, 7 Jan. 1938.

144   Depressed by the honour: JD, 18 Dec. 1937.

144   'pirate submarines': Owen Morshead to KC, n.d.

144   a public benefactor: Henry Lamb to KC, 15 Jan. 1938.

144   Doing more than anyone: Jack Beddington to KC, 3 Jan. 1938.

144   'the Garter is too gaudy': Logan Pearsall Smith to KC, 3 Jan. 1938.

144   Purchase not a mistake: KC to 'Ivor', 14 Jan. 1938.

145   Warm feelings for Berenson: KCB, 1 Jan. 1938.

145   His mingled feelings about the *Florentine Drawings*: KCB, 3 Dec. 1938.

145   'a new standard in art criticism': Eric Newton, *Sunday Times*, 23 July 1939.

145   'erudition with elegance': Raymond Mortimer, *New Statesman and Nation*, 5 Aug. 1939.

146   Gratitude for Berenson's praise: KCB, 22 Aug. 1939.

Chapter Twelve   Black as our Loss

147   Quotation: Edith Sitwell, 'Still Falls the Rain' (The Raids, 1940), in *The Canticle of the Rose* (New York: Vanguard, 1949), p. 167.

147   Confident Britain would win: *TOH*, p. 31.

147   a rank growth: JD, n.d.

147   civilization was crumbling: KCB, 20 Jan. 1938.

147   He would have no place: KCJ, 11 Sept. 1939.

147   he never lost his conviction: KC to Alice Clark, 27 Feb. 1940.

147   An essay in *World Review*: KC to Graham Bell, n.d., *c*. spring, 1941.

147   a battle to the death: KC to Graham Bell, n.d., *c*. Sept. 1939.

148   orders from Berlin: KC to Lord Balniel, 20 Sept. 1939.

148   First evacuation of paintings: KCB, 2 Oct. 1938.

148   'our respective teams "jumped to it"': Alan Clark (ed.), *A Good Innings: The Private Papers of Viscount Lee of Fareham* (London: John Murray, 1974), pp. 349–50.

148   The move to Gray's Inn Square: KCB, 12 July and 12 Aug. 1939, KCJ, 18 Sept. 1939.

149   Upton House described by their neighbour: Hiram Winterbotham to author, 20 Jan. 1981.

149   Jane's journey: KC to Alice Clark, 27 Aug. 1939.

149   A comfortable room at Garlands Hotel: KCJ, 1 Sept. 1939.

149   listening to Maggie Teyte: KCJ, 18 Sept. 1939.

149   A dog's fading wail: John Lehmann, *In My Own Time* (Boston: Little, Brown, 1955), p. 237.

150   'the unaccustomed darkness': ibid., p. 235.

150   He became impresario: 'London Carries On', *Manchester Evening News*, 21 Sept. 1939.

150   'an engaging and piquant figure: *Church Times*, 19 Jan. 1940.

151   Too crowded to sit: KCJ, 11 Nov. 1939.

151   'just jokes by incompetent': quoted in *London Evening News*, 18 April 1940.

151   dictator of the arts: ibid.

151   regretted some omissions: *London Evening News*, 19 April 1940.

151   Lively and stimulating: *Oxford Mail*, 19 April 1940.

151   The mentor for refugees, KCB, 14 Sept. 1939.

151   ignore the war: KC to Graham Bell, n.d., *c*. Sept. 1939.

151 artists begging ... work: KCJ, 11 Nov. 1939.

152 Dared to make radical choices: Mollie Panter-Downes, 'Letter from London', *New Yorker*, early 1940.

152 The Sutherlands' war problems: KC to Kathy Sutherland, 5 Sept. 1939.

152 'couldn't be away from things': interview with Henry Moore.

152 'I'd seen enough of war': ibid.

152 'women were undressing their children': ibid.

153 Jane Clark hoped she would live to see the day: JD, 4 Jan. 1941.

153 Difficult to have Moore appointed: JD, 7 Jan. 1941.

153 Role as head of films division established: *TOH*, p.10; KC to Lord Crawford, 1 June 1942, 31 Jan. 1940 and 20 Dec. 1939; to Gulbenkian, 19 Dec. 1939, and *Huddersfield Examiner*, 5 Feb. 1940.

153 the fate awaiting Jews: *News Review*, 25 April 1940.

154 teaching people their business: 7 April 1940.

154 'which has languished': *New Statesman*, 20 April 1940.

154 He should have gone into politics: JD, 2 Jan. 1941.

154 grateful to leave: Harold Nicolson's diary, 28 Jan. 1942.

154 'beautiful marble head': Harold Nicolson's diary, 8 Nov. 1940.

154 'we saw no end': Winston Churchill, quoted by Harold Nicolson, *Diaries and Letters, 1939–1945* (London: Collins, 1967), p. 114.

155 Blitz experiences: derived from JD, 6–9 Sept. 1940.

156 Life in the front lines: KCJ, 12 Sept. 1940.

156 Heartbreaking destruction: KC to Lord Balniel, n.d.

156 He was amazingly calm: JD, 15 Sept. 1940.

156 how far one could run: JD, 9 Oct. 1940.

156 fittings at Molyneux: JD, ibid.

156 breakfast in tears: JD, 11 Oct. 1940.

157 volunteering to be a firewatcher: JD, 15 and 18 Jan. 1941.

157 His closest call: JD, 17 April 1941.

157 a blue flannel coat and striped trousers: Harold Nicolson's diary, 17 April 1941.

157 Destruction of Gray's Inn flat: JD, 6 Nov. and 3 Dec. 1940.

157 Full court regalia on a tree: interview with KC.

158 Something had altered: JD, 21 April 1938.

158 worried about getting older: JD, 6 Oct. 1938.

158 The 'puffer' did not always work: JD, 30 April 1941.

159 'she gave him such a wigging': interview with Morna Anderson.

159 An infection in the autumn: JD, 8 Sept. 1938.

159 He was better than ever: KCB, 2 Oct. 1938.

159 'I don't think I was so bad': interview with Colette Clark, 28 Sept. 1979.

159 'schoolmarmish': interview with John and Myfanwy Piper.

159 obsessive ideas: Hiram Winterbotham to author, 20 Jan. 1981.

160 'as bad as mad persons': interview with Colette Clark.

160 'I had no idea': John Sparrow quoted by Colin Clark in interview with author.

160 'absolutely berated him': interview with Graham Sutherland.

160 'a screaming rage': interview with Alan Clark.

160 'it was hardly worth it': interview with Colette Clark.

161   'Oh no, no, no': interview with KC.

161   'a tacit understanding': interview with Alan Clark.

161   a stiff drink: JD, 16 June 1938.

161   He was her whipping boy: KCJ, 11 April 1942.

161   'He adored life': interview with Colette Clark.

162   upset about a film: JD, 27 June 1938.

162   There must be something wrong: JD, 19 Jan. 1941.

163   'when the war ends?': interview with Colette Clark.

163   Helpfulness of Eddy Sackville-West: Jane Clark to Lord Crawford, 25 June
       and 15 Aug. 1940.

163   'We'll all have coupons': interview with Kathy Sutherland.

163   'very puritanical and stiff': interview with Graham Sutherland.

164   'She was always thinking': interview with Kathy Sutherland.

164   An Aladdin's cave: interview with the Sutherlands.

164   Eddy Sackville-West did not want to leave: JD, 4 and 6 Dec. 1940.

164   A declaration of love: JD, 10 and 11 Jan. 1940.

165   Stood up and cheered: JD, 30 Jan. 1942.

165   'gentle in appearance': *Sunday Dispatch*, 26 Oct. 1941.

165   'more exciting than the first': *Spectator*, 14 Feb. 1941.

165   Planned to write on subject of nude: JD, 13 Nov. 1940.

166   Did not want to make a fuss: JD, 19 April 1941.

166   ring her up and comfort her: JD, 6 March 1941.

166   Jane was infuriated: JD, 17 March 1941.

166   No longer consulted: JD, 1 May 1941.

166   some tactful words: JD, 1 Dec. 1940.

166   it was over: JD, 10 Aug. 1941.

166   perpetually sad nowadays: JD, 11 Sept. 1941.

Chapter Thirteen   'Green Grow the Rashes, O'

167   tea at Portland Place: JD, 13 Dec. 1937.

168   An exceptional talent: KC to René d'Harnoncourt, 27 Nov. 1951.

169   'I remember her velvet skirts': interview with Colette Clark.

170   'desperately innocent': interview with KC.

170   began to withdraw sexually: ibid.

171   'she knew a great deal': ibid.

171   'three people in the world': interview with Colette Clark.

172   'You've been to see Mary Kessell': Jane Clark as quoted by Colette Clark in
       interview with author.

172   'willowy, sharp-featured, distinguished': James Lees-Milne, *Ancestral Voices*
       (New York, Scribner, 1975), pp. 165–6.

172   skirted deeper waters: *APW*, p. 253.

172   the most beautiful woman: KC to Rosamond Lehmann, 9 Dec. 1974.

173   passionate declaration: KC to Morna Anderson, 23 April 1949.

174   brazenness of women passengers: *TOH*, p. 149.

174   tried to cheer her up: KC to Morna Anderson, n.d., *c.* 30 Dec. 1948.
174   'We defended him': interview with Lady Anderson.
175   Mother's inhibitedness: *APW*, pp. 29, 74.
175   'a cold fish': interview with Sir Colin Anderson.
175   'stuffy, cold': interview with John and Myfanwy Piper.
175   'small and flinty': interview with Nancy Thomas.
175   'she bucked up', 'comes off very badly': interview with KC.
176   a human contact was developing: *TOH*, p. 124.
176   Alan was doing so well: KC to Alice Clark, n.d.
176   Colin making friends: ibid.
176   a store of furniture: ibid.
176   Ambition to become Slade Professor: KC to Alice Clark, 29 Oct. 1945.
176   Mother had a fall: *TOH*, p. 125.
177   Jane sent bulletins: KCJ, 15 Oct. 1946.
177   'an awfully sweet talk': interview with KC.

Chapter Fourteen   Art Completes

178   Dreams of a Welsh landscape: *TOH*, p. 8.
178   Bus queue decimated: *Oban Times*, 29 July 1944.
178   Tired of the National Gallery: John Rothenstein, *Time's Thievish Progress*, vol. 3 (London, Cassell, 1970), pp. 46–7.
179   'elder statesman': ibid.
179   a concept so tenuous: *KCJ*, 16 Sept. 1949.
179   writing seven times more: KC to Morna Anderson, 25 Sept. 1949.
179   Florence was glorious: KCJ, 22–23 Sept. 1949.
180   Berenson the ideal father: KCB, 31 March 1950 and 21 June 1955.
180   books would not conflict: KCB, 7 June 1954.
180   Lectures could become books: interview with KC.
180   Ruskin predominant influence: *TOH*, p. 79.
180   Kenneth Clark's inaugural lecture on Ruskin: *Ruskin at Oxford* (Oxford: Clarendon Press, 1947).
182   Title difficult to choose: KC to John Murray, 25 March 1948.
182   'one of the most interesting': *New York Times Book Review*, 19 March 1950.
182   'a fastidious sensibility': Herbert Read, *World Review* Feb. 1950.
182   Lectures so crowded: *Spectator*, 17 Feb. 1950.
182   'the most brilliant of lecturers': James Lees-Milne, *Ancestral Voices* (New York, Scribner, 1975), p. 270.
183   a freak gift: interview with KC.
183   It was too easy: Kenneth Clark, *Sunday Times Magazine*, 6 Oct. 1974.
183   had ruined his style: *APW*, pp. 183–4.
183   Points of contention did not matter: KCM, 30 Dec. 1968.
183   Pedantry useless: KC to Clive Bell, 9 Sept. 1947.
184   Transported to another plane: William Gaunt in *John O'London's Weekly*, 30 March 1951.

184 'factual, shrewd, ingenious': Frank Davis, *Illustrated London News*, 14 July 1951.

184 'a combination of excellences': Raymond Mortimer, *Sunday Times*, 25 March 1951.

185 a moment of divine inspiration: from interviews with KC; KCJ, 22 June 1965; KC to author, 10 July 1981; *TOH*, p. 87.

185 flashes of illumination: Somerset Maugham to KC, 2 Sept. 1954.

186 Mystical experience at Church of San Lorenzo: *TOH*, p. 108.

186 a divine source of inspiration: Kenneth Clark, 'Apologia of an Art Historian', *University of Edinburgh Journal*, Summer 1951.

Chapter Fifteen   Ministering to the Arts

187 Quotation by John Ruskin, Kenneth Clark (ed.), *Ruskin Today*, 191, 'For Television' (London: John Murray, 1967), p. 203.

187 'elegant and eminent': *Good Housekeeping*, Jan. 1945.

188 Hardly anything worth seeing: KC to the Earl of Rosse, 15 Oct. 1951.

188 Would he buy a ticket: KC to John Murray, 3 May 1950.

188 asked for her comments: KCJ, n.d.

188 'Jane thinks it's too long': Gill Ross interviewed by Ruth Taylor.

189 'a late supper party': *Good Housekeeping*, op. cit.

189 'With flashing ear-rings': ibid.

190 Her clothes choices: *News Chronicle*, 18 June 1952

190 A deep curtsy outside Claridge's: *News Chronicle*, 13 Nov. 1952; *Daily Mirror*, 13 Nov. 1952.

190 A royal fashion show: *TV Mirror*, 14 Nov. 1953, *Yorkshire Observer*, 12 Nov. 1953, *Birmingham Gazette*, 20 Nov. 1953, *Star*, 19 Nov. 1953, *Marylebone Record*, 26 Nov. 1953.

190 'Successful and brilliant occasions': the Recorder's Diary, *Recorder*, 19 Nov. 1953.

190 Resigns as president: Jane Clark to Norman Hartnell, 1 Jan. 1954.

190 improving but in poor spirits: KCB, 3 May 1947.

190 needed a major operation: KCB, 15 Oct. 1951.

191 more drastic than anticipated: KC to Kathy Sutherland, 27 Dec. 1951.

191 a tragic figure: KCB, 6 Oct. 1951.

191 his cue to fade out: KC to Morna Anderson, 25 Sept. 1949.

191 Mary's visit coincided with K's: interview with Derek Hill.

191 Ambivalent friendship: interview with René Massigli.

191 longed to be married: interview with Derek Hill.

192 'an art school girl': interviews with KC.

192 'Whatever has happened to Mary Kessell?': quoted by Colette Clark in interview with author.

192 barbed comments: interview with Janet Adam-Smith.

192 physically and mentally exhausted: KCJ, 28 Oct. 1953.

192 months late on manuscripts: KCS, 12 Dec. 1953.

193 Additional evidence: KC to Sir Alec Martin, 29 Oct. 1953.

193   bouts of self-disgust: KCS, 7 May and 22 Feb. 1954.

193   Magical beauty of Saltwood: KCS, 8 Nov. 1955.

193   needed a new challenge: KCB, 21 Oct. 1955.

193   Role of government in the arts: Kenneth Clark, 'Art and Democracy', *Cornhill Magazine*, 22 May 1945; and in the *Observer*, 2 April 1944.

194   desperate shortage of money: *TOH*, p. 136.

194   Disappointments of Arts Council job and reasons for remaining: Kenneth Clark's letters to Janet Stone, 1954–60.

195   'I like to be bothered': Joanna Drew interviewed by Ruth Taylor.

195   An exceptional propagandist: *Observer*, 30 March 1958.

195   'debase national taste': L. Marsland Gander, *Daily Telegraph*, 11 Sept. 1957.

195   Booed at Athenaeum: Kenneth Clark, 'From the Few to the Many', Granada Guildhall Lectures, Granada TV, 1966.

196   First day at the ITA: KCS, 4 April 1954.

197   One impossible Tuesday: KCS, 11 Sept. 1954.

197   officious Civil Servants: KCS, 17 Dec. 1954.

197   completely entranced: KCB, 10 Nov. 1954.

197   inspecting himself with a mirror: Lord McGregor of Durris to author, 5 Aug. 1981.

197   avalanche of grievances: KCS, 6 June 1955.

198   no interests of her own: KCS, 11 March 1957.

198   his lack of responsibility: KCS, 27 Jan. 1956.

198   Myfanwy Piper's prediction: *TOH*, p. 42.

198   way of declaring his love: KCS, 25 Oct. 1955.

199   attendance records were kept: KCS, 17 July 1953.

199   a beautiful friend: KCS, 8 Oct. 1953.

199   in a fish bowl: KCS, 12 Dec. 1953.

199   their plight: KCS, Feb. 1954.

199   limits to possibility: KCS, 25 Nov. 1954.

199   wholeheartedly in love: KCS, 18 Sept. 1954.

199   Private calls tapped: KCS, 2 July 1954.

199   his plans wrecked again: KCS, 29 Feb 1956.

200   he was ageing: KCS, 22 Feb. 1954.

200   Ashamed of his face: KCS, 17 May 1955.

200   He felt revived: KCS, 16 Aug. 1956.

200   wrapped in warmth: KCS, 22 Aug. 1956.

201   Barbarians had taken over: KCB, 23 Sept. 1955.

202   'arrogant and uncouth': draft for a history of the ITA by Bernard Sendall.

202   not willing to be reappointed: KCB, 12 May 1957, and KCJ, 12 Dec. 1956.

202   Standards could have been higher: Kenneth Clark to the Pilkington Committee, Paper No. 232, January 1961.

202   he dreaded the *Angst*: KCS, 3 March 1957.

202   a series of articles: KCS, 28 Dec. 1956.

202   Bad headaches described: KCS, 23 Jan., 21 Feb.., 22 Feb., 25 March and 9 May 1957.

202 He was not neurotic: KCS, 2 April 1957.
203 The cook gave notice: KCS, 31 July 1957.
203 two shrivelled peas: KCS, 25 April 1957.
203 Domestic atmosphere unpredictable: KCS, 26 April 1956.
203 hysterical recriminations: KCS, 16 May 1957.
203 becoming genuinely peculiar: KCS, 30 June 1957.
203 despairing state of his handwriting: KCS, 5 Sept. 1956.
203 Old, paunchy and grey: KCS, 29 April 1957.
203 two ambitions left: KCS, 14 Feb. 1957.

Chapter Sixteen   Another Side of the Alde

204 Quotation: interview with Graham Sutherland.
204 already overdone it: KCS, 20 Jan. 1961.
204 six men in search of a character: *New Statesman and Nation*, 18 Dec. 1954.
204 find himself being hounded: KCS, 3 July 1960.
205 intermittent panic: KCS, 13 Oct. and 7 Nov. 1957.
205 pontificating on pottery: KCS, 16 Dec. 1957.
205 how time-consuming it was: ibid.
205 First programme a failure: KCS, 11 Feb. 1958.
205 They should not condemn the medium: KCB, 5 March 1959.
205 the latent ham: KCB, 22 May 1958.
205 'Do we want more': *Daily Sketch*, 30 May 1958.
206 avalanche of attention: KCS, 26 Jan. 1959.
206 inundated with so many flowers: KCS, 17 June 1962.
206 Flower sellers' approval: KCS, 28 Feb. 1960.
206 Kenneth Clark, 'The Value of Art in an Expanding World', printed in *Hudson Review*, Spring 1966.
207 Was it his personal inability: KCS, 3 Nov. 1963.
207 He must retire or try to explain: KCS, 1 June 1960.
208 Not in his lifetime: Kenneth Clark quoted in the *Los Angeles Times*, 15 April 1962.
209 Art history concerned with subjects: Kenneth Clark in *Motives, Studies in Western Art*, ed. Millard Meiss (Princeton University Press, 1963), p. 190.
209 Immediate difficulties: KCS, 14 June 1961.
209 Could not develop the idea: KCS, 31 July 1961.
209 Abandoned with a sigh: KCS, 10 Jan. 1970.
209 An impossible moment to define: 'The Value of Art in an Expanding World', op. cit.
209 Confess his own inadequacy: Kenneth Clark, 'Apologia of an Art Historian', *University of Edinburgh Journal*, Summer 1951.
210 Aldeburgh sharpened his focus: Kenneth Clark, *The Other Side of the Alde* (London: Warren Editions – Jonathan and Phillida Gili, 1968), no pagination.
210 Watching *Noye's Fludde*: KCS, 20 June 1958.
210 The charms of Orford: ibid.
210 Advantages of visiting Maugham: KCS, 2 March 1957 and 9 March 1961.

210   Reminded of Matisse's interiors: KCS, 9 March 1961.

211   The Piper exhibition: KCB, 1 June 1960.

211   Graham Sutherland portrait sittings: KCS, 8 Jan., 26 Aug., 11 Sept. 1962; and interview with Graham Sutherland.

212   haughty and belligerent: KCS, 10 May 1965.

212   Descriptions of *Montaigne's Tower*: KCS, 1 Jan., 6 Nov., 4 April 1967; 12 Jan. 1960 and 4 Nov. 1962.

212   bouquets of lilies-of-the-valley: KCS, 11 May 1967.

212   Eradicating roots: KCS, 21 Aug. 1962.

212   Taking boys on tour: KCS, 15 Oct. 1957.

212   decidedly eccentric: KCS, 20 Jan. 1961.

212   very benevolent: KCS, 16 Aug. 1964.

212   spent four hours arguing: KCS, 5 July 1964.

213   Yellow room haunted: KCS, 13 March 1960.

213   Visits from bigwigs: KCS, 31 July 1967.

213   Happy to see people leave: KCS, 6 July 1959.

213   His tearful Christmas state: KCS, 17 Feb. 1964.

213   A negative verdict: KC, 29 Dec. 1957 and 29 Dec. 1963.

213   Absences a major issue: KCS, 26 Jan. 1959.

214   Might reach a stage: KCS, 13 March 1960.

214   did not intend to relinquish such happiness: KCS, 2 July 1961.

214   Bored at Arts Council: KCS, 21 Aug. 1958.

214   Sad to leave: KCS, 17 April 1960.

215   Recurrence of headaches: KCS, 29 Oct. 1959.

215   Felt unworthy and gross: KCS, 8 Oct. 1959.

215   Bouts of depression: KCS, 17 July 1958.

215   persecution mania: KCS, 25 April 1959.

215   He was normal: KCS, 9 June 1961.

215   great battles with Colette: KCS, 28 Jan. 1960.

215   Colette was insulting: KCS, 29 April 1963.

215   A row with Alan: KCS, 1 Oct. 1961.

216   Jane too drunk to object: KCS, 28 Dec. 1958.

216   Jane in bad form: KCS, 8 Oct. 1959.

216   A tranquillizer recommended: KCS, 26 Sept. 1960.

216   Assessing the cure: KCS, 16 Oct. 1960.

216   'used to look at it': interview with Kenneth Clark.

216   Jane turned to alcohol: ibid.

216   Colin questions version: interview with Colin Clark.

216   'My dear, she's drunk': interview with Colette Clark.

217   'clink and clank': interview with Violette Verdy.

217   'Oh no, my dear': ibid.

217   Effect of alcohol on her mother: interview with Colette Clark.

217   KC rebuffed: ibid.

217   Hypnotist's early success: KCS, 11 Jan. 1960.

218   Particularly well when Walton came: KCS, 3 Dec. 1961.

218   a sort of therapy: KCS, 29 Nov. 1964.

218   only half of him felt it: KCJ, 8 Sept. 1927.

218   made him breathless: KCJ, 10 Nov. 1927.
219   like Cézanne: KCS, 23 Nov. 1967.
219   'I didn't abandon myself': interview with Violette Verdy.
219   'did it without a drop': interview with Catherine Porteous.

Chapter Seventeen   Civilisation

221   Quotation: Kenneth Clark, *Civilisation* (New York: Harper & Row, 1969), p. 110.
221   severe personal stress: KCS, April and July 1966, April 1969, January 1970.
221   Start of 'Civilisation' series based on Kenneth Clark's letters to Janet Stone and interview with Michael Gill, producer of series.
224   Progress of filming: based on Kenneth Clark's letters to Janet Stone, Margaret Slythe and Jane Clark.
226   Friendship with Margaret Slythe: based on interviews with Mrs Slythe and KC's letters to her.
228   his autobiography: KCM, 16 Jan. 1969.
229   'false turnings and dissolving perspectives': Kenneth Clark, *Civilisation* (New York: Harper & Row, 1969), p. 177.
229   an elegy for a vanished past: Christopher Booker, *Spectator*, 11 Aug. 1979.
230   'the liveliest intellects': *Civilisation*, ibid., p. 346.
230   'the whole gamut of life': *The Times Literary Supplement*, 4 Dec. 1969.
230   'perceptive, sensitive and wise': *Burlington Magazine*, editorial, June 1969.
230   testimony to man's genius: *Daily Telegraph*, 19 May 1969.
230   'It is this underlying': ibid.
230   'a contribution to civilisation': *Sunday Times*, 25 May 1969.
230   'an expression of gratitude': *Civilisation*, op. cit., p. xvi.
231   being praised and flattered: KCM, 5 April 1969.
231   Jane swung at a producer: interview with Margaret Slythe.
231   Touching letters: KCS, 10 Jan. 1970.
231   Nine would-be suicides: *TOH*, p. 223.
231   in tears: KCS, 20 June 1969.
231   journalist's sense of timing: KCM, 22 June 1969.
231   six personal appearances: KCJ, 25 Nov. 1969.
232   Accosted by Americans: KCJ, 12 Nov. 1970.
232   buying an umbrella: KCJ, 10 Jan. 1970.
232   burst into tears: *TOH*, p. 225.
232   Experience of Anatole France: Theodor Reik, *Of Love and Lust* (New York: Grove, 1957), pp. 117–20.
233   go into a retreat: KCS, 24 Nov. 1970.

Chapter Eighteen   Other Parts of the Wood

234   Quotation by John Ruskin, Kenneth Clark (ed.), *Ruskin Today*, 67, 'Depression' (London: John Murray, 1964), p. 73.

234   People would not leave him alone: KCM, 12 Nov. 1973.

234   No essay for Picasso: KC to Herbert Mitgang, 28 Nov. 1971.

234   No comment on Watergate: ibid., 6 June 1973.

234   Kenneth Clark's speech at Winchester: reprinted in *The Wykehamist*, 3 June 1970, p. 474.

235   Still a little creep: KCS, 10 May 1970.

235   Decides against Tuscany: KCM, 1 Oct. 1970.

235   The model a success: KCS, 17 Nov. 1969.

236   detested the new house: KCS, 19 March 1971.

236   Nothing too emphatic: KCS, 10 July 1971.

236   signing-over of Saltwood: KCS, 15 July 1971.

236   Gall bladder operation described: KCS, Feb. and 16 June 1971; KC to Morna Anderson, 12 May 1971.

236   Jane's state of mind disturbing: KCS, 1 Aug. 1971.

237   Recording memories on the plane: KCS, 7 April 1971.

237   Original scheme changed: KCS, 1 Aug. 1971.

237   Should have looked deeper: KC to Rosamond Lehmann, 9 Dec. 1974.

237   Not out of the wood: KCS, 9 Sept. 1962.

238   The same phrase used: KC to Juliette Huxley, 11 Feb. 1974.

238   'to arrive that way': quoted by Lady Gladwyn in interview with author.

238   fell and broke two ribs: KCS, 8 Nov. 1964.

238   cut her head: KCS, 1 July 1966.

239   black eye: KCS, 3 July 1966.

239   a suspicious number of calls: KCS, 8 July 1966.

239   a really terrible accident: KCS, 17 Dec. 1967.

239   'I believe in courtesy': Kenneth Clark, *Civilisation* (New York: Harper & Row, 1969), p. 347.

239   he never could exclude her: KCS, 17 Nov. 1967.

239   advised him against a confrontation: KCS, 1 Aug. 1957.

240   vomiting on the train: interview with Colette Clark.

240   in some ways he preferred her drunk: ibid.

240   'You mean it's my fault': interview with Leonard Lindley.

240   never watched television: KCS, 26 Sept. 1971.

241   trying to make tea: interview with Diana Menuhin.

241   free to continue: KCS, 12 Feb. 1972.

241   did not know how it would all end: KCS, 18 March 1972.

241   Images of Kandinskys: KCS, 3 April 1972.

241   Bath television script: KCS, June 1972.

242   the uncut *Don Carlos*: KCS, 5 May 1972.

242   marvellous shot: KCS, 7 Aug. 1972.

242   destroying his creative powers: KCS, 10 Aug. 1972.

242   Another visit to Jersey: Jane Clark to the Andersons, 15 Dec. 1972.

242   Family background provided by Nolwen Clark.

243   'fine desperado': quoted by James Fox in *White Mischief* (London: Cape, 1983), p. 33.

243   'It is my secret': quoted by Andrew Barrow in *Gossip, 1920–1970* (New York: Coward, McCann & Geoghegan, 1979), p. 32.

244 submerged and incomprehensible: KCS, 7 May 1973.
244 Party at the Café Royal: *TOH*, p. 233.
244 Not the party she suggested: KCM, Summer 1973.
245 Hoped she would enjoy it: KC to Nolwen Clark, 11 Nov. 1973.
245 excited by the challenge: KCS, 28 Sept. 1973.
245 signs of distress: ibid.
245 Description of Smithsonian cruise: *TOH*, pp. 234–9 and KCS, Oct. 1973.
246 talked to Henry Moore: KCM, 6 Feb. 1974.
246 Getting back to work: KCM, 19 Feb. 1974.

Chapter Nineteen   The Last of the Roses

247 'I look upon it with some distress': KC to author.
248 Kenneth Clark's timetable: author and Margaret Slythe.
248 'Dammit, here they are!': KC, as quoted by Mrs Slythe.
248 'some avocados and the sole': ibid.
249 not encouraged to ask for more: ibid.
249 'like a train shunting': ibid.
249 howling as if possessed: KCS, 11 June 1974.
250 Jane's decline based on Kenneth Clark's letters to Janet Stone and Margaret Slythe, 1974–76.
250 'a martyrdom for him': interview with Derek Hill.
251 'two tickets to the Gala': interview with Catherine Porteous.
251 'marvellous, blazing integrity': Margaret Slythe to author.
253 Jane's death: interview with Margaret Slythe.
254 His travelling plans: KC to Nolwen Clark, 20 Dec. 1976.
254 The difficult time of day: KCM, 29 Dec. 1976.
254 Trip to Basel: KC to Nolwen Clark, 16 Feb. 1977.
254 Free taxis more useful: KC to Morna Anderson, 30 May 1977.
254 were all married: KC to author.
255 He must reform: KC to Nolwen Clark, 6 Aug. 1977.
255 Ailments imaginary: KCM, 14 Aug. 1977.
259 'I'll take him on any terms': Nolwen Clark to author.
260 'Rembrandt is the only artist': Kenneth Clark, *An Introduction to Rembrandt* (New York: Harper & Row, 1978), p. 7.
261 'a spine-chilling book': Christopher Booker *Spectator*, 12 Nov. 1977.
261 'This was nothing like it': interview with Diana Menuhin.
262 Death of Kenneth Clark: from information provided by Nolwen Clark, Margaret Slythe and Leonard Lindley.
263 'what I have long been wanting': James Lees-Milne to author, 5 Nov. 1983.
263 commitment was of long standing: *The Times*, 15 Oct. 1983.
263 He did not desire it: Sir William Keswick to author, 7 Nov. 1983.
264 'a resonance that seems to make': editorial, *Burlington Magazine*, June 1969.
264 'dealt a marvellous hand': Stuart Preston in *ARTnews*, Sept. 1983.
265 To Orford and Sudbourne: trip made with KC, 30 Sept. 1979.

Books by Kenneth Clark

The Gothic Revival, Constable, London, 1928, revised edition 1949;
Scribner, New York, 1929; John Murray, London, 1962, 1970, 1973,
1974, 1975, 1978; Penguin, 1964, 1968.

A Catalogue of the Drawings of Leonardo da Vinci in the collection of His
Majesty the King at Windsor Castle, Cambridge University Press, 1935;
Phaidon Press, Oxford, 1968.

One Hundred Details from Pictures in the National Gallery, London, with
an introduction and notes by Kenneth Clark, National Gallery:
Longmans, London, 1938

Last Lectures by Roger Fry, with a preface and introduction by Kenneth
Clark, Cambridge University Press, 1939.

Leonardo da Vinci, an account of his development as an artist, Cambridge
University Press, 1939, 1952; revised edition, Penguin, 1959, 1967.

More Details from Pictures in the National Gallery, London, with an
introduction by Kenneth Clark, National Gallery, London, 1941.

Paintings of Graham Bell, with an introduction by Sir Kenneth Clark, Lund
Humphries, London, 1947.

The Idea of a Great Gallery, Speciality Press, Melbourne, 1949.

Praeterita, outlines of scenes and thoughts perhaps worthy of memory in my
past life by John Ruskin, with an introduction by Kenneth Clark, Rupert
Hart-Davis, London, 1949.

Landscape into Art, John Murray, London, 1949, revised edition, 1976;
also published as *Landscape Painting*, Scribner, New York, 1950;
Penguin, 1956, 1961, 1966; Harper & Row, New York, 1976.

Piero della Francesca, Phaidon Press, Oxford, 1951, 1969, 1981.

Drawings by Charles Keene 1823–1891, introduction by Sir Kenneth Clark,
The Arts Council of Great Britain, London, 1952.

The Nude, John Murray, London, 1956; Doubleday, Pantheon, New York,
1956; Anchor Books; Penguin*, Aldo Martello, Milan*.

Looking at Pictures, John Murray, London, 1960; Holt, Rinehart and
Winston, New York, 1960.

* date not available

The Other Side of the Alde, Faber, London, 1963 ; Warren Editions,
    Litton Cheney, 1968.

Ruskin Today, chosen and annotated by Kenneth Clark, John Murray,
    London, 1964 ; Holt, Rinehart and Winston, New York, 1964 ; Penguin
    Books, 1967.

Forty Years with Berenson, Nicky Mariano, with an introduction by Sir
    Kenneth Clark, Hamish Hamilton, London, 1966 ; Alfred A. Knopf, New
    York, 1966.

Rembrandt and the Italian Renaissance, John Murray, London, 1966 ; New
    York University Press, 1966 ; W. W. Norton, New York, 1968.

Civilisation, John Murray, London, 1973 ; Harper & Row, New York, 1973.

Another Part of the Wood, John Murray, London, 1974 ; Harper & Row,
    New York, 1975.

The Other Half, John Murray, London, 1977 ; Harper & Row, New York,
    1978.

Animals and Men, Thames & Hudson, London, 1977 ; William Morrow,
    New York, 1977.

Introduction to Rembrandt, John Murray, London, 1978 ; Harper & Row,
    New York, 1978.

Aubrey Beardsley, John Murray, London, 1979 ; in New York, available
    through Thames & Hudson, 1979.

The Florence Baptistry Doors, with an introduction by Lord Clark, Thames
    & Hudson, London, 1980.

Feminine Beauty, Weidenfeld & Nicolson, London, 1980 ; Rizzoli, New
    York, 1981.

Moments of Vision, John Murray, London, 1982 ; Harper & Row, New
    York, 1982.

The Art of Humanism, John Murray, London, 1983 ; Harper & Row, New
    York, 1983.

Index

K stands for Kenneth Clark.